William Henry Thomes

Life in the East Indies

William Henry Thomes

Life in the East Indies

ISBN/EAN: 9783337317904

Printed in Europe, USA, Canada, Australia, Japan

Cover: Foto ©Andreas Hilbeck / pixelio.de

More available books at **www.hansebooks.com**

# OCEAN-LIFE SERIES

- GOLD HUNTERS IN AUSTRALIA
- BUSH RANGERS
- GOLD HUNTERS IN EUROPE
- A WHALEMAN'S ADVENTURES
- A SLAVER'S ADVENTURES
- LIFE IN THE EAST INDIES

Wm. H. Thomes.

LIFE IN THE EAST INDIES.

BOSTON,
LEE & SHEPARD.

Entered, according to Act of Congress, in the year 1872,
By LEE AND SHEPARD,
In the Office of the Librarian of Congress, at Washington.

STEREOTYPED AT THE BOSTON STEREOTYPE FOUNDRY,
No. 19 Spring Lane.

BOOKS BY THE SAME AUTHOR.

THE GOLD-HUNTERS' ADVENTURES IN AUSTRALIA.

THE BUSHRANGERS; or, LIFE IN AUSTRALIA.

THE GOLD-HUNTERS IN EUROPE; or, THE DEAD ALIVE.

A WHALEMAN'S ADVENTURES IN THE SANDWICH ISLANDS AND CALIFORNIA.

A SLAVER'S ADVENTURES ON LAND AND SEA.

LIFE IN THE EAST INDIES.

All Handsomely Illustrated.

LEE & SHEPARD, PUBLISHERS, BOSTON.

CONTENTS.

CHAPTER I.

Manila and its People. — An Explanation. — Agreeable Quarters. — A Spaniard's Home. — Field Sports. — Visitors. — A Handsome Lady. 9

CHAPTER II.

The Search for the Outlaw. — An Obstruction. — The Monkeys. — The Ladrone. — The Fight. 38

CHAPTER III.

Don Arturo's Dreams. — A Moment's Absence. — An Excursion. — A wonderful Spring. — The Ladrones. 93

CHAPTER IV.

A Night in the Convent. — A sudden Death. — Surprise and Consternation. — Father Juan. — Suspicions, and what they amounted to. 117

CHAPTER V.

A Warning. — Father Juan on the Trail. — Tom and Donna Teresa. — The Supper, and what come of it. 145

CHAPTER VI.

A surprised Husband. — A cool Priest. — An Explanation. . . 172

CHAPTER VII.

Teresa's Aunt. — Her Ideas and Confessions. — How the Search proceeded, and what was the Result. 188

CHAPTER VIII.

The Inn. — Our Coffee. — The Ambush. — The Attack. — Its Failure. — The Examination. — The Result. 230

CHAPTER IX.

The Search of the Ladrones. — The Fire. — A bad Predicament. — Looking for a Wife. 253

CHAPTER X.

Gracia's Father. — A Confession. — On the Trail, &c., &c., &c. . 281

CHAPTER XI.

Meeting one's Wife. — A long Conversation. — The Discovery. — Plans for Escape, &c., &c., &c. 328

LIFE IN THE EAST INDIES.

CHAPTER I.

MANILA AND ITS PEOPLE. — AN EXPLANATION. — AGREEABLE QUARTERS. — A SPANIARD'S HOME. — FIELD SPORTS. — VISITORS. — A HANDSOME LADY.

THERE is not a more pleasant city, whether for love, fun, or adventures, in the Eastern world, than Manila, the principal port of the Philippine Islands. It is under Spanish rule, and has so remained for the last two hundred years, and presents all the peculiar features of a large Spanish city, with its costumes and its customs, its trade and its convents, its loves and its jealousies, its handsome women and delicious fruits, its peculiar dishes, and its haughty Dons and insolent soldiers. Manila is only three days' sail from Hong Kong, and the merchant princes of the latter city are often glad to leave their busy cares and the dreary wastes of that portion of China, and steam over to the Spanish province, where youth and beauty are sure to greet them, and luxurious living and enticing amusements repay the truants for their trip.

The climate, during the dry season, which lasts about seven months in the year, is delightful. A clear sky, and a delicious breeze, which sweeps over the city, fresh from a magnificent bay, cooling the atmosphere both morning and evening, render the sunset promenade upon the Calsarda so attractive, that a foreigner would sooner think of foregoing his cheroot, than miss directing his steps across the stone bridge which spans the Pasig, regularly after dinner, between five and eight o'clock.

At those hours the regimental parades take place, and the brass bands discourse music for the edification of the gay throng, who ride and saunter along, exchanging the compliments of the day, retailing the latest scandal or the most remarkable news.

Dark-haired ladies, with eyes like liquid fire, lean back in their carriages, and a flash of their bright optics tells more than their lips dare to confess.

Wrinkled mothers and duennas watch the gallants, and are extremely officious to prevent lovers from exchanging a single word in private; but in defiance of their precautions, stolen glances and secret signs convey meaning known only to those intended, and many a private rendezvous is agreed upon, while parents imagine their daughters little think of lovers, or aught else but confessionals and repentance.

Still the gay throng passes onward, and with the crowd mix priests and men of all nations. The Englishman, with his bold, defiant air and sandy whiskers; the American, with his thin face and care-worn brow, wondering whether the cargo upon which he has ventured half his fortune will arrive at its port of destination in safety; the mercurial Frenchman, thinking of nothing but love, adventure, and pleasure; the swarthy Spaniard, with dark looks and sullen aspect, if a gallant regards the lady of his love with more than usual interest, or presumes to smile upon her in any other capacity than a friend of the family; the awkward Chinaman, with his pig-tail and wide trousers, meditating upon the profits which he expects to reap by a sale of paddy, and appearing courteous to all, while in his heart he despises the throng for its waste of money in riding in carriages as long as feet are able to support the body; Mestiza girls, with scanty clothing and voluptuous forms, and long, dark hair nearly reaching to their knees, flowing in the most profuse *abandon* over their necks and shoulders, chewing betel-nut, and spitting a blood-red secretion, which more than once has been mistaken by foreigners for the vital fluid from the lungs, — all these characters, and many others, can be seen of a pleasant afternoon upon the Calsarda, for then the wealth and beauty of Manila are abroad, and all flock to that celebrated promenade as readily as our citizens seek the Common, or Londoners Hyde Park.

I will tell you, however, before I proceed farther, how I happened to become a resident of Manila; for I have nothing to conceal, and much to reveal, and it is necessary that the reader should understand my position, and the reason why I, a stranger, leaped from a ship, and got quartered with one of the richest and most influential Dons of the town.

The house with which I was connected at Hong Kong made up its mind that money could be gained by purchasing rice at Manila and shipping it for China; but to carry on the business extensively, it was necessary that one of the partners, with a knowledge of the Spanish language, should reside at Manila, watch the market closely, and purchase at the best advantage.

I was luckily selected, and, armed with letters of credit and introduction to our correspondent, Don Arturo, a wealthy Spaniard, with immense pride and a pretty wife, and also with notes to Messrs. Russell Sturgis & Co., I bade a joyful farewell to China, and after four days passage arrived in safety at the place of my destination.

Of course, the instant I presented myself at the residence of Don Arturo, whose spacious mansion was located in Binondo, separated from the city proper by the Rio Pasig, I was welcomed with all the hospitality of a true son of Spain, and in spite of my strong declination, was compelled to take up my quarters with him, where I spent many pleasant hours, and quite a number of wretched ones, yet wholly unable to escape without giving serious offence to the Don and his fair wife.

At length I made new acquaintances, and under the pretence of desiring a week's shooting, would leave the house of my entertainers and remain absent until courtesy compelled me to return.

On the left bank of the Rio Pasig, about five miles from Manila, surrounded by cocoa-nut trees, mango trees, and luxuriant vegetation, such as only the most rich tropical climates can produce, stands a number of whitewashed buildings; and during the long summer afternoons, when the river boatmen have ceased their songs, and the washerwomen suspended their clothes-thrashing upon the smooth rocks, the buzz of a thousand spindles, and the panting of a steam engine as it regularly performs its work, can be heard, and creates feelings of intense surprise in the minds of strangers, who are aware of the Spaniard's aversion to labor saving machines, or to any innovation upon the forms of his ancestors.

The engine and the spindles are engaged in the manufacture

of rope of all sizes, from the mighty hawser to the finest lead line, and is the only cordage factory of any magnitude in the Eastern world, or was, at the time I write, in the years 18—. The enterprise was formed by American energy, carried through by American intelligence, and was then, and is now, for all I know to the contrary, entirely under American control, and owned entirely by American capitalists.

The machinery was purchased in Massachusetts; the long rope-walk was built, and then taken apart and put on board a vessel that sailed from Boston; and lastly, Massachusetts mechanics were employed to go to Santa Mesa, put the whole in complete order, and remain in the country and superintend the works, with the condition of owning a certain number of shares in case the enterprise was successful, of which there was some doubt, owing to the superstition of the natives and the jealousy of the government, which feared to give Americans a fair foothold in the country, on account of the peculiar ideas which our countrymen entertain respecting liberty of speech and action.

The enterprise was successful. After a sickly existence at first, Messrs. Huckford & Allen, who were the resident superintendents, gradually found that their wealth was increasing with their experience, and that at the end of their engagements they could return to the United States comparatively wealthy, and no longer sleep with weapons under their heads for fear of midnight attacks, or carry concealed pistols during the daytime to defend their lives, in case a workman should take a fancy to the clothes or the watch which they wore; for a more treacherous race of scamps never existed upon the face of the earth than the Manila Mestizos, or half-castes.

They will cut your throat for a dollar, if they can do it without being required to display bravery; they will steal all that you own, if your back is turned, even if ten minutes previous you had saved their lives from an anaconda or a wild buffalo; they will cheat you with unblushing impudence, and lie to screen themselves; they will murder you for having an amour with their wives or daughters, and then sell both to the next European they chance to meet; they will gamble their last shirt away, and steal their neighbor's; they will quarrel among themselves for hours at a time, and yet not come to blows; and lastly, they will share their plunder with the priests, who coolly take their portion, and give absolution with an unconcern for the crime that is truly refreshing in so warm a climate.

Such are a few of the peculiar characteristics of the race which the Spanish hold in subjection by the pure force of military despotism; and perhaps it is as well that the natives have cruel masters, for kindness is entirely thrown away when meted out to them.

At Messrs. Huckford & Allen's residence, at Santa Mesa, I was a welcome guest, for Americans were scarce upon the island, and what few there were were as clannish as Scotchmen.

Frequently would I mount my horse, and leaving word for my servant to follow in a banco with a change of linen, escape from the heat and bustle of Manila for a quiet residence of a few days at the factory. Then Allen, who was my senior by three years, would lay out the sport which we should pursue, and was never so happy as when, with dog and gun, we paddled up the river and shot pigeons, deer, or got a crack at deer. And when we returned, Mr. Huckford would lean his head upon his hand and listen to the recital of the sports of the day with all the enthusiasm of a true disciple of Nimrod — happy to think that we had enjoyed ourselves, yet never for a moment regretting that he was unable to leave the factory while Allen was absent, so that he could participate in the sports.

"What plans have you laid out for to-morrow?" inquired Mr. Huckford, as we drew back from the tea table and lighted our cheroots by a flickering flame fed by cocoa-nut oil.

We had returned home after a hard day's tramp, during which we had slain two deer and a number of birds with plumage like a rainbow, but which the cook had seized with guttural expressions of delight, and uttered a promise to prepare them for breakfast with curry and rice.

"We think of trying the woods just above San Pedro Macati. We met a lancero this afternoon, who stated that he had seen large numbers of deer there within a few days," answered Allen.

"Then you had better start before daylight, for the deer will seek the most sheltered spots before the sun gets high, and I don't think that it is safe within the darkest recesses of the woods," replied Mr. Huckford.

"Danger?" cried Allen; "why, what danger can there be to two well-armed men? If you mean *ladrones*, we should not fear a dozen, even armed with muskets of the most approved Spanish pattern."

"The ladrones will not trouble you," replied the head superintendent, "simply because men on gunning expeditions carry but little money upon their persons. No; I allude to a more serious consideration. The anaconda is a dangerous fellow to meet in a wood, and you know that he seldom gives warning of his attack."

I could not suppress a shudder, for I had seen the monsters in all their wildness and power during my residence in the island, and I confess that a close inspection was not agreeable.

"I think that I shall leave the forest of San Pedro to more mighty hunters than myself," I said, after a moment's hesitation. "I have no nerve for encountering the eyes of a serpent. The fate of all Englishmen who would not take advice is still in my ears."

"Bah!" replied Allen, with a smile; "I know of a pair of eyes that are much more dangerous to you than those of an anaconda. With a steady hand and a good rifle a snake can be overcome; but whoever heard of a second Joseph in this enlightened and uncommonly fast age?"

I observed a peculiar smile upon Mr. Huckford's face, and I was just about asking Allen for an explanation of his words, when the dogs in the yard set up a loud yelping, which betokened the presence of strangers. A moment after, the sound of carriage wheels was heard, and in a few seconds the vehicle stopped in front of the huge gate, which was always closed at night.

"Who can have arrived at this late hour of the night?" Mr. Huckford inquired.

"Can't you guess?" Allen replied; and I thought that the words were accompanied by a significant look which Mr. Huckford seemed to understand, for he rested his head upon his hand and looked at me as though he had some trouble, which he was anxious to confide under strict injunctions of secrecy.

"They must come in, I suppose," Allen said; and then raising his voice, he shouted to the servants, who were in the next room, to bring lights and open the gate to admit the visitors.

"*Ho, el casa!*" shouted a voice that I thought I recognized.

"Well, what is wanted?" replied Allen, stepping to the door which overlooked the outer court-yard; and shading the light with his hand, he allowed the flame to flash full upon the dark carriage beneath.

"My noble master, Don Arturo, is your visitor, and would fain speak with you right speedily," replied the coachman, who had served the old gentleman for many years, and had been drilled like a marine during that time for the purpose of delivering messages with proper pomposity.

"Is he alone?" Allen asked; and I thought that I detected a sneer in his tone as he inquired.

"His lady is with him, senor," replied the man.

"Did I not tell you?" Allen asked, turning to Mr. Huckford; but what he meant I didn't understand.

The old gentleman did not reply, but made a gesture of impatience, and lighted a fresh cheroot.

"What can have brought my friends here at this hour of the night?" I asked. "The road is none too secure between Mesa and Manila, and the diamonds which Donna Teresa wears would prove a prize to a gang of ladrones. Her husband has but little courage, and his hands tremble when excited."

"The night air is pleasant, and the lady needs exercise, I suppose," replied Mr. Huckford.

I did not consider the reason a valid one, but went to the head of the stairway and heard the servant drive away the savage dogs and quiet them, and then unlock and unbar the gate and admit the carriage.

I heard the voice of my old friend as he left the vehicle and was welcomed by Allen, and then I recognized the low, sweet tones of his wife, as the gallant Spaniard assisted her to alight, and led her up the stairway, preceded by the servants with lamps.

"Ah, Guillermo, my friend, we find you at last!" exclaimed Don Arturo, grasping my hand with much warmth. "We are very dull at home without you, and this time you have been absent for many days."

I returned his warm grasp and bowed low, as the wife, in all her queenly beauty, swept past and acknowledged my salute with a flash of her bright black eyes, that was like a shock of electricity to my nerves.

The servants placed chairs for the visitors, brought fresh coffee and additional cigars, and then vanished like ghosts.

"By all the most holy saints, but you have treated us most coldly, Guillermo," the Spaniard said, while sipping his coffee. "Six days absent, and not a word during all that time. *Diablo!* I began to think that something serious had happened."

"And did you imagine that we were incapable of taking care of our friend?" Allen asked, turning to the lady and regarding her beautiful face keenly.

"*Santa Marie!*" she replied, with a careless smile; "I had but little thought of the matter."

"I have passed a number of days in hunting and roaming through the forests," I said, "and have yet a few engagements with Senor Allen, who has promised to find me deer in abundance."

"And you forget that I promised to show you to-morrow the prettiest Mestizas girl in Santa Mesa," cried Allen.

I saw the blood flush into Donna Teresa's face, and her eyes sparkled like diamonds as she listened.

"For shame!" I said in English; "the lady does not understand such kind of jokes. Don't make me worse than I am in her eyes."

"Did you not say that a gentleman wished to see the Senor Guillermo in Manila?" the lady asked, turning to her husband, and speaking in subdued tones.

"To be sure; and I nearly forgot to mention the matter. A Chinaman is desirous of disposing of ten casco loads of rice, and will sell cheap for cash. You must see him in the morning without delay."

"I have already done so: to-morrow he will present drafts on your house for payment," I replied.

I saw a shade of disappointment cross the face of the lady, and I wondered at it. Don Arturo required an explanation.

"The Chinaman, learning that I was at Santa Mesa, took a banco, and came up the river this afternoon. I found him here when I returned, and completed the bargain in ten minutes."

"Then our journey has been useless," replied the Spaniard, turning to his wife; but she did not answer. She seemed occupied with her own thoughts, and her glorious eyes, veiled by long lashes, were cast upon the floor.

"No, not useless," I replied, "for I am positive that Señors Huckford and Allen are grateful for the pleasure of your company.

This house rarely opens its doors to give admittance to ladies, so that when they condescend to visit us we extend a hearty welcome."

The lady raised her eyes, and darted a glance, rapid as lightning, at my face; but, quick as she was, Allen saw it.

"Let me see," I continued, in a musing tone; "I have been here six days to-day, and during my absence from the city I have not exchanged a word with lady or Mestizas before this evening."

"You are mad," muttered Allen, in English, "and are doing all you can to feed —"

I did not comprehend him, and indeed I was regarding the wife too closely to pay much attention to his words; and I felt happy when I saw that she smiled upon me for my virtuous habits, and that her eyes looked more soft after receiving the information.

"We must return to the city," the Spaniard said at length, glancing towards his wife; but she made no response.

"You will remain with us till morning," Mr. Huckford said, although I thought he spoke rather coldly.

The Don looked towards his wife for instruction.

"If we return we must have an escort, for the hour is late for travellers," she replied.

"If you will go I shall accompany you," I said. "We cannot think of letting so much beauty run the risk of insult from every roving band of ladrones."

"But you forget that I accompany her," cried the old Spaniard, with dignity; and had I not known him I should have certainly thought that he was a man to fight to the death.

"True, but what can one man do against a dozen?"

"Die," answered the son of Spain, solemnly, placing his hand upon his breast like a knight of St. Louis.

"Let us end this discussion," the lady exclaimed, with a haughty wave of her jewelled hand. "I cannot think of exposing the life of my husband. We will accept of the hospitality of our friends, and remain here for the night."

"I supposed it would come to that in the end," muttered Allen, in English; and as he spoke he rose, and gave the necessary orders to prepare the best room in the building, and to put the horses up for the night.

I had always classed Allen as a cold and distant man in the

2

presence of ladies, and more than once I had joked him on his evident dislike to Donna Teresa. He had always repelled the imputation; but still I was satisfied that there was ill feeling between the lady and him, and that I was in some measure the cause. At any rate, on the evening in question, after the lady had decided to remain all night, not the most punctilious could find fault with Allen's deportment. He was kind and attentive, and even brought out his harp, which the servants were forbidden to dust or look at, and placed it before the haughty beauty, begging in humble terms that she would honor him by touching the chords with her delicate fingers.

"Do you wish to speak with her alone?" Allen whispered, as he passed me.

I looked at him in astonishment, and did not understand the meaning of the question.

"It's all right, my boy; I'll find an opportunity," he continued, mistaking my silence for assent.

"*Ho muchachos, traer vino,*" Allen shouted; and as the lads entered with decanters and bottles, the old Spaniard rubbed his hands with glee, and, regardless of his wife, challenged Mr. Huckford to drink the health of every person of note on the island.

I loved the music of the harp better than wine, and while the rest were drinking glass for glass, leaned over the back of Donna Teresa's chair, and chatted with her in a low tone.

"Tell me," said Donna Teresa, while she was carelessly drawing her hand over the harp, "what Senor Allen meant when he spoke to you in English this morning."

"Upon my word, I have forgotten," I replied. "The subject was too trivial to occupy my attention when a lady was present."

She darted a sharp glance at my face, as though to judge of my sincerity; but as she met my gaze of admiration, she colored, and swept the harp a few times as though endeavoring to recall a favorite air.

"Will you never give up this dangerous pastime of yours? Can hunting be so fascinating that all society is forgotten, and all business neglected?" she asked.

"I have few friends in Manila," I replied, "and I sometimes think that the less they see of me, the more of their esteem I shall possess."

"You wrong your friends and do great injustice to my husband, who is never happy unless he can converse with you after the business of the day."

"How can a man be unhappy, possessing so beautiful a wife?" I asked.

She cast a reproachful glance at me, and then remained silent so long that I feared I had offended her, and was about to apologize, when Don Arturo, who was being plied with wine by Allen, and whose weak head was incapable of carrying all that he swallowed, volunteered to sing a song, and commanded silence accordingly.

"By the mass, I know not if I can recollect it, for 'tis forty years since I learned the lines while coming from Spain. Let me see; it begun thus: —

"'The king has forty galleons laden deep with ore;
Our queen is full as rich, for she has many more;
The Spanish ships are manned with braves—'"

Here the worthy Don grew inharmonious and hoarse, and while trying to recover the tune, forgot his song, plunged his head into a huge glass, and drained its contents.

"You see how happy he is, and how much I am prized when wine is on the table. I should be proud of my husband — should I not?"

How scornful she looked at the old man, who had bound her to himself by vows which she could not break, much as she fretted under them.

"You will return to the city with us to-morrow — will you not?" she asked; and when she spoke to me I noticed that her voice was soft and gentle, and that her hauteur was gone.

"Not to-morrow," I replied. "Before your welcome arrival, we laid out our plans for a day's shooting in the woods of San Pedro. I must not disappoint *amigo* Allen."

"Of course he is of more importance than myself. Go by all means."

She struck the harp a number of energetic blows, as though she felt indignant at the carousal of her husband; but in a few minutes all expression of displeasure passed from her face, and she was as handsome as ever.

"I wish that you had never met with these people," she said

at length. "Who knows but something may happen to you while on expeditions of a dangerous nature? and then my husband would be blamed by your friends."

"No fear of that," I answered, laughing. "My friends know that I am able to take care of myself."

"Hark," she said, suddenly, directing her attention to the table. "Don Arturo is talking of hunting."

The old gentleman was listening as well as he was able to Allen's details of the day's sport, and he grew enthusiastic as he thought of the tramp through the woods, and the trophies to be gained by a good shot.

"I go with you to-morrow, senors, and will do my share of the labor. I used to know a hunting song which I fain would sing when I awaken in the morning, but it has slipped my brain."

"But your fair wife may object to your exposing your precious life," Allen said, with a glance towards the lady, which caused the rich blood to mantle her cheeks until they seemed to burn.

"I shall be very sorry if Don Arturo undertakes any such expedition," she said.

"Bah! you women know not the pleasures of a hunter's life," cried the Spaniard, contemptuously. "My friends, we will start at daylight; we will kill many deer and much game, and when we return my wife will welcome us as heroes, and wreathe garlands for the most successful hunter."

"I shall do nothing of the kind," she said, firmly. "If you go, 'tis without my consent, and if you return —"

"'Tis without your wish, hey?" Allen said in English.

The lady turned to me for an explanation, and I could see by her flashing eyes that she thought the remark one calculated to humiliate her.

"He says," I whispered, — and Heaven forgive me the lie, — "that if he had a wife as beautiful as yourself, all the deer that roam in the forest would not tempt him from your presence."

The beauty pouted for a moment, as though she was not quite satisfied with the interpretation; but just at that moment old Maje, the best deer hound that belonged to the house, uttered a sharp cry, arose from the corner where he had been lying in the room, and looked wishfully in the faces of his masters.

"What is it, Maje?" Mr. Huckford asked, patting the animal on his head.

The dog looked in his face with a wishful glance, and then uttered a prolonged howl.

"There's death in the night wind," Mr. Huckford said, thoughtfully, pushing back his full glass untasted, and glancing uneasily at the open windows.

"How do you know that?" Don Arturo asked, with a shudder, as he rapidly crossed himself.

"The dog can scent death an hour before it arrives, and he has never yet deceived me by his warning. Pray Heaven that none here are doomed."

"Amen! May the saints preserve us. I wish that I was safe at my residence in the city, for I like not the quiet gloom that reigns here," muttered the valiant Spaniard.

"Heaven overlooks us all," Mr. Huckford said, piously; and while speaking he drew a pair of pistols from his pocket, and examined the charges. "You are as safe here as you would be surrounded by a regiment of the best soldiers of Spain. If your time had come, force could not save you."

"Go find 'em, Maje," Allen said; and the dog, with grave dignity, walked to an open window that faced the Pasig, put his paws upon the sill, and snuffed the night air three or four times, but without uttering a cry or manifesting uneasiness.

"It's not in that quarter," the superintendents said, exchanging glances.

The hound retired from the window, and went to the second one, which faced the city. A line of sheds, under which workmen prepared the hemp for the factory, was in view, enclosed by a high wall built of baked *adobes*. An active man could have scaled it without much trouble; but the instant the yard was gained a crowd of ferocious dogs, trained to make war upon the natives in the night time, would have devoured an intruder before he could have secured a foothold.

For five minutes the hound stood at the window, snuffing the cool breeze, which just stirred the leaves of the mango trees in the yard; but at length he retired from the casement, and wandered slowly around the room, as though he was uncertain what to do next.

"Senor Allen, is there any danger?" inquired the Spaniard,

who seemed sobered by the sudden stillness of the room, and the mysterious proceedings of the dog.

"We hope not," replied Allen, with an attempt to seem indifferent.

"I care not for myself, but for my wife," Don Arturo muttered, with a glance towards the lady which she seemed not to heed.

"There is no danger," Allen said, cheerfully; "and even if there is, we are strong, and can protect her as well as ourselves. Let her retire with her husband to her room, and in the morning she will smile at the perils of a night at Santa Mesa."

"Yes, yes; let her go to her room!" cried the Don, eagerly; but whether to shelter himself or his wife was then a difficult question to solve.

"I shall remain here," she answered, firmly; and all our urging could not change her resolution.

"Perhaps the servants may account for the singular conduct of the dog," Allen remarked, as he strode across the room, and opened the door leading to their apartment.

He called the names of the men, but there was no answer. The lights in the room were extinguished, and the fire upon the hearth was out.

The hound had followed his master to the door, and after a snuff or two, uttered a fierce howl, and attempted to dash into the vacated room; but Allen prevented him, and shutting the door, bolted it.

"They are there," he said, in answer to Mr. Huckford's look of inquiry.

"Then we must arm ourselves, and if an attempt is made, repel it," was the firm response.

Allen seized a light, and from a closet brought out a miscellaneous collection of arms, from which each man selected what he desired, and began to prepare them carefully.

Don Arturo looked on in astonishment, but did not offer to assist us.

"Tell me what all this means, Senor Allen?" the lady asked, somewhat bewildered at the novelty of our preparations.

"It means, lady, that the ladrones have heard that a lot of silver was brought here to-day, and they have a st___ desire to possess it. The scamps are already in the house, and mus___ have entered while your carriage was occupying the attention of the boys at the gate."

"But the servants should have given an alarm," she said.

"The servants may have given the information, and therefore expect to reap a portion of the benefits of the robbery; or they may have been warned, and fled hours ago; again, they may be bound hand and foot, and kept quiet by means of a knife. At any rate, I would not swear that the fellows are not concerned with the ladrones."

Even while Allen was speaking, he was employed in ramming down bullets and fitting caps to his guns and rifles.

"This is dreadful," murmured Donna Teresa, pale as death.

"It is all your fault — you would come here to-night!" exclaimed the Spaniard, pettishly.

"Peace," she said, so sternly, and with such a flash of her eyes, that the husband held his tongue, and watched the proceedings with considerable apprehension.

"Now, then, out with the light, and let us wait patiently the result," Mr. Huckford said; and in obedience to his orders we sat in the dark for half an hour, and yet not a sound was to be heard excepting the dogs in the yard; and they appeared uneasy, and growled at intervals, as though not exactly satisfied with the state of affairs.

I took a seat by the side of Donna Teresa, and I suppose that she mistook me for her husband, for I felt one of her hands laid lightly upon my shoulder, while the other sought my grasp, and remained there, with pulse beating much more regular than my own, although her flesh was full as warm to the touch; and I must confess that I felt as though suffering from a fever. I did not dare to undeceive her. I sat there and listened and held her hand, and thought that I should not object to remaining in the same position through the night.

"Hush!" whispered Mr. Huckford; "I hear the villains stir in the next room."

"May the saints forgive me all my sins," murmured the Spaniard, who was seated a few steps from his wife.

I supposed that she would withdraw her hand from mine when he spoke; but she must have been busy with her thoughts, and not noticed the remark.

I placed my pistols in my belt, and moved my chair silently and carefully nearer the lady, for she leaned heavily upon my chair and seemed to sleep. Quietly I put my right arm around her waist, and drew her towards me; and then upon my shoulder fell her head with its profusion of hair, that was soft as silk, and wavy as Manila Bay during a typhoon. I felt her sweet breath upon my cheek, and the temptation was too great to be overcome; if all the moralists in the world had lectured me upon the enormity of my crime, I could not have resisted pressing my lips to hers.

"There they are," again cried Mr. Huckford; but I have an impression that he was mistaken that time, for the noise sounded to me like a kiss.

The lady did not move her head from my shoulder; but the devil instigated Don Arturo to think of his wife just at that moment.

"Where are you, Teresa?" he asked; "at this hour of danger I should be by your side."

I expected that the beautiful head would be withdrawn from my shoulder with a slight scream; but to my surprise it remained where I had placed it, and the owner exclaimed, —

"Remain where you are, dear, for I fear, if you move, that you will betray your presence to the ladrones, in case they are listening for a moment."

"And Guillermo — where is he?" queried the old gentleman, with friendly interest.

I was just about to speak, when Allen came to my rescue, and prevented my whereabouts from being known to the husband.

"He is sleeping in a chair near me," Allen said; and then continued in English, "I hope that the old fellow hasn't got a lucifer match in his pocket; if he has, you'd better look to yourself, my friend."

I made no reply; but I pressed the beautiful form which I held in my arms closer and closer, and my heart beat wildly, when I found that she did not resist.

At this instant a hand was laid lightly upon the latch of the door leading to the servants' apartments, and a gentle pressure was made to force the door open. Not succeeding, all remained quiet for a few minutes, during which interval I could hear the beating of the lady's heart.

"What will be their next move?" Allen asked.

"I suppose that they will stave the door open, or else batter down the partition. If we only knew how many there were I should feel like giving battle without this delay," Mr. Huckford said.

I thought of a plan that would be successful; but I did not dare communicate it while I was sitting, for fear of revealing my position to Don Arturo. As delay was dangerous, I gently withdrew my arms from the lady, and bestowing a second kiss on her red lips, crept silently across the room to Allen.

"There's some one moving across the floor!" cried Don Arturo, in alarm.

"Be quiet, my friend; 'tis but the dog," Allen said; and the explanation was satisfactory, although I heard the Spaniard mutter,—

"I had no idea he was so large."

"Let us not wait for the ladrones to begin the attack," I whispered to Allen; "because it's possible that they may send for recruits, finding us prepared for battle. We shall be kept here in a state of suspense until daylight, and perhaps while we are nodding, an entrance may be effected."

"The only thing that we can do is to escape, and leave the building for the scamps to plunder, for which they would thank us, and repeat the experiment the first time that money was known to be in the house. That wou't do, as long as there's three able-bodied men ready to fight a little," was Allen's response.

"But what say you to calling in the dogs quietly, and after they are all mustered, open the door and let them war with the black scamps. We can use our pistols, and by firing at random help the brutes considerably."

Allen thought of the plan for a moment, and at length suggested it to Mr. Huckford, who agreed that unless the natives mustered in large numbers it would be successful.

The only thing he feared was, that the ladrones would make a rush and carry the building before we could repel them. We at length convinced the old gentleman that the rush of dogs would so dismay the ruffians, that safety would be sought in flight, and that all attempts to rob the house would be abandoned.

"Let the lady and her husband retire to the closet, and we will try the experiment," Mr. Huckford said. "The dogs will be likely, in their excitement, to bite them instead of our enemies, and that we must guard against. The lady is too fair to suffer ill treatment."

Allen lighted a lamp, and its beams fell upon the terrified countenance of the Spaniard, who, seated some distance from his wife, was waiting for the termination of events, and counting his beads with trembling hands; while the lady, with her dark mantilla drawn around her neck and shoulders, and her form straight as an arrow, sat without manifesting visible signs of fear, although but a few feet from us were ruffians who would not have respected her high position, beauty, or wealth, and would have torn her diamond ear-rings from her ears, and laughed at her cries of pain, had she been sensible of the indignity.

There was a striking contrast between the woman and the man, and I forgave her the look of contempt which she bestowed upon Arturo, even if there was but little conjugal tenderness in it.

"Three silver candlesticks and a gold one will I give to the Church of the Saviour if I escape from this gang of thieves without a scratch, or loss of money," muttered the Don, as Allen approached him.

"Then come with me without a moment's delay. Guillermo, look to the lady and explain our plans. She can understand them, and will remain quiet."

I needed but a few words to relate our project, and she listened so calmly that I could have embraced her for her heroism, had I had a brother's or a husband's right to have done so.

In the large apartment where we were besieged, and which was on the second floor, the lower part being devoted to business purposes, was a closet where clothes were hung, and many valuable odds and ends thrust for convenience and security.

It was large enough to hold half a dozen persons as long as they were inclined to assume a perpendicular position, while two could sit upon chairs, and experience no inconvenience, even if compelled to remain there for hours.

I removed all the weapons which the closet contained, for I feared that Don Arturo might not be the most proper person to use one in case of excitement, and then I handed the lady to her allotted place, and was rewarded by a look that bespoke volumes of gratitude.

"You will be careful, Guillermo," she whispered.

"Do not fear, lady. I will sell my life before the ruffians shall reach your retreat;" and I think I meant what I said, for somehow, I began to look upon Donna Teresa no longer in the light of an acquaintance, cold and distant, but as a lovely woman, capable of inspiring a stoic with passion.

"I mean not that," she cried, hastily. "I allude to your own danger. Be not rash and headstrong. I would rather give half my fortune than know that blood is to be spilt."

"I'll give five candlesticks," muttered her husband, who thought that she was beseeching the saints for protection. "Five candlesticks — one of solid silver, and the others excellent imitations. If that offer don't save us, there's little use in having saints."

A noise in the adjoining room, as though the ladrones had thrown off all disguise, and were determined to carry our quarters by assault, quickened our motions. With a hurried word of courage to the lady I closed the door, and was just in time to see Allen admit six huge dogs, of the mastiff and bloodhound breed, with strong jaws and powerful chests, ferocious as wolves starved for food, and capable of tracking a native even into the busiest portions of the city.

They prowled around the room with sullen looks, and even appeared anxious to effect an entrance into the closet where we had concealed the Spaniard and his wife.

"They are in a delightful humor to-night," Allen whispered, "and will bite and tear like tigers. They scent the black devils, and are eager for a fray as the deer hound, which has to stand back when the others are disposed for a fight."

The brutes did not utter a whimper to give warning to the rogues of the surprise which we intended, being kept in subjection by the short whip which Allen held in his hand.

"We are all ready," Allen said, addressing Mr. Huckford; and he was just about to give the signal for the bolt to be withdrawn from the door, when a tremendous blow was struck against the partition, that caused the building to shake from its foundation.

"They are showing their hands in earnest," muttered Allen. "If we would only run for it, I dare say that we should find the road free of our obliging friends, and they would only be too glad to get rid of us."

"The instant the door is opened," Mr. Huckford said, finding that the dogs were no longer disposed to remain quiet, "give the scamps a broadside from your pistols. As for me," he continued, holding up an old musket, with a bore like a blunderbuss, "I have put in a few handfuls of shot here, which I expect will scatter and do execution. The Lord forgive me if I am acting wrong."

The dogs were collected near the door, and watched with glowing eyeballs for the signal to commence the attack. The light in our room was extinguished to prevent the ladrones from picking us off before we had time to serve them with the surprise which we had prepared, and we ranged ourselves in such a manner that there was no danger of our shooting each other.

Again was there a stout blow upon the partition, and I heard the boards crack, and the dust descend in showers upon our heads.

The dogs, no longer seeing the whip, uttered simultaneous howls of rage, and dashed against the door as though they desired to be at the bloody work without delay.

"Let them go," shouted Mr. Huckford; and at the word the bolt was slipped, and the door thrown open.

"Seize them!" we yelled; but the dogs did not wait for the words. With ferocious yells they sprang into the room where the ladrones were assembled, and then, for a moment, I was stunned by the discharge of our pistols, which we fired in rapid succession without provoking a single shot in return.

The yells of the frightened Mestizos, as they sought to escape from the fierce charge, and the groans of the wounded, who had fallen and were trampled under foot, were frightful. Down the stone staircase we could hear them stumble, as they rushed over each other; but loud above all, the savage growls of the dogs as they bit, and shook, and worried their victims, were most appalling.

At length all was quiet, excepting the fierce snarling of the dogs; and when we ventured to light a lamp and inspect the scene of the slaughter, it made our hearts turn sick to witness the spectacle.

It required the use of the whip, used with no gentle hand, to beat off the brutes, and turn them loose in the yard, where they attempted to follow the footsteps of the flying enemy, but were prevented by the high walls, over which the natives had sprung with but little difficulty, and made their escape in the wilderness beyond.

On every side were wounded natives, bleeding and mangled b

dog and bullet, while the brick floor was slippery with blood, and covered with remnants of clothing, torn from the persons of the robbers, as they sought to escape from their ferocious enemies. Pieces of black cloth, about the size of the face, with apertures for the mouth, eyes, and nose, were also found in abundance, which showed that the ladrones had taken their usual course to keep their countenances from being known in case of a collision where there were lights.

As there was no danger of another attack that night, we released the lady and her husband from confinement; but the Don was too terrified to utter any words excepting praise for his wonderful escape; and the only way we could bring him to his senses was to pour half a dozen glasses of wine down his throat, and then make him take up his quarters upon a mattress in the sitting-room, which was free of all marks of violence, and much more comfortable than a distant chamber, after the scenes through which we had passed, and were still to pass.

As for Donna Teresa, she was composed as a heroine; and I think that she would have even offered her services to attend the wounded, had she not known that we would have rejected them.

Humanity demanded that we should relieve the sufferings of the miserable wretches, who were crawling upon the floor, moaning for aid, as much as possible; but we could do but little until daylight, as none of us liked the idea of driving or paddling to Manila for a physician at that time of night, and run the risk of getting murdered to pay us for our charity. But we did the best we could; and while binding up the fellows' wounds, we were careful to get a good view of their faces, and found, as we expected, that many of them were workmen who had been employed in the factory ever since its commencement, and received wages which they could not obtain at any other business. One of the wounded men in particular, named Maquil, who had been appointed as a sort of overseer of a division of spinners, and who had always manifested the utmost attachment for Mr. Huckford and Mr. Allen, was found with a charge of shot through his right leg, and several bad-looking marks upon his arms and body, where the dogs had buried their teeth, and in one or two instances, torn whole pieces of live flesh from his limbs.

"There is a man," said Mr. Huckford, pointing to the groaning wretch, "who has always received favors at our hands; yet if I question him in regard to his being here, he will lie most outrageously. Listen and hear him."

"You are badly hurt, Maquil," my host said.

"Si, senor," replied the fellow, with an attempt at a smile, which was sadly out of place.

"And you came with the others to rob your old friends?"

"O, no, senor; I came to help you, but arrived too late to get the ladrones to retire. I did not hear of the attack until an hour since, and then hastened here to save or die with you. The senor has been kind to Maquil, and he don't forget it. The saints have had you in their keeping."

"Did you ever hear a cooler lie told in your life?" Mr. Huckford asked, in English; and I must confess that the fellow's impudence staggered me, but I should have believed him if I had not known the treacherous character of the natives.

"Can you help the soldiers arrest the ladrones who escaped?" Mr. Huckford asked, in a low tone, so that those who were in the room should not overhear the remark.

"Shall I get paid for it?" the wretch asked.

"Perhaps."

"Then I think that I can; but I must have the silver before I perform the work."

We left the liar and traitor to his sufferings, for it would have been useless to have induced the government to send in pursuit, even if good evidence had been offered, exposing the principal actors in the drama. We could only feel grateful that we had repelled the attack, and inflicted such injury upon our assailants as would cause them to remember it for many days, and be cautious how they struck a blow in future.

"Donna Teresa feels a little nervous; perhaps you had better comfort and cheer her," Allen said, while we were clearing the room of the injured.

"What can I do for her happiness?" I asked.

"Well, that is a question that I am unable to answer, and it is probable that she would be in the dark as much as myself, if interrogated," was the dry reply.

I saw that I could be spared from the work which I had helped perform; so cleansed the stains from my hands, and once more sought the presence of the lady, whom I found seated by the side of her husband; and the latter, as though to show his contempt for the danger through which we had passed, was snoring most unmelodiously, having drank freely of wine to drown all recollection of the fight.

Donna Teresa was leaning her face upon her hands, and did not see me until I spoke.

"There is no longer any danger," I said; "the ladrones have fled, and will not return. You are as safe here as you would be in Manila, surrounded by a regiment of the line."

"And for my life, and that of my husband, I have to thank you and the other brave Americans. I should like to live in a country that produces such brave men," she said; and by the dim light I thought that she directed a look of contempt at the sluggard by her side. "Tell me of your home," she continued, laying one of her delicate hands upon my own, which was hard and rough through arduous sports in the forest and mountains; "I would know more of America than I do; I wish to hear of its customs and inhabitants, its climate and ladies."

"What shall I tell you of the latter?" I asked her.

"Tell me of their beauty, for I know that they must be handsome."

"They are fair," I replied, "and very delicate; for our young ladies entertain an idea that health is not compatible with beauty."

Donna Teresa opened her large eyes with astonishment, and was inclined to be incredulous. Enjoying the most perfect health herself, and taught from an early age that illness was only to be avoided by plenty of exercise in the open air, to which add bathing and a regular diet, it is no wonder that she was inclined to pity the women of America, and wonder that they should fear the air at any hour excepting the night.

Time flew rapidly while we were thus engaged, and I was surprised to see the light turn pale, and the gray shadows of morning steal into the room, while I supposed that it was near midnight, and that three or four hours still remained for conversation.

"I am sorry to disturb your tête-à-tête," Allen said, rousing me from my dream of love and happiness; "but it is necessary that some one should proceed to Manila and inform the mayor of what has taken place, and request a military commissioner to visit the factory without delay, and remove the dead and wounded to the hospital."

The lady started at the sound of his voice, and hastily drew her hand from mine; and I could see that she colored to her eyebrows, when she caught Allen's look of mischief.

"The Don has slept most soundly, I should judge, if he has snored at that rate all night," Allen said, with a malicious grin, which we were too wise to notice. "If we can start your husband, senora, he would confer a favor on us by proceeding direct to Manila, and stating the particulars of the attack. He could benefit us much, and save us thousands of questions, which as foreigners we should have to answer, but which he, being so well known, would escape. Dare you wake him, lady?" Allen asked.

She looked her disdain at the question, before she replied.

"'Tis a piece of work that I leave for the most robust," she answered. "Shake the senor, and not lightly, for he sleeps soundly."

Allen followed her advice; but the husband only tossed arms about his head, as though fighting desperately with overpowering numbers.

"Ho, Don Arturo, awake! we need your aid!" shouted Allen.

"One glass more, and the last. To the health of my wife," murmured the sleeping man.

"You see, madam, that he thinks of you always. He is a constant husband — is he not?"

She did not reply, and Allen seemed ashamed of the question, for he laid violent hands upon the Don, and in spite of growls and protestations, soon had him in a sitting position.

"You sleep sound, Don Arturo, after your hard night's work. Come, drink a single glass of wine, and then you will be thoroughly awake."

The old gentleman made no objection, and the liquor seemed to revive him.

"I dreamed," he said, "that I had fought desperately with ladrones, and that I had slain half a dozen in defending my wife."

"The dream was more real than such fancies are apt to be. Come, we want you to proceed to Manila, and lay the circumstances of the case before the mayor, and then hasten back with a physician."

"My horses and servant," muttered the Don.

"Are in the yard and waiting. Your coachman pretends that he slept through the fight without hearing anything of it; but we may believe as much of that as we please."

The Spaniard looked towards his wife, as though undecided what course to pursue.

"Leave her with us until you return. She is nervous, and needs rest," Allen said.

"No doubt, no doubt!" Don Arturo exclaimed, as he rolled his rich blanket around his form, and prepared to start; "she feared that I would expose my life to the knives of the assassins, and I believe that I was rather reckless during the fight. I will return in two hours' time, and then talk further of the matter. I will have soldiers here to investigate, or I'll give the mayor a piece of my mind that will last for a twelvemonth. Farewell, Teresa, and don't be uneasy at my absence;" and with this parting show of tenderness, the Spaniard vanished, and in a few minutes we heard his carriage rolling over the hard road on its way to Manila.

"Your room has been prepared, senora," Allen said, "and as you have passed a sleepless and terrible night, perhaps it would be better if you refresh yourself with a little rest."

Even if she was disposed to decline the offer, which I hoped she would, she could not overcome Allen's solicitations, and therefore retired with a stately grace that was charming to contemplate, while her adieus were uttered in a voice sweet as a first-class dulce.

"That is hardly fair," I muttered, as she disappeared; "I was anticipating an interview two hours long —"

"So I supposed; but believe me, it is safer to have her in her chamber with you on the outside, than to be sitting within a few feet of each other during the husband's absence. Too many prying eyes would watch your motions, and carry reports to Don Arturo, and it would need but a word to rouse his jealousy to fever heat."

"But we are alone," I said.

"We are now, but in a few minutes our servants will return, and they are quick to observe, you know."

"Do you mean to say that you will receive the scamps, after they deserted you as they did last night?"

"To be sure," Allen answered; "they are acquainted with our ways and wants, and even if we change, we should get men just as bad, if not worse, besides having the trouble of teaching the fellows their duty."

"But the rascals have been leagued with the robbers," I suggested.

"To tell you the truth," my companion replied, "I am inclined to think that they were; but we can't prove it, and of course the rascals will deny that they knew an attack was to be made. I hear Mr. Huckford at them already. Let us go and listen to their excuses."

We passed to the room used for the kitchen, and there saw three knaves, with marks of astonishment upon their faces, listening to the scolding which the superintendent was administering, and looking at the wounded and dead Mestizos, yet there was no sign of sympathy for their countrymen, because they had made an attack and lost, and therefore were not in a condition to share the plunder which they expected.

"Which of you informed the gang that there was silver in the house?" Mr. Huckford demanded.

"The senor is laughing at us," they whined. "We love the senor and his friends, and would have given information had we known that an attack was expected."

"Why did you leave the house?"

"We knew that there was to be a dance the other side of the river, and we went, because we supposed that the senors would not require our services longer. We feel sorry at what has happened, and will be more careful in future."

"We will pardon you on one condition," Mr. Huckford said.

"The senor is kind — let him mention the favor that he desires."

"Discover the name of the ladrone who led the attack last night, and where he can be found."

With one accord the scamps declared that they knew nothing of the business, and that they should excite the hostility of their neighbors if they made any such movement; but we took no notice of their protestations, and pretended that the soldiers whom we had sent for would seize them as witnesses, and at length banish them from the island as murderers.

Then they hesitated and whispered together, and at length requested permission to talk with the wounded men, which we granted; and after the lapse of half an hour, they reported that the man who had planned the attack and led it, was one Juan Baptiste, a fellow who had been the terror of the neighborhood for the last two years, and who held the natives in such subjection that there was not one who would refuse him a helping hand through fear.

The Spaniards dreaded the fellow, for he had inflicted much injury upon the wealthy residents of Santa Mesa, and many attempts had been made to capture him, yet without success; and there was even a reward of two thousand dollars offered for his apprehension at one time, for a daring robbery and murder, which he had alone committed some ten months before the attack upon the factory. The natives would gladly have betrayed the rascal for that sum, but were fearful of the vengeance of his friends, who shared his spoils, and warned him of danger when it was near.

"Where does this man find shelter?" Allen asked.

"He has lately lived in the swamps of Sar. Macati, where no one dares venture but those acquainted," was the reply of the servants, with ominous shakes of their head, as they thought of the dangers.

Allen motioned me to accompany him to another room, where we could converse without danger of being overheard.

"Well," he said, "what do you think of allowing Juan to continue his career unmolested?"

"How can we help ourselves?" I asked.

"By following him to the swamp, and making an effort for his capture."

"The undertaking is dangerous and difficult," I replied.

"Not so dangerous as it appears at the first glance. We can take our three best dogs, and they will follow him through the swamps, and corner him, unless he is smarter than I think he is."

I reflected on the matter for a moment, and then consented to accompany Allen on his disagreeable expedition; but first it was necessary that we should secure the consent of Mr. Huckford, and that we should start without delay.

The superintendent was unwilling that we should incur the

risk; but at length Allen talked him over, and we made ready for the journey, taking good care that the servants should know nothing of our proposed expedition, for fear that they should manage, in some way, to communicate the alarm, and thus defeat our object.

We hastily swallowed our breakfast long before the sun was visible, and then equipped ourselves in costumes suited for the business which we were about to enter upon; for the character of the swamp was too well known to us to expect to find easy travel, and no obstacles of a serious nature.

We wore blouses made of linen cloth, which fitted tight to our bodies, while for pants we selected the thickest that we owned, and found that they were none too strong before our return. To protect our feet we wore heavy sea boots, with long tops, into which we thrust our pants, as much to keep them out of the way as to prevent snakes from seeking a refuge on our bodies, and rendering themselves disagreeable.

Our next business was to see that our rifles were properly loaded, and that our knives were in good order; and by the time we had accomplished that task, Mr. Huckford joined us, holding in his hand a shoe made of untanned leather, and of monstrous dimensions.

"I found this in the yard near the wall," he said, "and I am told that it is the property of Juan, who in his flight dropped it. I think that the story is correct, for I recollect of seeing no native in these parts who has so large a foot. It will be useful for the dogs, in finding the fellow's trail."

While Allen and Mr. Huckford were discussing the subject, I slipped quietly out of the room, and knocked timidly at the door of Donna Teresa's chamber. I expected that she was asleep; but to my surprise, she opened the door, and looked somewhat astonished when she saw my costume.

"How now, Guillermo!" she said; "what is the meaning of your strange dress?"

"I shall be absent from the factory for a few hours," I replied, "and I desired to pay my respects to one whom I esteem so highly before I go, fearing that you may be in Manila when I return."

"But where are you going?" she continued, her color slightly changing while she spoke.

"But a few miles from here. I shall return before night, and hope to have a story of interest to relate to you this evening, if you will promise not to leave the factory."

"I promise," she said, as she laid her hand upon mine, in proof of her sincerity; and I thought that I felt a gentle pressure, which I ventured to return. "You will not expose your life while absent, for if you should, Don Arturo will be miserable. Remember that he takes a great interest in your welfare."

I promised, and yet I was still reluctant to leave her, for she looked so melancholy that all my resolutions were forgotten, and I was more than half inclined to tell her that I loved her to distraction, and to ask her compassion.

"Say no more now, but go!" she exclaimed, hurriedly, hastily withdrawing her hand, which I had forgotten to relinquish.

I turned to discover the cause of her alarm, and saw one of the servants hastily retreating through a door which was nearly opposite to where we stood. I ran after him to discover if he had listened to our conversation; but before I could cross the corridor he had disappeared, and further pursuit would have been useless.

I returned to the lady, and assured her that no one was acting the part of a spy on our actions; but she did not seem much comforted by the assurance, possibly because she knew the Mestizo race better than I did.

"There is not one of them in the house," she said, hurriedly, "but would sell us for a piece of silver, unless he thought he could make more by keeping silent. Not," she added, with extreme hauteur, "that I have anything to conceal from my husband; but he is old and jealous, and trifles disturb him. Now go, and let me meet you at dinner, or even before, if possible."

She extended her hand as she spoke, and after a warm pressure I left her, more in love than ever, and inwardly cursing the expedition which was to take me from her society, even for a few hours. I found Allen in the court-yard waiting my appearance; but he made no remark, and in a few minutes we had the dogs which we desired selected from the pack, and put them on the scent.

The animals understood their business, for they had been trained when young, so that we found no difficulty in getting upon the track of Juan, or, at least, the owner of the shoe.

The dogs led towards the river, which was about one hundred

and fifty yards from the factory; and as Allen had expected that would be their course, he had ordered a banco to be stationed at the landing, so that we could cross without delay.

The brutes, after gaining the edge of the water, did not utter impatient howls, but stood there in sullen silence, with their noses to the ground, or else looking wishfully to the opposite shore, as though longing to be again upon the trail.

"They are in splendid humor this morning," Allen said, as he patted old Maje upon the head, and noted the fierce looks of the animals. "They tasted blood last night, and now they wish for more, and I sincerely hope they will be gratified; for if we can get hold of Juan we shall put a stop to this system of pilfering which has been carried on for years, and yet never received a check excepting when administered by the people at the factory."

While Allen was speaking, he called the dogs into the banco, and then we shoved off, and paddled across the stream. We preferred to labor at the oars, so that the natives would not suspect our mission, and communicate it to the one we were in search of.

Upon gaining the right bank of the Pasig, the dogs were sent on shore, but they gave no indication that the robber had landed at that point; so, leaving the animals to follow along the bank, we reached San Pedro Macati, which was not more than half a mile distant from the great swamp, where it was reported the outlaw kept secreted.

CHAPTER II.

THE SEARCH FOR THE OUTLAW. — AN OBSTRUCTION. — THE MONKEYS. — THE LADRONE. — THE FIGHT.

"Look at the dogs," Allen remarked, a few moments before we landed; and by their actions it was evident that they had got on the scent, and only waited for the command to lead us in the direction of the swamp. "The rascal must have swam the river, and then escaped under cover of darkness to his retreat,

Probably he is sleeping off the effect of his night's labor, so that, if we are lucky, we shall take him unawares."

We secured our canoe, then gave the impatient dogs the signal to start, and with heads lowered to the earth, they followed each other, stopping every few minutes and looking back at us with angry glances for not moving at their speed, until the river was lost to view, and we began to enter a wild and uncultivated region, where pedestrianism was extremely difficult, and where our long-legged boots began to be of service.

"Here is where we are to take leave of the sun for the present," Allen said, calling to the dogs, and checking their course at the very edge of a dense jungle, which did not look very inviting, and seemed as though it was capable of harboring all the ladrones in the country, as well as all the wild animals and serpents. "Have you a fancy for visiting convents?" Allen asked, while we stood resting upon our rifles.

"That is a question I cannot answer, simply because I never saw the interior of one," I replied.

"Then some leisure day we will visit the large building which you see in the distance, and which is called the Convent of San Pedro, and is under the charge of a holy father named Bonventuro. He is a particular friend of mine, and entertains for me a profound respect, because I have sent him to bed on several occasions with more of a load in his stomach than his head could carry."

"He is not a believer in cold water, then?" I asked.

"He believe in cold water?" repeated Allen. "Why, he hasn't made use of a drop except to float his banco, and make coffee, for ten years; and if he lives ten years longer, he will have consumed more wine than any man on the island. He is a jolly old fellow, and can sing an amorous song or mournful ditty with admirable grace. I shall be happy in making you acquainted."

"Provided we return in safety from this expedition," I muttered, as we shouldered our guns; and shoving aside the tangled boughs, we entered the great swamp, which was rarely visited by the Spaniards, for they entertained a correct idea that there was danger in its dark recesses and stagnant pools of water, and that it was safer to suffer the visits of ladrones than to expose their lives by hunting them in such a suspicious place.

The dogs led the way with glowing eyes, and we followed as

fast as possible; but the soil was soft and spongy, and although it received the impression of our feet, the tracks were soon erased, or filled with dark water, rank with vegetation and slime. We were positive that we were on the right track, for we frequently met with broken twigs, and a brief examination showed that the sap was still fresh and running, and that they must have been disturbed but a few hours before. I also entertained an impression that the course we were pursuing had been passed over many times, for we were comparatively free of briers and underbrush, as contrasted with the foliage each side of us.

On we passed, bending low at times to escape the branches of trees, or else cautiously peering into a thicket to discover the cause of the sudden rustling which we detected among the leaves, and, perhaps, while we listened, hearing the low, angry hiss of a snake as it glided into the darker recesses of the swamp, or plunged with sudden motion into the pools of stagnant water, and with head erect, wriggled to its hole, or disappeared amid the bushes.

Sometimes it was necessary for us to leap from knoll to knoll to escape the bog-holes, or else crawl upon our hands and knees through thickets almost impenetrable, while the dogs took the easiest course, and swam the broadest places, yet were never baffled or thrown off the scent, and seeming more fierce and eager as we proceeded.

Suddenly Allen stopped and examined marks that attracted his attention, and we had no difficulty in tracing the footprint of a man who had passed that way barefooted; and by comparing the shoe which we carried with the impression upon the soil, we found that they corresponded.

"Here, Maje, tell us what that is," Allen said, addressing the hound, which hardly stopped to take the scent, when the brute looked in our faces and uttered a low, peculiar cry. "That will do, old boy, that will do. We want as little noise as possible in this place. I have a notion that too much would defeat the object of our visit. Go on, now, and be a good dog."

The animal seemed to comprehend the words, and trotted along with his usual dignity, while we followed as rapidly as possible, until suddenly the dogs uttered a suppressed howl, and, with tails between their legs, retreated towards us.

"There is danger in our path of some kind," muttered Allen,

stopping and scrutinizing the trees in our vicinity; but nothing was to be seen, and we attempted to urge the hounds along, but they obstinately refused to proceed, and nothing but fear of the whip prevented them from breaking out in a chorus of howls, which would have alarmed the person we were in search of.

"Remain where you are for a moment, and have your rifle ready for instant service, while I make a short circuit, and see if I can find out the trouble. Don't fire on any account, unless compelled to, and then be careful that your shot tells."

I did not like the idea of being separated from Allen, but I wisely kept my fears to myself, although I watched his form until lost to view among the thickets, and half resolved to follow, on the ground that it was expedient for us to keep together in so dangerous a place.

The dogs had left me for the company of my friend, and I was alone, with a death-like stillness reigning over the swamp, and my imagination conjuring up all sorts of diseased fancies. I leaned against a tall tree, with leaves so thick that the sky could not be seen above it, and awaited the return of my companion; but while I meditated upon the madness of the undertaking before me, I saw a sturdy limb of a tree move and shake as though agitated by a violent blast of wind.

I did not stop to think that when we entered the swamp the air was quite calm, and no sign of a gale visible, because my thoughts were otherwise engaged; and I don't know that I should have moved from my position under the tree, had not a chattering monkey upon a sapling, a few rods off, suddenly appeared, and after staring at me for a moment, made a gesture of fright, and with a fierce cry disappeared.

I started in the direction that the animal had taken; but before I had gone two steps, the tree, against which I had leaned, was shaken from its trunk to the topmost branch, and a rain of leaves fell upon my head. Then I began to suspect that I was in a dangerous neighborhood; and hastily glancing over my head, saw something, I could not tell at first what, whirling among the leaves, twisting and turning like gleams of lightning, and cracking the tender branches in its movements, and showering down leaves like flakes of snow.

I think that I was not more than five seconds in placing the distance of a rod between myself and the tree, and I don't remember to have once turned back to see whether I was clear of the danger that threatened me. What it was I knew not, but suspected that a wild animal had taken possession of the tree, and was calculating the propriety of making a meal of me, when its eagerness caused an alarm.

I was not, on the whole, sorry when Allen made his appearance and reported that the path was clear, but that the dogs still manifested symptoms of alarm, and appeared ill at ease for animals like them.

"You don't look any too lively," Allen said, after a glance at my face; "what is the matter? Don't feel tired — do you? Take a drink of this;" and he offered me his flask.

I did not refuse, although, while the bottle was at my lips, I kept my eyes fixed upon the tree, expecting to see it move every moment.

"It strikes me," I said, returning the flask, "that the cause of this alarm is in yonder tree, and that the leaves hide something disagreeable to view. If you don't believe it, go and look."

"I will do better than that; I will send Maje, for he seems as uneasy as a young woman without a lover, or a young wife with an old husband."

The dog was directed to the tree, and made one or two efforts to obey orders; but all ended with a feeble yelp, and then he retreated behind us.

"Blast the dogs! have they lost all their courage!" exclaimed my friend, pettishly; "they are frightened at their own shadows. If they won't go I will;" and cocking his rifle, he started forward, and gained a position where he could command a view of the tree.

I tried to dissuade him, but without avail; and for fear that he would think me but an indifferent sportsman, I moved a few steps in the direction which my friend had taken.

"I don't see anything," Allen exclaimed, with great self-confidence; but just at that moment the leaves of the tree rustled as though some large body was moving amid the limbs. The dogs uttered a suppressed howl, and retreated with their tails between their legs, and I heard Allen say, —

"By jingo, it is!" an exclamation that was emphatic, but hardly explanatory; for he stepped back, regardless where he put his feet; and the consequence was, he fell into a miniature lake, and for a moment disappeared from view, but only for a moment. He came to the surface of the green water like a sperm whale that had been exploring the domains of Neptune for an hour or more, but, unlike the huge monster, he didn't look clean or comfortable.

"Well, you are the dirtiest looking white man that I ever saw," I cried; and I could not restrain my laughter at his ludicrous appearance.

"Curse appearances!" he shouted, spitting the water from his mouth, and scrambling upon dry land.

"I should say so, to judge from your looks. You have grown green within five minutes."

"I can't stop to thank you for your complimentary remarks," Allen said, picking up his rifle, which he had thrown from his hand when falling, and thereby saved it uninjured, "because in yonder tree is secreted the biggest anaconda that I ever saw."

It was now my turn to jump; and I think that I placed about twenty feet between myself and the tree in less than two seconds, and even then did not feel safe from harm.

"I should judge that the animal desires a breakfast off of the dogs; but perhaps he would not object to a man, if fat and tender."

"And clean," I cried, "and you have described me to a hair. There is no danger of the snake's troubling you, if at all particular about his food, for your looks are repulsive."

Allen smiled in a ghastly manner, and walked to a favorable position for getting a shot.

"What do you mean to do?" I asked.

"See how near I can come to the brute's eye at a rod's distance," was the reply.

"Then I wish you a good morning, and will thank you to show me the nearest way out of this mud-hole."

"There's not half as much danger as you imagine," my friend said. "We can stand here and give the reptile a few shots, and see how he looks when wounded."

Perhaps the anaconda understood his meaning, and was disposed to begin the fight, and not remain in the tree like a coward; for suddenly there was a whirl of the leaves, and they fell thickly to the ground. While we were watching, a head with flaming eyes was thrust from the foliage, and then followed a neck, and about six feet of the body. The reptile's mouth was open, and displayed two huge fangs set well back in the jaws, while a tongue, red as blood, darted back and forth, as though extremely desirous of tasting our flesh, and judging of it by actual mastication.

For a few minutes the head waved back and forth, with its eyes still fixed upon us, or the dogs — we couldn't tell which; and those ponderous jaws, opening and closing, as though desirous of commencing a fight, if we were really disposed to begin one in earnest.

The spectacle was truly a fascinating one, and I could think of nothing but how I should escape from such an unwelcome neighbor without exchanging blows; for I imagined, with good cause, if the anaconda could show six feet of length by the way of a joke, that there must be some twenty-five feet more out of sight, coiled upon a limb, and ready to be used if occasion should require it, although it rather seemed to me that we were looked upon with some contempt, as though unworthy of much attention.

Even the dogs were not disposed to provoke a fight, for they kept at a respectful distance, and only showed their disgust by snarling and exhibiting their teeth, powerless against a monster possessing the strength and quickness of an anaconda.

A few yards from us a troop of monkeys were assembled, watching our motions with some interest, and expressing their hatred of the anaconda by furious grimaces and insulting gestures, yet taking very good care not to venture near the snake, and always skipping nimbly from their position to a better one, if the reptile offered to move from the place where he had taken up his quarters. One old fellow, who seemed aged enough to be the grandfather of the party, was quite human in showing his dislike; and his family watched his proceedings with grave satisfaction, and applauded him like a gang of first-class *claqueurs*.

The old monkey, after chattering for a few minutes in a high key, would seem to choke with choler, and, unable to proceed for want of breath, or words, would then shake his hairy fists at the snake, and clutch handfuls of leaves and hurl them at the monster; and all the monkey tribe would chatter their applause, and encourage the old fellow to renewed attempts at insulting their enemy.

The snake seemed to care as much for the monkeys as he did for the dogs, and continued to move his head back and forth, regardless of the leaves that were hurled at him, or the scoldings he was receiving.

At length the gray-headed monkey exhausted his invectives, and turned his attention to Allen and myself, and as near as we could understand the language he used, he seemed to say that we were cowards and did not dare to assail our equals; and we even got pelted with leaves; and what was of more account, some of them dropped upon our heads, which seemed to please the juvenile members of the troop very much, for they chattered with delight, and every one commenced plucking leaves and hurling them at us; and during the contest the snake was forgotten by our apish friends, although I never lost sight of him for more than a second at a time.

On any other occasion I could have enjoyed the contest, and entered into the sport with a keen relish; but knowing that a twenty-five feet anaconda was regarding us attentively rather detracted from the amusement, for I did not know how soon the snake would commence unfolding his tail, and desire close quarters.

" Well, are we to stay here all day?" I asked, watching the snake in the tree, " or shall we make the best of our way out of this swamp?"

" We are hardly prepared to leave yet," Allen said, " because we have not accomplished the object of our expedition. I intend to try the effect of a bullet on the snake's head, and then I am with you."

As Allen spoke, the whole troop of monkeys remained silent; but the instant he concluded his remarks there was a wild clatter of contempt, and leaves were again hurled at us with renewed energy.

Allen raised his rifle, and waited for the snake to remain stationary for a few moments, when he fired. There was a wild scream of terror from the whole troop of chattering monkeys, and they disappeared amid the trees like lightning.

The ball struck the anaconda near his flaming eyes, and a jet of blood spurted out and fell upon the leaves beneath like huge rubies. The tree upon which the snake rested was shaken to its very roots, and swayed to and fro as though a hurricane was raging. Branches were broken off, with reports as loud as the discharge of pistols, and those limbs which were too large for even the reptile to contend successfully with, were stripped of leaves as completely as if done by hand.

The struggles of the monster were terrible, and more than once I felt like imitating the monkeys, and disappearing as fast as possible from the scene. It seemed imbued with mighty strength, for it uncoiled its tail, and after thrashing it about the body of the tree for a few moments, recoiled it around the trunk, and tightened it until I thought the very sap would exude.

"Now is your time," cried Allen, who was quietly loading his rifle. "Fire, and see how quick he will relax his hold."

I took deliberate aim, and fired. The ball struck one of the folds, cut its way through, and penetrated the tree. The coils were quickly unwound and concealed for a moment, for the snake was now roused to madness, and seemed determined to destroy everything within reach. The saplings in the vicinity were knocked down, the bushes were torn up, and showers of dark water were scattered upon us as the monster struck at everything it could reach.

"End the contest," I cried, as the head of the anaconda rested for a moment, covered with its blood, and the fierce eyes glared upon us more wicked than ever.

"Pooh!" cried Allen; "we haven't begun to see the fun yet."

If he called it fun to look at the snake's contortions, I wondered what he would consider serious business; but before I had time to ask the question, the reptile gave a convulsive twirl with its tail, and as it did so a huge piece of decayed wood was struck, and sent with considerable force into the air.

"He's in his flurry," shouted my friend, using the expression of a whaleman; and like those gentlemen who search the seas for *light*, he crowed somewhat too quick; for the stick of wood descending with a velocity in accordance with natural causes, struck Allen upon his head, and broke into a thousand different pieces; but the dirt and dust adhered to his face and shoulders, and if possible he was a dirtier-looking man than when he emerged from the stagnant water.

To add to his perplexity, the blow was sufficient to prostrate him; and as he sat upon the damp earth, hardly conscious what hit him, I could not help laughing; and I thought the old gray-headed monkey would have joined in my mirth and chuckled with delight.

"Darn it, I don't see anything to laugh at!" cried Allen, pettishly, as he cleared the dirt and the dead wood from his face.

"If you had a looking-glass you would say different," I cried, still watching the snake.

"I have no doubt that I am a picture at the present time; but I look full as well as you did last night when kissing Donna Teresa in the dark. Come, I've got you there."

"Say no more, and I'll promise not to laugh again for a fortnight. What I did last night was accidental."

"I know it was, and so was the falling of the stick of wood upon my head; yet you see how disastrous it has been, and how soiled my clothes are. There can be a moral deducted from the affair that will benefit you, if you will only profit by it."

"This is no time to study homilies," I replied, not relishing the conversation. "Kill the snake, and let us continue the tramp, for time is flying fast."

Allen shook his form, and then cleared his rifle of the dirt and dust. The anaconda had revived considerably by this time, and was now engaged in gnawing the tree upon which it was coiled, yet not working with energy; for it had shed much blood, and was growing weak rapidly.

"I will bet an ounce that I put a ball within one inch of his left eye," Allen said, slowly raising his rifle, and turning to me to see whether I took the wager.

I nodded my acceptance, for I was tired of the sport, and wished to end it.

My friend fired, and the head of the anaconda, after one convulsive struggle, fell to the ground and remained motionless; but the tail still continued to work as though life was too dear to be relinquished by a few small wounds.

Almost with the fall of the snake the troop of monkeys reappeared upon a neighboring tree, and chattered and crowed with delight; and the old gray-headed rascal once more gathered leaves, and while he made grimaces at us, did not fail to fling them at his defunct enemy, and boxed the ears of his numerous progeny because they did not follow his example, instead of staring at us like greenhorns who had never been from home or seen a stranger during their brief existence.

We waited for a few minutes to see whether the anaconda was not playing a deep game for the purpose of getting us within its reach; but its head remained quiet, even if the tail had not ceased its convulsive workings. At length we ventured near enough to punch the fallen monster with sticks; but it gave no sign of animosity at the indignities which were heaped upon it, and taking courage from its dormant state, we examined our prize, worthless to us, but of great value to the natives, who consider its fat as inestimable for the cure of certain diseases; and had they known that an anaconda was lying dead within three miles of the factory, hundreds of the Mestizas would have flocked towards the great swamp for the purpose of securing a titbit and carrying it home in triumph.

The dogs could not be induced to approach the carcass, although we endeavored, by threats and kindness, to get them to do so; while the monkeys, on the contrary, ventured as near as they possibly could and keep out of our reach, but they watched our proceedings with great interest, and chattered as we moved about as though speculating what we would do next. Re-enforcements of the saucy knaves continued to arrive every minute, and in less than half an hour after the death of the snake, there were at least five hundred, of all sizes, swinging from the trees and demanding of the gray-headed veteran how their enemy perished. Such a chattering and screaming could only be equalled by an immense concourse of people, talking on some subject dear to their hearts, such as a new bonnet or a bit of scandal.

A few of the boldest of the tribe even ventured upon the tree, around the trunk of which the snake was coiled, and sat upon the branches and made faces at us, or else imitated our gestures, and looked so cunning that for some time we committed many absurd acts simply for the pleasure of seeing the troop endeavor to comprehend and imitate them. But the dogs began to grow impatient, and time was too valuable to waste playing with apish visitors. We saluted them with a polite bow, and a hundred heads were ducked in acknowledgment of the compliment, and a hundred shrill cries were uttered, which sounded like sardonic laughter; and I know that the scamps told each other that we had braved the danger, and that they were to reap the benefit.

The old grandfather uttered a parting benediction, and hurled a handful of leaves at our heads, as we called our dogs, and once more put them on the trail, while we followed close at their heels in pursuit of the ladrone Juan, whose capture we had neglected for the purpose of destroying the anaconda.

The dogs took to the trail quite readily, and seemed much relieved when the dead snake was left far behind. The brutes, perhaps, had learned from instinct that the anaconda was a very bad enemy to meet in the forest, and that courage and ferocity availed but little against the enormous strength and rapid movements of the snake, whose power is so great that even the stoutest buck that roams the valleys is no match in a fair fight, when the anaconda has the protection of a tree, and uses it as a retreat.

The natives tell wonderful stories of the power of the anaconda in the eating line, and quite a number of Mestizas, who pretended to know all about the habits and disposition of the snake, were ready to swear that they had seen them gorge deer that weighed at least one hundred pounds each, first preparing them by breaking every bone in their bodies, until the mass was a complete jelly, and after covering it with slime, slowly swallow it, and then lie dormant for a week, awaiting digestion.

At such times the anaconda is incapable of offering resistance if attacked by wild beasts, or natives armed with lances and knives, and quite frequently the monsters are destroyed in this manner. But I am inclined to think that the natives have, with their usual exaggeration, magnified a doe of two months old into a full-grown deer; for, during my residence in Manila, and while on hunting excursions, I probably met with eight or ten anacondas, — not torpid things, such as are shown in cages and boxes in this country, and are called full-grown boas, but powerful snakes, twenty-five, and even thirty-five feet long, and measuring in circumference as much as a man's thigh. I have watched them for hours in the dark forests of Macati, while they sported upon the branches of a tree, or else lay dormant, and with eyes that seemed half closed, watching the sports of monkeys as they played within a few feet of their retreat, and provoked an attack by their boldness.

I have seen the listless monsters suddenly raise their heads, and like lightning dart upon the unlucky ape, and after one shrill scream of terror, its life would be crushed out as easily as a cook can break an egg-shell.

It sometimes happens that an anaconda, tempted by the fine weather and the warm sunshine, or else in search of a dinner, will stray towards some native village, and take up its quarters in a mango tree, where it will remain for hours, waiting with exemplary patience for the approach of a dog, child, or even full grown native; and woe betide either of the above named, if they venture within the circle of the anaconda's reach, for it can dart with the quickness of thought upon its prey, and give no warning of its intentions. But death speedily follows the attack, for the enraged natives muster in strong force, hurl sticks and stones at their torpid enemy until it is incapable of mischief, then sharp knives complete the work.

The dogs grew more excited at every step, and it required a stern word to prevent them from breaking out in a cry, and starting in hot pursuit of the robber.

Suddenly we emerged from the trees and brush, and reached a sheet of water which contained a small island in its centre, nearly destitute of trees or bushes. The land was high, and looked very rich and inviting, and we thought that we could discern signs of cultivation in small patches upon the side that greeted our point of observation.

"On that island," said Allen, "is Juan Baptiste."

"Your reasons for the supposition?" I asked, refreshing my inner man with a drink from a flask, and after a careful observation of the neighborhood, taking a seat under a tree, where I lighted a cheroot, and prepared to enjoy myself.

"My reasons are these," replied my friend: "you observe that the dogs have led us to the edge of the water, and make no effort to find another trail. This shows that the man we are in pursuit of embarked on a raft or boat, and, it is probable, has a home on the island. Reason number two is, that the lake is full of alligators, which makes his retreat much more secure."

"Tell me how you know that the lake contains alligators, and I'll agree to your reasons," I said.

"Willingly. You see that the dogs don't offer to take to the water, and that they stand quite a number of feet from its edge, and eye the lake with suspicion."

I acknowledged that I had noticed the circumstance.

"Well, the brutes know much more than they can express; be assured that whenever you see dogs, in this country, refusing to follow up a scent by crossing water, it means that black monsters, as dangerous as anacondas, are lying at the bottom of the water, and that the hounds know it."

"Convince me that your reasoning is just, and I'll believe it," I said.

Allen picked up a piece of bamboo, and threw it into the water so gently that but a slight splash was heard.

Before the ripples upon the water had spread to the circumference of a quarter-acre lot, a dozen black spots were seen upon the surface, where they remained dormant, as though without life or animation.

"Are you satisfied?" Allen asked.

"Hardly," I answered. "The black spots which you claim as alligators' heads may be logs of wood."

"Then plunge into the lake, and I'll bet you any money that you will never leave it alive."

I declined the wager on purely personal considerations, for I began to have an inkling that Allen was right. To further test the matter, I hurled a stick of wood into the lake, and as it struck the water, the black heads disappeared, but, after a short lapse of time, re-appeared, and remained silent and motionless as before.

"What sport we could have," Allen remarked, "if a dead buffalo was lying at the water's edge, and we had no business before us. We could then witness a struggle and a war that we should remember for many months. Huge fellows, with tails as powerful as young right whales, and jaws filled with ivory, would attack alligators smaller than themselves, or else struggle with their equals, and sink to the bottom of the lake in mortal combat. Then we could sit here and test our skill as marksmen by firing at their eyes or under their flippers — the only places, I believe, that a rifle bullet can make an impression."

"Don't conjure up such sporting scenes until our present enterprise is completed, for, to tell you the truth, I have a desire to sleep at the factory to-night. If we do not reach home, Mr. Huckford will feel concerned at our absence."

"Is there any other person at Santa Mesa who will feel disappointed unless you return?" asked Allen, with a slight laugh.

I suspected his motive in asking the question, so disdained to reply, but puffed out volumes of smoke from my cheroot, for the purpose of hiding my confusion.

For a few minutes neither of us spoke. We sat watching the island, and the dark heads of the alligators, as they moved about the surface of the water, eying the party on shore with wishful looks, as though they hadn't had a real feast on dog or man for many days. At length Allen threw away his cigar, and drew his huge hunting-knife, as though he meant mischief.

"We have wasted time enough," he said. "Now let us begin the dangerous and difficult work before us."

"Do you expect me to swim the lake, with a knife between my teeth, to defend myself against the alligators, or will you perform that service?" I asked.

"I anticipate nothing of the kind," Allen answered. "I expect that you will help me cut bamboos, and from them we can build a raft that will carry us in safety to the island."

There were no other resources, and the idea seemed practicable, although I had much rather have had a good stout banco in which to trust my precious self, for I thought that it would require but slight exertion on the part of the monsters of the lake to interrupt our voyage, and give it a disastrous termination. If Allen had any such fears, he did not show them, for he went to work with a will, and almost before I was on my feet, half a dozen strong bamboos had fallen, and awaited trimming before launching upon the lake.

We continued our work with energy, and yet with so much stillness that not a sound was heard three rods from where we stood, although we often glanced towards the island to see if there were any signs of life, and if any person was watching our movements; yet we as often failed to detect the presence of a human being, and I was almost ready to swear that Juan was no longer on the island.

Our raft was speedily constructed, and in a thorough manner, for bamboo, noted for its buoyancy, was plenty, and large enough to answer our purpose.

The largest sticks were placed as stringers, and on them we piled the smaller ones, securing all with twigs of the same material, until our raft was twenty feet long, ten wide, and about six inches deep.

After it was built it required but little strength to launch it, and this we were enabled to do in spite of the alligators, which were prowling around in shallow water, and even rubbed their noses against the raft, as though desirous of testing its strength.

"Are we to take the dogs?" I asked.

"Of course; we shall find no difficulty in coaxing them on the raft, and after we reach the island they will be of great service."

"But suppose we are attacked while on the voyage? We can't use our rifles without giving an alarm, and that would defeat the object of the expedition."

Allen mused a moment, and then announced that he had a plan that would give us the advantage, decidedly, over the denizens of the lake, in case they were disposed to impede our progress. He lashed his knife to a bamboo, and held it up in triumph.

"What do you think of that for a weapon?" he asked.

"I will tell you after I have seen how it operates," I replied; "if it will keep the scaly devils from carrying our raft by storm, I'll praise your ingenuity, provided, of course, I live long enough. If I don't, you must apply to my executors."

We secured two long poles to propel our raft, and then, partly by force and partly by persuasion, got the dogs upon it and shoved off; and never did mariners upon the ocean, with but a few spars to cling to, exercise more care than Allen and myself, as we slowly pushed our way towards the island, surrounded by dozens of alligators, who swam round the raft and eyed us with no good will for our boldness in thus invading their domains.

One fellow I noticed in particular, for he seemed like a monarch whom none dared to approach; and as he swam around the raft his companions made way for him by darting one side, as though there was danger in being too familiar. He was a magnificent specimen of the alligator race, and must have measured at least twenty feet in length, while his jaws were ponderous, and seemed capable of crushing a man with but one bite, and swallowing the pieces without mastication.

"Don't you think," I said, turning to Allen, "that the attentions which this black rascal is bestowing upon us deserve some return?"

"He won't trouble you," Allen replied. But just at this moment, as though to show that he spoke without authority, the monster struck his head against the raft with so much force that it staggered us, and the dogs uttered a low whine of terror, and clung to the bamboos with tooth and nail, as though they knew what their fate would be if precipitated into the water.

"Don't stop," Allen cried, still urging the raft through the water; but the alligator could move ten feet to our one, and as we neared the shore the old fellow seemed disposed to dispute our passage, for he gave us another gentle rap with his head, and then dove under the raft and lifted it nearly a foot out of water.

"Cuss him, I can't stand that!" muttered Allen, who was nearly thrown overboard by the collision; and grasping his long pole, with the knife at the end, he watched for an opportunity to use it; and he did not have to wait long. The alligator slowly rose to the surface, and eyed us with a look which seemed to ask, "How do you like it?"

Allen watched a good chance, and as the side fin was raised for a moment, made a lunge, and buried the whole length of the blade in the mouster's body.

Instantly the tail of the animal made its appearance, described a curve, and before I could understand how the thing was done, one of our dogs was flying through the air, all doubled up in a heap, as though paralyzed by the powerful blow which he had received. The poor brute struck the water a couple of rods from us; but before he had time to utter a yell, or to swim a stroke, a dozen black snouts suddenly appeared, and dragged him to the bottom of the lake. I glanced hastily towards the spot, and saw a few bubbles and a slight tinge of blood upon the water; and then, a moment afterwards, the monsters were swimming around the raft, looking more greedy for the slight taste which they had obtained of flesh.

"That tail might have hit one of us," I remarked to Allen, as I urged the raft along towards the island, anxious to escape from such disagreeable company.

"It might," he answered, laconically.

"Your friend is about to pay you another visit," I cried, as I saw the alligator which Allen had wounded suddenly re-appear from beneath the raft, and slowly work his way to the point where Allen was standing.

"If he will let me alone, I'll promise not to molest him again. I think that he has the advantage, for with one fair blow of his tail he could sweep the raft, and then where should we be?"

It did not require the aid of a prophet to guess, and as the subject was one that was not debatable, I plied my pole as hard as possible; but the monsters seemed to gain strength, and made the water look ten shades darker by their presence, as they darted to and fro beneath us. Two or three times my pole was seized by younger members of the family, who were apparently not sufficiently enlightened to distinguish between a piece of bamboo and a human leg; but a slight bite was sufficient to convince them that they had made a mistake, and that wood was not very nutritious.

As we neared the shore our escort grew bolder, and even thrust their heads upon the raft, to the great terror of the dogs, and the exceeding discomfort of two human beings, who wished with all their hearts that they were safe at Santa Mesa, drinking wine and eating mangoes, or else chatting of romance and chivalry with Donna Teresa. More than once I glanced towards our rifles, thinking that the time had arrived for their use, even if the reports did give the one we were in search of warning of our approach, and thus defeat the objects of the expedition. But Allen shook his head and urged more activity in pushing for the shore, and I was willing to run a little more risk for the sake of capturing Juan, and thus revenge ourselves for his audacious attack upon the factory.

"A few minutes more and we shall be beyond their reach," whispered Allen, lancing with his knife the boldest of the monsters as they thrust their heads upon the raft, or else dove under it for the purpose of shaking us off; but if one was driven off wounded, another was ready to take its place; and thus we fought our way to the shore, which we gained with thankful hearts, too anxious to escape from the dangers of the water to think of the terrors of the land, for a resolute man could have held us completely at his mercy while we were securing the raft and examining our rifles.

The dogs bounded to the shore with many expressions of delight for their escape; and as soon as we were ready, they set themselves to work to find the spot where the outlaw was in the habit of landing. This was but the labor of a few minutes, for the scent was still fresh, and the dogs eager for action, and ready to show that they were willing to make atonement for their display of cowardice when we encountered the anaconda and the marine monsters.

The brutes led us up the steep slopes of the island, through a grove of bamboo; when we suddenly emerged upon a cultivated spot, where yams and sweet potatoes were growing in profusion, but there were no signs of a house, or a habitation of any kind. The dogs trotted on, and we followed as fast as possible; but the brutes were too eager to await our motions, and we lost sight of them for a few minutes, when we were suddenly startled by their deep baying, which told that they had run their game to a stand.

Instead of following the trail of the dogs, we diverged to the right, and moved carefully to a point where we could get sight of the animals and whatever object they were looking at. For five minutes we crept through underbrush and rank grass, until at length we gained a small clearing, in the centre of which was a huge mango tree; and amid the branches, twenty feet from the ground, we saw a bamboo hut, thatched with leaves, and evidently intended as a habitation by the person we were in pursuit of.

The dogs were howling most merrily when we reached our point of observation; but no signs of life could we observe in the hut, and we should have supposed that Juan had left his quarters before our arrival, had we not been certain that the dogs were not liable to make mistakes. As the hut contained numerous apertures, we were not positive that the outlaw was not watching our movements from one of them; and as he was known to be a good shot, we thought that it behooved us to remain quiet, and see what course he would take.

For half an hour we remained concealed, but there were no signs of life in the hut, and I began to grow wearied with the siege, and once more wish myself back at Santa Mesa.

"This is as bad as battling with alligators," I cried, yawning, and incautiously exposing my body above the bushes.

I had hardly spoken when a loud report was heard in the tree, and a ball whizzed within six inches of my head, and was buried in the earth twenty yards beyond.

"That is not a bad shot for a musket," coolly remarked Allen, and I agreed with him most heartily, as I dropped behind a clump of bushes.

" Lucky the fellow used a musket instead of a rifle, or this day would have ended your adventures," was all the consolation which I received from my friend.

" I can't believe that he can shoot as well the second time," I remarked. " Just stand up for a moment and see."

Allen declined the pressing invitation, and for half an hour longer we watched the tree and the hut in hope of getting a glimpse of the outlaw; but he was too careful of his person to expose it to strangers.

" Why don't he shoot the dogs?" I asked, half inclined to do so myself, for I was getting tired of their infernal din.

" That is a question that I have asked myself half a dozen times, but I cannot answer it. Of course the brutes are too well trained to stay there and be shot at; but the fellow might kill one, at any rate, before the other would take the hint and retire from the range of his gun."

" Bamboo is light," I said, glancing at the hut and then at my rifle. " Who knows but a chance shot might tell?"

Allen took the hint, and nodded his head in approbation. I took a careless aim and fired. The ball crashed through the bamboo, and the dogs, recognizing the report of the rifle, redoubled their howls, and sprang wildly upon the tree, as though they would tear the occupant limb from limb, if he would only give them a chance. The outlaw made no movement to show that he was affected by the shot, and I suggested to Allen that perhaps I had killed him.

"That don't look much like it," my friend remarked, as a ball struck the bushes in front of him, and then, glancing, whizzed to another part of the island. " *Diablo!* this is far from interesting!"

" A very good shot for a musket. Keep quiet, and don't move. Lucky it wasn't a rifle," I cried, using the same language which he addressed to me when my head was in danger of flying lead.

We were glad enough to crawl on our stomachs to a new spot, where the outlaw would not be likely to suspect our presence, and thus escape from his chance shots; and I will confess that I wished the fellow to the devil with hearty good will, and inwardly vowed that I'd never undertake another expedition, even if Charley Allen made one of the party to seduce me with his plausible reasons for everything that he desired to engage in.

The sun poured down with awful warmth, for it was noon, and not a breath of air was stirring; and to add to our discomfort, the mosquitos began to find our retreat, and were inserting their bills with fearful effect upon every portion of our body that was not encased in strong cloth; and I will add that I was rejoiced with exceeding joy when I saw a cloud hovering over my friend's head, and half a dozen endeavoring to find lodgment upon his nose, to prevent which he was constantly employed with both hands, and sometimes with his feet.

"How do you like the fun?" I asked, with a malicious grin; for I had taken the precaution of bringing a pair of stout gloves with me; so my hands were well protected.

"O, I don't mind these few," he replied, with an attempt at calmness. "When night sets in we shall probably have clouds of the insects to contend with, and until then I mean to retain my good nature."

To hear a man talk about stopping all night on the island, when everything that was dear and pleasant was miles away at the factory, was not to my fancy; so I grew desperate, and resolved to end the contest as soon as possible. The dogs had barked themselves hoarse, and were lying at the foot of the tree motionless, as I could see by pushing the bushes one side; but even my movement, slight as it was, roused them, and they were all attention and ready for work. But I saw something of more importance than the dogs, and I was not slow to bring my rifle to my shoulder, when Allen interrupted me.

"What is it?" he asked.

"Do you not see the face of the ladrone peering at us from one of the windows of the hut?" I said.

Charley did not answer, but snatched up his rifle, and after a hasty aim fired.

"Missed him, I'll bet a dollar," I cried.

"I'll take the wager," was the quiet response.

"How shall we settle it?"

"That is easily done. Do you hear the dogs recommence their baying fiercer than ever?"

I nodded, but still kept my eyes fixed upon the tree and the hut, in hopes of getting another view of the robber.

"Well, be assured that they smell blood freshly shed, and that Juan has got a wound that will prevent his escaping from us, even if he should kill the dogs."

I did not reply, for at that moment I saw a limb of the mango tree shake as though an anaconda was winding its heavy folds around the branch, preparatory to making a dart. "The Lord preserve us from another snake," I thought, for I had had quite enough of them to last me for one day.

Suddenly the branch of the tree, which I was watching, sprang up to its proper place, and then I heard a heavy body strike the earth. The dogs uttered terrific yells, and seemed to change their position from the foot of the tree to one farther off.

"The ladrone is escaping," I cried, the thought suddenly recurring to me that he had dropped from the tree as a last resort, and intended to make for some secret hiding-place on the island.

"It can't be possible!" exclaimed Allen, starting up. "The dogs would tear him to pieces before he had run ten steps."

"He has run more than a hundred, and yet you hear the brutes in full cry."

Allen listened for a moment, and then seized his rifle and started in pursuit, closely followed by myself. When we gained the tree where the outlaw had built his hut, we were enabled to command an uninterrupted view of the island as far as the water's edge, and within thirty rods of the lake we saw the form of the robber running with extraordinary speed directly towards the water. The hounds were close to him, however, and every moment we expected to see old Maje make a spring and bear the native to the earth, and hold him until our arrival. But in this we were disappointed, for Juan was as nimble as a deer, and every bound that he made took him clear of bushes and rank grass as completely as though he was flying through the air.

We could have sent a bullet whizzing after him, and with a tolerable certainty that it would have maimed him, or else ended his life; but we were so sure that the dogs would overtake him, that we reserved our fire, and watched the race in breathless suspense. The outlaw was within a rod of the water, and the hounds, instead of quickening their pace, subsided into a trot, which was conclusive evidence that they had not forgotten the lesson taught them a few hours before, during the encounter with the alligators.

"Heavens! it can't be possible that the fellow is about to throw himself into the lake!" cried Allen; but it seemed as though he was resolved to risk it as a chance for life, for Juan shaped his course towards the nearest water, and for a while he was hid from our view by a small knoll.

We followed in pursuit as fast as possible; but before we had taken ten steps from the tree we heard a loud splash in the water, and then the sad wail of the dogs as they howled a death chorus.

"He is in the lake, and will be food for alligators," cried Allen, trembling so violently that he could hardly run. "Why didn't the devilish fool surrender in the first place, and not give us all this trouble."

Even while my friend was speaking we reached the knoll, which overlooked the lake, and saw the outlaw upon the surface of the water, striking out with vigorous strokes for the main land, which was near a third of a mile from the island, while the dogs stood upon the shore and howled their rage at thus losing their prey, yet did not dare venture in pursuit.

For a few moments we stood in silence, expecting that the ladrone would be seized and dragged beneath the water; but on he went unharmed until Allen thought that it was time to bring him to, and for this purpose mild measures were resorted to.

"Ho, Juan!" he shouted; "return to the land, and surrender like a man."

"Never," answered the outlaw, looking back and shaking his clinched hand in defiance. "Juan can die like a man, but he will not surrender to end his days in a Spanish prison, or work like a dog in the chain gang."

"Your death is certain unless you return. The lake is full of alligators, more ferocious than the Spaniards or your midnight ladrones."

"I make a bold venture for my life," returned Juan, "and, if I escape, will leave this part of the country forever. If I die I will curse you with my last breath, for none but Americanos would have dared pursue me to this spot."

The outlaw waved his hand in token of adieu, and then turned and recommenced swimming vigorously.

"Can it be possible that the alligators will let that man pass through their dominions unmolested?" Allen asked, and it seemed possible, for the outlaw continued on his way uninjured; and more than once my friend glanced at his rifle as though undecided whether he should test its efficacy, or let the ladrone escape. "The rogue deserves to get clear for his boldness; but if he does, the old factory will have to suffer in retaliation for this visit. I hardly think it would be right, considering the tramp that we have had, to return home without accomplishing some good. See how the scamp swims, and glances over his shoulder as though he expected a bullet every moment; and faith, 'tis a pity to disappoint him."

Allen raised his rifle slowly, and was about to fire when I struck up the weapon and pointed to the water. Two black heads were observed within a rod of Juan, motionless, as though uncertain from whence the sounds they heard proceeded. The outlaw saw the alligators, for he changed his course and swam away from them, and I noticed that he glanced frequently towards the motionless snouts, as though to be certain that they did not pursue him. Suddenly four other heads were seen directly in front of the fellow, and once more he altered his course to avoid them; but hardly had he done so, when the lake seemed alive with alligators, all heading towards the swimmer, who no longer strove to reach the land, but seemed to become bewildered at his situation, and swam around in circles which grew more contracted every moment. The monsters did not seem in a hurry for their prey, but actually sported with the man, for three or four times we saw him raised from the water as though one of the alligators had poked him with its nose for the purpose of provoking a fight; and then the huge animals would lash their tails upon the surface of the water as though applauding the performance, like a party of gentlemen at a French opera. All of our fierce animosity vanished as we witnessed the condition of the outlaw, and we would have given a reasonable sum of money if we could have had the power to save him unharmed. Once we started towards our raft; but the idea was abandoned almost as soon as formed, for we thought that before we could propel the structure to the spot, there would be nothing left of Juan but a few stains of blood upon the surface of the water.

Once the Mestizo seemed to have resolved to sell his life as dear as possible, or else cut his way through the scaly circle that encompassed him, but speedily relinquished the idea, and the long knife which we saw in his hand for a moment was dropped, and he recommenced swimming more violently than ever, but still in a circle, which grew smaller every moment.

"Save me, senors!" suddenly shouted Juan, raising his body from the water and waving his arms towards us. "Save me from this dreadful fate, and the Virgin will reward you."

We were powerless, and could only pity the man and hope that death would speedily end his troubles; for if we had fired, and even wounded the alligators which were upon the surface of the water, there were, no doubt, dozens in the lake ready to rush in for a share of the feast, and fight until they obtained it.

The strokes of the swimmer grew weaker and weaker, as though his strength was nearly exhausted, and still that circle of black heads continued to press towards him, and they were almost within two yards of their prey, when we were surprised to observe a movement that looked as though the monsters had altered their minds, and were disposed to let the outlaw escape; for the circle was broken, and we saw many heads disappear, and others sheer off to a convenient distance, and wait as though for further orders. From this the outlaw gained courage, and struck out for the land as rapidly as possible; and I really hoped that he was destined to escape; but before the unfortunate had swam a rod, a monster head was thrust out of the lake, and after a short survey of the swimmer disappeared.

"'Tis the same one that you lanced," I said, turning to Allen, who nodded; for he was too much occupied in watching affairs upon the lake to speak.

Hardly had I spoken before the outlaw suddenly sprang half his length from the water, uttered a yell so shrill that it could have been heard at Santa Mesa, and then disappeared from the surface of the lake.

"That's the last of him," muttered Allen, drawing a long breath, as though a weighty matter was removed from his mind; and although we watched the spot where the Mestizo had disappeared for nearly half an hour, we never saw him again. The surface of the lake remained smooth, as though never agitated by storms or living monsters. All seemed calm and quiet, and from the main land we could hear a colony of monkeys quarrel and make love much after the fashion of the human family.

We slowly retraced our steps to the hut from whence the outlaw had escaped, and found that he had been well provided with cooking utensils, and food enough to last him several weeks; for there were three or four goats confined in a pen, besides quite a number of fowls, which he had undoubtedly raised to use in case there was danger in seeking for food at the villages. After a brief survey of the grounds, we cut some poles and made a ladder, so that we could ascend the tree and reach the hut. This we accomplished after a little labor, and found that Juan was in the habit of getting up in the same way, and then drawing his ladder after him; for we saw a very good bamboo ladder stowed away amid the branches, and almost concealed from sight by the thick leaves.

In the hut we found but little to repay us for our trouble, with the exception of a few pieces of silver plate, stolen from some gentleman's house, and the gun and other weapons, which were used for nocturnal excursions. These we took as trophies of victory, and then prepared to leave the island, and hasten back to Santa Mesa, so that we could reach the place before night, and not get caught in the great swamp, and be obliged to consort with wild beasts, and more terrible still, be eaten by mosquitos. Of ammunition we found none — every charge in the powder-horn being exhausted.

As we expected to encounter some opposition in crossing the lake, we seized three of the goats and fastened them to the raft, and then coaxed our dogs on, and started for the place from whence we had embarked two hours before.

I rather think we should have crossed without attracting the attention of the denizens of the lake, had not the goats commenced bleating as though desirous of provoking their fate. But we were not more than half over, when first one ugly snout and then another was raised above the water, and after listening for a moment disappeared; and the next time we saw them the monsters were swimming beside our raft, and looking at us most knowingly.

We paid no attention to our visitors until they exhibited signs of pressing impatience and hostile symptoms, when we cut a goat loose, and in despite of its struggles urged it into the water.

The poor animal swam after us for a few moments, while the alligators were tampering with it, and we improved our opportunity to urge the raft through the water as fast as possible. Suddenly we heard a pair of jaws crash together, and I glanced over my shoulder and saw that the water a few yards astern of us was all of a foam, and that the goat had disappeared.

For a few minutes we were clear of the monsters; but when five rods from the shore, they reappeared, more ferocious and more numerous than ever.

"Over with them!" shouted Allen, and over the goats went.

There was a rush and a struggle, and the water boiled up as though there was a whirlpool in the lake, and before it had cleared away, our raft, thank God, struck the shore.

The dogs bounded to the land with yells of delight, and we were none too quick in following their example; for the alligators, after their meal of goats' flesh, were ravenous for more, and followed the raft even to the edge of the water, and thrust their long noses upon it, and grunted their displeasure when they found that we had escaped. Conspicuous for his ferocity was the huge monster who had commenced the attack upon Juan, and the same one that Allen had wounded with his knife while we were making the best of our way to the island.

The rage of the old fellow, when he found that the raft was deserted, was so intense, that he snapped at his brethren whenever they ventured near him, and once or twice I saw that he left marks of his teeth upon the tails and fins of his less fortunate companions, and then, to complete his work, gave the raft a gentle brush with his powerful tail, that broke the sticks and poles into a thousand pieces, and sent them flying in all directions, both on shore and on the lake, while the mud was showered upon us in torrents, and for a moment we were blinded by the spray.

As soon as we could clear our eyes, we saw the huge brute lying upon the surface of the water, looking at us with his twinkling eyes; and they said, as plain as possible, —

"How do you like that? There's more of the same sort left, if you would like to try it."

"Did you ever witness such a display of cussed impudence?" muttered Allen, who had been engaged in picking a piece of mud out of his left eye, and therefore was not in the most amiable temper just at that time.

"Why don't you rebuke it?" I asked, laughing at his streaked face.

"Cuss me if I don't," he replied, snatching up his rifle, and taking deliberate aim at the eye which was still leering at us, as though in triumph.

He fired, and for a moment I thought that there was an eclipse; for the sun was obscured by the sheets of water and mud that were raised by the monster in its struggles, and I'm sorry to state that we got the most of the spray, for we stood near the lake, and directly within full sweep of the alligator's tail.

But that was the last splurge that the huge animal ever made, for it was his death throe; and when the foam cleared away, there lay the ugly fellow upon the top of the water, motionless, and ten or a dozen little ones were cruising in his immediate vicinity, as though to assure themselves that he was not playing possum for the purpose of getting them within reach of his ponderous jaws; and by watching we saw how in death he was insulted by those who, in life, had paid him all due deference and honor. We shouldered our rifles and left the scene.

As we neared the place where we had killed the anaconda, the dogs made a circuit to avoid the spot; but as our trail lay past the tree where the dead snake was coiled, we went as near to it as possible, and were greeted with a most unnatural yell; and to our surprise found that the trees in the immediate vicinity of the anaconda were covered with monkeys, from the little fellow not more than a month old to the venerable old grandfathers with gray heads and white beards. They seemed to be holding a council of war over the fallen foe, and, instead of regarding us with mistrust and fear, they actually maintained their places on the lowest branches of the trees, and even when we brushed past them, only made faces of derision, and showed their long, white teeth, and chattered defiance, or perhaps welcome, for they used a language that we did not understand or care to interpret. At any rate, there was great rejoicing over the destruction of their enemy, and it appeared to us that intelligence of the event had been sent to every tribe in the great swamp during our absence, and that they had speedily assembled to debate in council what action should be taken in the premises.

After two hours' hard walking we gained the edge of the swamp, and saw the white walls of San Pedro in the distance,

5

the sun shining upon the horn windows with all its intensity, as though to melt them to glue, and set the inmates of the building free; and not until then did we feel that we were safe, on our return from the dangerous expedition of hunting an outlaw, or ladrone. We found our banco where we had left it, and casting off the painter, quietly paddled down the river, exchanging salutations as we drifted along with the crews of cascas which had been a few miles above for the purpose of filling their crafts with fresh water for the shipping in the bay, or else receiving our full share of jokes from some washerwoman who was pursuing her calling upon the banks of the river, and beat her clothes upon rocks, as though they were made of iron.

At times we came upon a bevy of young girls, who were taking their afternoon bath, and sported in the water like sea-nymphs, without thinking that they were violating the laws of decency by not using bathing dresses; but had such useful articles been suggested, great would have been the astonishment, and greater still the laughter. Numerous were the invitations we received to join them in their gambols in the water, and had we done so, a nice ducking we should have got, unless we were quick enough to keep out of their way, or were swimmers good enough to stand a fair battle, where no mercy would have been shown. Many fair-shaped limbs were thrust above the water as we declined the invitations, and many a laugh from the girls told us that they were making merry at our want of gallantry in thus refusing to gratify their caprices.

The scenes were too attractive to be passed hastily, and I am ready to acknowledge that my paddle was lying idle while we gazed at dusky necks and shoulders which glanced above the water and disappeared as quick as meteors in the sky. A bath would have improved our appearance, and been relished keenly; but time was an object just then with us, for we desired to reach the factory before sundown, for the purpose of relieving all anxiety on our account.

But the generous invitations of the Mestiza girls were not wholly rejected, for many times afterwards did Allen and myself steal away from the factory, and sport in the cool water for hours, while dozens of black-haired girls were on every side of us, and ready to swim a race or try their skill in ducking. And yet we thought less of sin than the thousands who line the sho

Newport and Cape May, with all the circumspection of dress and sober faces.

As we neared the landing-place at Santa Mesa, we saw old Pedro, who had long been in the employ of the factory company, standing upon the bank of the river, watching for our return; and whether he was glad to see us, or was tired of waiting, is more than I can tell, but a smile of satisfaction was upon his face when he saw us safe, and he welcomed us back with an expressive grunt.

"How are things at the factory?" Allen asked, as soon as he had secured the banco.

"*Muy bueno, Senors,*" was the answer; "the soldiers have been here, made a few inquiries, and carried off all the dead and injured, and sworn that every ladrone shall be caught, dead or alive, before next feast day."

"A threat that they have forgotten before this time," muttered Allen.

"There are visitors at the house?" I suggested, burning to know whether Donna Teresa and her husband had left for the city.

"*Si, Senor,*" replied the fellow, promptly; "the holy father of the convent of San Pedro heard of the attack to-day, and he instantly ordered his banco, to pay a visit of condolence. His banco has returned up the river, so that I think he will remain over night."

"No others present?"

"The old Spaniard and his wife, senor. The old gentleman felt grieved to think that you should have hunted without his company, and he swore that he would stop until he had shot a deer, if he remained a week."

"That is good news — is it not?" Allen asked, in English, handing the rifles on shore, and smiling most maliciously.

I made no reply, for I felt too pleased at the information to feel angry with my worst enemy, just at that moment. But I glanced at my soiled hands and clothes, and thought how shocking it would be to meet the lady until a change of dress had restored me to my usual condition of cleanliness. As Allen started towards the house, I stopped him.

"We look none too clean to mingle with company. Let us

send Pedro for a change of garments, and while he is gone, have a swim."

Allen cared but little for his appearance after a hard day's hunt, and I knew it; but I succeeded at length in convincing him that the company at the factory would look upon the change in the light of a compliment; so Pedro was despatched for clean linen, and brushes and combs, while we washed from our persons the accumulations of the Great Swamp; and never did the water seem more refreshing to our tired limbs than after that hard day's work in hunting the outlaw. And then how different I felt when dressed in a white linen shirt, with thin shoes and white stockings, and hair arranged in the most telling style, and which was intended to tear Donna Teresa's heart to atoms, and not leave one little piece that she could call her own or her husband's.

Lamps were lighted in the dining-room as we walked towards the house, for we had squandered much time at the edge of the river; and as soon as we reached the court-yard we heard a hearty laugh, which seemed to shake the very walls of the building. It was something between a growl and a roar, as though the utterer was endeavoring to restrain his animal spirits while relating his jokes, but finding it impossible, was obliged to yield to the pressure, and give his voice full vent, or take the chances of strangling.

"That," said Allen, in reply to a glance, "is the holy father, Benventuro, who can sing or pray, feast or play, as well as the most zealous in the land. He is loved by the natives, and feared, at the same time; for the holy father, in spite of seeming indifference, carries an iron hand, and when it falls, a native goes with it. He is a profound admirer of Americans and America, and if the crown of Spain would appoint him governor general of the islands, their prosperity would rival that of Cuba in five years. He knows what is required to develop the resources of the country, and if he had position he would put his knowledge to some use. As it is, he lives a careless, jovial life, without one thought of the future, and entirely indifferent whether he conforms to all the customs of the church or not."

We ascended the steps leading to the second story, and found the holy father seated at a table which was well spread with substantial food, while opposite to him were Mr. Huckford and Don Arturo.

Gazing from the window, with her back turned to the company, was Donna Teresa; and even when we entered the room she did not turn to greet us, but remained motionless as though too busy with her thoughts to notice our arrival.

"Ah, praise to Bacchus and Venus, the wanderers have returned!" shouted the priest, as he caught sight of us. "I have fasted for such a length of time that my stomach is as empty as my wine cellar, and my temper was growing as bad as Father Vidas'; and they do say — although I tell you this in confidence, mind, and it must not go further — that he never speaks a pleasant word except on Sundays, and not then, unless two things happen."

"And what must happen to bring forth such an expression of benevolence?" Allen asked, as he shook hands with the jolly-looking father, and presented me in due form.

"Why, his fighting cock must win a battle, and a pretty girl confess her sins and her little peccadillos, and promise to reform; but faith, I have always found them ready to promise, but slow to perform."

I glanced towards the swelling form that stood at the window to see what effect such conversation would have upon her; but she remained motionless, and apparently unheeding.

"The supper, the supper! bring in the supper!" shouted Father Benventuro, slapping the table with his fat hand until the crockery ware danced, and threatened dissolution. "Why, I have not broken my fast since morning, and I feel like a boa that has lived on air for a month. Senor Huckford, I hope your cook has lost none of his skill, and that he knows I am to stop for supper."

"You shall be satisfied," Mr. Huckford replied, with his melancholy smile, which was as habitual to his face as though he had a presentiment that he should never see his home again. He touched a bell as he spoke, and the servants entered the apartment with steaming coffee, and curry, and rice, and young chickens, delicately broiled and browned without being burned, while there was game cooked in various ways, and vegetables swimming in fresh butter.

The priest rubbed his hands, and tucked a huge colored handkerchief around the neck of his black robe of office, and even the sunken eyes of the old Spaniard lighted up with fire as the fumes of the food assailed his nostrils, and provoked his appetite. While the servants were arranging the dishes I hastily passed to the side of Donna Teresa, and laid my hand lightly upon her exquisitely moulded arm, so round, and smooth, and delicate, that it looked like wax-work, encircled with heavy hoops of gold, some of them studded with diamonds and precious stones, which glittered in the light like stars in the heavens, to which her large black eyes were directed. She must have felt my touch; yet she did not move or withdraw her arm from the position in which she held it.

"Can I not obtain one word of welcome from Donna Teresa?" I asked, in a low tone.

For a moment she suffered her eyes to wander to my face; but when she saw the look of admiration that I could not restrain, she turned her head, and the rich blood mantled her cheek as she asked, —

"What kind of a welcome does Guillermo desire at my hands?"

"The welcome of a friend," I replied, still speaking in a low tone.

"Friendships are dangerous at times, and lead to unfortunate results. Would it not be better that I should extend to you a sisterly welcome, or one cold and formal like a new acquaintance?" she asked, after a moment's thought.

"What have I done to deserve this?" I inquired, in surprise; and placed my hand upon hers to enforce attention. She did not repel the liberty, but looked grave and stately, as I had seen her when presiding over her husband's dinner table, surrounded by the most distinguished company that the island could produce.

"You have done nothing that I can condemn, and much that I regard, since our acquaintance commenced, Guillermo," she said slowly and distinctly, as though she was weighing each word, or was uttering them very reluctantly. "I have been alone all day," she continued, "as I told you that I should; and I have thought much of my past life, and endeavored to fancy what the future would be like, and whether it would be as unhappy as the past few years of my existence."

"You should be happy," I remarked, "for you have youth, beauty, and immense wealth. What more could you desire?"

How reproachfully her dark eyes appeared, as she looked at

my face to see whether I was speaking ironically, or from my heart.

"Wealth!" she repeated, bitterly; "were it not for my gold and lands I should now be free from all matrimonial control. Would that the earthquakes had destroyed all that I possessed. sooner than a husband."

"I thought you married of your own free will and accord," I said.

"Then you thought wrong, and 'tis but right that I should undeceive you."

She glanced towards the table, and saw that the servants were still arranging the dishes and removing the wine from the coolers, and that her husband was listening to a story from the holy man.

"When my father died, four years since," the lady said, "he left me under the care of Don Arturo, his oldest friend, with directions in his will that at fifteen I should marry the Don, or enter a convent. In the latter case my wealth was to be divided: one half was to enrich the convent that I entered, and the other half to belong to Don Arturo. After my father's death I was debarred seeing any one excepting such friends as Don Arturo designated, and those, of course, were loud in praise of his goodness and amiable qualities, insisting that the woman who was blessed with his hand would have great cause for rejoicing. I little thought that he would adhere to the obligations of the will; but he did, and you see the result before you. For two years I have been his wife, and two long years of woe and misery they have been. Had I been dependent upon the charity of relations, I could have used my eyes, and exercised my own choice in the selection of a husband; but unfortunately I was not poor — more reason for sorrow."

I pitied her from my heart as she told her griefs, and would have given all the wealth I possessed to have been able to have comforted her, or to have held her in my arms and called her wife; for I could not help thinking that we were much more suited to each other in age and disposition than Don Arturo and herself.

"You now know why I say that friendships are dangerous; and believe me, Guillermo, I weigh every word when I repeat to you that we must in future meet as seldom as possible. It is for your sake that I make the request, for I am young, passionate, and easily swayed to good or evil, and may the Virgin help me to avoid the latter."

She laid her soft hand on mine as she spoke, and I felt my blood bound through my veins as though each drop was a race-horse. It seemed to me, as I heard her speak, that the earth was less beautiful than before, and that the stars were less bright, and that if I could steal from the room, I would mount a horse and dash off through the darkness, regardless of danger, or where I should finally stop. Yet I knew that she was right, and that to cure my infatuation, absence from the shrine at which I had worshipped so many months, was the only remedy, and I endeavored to nerve myself for the contest.

"Guillermo," she said, in a low whisper, and with a soft pressure of her delicate hand, "you are not offended with me for speaking thus plainly? I mean for the best."

"May the saints preserve you," I said, although I felt my heart rise in my throat while speaking. "I have long felt the danger of my position, and will now avoid it. The first ship that leaves for China carries me as a passenger; but I go with a broken heart."

"No, no!" she cried eagerly; "remain in Manila, and let us meet as often as once a week, or even more frequently, There can be no harm in that. We can always see each other in company, and exchange a few words."

I shook my head, for I doubted the expediency of such a course.

"Do not answer now," she said, hurriedly; "but meet me to-night in the corridor, while the company are flushed with wine, and will not miss your presence. Drink sparingly, and still think of me kindly."

As she concluded, the holy father was shouting loudly for his long-expected dinner; and Don Arturo was glancing round the room to find his wife.

"Ho, Senor Guillermo!" shouted the holy father, striking the table with a bottle of hock of an excellent brand, a liquor of which the good man was excessively fond. "Have you turned priest, and are you assuming my prerogative by confessing the fair Donna Teresa. By the good St. Veritus, but I shall interfere in the matter."

"The lady's thoughts and petty sins are still her own," I said, advancing to the table, and seating Teresa by her husband's side. "She would not make confession to a heretic; so I was obliged to entertain her with an account of our adventures this day in the great swamp, and they have amused her, and perhaps excited her pity."

The cloud which I saw gathering upon Don Arturo's brow disappeared under the strength of my reasoning, or the fumes of the supper table, I could not tell which; and to tell the truth, I did not care, for my spirit, from being crushed by the decision of the fair lady, had suddenly assumed a buoyancy at her change of opinion that was entirely unusual.

We were soon in our places at the table, Allen on my right, and Donna Teresa on my left, while opposite to us were Mr. Huckford and the holy father Benventuro, the latter with an appetite like a hunter, and a digestion like an ostrich.

His eyes glared like those of a sensualist, as they wandered over the rich viands which loaded the table; and knowing his disposition well, our host was not backward in helping him first, even to the exclusion of all but the lady.

"The church," said our host, as he sent the servant with a huge plate, loaded with the best that the table contained, "must and shall be respected. If the worthy father does not eat heartily, I shall think he is not hungry, or else dislikes our slight entertainment."

"May the saints forgive you for your groundless suspicions," muttered the priest, seizing his plate, and squaring his shoulders for the contest, like a hunter before taking a dangerous leap; and for fifteen minutes he did not speak a word, but used his knife and fork with as much skill as the best tactician could desire.

"By the way, we have not heard the adventures of the day," the father said, pausing in his exertions, and emptying his wineglass, and then immediately challenging Donna Teresa to do the same; but the lady was prudent, and merely wet her red lips in the generous liquor; and the priest was too busy with his own affairs to notice that she had not done justice to his pledge.

"Yes, let us hear the adventures of the day," cried the Spaniard; "and remember that I have not forgiven you, young gentlemen, for leaving me out of the party. I had a right to expect an invitation after the assistance that I rendered last night."

"We had no time to lose," Allen said, "or we should have

been pleased with your company and valuable aid. We were obliged to take the field before the dew was off the grass, or else forego an important business."

"But remember I am not to be put off in that way," cried Don Arturo. "I came here for a hunt, and shall remain here until I have accomplished my object. If my wife does not like that plan, she can return to the city in the morning."

I mentally hoped that she would take kindly to the arrangement, but was somewhat disappointed when she objected, and hinted that it would be better if both returned to the city as soon as possible, as she feared that some accident would happen if he persisted in his dangerous expeditions.

This was sufficient to excite the obstinacy of the Don, for he had been drinking freely, and thought that it was necessary for his reputation that he should show becoming contempt of all danger.

"I tell you, Teresa, that here I remain until I have had my hunt, and here you remain until you have witnessed my exploits. It is useless to remonstrate, for I am just as firm as a rook on this point."

I bent my eyes upon the table, and strove to moderate the transports which I felt at the old man's decision, for I knew that the holy father was scanning my face with his glittering eyes, as though he was endeavoring to read my very thoughts.

I remained immovable and impassive under his scrutiny, and at length I heard him mutter, as he plunged his face in a huge glass filled with sparkling wine, —

"*Diablo!* I must have been mistaken."

"At what?"

"In thinking that this was hock instead of champagne," he replied; and then, to change the subject, loudly called for a detailed statement of our adventures, and while Allen was relating them, the good father would frequently interrupt him to propose the health of the hunters, or the health of our host, or the lady, or Don Arturo; but I noticed that the priest was more particular in seeing that my glass was filled to the brim than the rest of the company.

At first I imagined it was owing to a sudden friendship he had contracted for me, and that the holy man wished to cement the bonds thus formed in the juice of the grape; but as I noticed his continued partiality, I had a slight suspicion that my brain was to be tested, and while in a state of intoxication I was to be sounded in relation to my feelings for the wife of the old Spaniard.

The more I watched his proceedings, the stronger I felt assured that it was the case, and I formed the resolution of letting the good priest see that an American possessed as stout a head as himself, and that in the end he would be baffled in his attempt to extort my secret.

I never fancied a drinking bout, and was, usually, extremely abstemious, rarely taking liquor unless at a dinner-party, and never then unless forced to do so by the custom of the country. But what was most extraordinary, I possessed a head and brain that were never known to yield to the influence of liquor, and were I so disposed, I could drink for hours, and yet rise from the table, and even the most fastidious lady in the land would never know that wine had passed my lips, unless she came in close contact with them.

Knowing as I did that I could drink the priest under the table, I responded to his toasts, and proposed others, and mixed his liquors until at length I got him to swallow half a tumbler of French brandy, under the impression that it was wine; and faith, I don't think that he discovered his mistake. I could see the little gray eyes grow more luminous as the revel proceeded, and to disarm the holy father of all suspicions, I pretended to be nearly oblivious of all that was transpiring around the table.

Twice I stole glances at Donna Teresa's face, to see how she was affected by the scene; and each time that I did so I met the full gaze of her large, melancholy eyes, as though reproaching me for my want of discretion.

"Let me sing you a song, senors," cried the holy father, struggling to his feet, and insisting that all should join in the chorus.

"But first let me retire," interrupted Donna Teresa, hastily rising, with some alarm, for she probably imagined that the songs sung by an intoxicated man were hardly fit for a modest woman to listen to.

"Go by all means," stammered her husband, who was too far gone to assist the lady or himself.

She bowed coldly to the company, and accepting my arm, was escorted to the door.

"I shall not fail you," I whispered. "At twelve I will be on the corridor."

I spoke without the least show of intoxication; and I could see a gleam of joyful surprise pass over her face as she listened. With an inclination of her proud head, she passed through the open door, and retired to her chamber.

"By all the saints in the calendar, but she is the fairest lady in Manila," cried the holy father, with enthusiasm; "and I will propose a toast which all must drink, or I'll excommunicate them from this blessed company, and compel them to drink river water for the remainder of their lives. Fill, *caballeros*, and drink to the health of the fair Donna Teresa and her gallant husband."

The priest's eyes were on me as he spoke, and in spite of his seeming intoxication, I could see that he was studying my motions and face to judge how I liked the toast.

"I propose an amendment to the sentiment," I cried, just as the company were raising their glasses to their lips. "Long may they live, and long may they love each other."

"I accept the amendment," shouted the father, and with enthusiasm we drank the toast, and were then bored for fifteen minutes with a speech from the husband; but what it referred to I have no recollection, for I was thinking of my appointment, and wondering how soon the Don and priest would lie under the table, where I most sincerely wished them.

During the confusion, and while the priest was relating a story, our host slipped off to bed, and the servants retired one by one, until we were unattended.

But the wine was close at hand, and we could spare them; and the only consequence of our host's absence was to draw our chairs closer together, and smoke and drink more fierce than ever.

"Did I ever tell you, Senor Allen, how the Mestiza girl played a trick upon the good, but extremely cross father Vidas?" asked Benventuro, as soon as the Don had concluded a story, which every one laughed at, but no one thought funny.

"Never; let us hear it without delay."

"Fill your glasses, and I'll commence. One day, three months since, the worthy father was told that a young girl desired the benefit of confession, but had neglected to bring the usual offering, a present, and the fair penitent was sent home sadly troubled, and uncertain what to do.

"I heard of her application, and determined to administer a rebuke to the old tiger for his selfishness. I took occasion to visit the girl, and gave her a few hints, and the next day she called upon father Vidas, and reiterated her request; and as she did so, she held something in her hand, covered with a piece of paper.

"'Ah, this time you have brought something—have you?' he said; and the girl acknowledged that she had, but took care not to mention what it was.

"She made a full confession, and got pardoned for all the sins she had committed, and then my brother held out his hand for the expected reward.

"'I'm very poor, holy father,' she said; 'and so are my parents, and my lover, Pedro; but I determined to bring you an offering that would please you.'

"Vidas rubbed his hands, and expected a peso at least.

"'I heard,' the girl continued, 'that last Sunday your favorite game cock was killed in a fight, and that you lost much money on the result.'

"The good man growled like a tiger as he acknowledged that such was the case.

"'Knowing that you would lament the loss, I took the trouble of getting my lover to cut the spurs from his legs; and here they are, neatly polished.'

"She placed the paper in his hand, and fled from the church; and for two days the good man did not make his appearance in public, but endeavored, by fasting and prayer, to subdue the feelings which were in his heart. But he has not forgotten the circumstance, and even now it is dangerous to mention spurs to him."

The story was told with many hiccups and expressions not necessary to be repeated here; but when it was concluded, I saw that the priest expected me to laugh; so I did, and thereby won some portion of his esteem. Don Arturo, who had hardly understood ten words that were uttered, swore that it was the best thing that he had ever heard, and in endeavoring to get up and shake hands with the narrator, lost his balance, and fell under the table, and by the time that he struck the floor was snoring most unmusically.

"See what a sot a man will make of himself!" pathetically muttered the priest. "Wine is a harmless beverage when not taken in immoderate quantities, and I always recommend it to those who can afford to drink it, but not otherwise. The Don's head is weak, and he should be restrained by his friends from over-indulgence."

The good father staggered to his feet, and assisted to raise the insensible body, and across the room we swayed, the holy father with the thin legs of the Spaniard in his grasp, while Allen and myself held on to an arm apiece; and as each of us was disposed to deposit him in different places in the room, of course there was some pulling and hauling of the unfortunate man, which he never would have submitted to had he been in his sober senses.

"Well," exclaimed the priest, suddenly dropping the legs of the poor Don, and wiping his brow with his fat hand, "if you two are not going to pull one way, I'm going to stop and rest; because the man's joints are small, and will probably yield in the pressure. Now, the question naturally arises, what shall be done with him?"

"Carry him to his wife's room," promptly suggested Allen, who had drank more than he should have done; and yet was nearly as sober as myself.

"Monstrous proposition!" thundered the holy man, waving his hand at Allen as though it was a war-club. "What! place this imbiber of liquor — this drunken sot — by the side of an angel, and not expect an earthquake to occur? Think you that Venus would submit to be outraged in that style?"

"But Venus has nothing to do with the matter, and therefore can't interfere," replied the matter-of-fact Allen.

"Don't blaspheme in that manner," cried the holy man. "All insults of such a gross nature to a handsome woman are recorded in the Venus calendar; and sooner than assist to lay him upon a bed with Donna Teresa, I'd throw him out the window. Mind you, only upon compulsion, or with the above proviso."

"And sooner than allow such a thing," Allen exclaimed, "I'd drown you in the Pasig, and thus poison the river."

"Don't introduce the lady in your brawls," I said; for I felt perfectly indignant that the noble and high-minded woman should be thus insulted by a fat priest, and my own particular friend, who was trying to bring him out.

At length it was resolved to lay the insensible Don upon a mattress, and Allen and the priest left the room for a moment to find one. While they were absent I looked at my watch, and found that it was quarter past eleven o'clock, and I had but three quarters of an hour to finish my friends so that I could keep my appointment with Donna Teresa, and have them suspect nothing of what was going on. I was in despair, for the priest seemed as though capable of drinking a barrel of wine, and yet retaining his senses; but a sudden thought occurred to me, and I prepared a dose for him that even the most adamantine head would have acknowledged and yielded to. I emptied the decanter of brandy into the champagne and hock bottles, and by the time the mattress was brought into the room everything was prepared for the experiment. The Don was rolled on his bed and once more we took our seats at the table.

"Ugh," grunted the holy father, filling his glass, which would hold half a pint, with the mixed liquor; "how thirsty I feel after the fatigue of putting that sot to bed! He is one of that kind of men who cannot drink in moderation and feel satisfied, but must drown his stomach and senses with generous liquor which he knows not how to appreciate. Let us drink to his wife, and wish her a better husband."

I watched him narrowly while the glass was at his lips; but he did not appear to notice that his liquor had been tampered with, and I had the satisfaction of seeing the last drop disappear down his insatiate throat, and that he re-filled his goblet as though he rather liked the change.

The priest attempted to sing a song, but failed; and thinking that it was owing to his thirst, up went his glass a second time, well freighted with brandy, which had never seen water, and strong sherry; but the second dose was as strong as the first, and in a few minutes I saw his head fall upon his breast; but he raised it again and strove hard to appear unconcerned; but the eyelids were heavy, and refused to remain open, and down with a crash went the holy man's pate upon the table, and such sounds proceeded from his nose that I no longer questioned his insensibility.

Allen stood the siege a little better; but when he saw that his old friend was entirely used up, he attempted to make a few remarks upon the impropriety of drinking to excess; but before he had finished, he forgot what he was talking about, and concluded, just five minutes before twelve, to sink into a quiet slumber, and he did; for which I was thankful, although all three snored so loudly that I was fearful they would wake each other.

I left the table and plunged my head into a bowl of cold water, bathed my temples until I felt my pulse reduced to a healthy throb, and then, extinguishing all the lights excepting one, opened the door that led to the corridor, closed it carefully, and after listening for a moment and hearing no sound excepting the outrageous snoring that the Don, the priest, and Allen were indulging in, stole quietly along through the passage-way, turned to the right, passed Donna Teresa's room, and then found myself in the corridor, at one end of which was a grated window, that had remained there from the time the old building was a convent, a hundred years or more. The only light that penetrated the long walk was from this single window; so that I was compelled to grope my way along carefully for fear of stumbling over the numerous antique settees which were placed in the corridor, more for the purpose of getting them out of the way than for family use.

Suddenly my outstretched hands came in contact with something that felt soft and warm; and by the dim starlight I saw before me a vision in white, which I was inclined to fall down and worship.

"Guillermo," said the vision, in the low, sweet tones of Donna Teresa, "how late you are! I feared that something had happened to prevent you from seeing me as you requested."

I did not tell her that she had made a slight mistake, and that I was too modest a lover to have ever requested an interview at that hour of the night. However, I managed to muster courage enough to take her hand, and to plead that the hour was just twelve, and that I was unable to see her before.

"I granted you this interview," Teresa said, making a slight effort to disengage her hand, "to ask you not to leave Manila at present, and to know if you will feel satisfied with my friendship, cold and distant, but still true."

"If you so will it," I answered promptly, for it struck me that the lady was acting the coquette on a grand scale, and that she should be met as such. I no longer made an effort to imprison her hand, but kept my distance, cold, but courteous. There was a long silence, and I could see, by the starlight which entered the grated window where we stood, that she was troubled at my indifference.

"The hour is late," she said at length. "I feel tired, and will retire. We shall meet in the morning — shall we not?"

This time she extended her hand, and I could see her dark eyes fixed upon my face as though reproaching me for my coldness. I pretended not to notice her glance, but leaned against the window and looked into the garden. I heard her take two or three steps towards her room, and then pause and hesitate, as though uncertain how to act.

"Good night, Guillermo," she repeated.

"Good night, Teresa," I replied; and again there was a pause.

I trembled for fear her haughty spirit would prompt her to leave me, in which case I should have had to yield, and made ample protestations that I was not offended.

She still remained undecided what to do; but at length, to my intense joy, I felt her hand laid upon my shoulder, and then her head, with its wealth of dark hair, was laid against my breast, and for the first time I heard Donna Teresa weep.

I threw my arms around her and pressed her close to my heart, which was beating so wildly that it seemed as though it would break; and thus we stood for many minutes, silent and motionless, for the lady made no attempt to disengage herself from my embrace.

"You are angry with me," she said, at length, raising her large black eyes, and looking at me so mournfully that I felt sorry for my conduct.

I called Heaven to witness that I was not, and added a few endearing words, which I have now forgotten.

"Let us be friends, very dear friends," she said; "but for my sake, let us meet hereafter as seldom as possible."

"And for my sake let us meet as often as we can," I replied.

She made no reply, but gently unclasped my hands and removed her head from my bosom.

"Answer me one question," she said at last; and I could feel her hand placed upon my shoulder to enforce attention.

"A dozen if you wish."

"Do you love me?"

"As I hope for heaven, I do," I replied.

"I do not mean such love as most men profess; but a sincere passion, pure and true — for you must recollect that I am bound to a man whom I call husband, and that I would suffer death sooner than live with him much longer."

"With my whole heart, Teresa, I love you," I replied, after a moment's pause; "were you single, and would accept of me as a husband, I would devote my life to your happiness, and cherish you with such passionate love that even your exacting nature could find no cause of complaint."

Her arms were around my neck again, and no opposition was made to the warm kisses which I showered upon her red lips.

"You will not leave Manila," she murmured.

"Not unless you go with me," I replied.

"That I would do willingly; but my fortune is so disposed that I cannot convert it into ready money."

"I do not ask for your fortune — let your husband enjoy that to his heart's content. I ask for you, and unless you are mine at no distant day, life will indeed be a burden."

"Better have patience, until I can come to your arms an honored wife," she said, starting back at my energy. "Let us remain as we are for the present, and while we can be friends to the world, we can love in secret."

"Do you promise me this?" I asked.

She laid her smooth cheek against my bearded face, and her lips met mine in token of assent.

"Do you truly love me?" I asked, intoxicated with my happiness.

"I have loved you from the time I first saw you," was the reply; and I believed her, and swore an oath that I would be true to her, and love her faithfully until death.

"Amen," cried a deep-toned voice at the end of the corridor; and then I heard steps as though some one was making a rapid retreat to the sitting-room.

"We are lost!" cried Donna Teresa, clinging closely to me in her terror, thus preventing my following in pursuit.

"Remain here for a moment," I said, striving to unclasp her arms; but she only held me the more close in her embrace; so I raised her with my right arm, and ran rapidly through the corridor

AN INTERVIEW WITH FATHER BENVENTURO. Page 83.

until I reached the lady's chamber, the door of which I opened, and saw that a light was burning dimly within.

I found that Teresa was nearly insensible with fear; I laid her upon a bed, and hastily whispered that I would return in a few minutes, and announce who had dared to listen to our conversation.

Drawing a dagger I stole quietly from the chamber, and then laid my hand upon the latch which led to the room where we had dined. For a moment I paused to listen, but heard only the deep breathing of those who had drank so deeply that night at the table, and whom I could hardly suspect of being sober enough to play the spy, and yet I could think of none others.

I pushed open the door and entered, and to my surprise saw half a dozen lamps were burning, and that seated at the table, looking perfectly sober and self-possessed, yet still drinking freely, was the holy father, Benventuro.

"Ah, Guillermo," he cried, when he saw me enter, "have you returned to help me finish the bottles? You have acted wisely. Draw up your chair, and I will open a fresh one."

"I am in no humor for jesting," I replied, taking my position in front of the priest, and regarding him sternly.

"No, I should think not. People seldom jest with a knife like that in their hands," he answered, quite composedly, pointing to the dagger with one hand, and raising his full glass with the other.

"I have a few questions which I wish to put to you," I said, still regarding the holy man sternly; but I could not perceive that he was discomposed in the least.

"Are they of a pleasant nature, or of a theological turn? I prefer the former to-night, for my blood is heated with wine, and my thoughts are all concentrated for the good of myself and people. Let the questions be brief and humorous."

"Have you left the room within fifteen minutes?"

"Yes."

He answered promptly, his black eyes fixed upon my face as though he would read whether there was murder in my thoughts.

"During your absence did you overhear a private conversation?" I demanded, my blood beginning to boil, and my thoughts growing more wicked.

"I did overhear a conversation between —"

He lowered his voice, and bent over the table, so that I was just enabled to hear him whisper the words, —

"Donna Teresa and yourself."

I don't know what made me withhold my hand, and prevented me from striking him dead; but by a mighty effort I was enabled to do so.

"Your motive in playing the spy?" I demanded, fiercely.

"To benefit the lady, you, and myself," he answered, laconically.

"Explain."

"Take a seat and I will," replied the priest, quite coolly.

I complied with the request, for the priest maintained so mysterious an air, that I deemed it best to hear what excuse he had to offer for intruding upon the privacy of Donna Teresa and myself.

"Go on with your explanation," I said.

The holy father was about to comply with my request, when a loud snore from Don Arturo attracted his attention.

"What I have to say to you must be known to us alone. Help me to remove Allen and the Spaniard to another room. We can accomplish our work carefully, and not awaken them."

I assisted the priest to lift the mattresses upon which the men were sleeping, and we deposited them carefully in an adjoining room, closed the door, and again took our seats at the table.

"A glass of wine together before I begin," father Benventuro said, holding out a bottle; but I feared treachery, and declined.

"As you please — there's the more left for me. Your health and long life," he exclaimed, nodding his head as he drained his glass.

"Your explanations," I cried, impatiently.

"Are these," the priest said, sinking his voice to a whisper, and speaking earnestly. "I suspected this evening, when I saw you and Donna Teresa standing at the window, that love was at the bottom of your friendship; so I resolved to watch you. Don't frown, for I had no motive but curiosity, and little thought that the subject would ever occupy my attention. I have had some weaknesses in my eventful life, and am not disposed to chide when others are guilty of a little sin. I did observe you, even while I was pretending not to; and the final result was, that I became more and more convinced that the lady was indifferent to her husband, and loved you with all the warmth and fervor of a Spanish girl. I also saw that your cold, northern blood had been stirred by the black eyes of Donna Teresa, and that you, too, was devoted to her. So far so good. I looked upon you as a friend, and was not disposed to interfere, for a few years since, even I should have rebuked such presumption, had I been engaged in a suit that promised successful results."

"Why do you interfere, then?" I demanded.

"Patience, and I will let you know," was the soft answer, as the priest refilled his glass. "I did not know certainly how long you had been loving, and whether the pursuit was as profitable as you could wish; but I thought that this night there would be a meeting between you, and I was the more convinced of the fact when I saw you change the liquors, while I was engaged in looking after Don Arturo's welfare."

"You saw me do that?" I stammered.

"To be sure I did, my boy; but I don't complain, because, in the first place, I pretended to drink the mixed liquor, and I think convinced even you that I did; but if you had watched me closely, you would have seen that I bowed my head upon my breast, and all that my mouth contained was discharged between my cassock and under-clothes. It was disagreeable, and a great waste of good stuff. But what was I to do? Be outwitted by an American, or suffer the sharp practice, which I learned at a Jesuit college, to fall into disrepute? No, my son; you did well, and deceived Allen into the belief that he was drinking champagne instead of strong brandy; but a priest never leaves a table, if he expects to return, without first noting how full his glass is, and its exact position; and if, during his absence, it has been changed, he drinks no more at that table. You see I am frank with you, my son, because I expect that we shall be good friends hereafter, and serve each other with fidelity and zeal."

"To what does all this tend?" I asked.

"I have not reached that portion of my confession, my son," replied Benventuro, mildly, refilling his glass, and again offering to supply me with liquor from the same bottle from which he was drinking; but I feared treachery, and once more declined. The holy man smiled, and continued his conversation.

"I believe that I convinced you I was drunk, as I certainly intended to, and had the satisfaction of seeing you make preparations for leaving the room, as sober, I believe, as when you entered it last night; and I could not help, as I lay upon the floor watching your movements through half-closed eyes, paying you a high compliment for your discretion — for remember, my son, that a lover should never meet his mistress intoxicated, as he is apt to say something which he would often repent of in his sober moments. Besides, all the pleasures of an interview are lost while the senses are clouded with liquor. I am too old a man not to know the joy which lovers feel after being separated for a few days. "Therefore, I repeat, always abstain from liquor while contemplating a visit to a mistress; and believe me that in this instance you will find the advice of a priest worth regarding."

I could but agree with him; so bowed and suffered the priest to fill my glass, although I was careful to note that the goblet was perfectly clean and dry, and had not been tampered with.

"Now you display sense, and I feel my heart yearn towards you as though I had known you for years," the priest said, rubbing his hands with an expression of cordiality that I found was infectious, and almost regretted that I had drawn a dagger for the purpose of ending the days of one who seemed so good a friend.

"Finish your story," I said, putting the dagger in my pocket — an act that the priest paid not the slightest attention to.

"All right. Let me fill your glass again. The saints forgive me for drinking as I have to-night; but the liquor is good, and the company pleasant, and I have been sorely tempted to an indulgence. It is a sin, and I know it well enough; but I don't like to inflict penance upon myself, even if I have to upon others; so that I am fearful I shall never be cured until all the vintages fail. But I see that you are impatient; so we will despatch our business without unnecessary delay; but first let me ask you a few questions, and I will tell you candidly that much depends upon your answers. First, do you really love Donna Teresa? Take time to answer. I don't mean, do you love her because she is Don Arturo's wife, and not your own, for a gallant's love is not as stable as a mountain, or as fiery as a volcano, although to hear him swear one would think so.

"Do you love the lady with that disinterested love which would prompt you to marry her were she a maid or a widow, without wealth?"

"You have no right to ask the question," I said, coldly.

"I acknowledged that some time since, my son, and must put but one interpretation upon your conduct. You love the lady because she is another's."

"By all the saints that a good Catholic swears by, I love the lady for herself alone, and would take her to my arms as my wife this very night, were I able to do so."

"Spoken like a man," replied the priest, his black eyes flashing with excitement; and his hand trembled as he filled my glass and his own. "You love the lady, and she loves you. That I know, for I overheard her confession to-night, and what I suspected before I am certain of now. She is worthy of the love of a king, and I am glad that she has found favor with an American sovereign."

"What else do you want?" I asked, somewhat impatiently. "You have a motive in questioning me, and I must exercise the same right. You know that I am a Protestant, and that I cannot marry Donna Teresa, even were she a widow, without changing my religion."

"That is the point to which I wish to bring you," cried the priest, lowering his voice to a whisper, and leaning over the table. As he did so a large wooden cross, which he wore around his neck, struck the dishes and attracted his attention. "Here," he exclaimed; "swear upon this cross an oath, solemn and impressive, that you will marry Donna Teresa in three months after she is a widow."

"What do you mean?" I asked, in amazement. "She is not a widow, and not likely to be one for these ten years. And even if she were, my religion would prove an objection."

"You shall remain a Protestant as long as you live, in your heart and feelings, and the lady can do the same in regard to her Catholicity. I don't think you will make the lady any the less happy on account of religious difference."

"You are trifling with me," I said, with some show of anger.

"I swear to you that I am not; and I further swear that I mean to act for the happiness of Donna Teresa and yourself, and in such a manner that you will both bless me."

I smiled in scorn at the words, and the priest noticed it.

"Listen to me for a moment, and then judge whether I will perform the part which, with your consent, I intend to play. Don Arturo is an old man, nearly seventy years of age, and is troubled with disease of the heart, which is liable to take him to a better world at any moment. This he knows, and has made all due provision for a sudden exit. When he dies, his immense wealth will revert to his widow, for most of it belonged to her father, an excellent man, but a great fool to suppose that his beautiful child could ever find happiness in the arms of a person old enough to be her great-grandfather."

"How do you know all this?" I asked, with more curiosity than I had yet felt.

"Through his confessor, Father Juan, of the Sebastian Convent. You have seen him, and he has seen you; and let me whisper this in your ear in confidence — he looks not upon you with any degree of favor."

"I never exchanged ten words with him in my life, for I like not his looks," I replied, with a vivid remembrance of the suspicious glances which I had seen him cast upon me when in the company of Donna Teresa and her husband.

"But he fears your influence upon the lady in case her husband dies. Another secret let me confide to you — the holy father suspects the passion which you cherish, and he is watching with Argus eyes for developments. Even a servant in this house is in his pay to spy your proceedings; so let me again caution you how you act when in the presence of the lady."

"But what benefit can Father Juan expect to derive by interposing between us?" I asked.

"Wealth and promotion," was the brief rejoinder; and Father Benventuro filled his glass, and smiled.

"Explain your meaning."

"Nothing more easy. When Don Arturo dies, the good Father Juan hopes to persuade Donna Teresa to enter the convent of St. Sebastian; and, if she should, her wealth would make the convent the most rich and influential in Manila, and plain Father Juan would be made a bishop for his services in securing so much money to the holy church."

"There is no fear of Donna Teresa's entering a convent," I said, confidently. "She desires to see the world and enjoy life."

The holy man smiled disdainfully, and even swallowed a full goblet of wine before he could compose his reply.

"Let me ask if such would be the case, if any accident should happen to you, whom I have reason to believe she loves with all the devotion of a first love. Suppose, for instance, you should soon follow the old Spaniard, and while her grief was fresh, a proposal was made that she should enter a convent, and devote her life to religious duties, as the surest way of meeting you hereafter. Think you that she could withstand the pressure that the holy church would make, not to secure her happiness, but the millions she could command?"

"But I flatter myself that no accident, as you term it, is about to happen to me," I replied, confidently.

The good priest smiled, and drew from his pocket three silver dollars, which he placed upon the table.

"With such a paltry sum could I purchase your life, and the most rigid investigation would never lead to my detection, simply because the tool that I should employ would suppose that all chance for future happiness would be lost, should he betray a pillar of the church. Think you that I am the only priest in Manila, or on the island, who possesses the same power?"

Well might I feel startled at so candid a confession; and for a few minutes I could only ruminate upon such a fate as my companion had pictured becoming a reality.

"Drink, Guillermo, and don't let what I have said prevent you from continuing to love the lady as warmly as ever; for upon this holy cross I swear that if you will comply with my demands, and take an oath to that effect, I will shield you from all harm, and never cease to work until you and Donna Teresa are one."

"Who would marry a high-born Catholic lady to a Protestant?" I asked. "It is in direct violation of your instructions from the archbishop; and even if the marriage was legal, the priest would be degraded, and perhaps dismissed from the church."

"I grant that," replied the holy man, composedly. "But if you are first married by the American consul, and then by me, or any other Catholic priest, I would like to see the court or the bishop that would dare to interfere with your happiness."

"But how could you shield yourself from the archbishop's wrath?" I asked.

"In a very simple manner," the priest said, smiling. "I believe that he has some love for me, and he has shown it many times, even if I do like a bottle of wine once in a great while. The archbishop is but human, after all, and if I should appear before him after I had concluded the ceremony, — which, by the way, should be performed in the presence of your friends, and a few of the lady's; and even they must not know for what purpose they are assembled, — and should say, My lord, I have married the widow of Don Arturo to a Protestant, because I think that she will convert him in time to the true faith, and because he generously presented the church, of which you are the head in this country, with five thousand dollars — "

"But you know, and I repeat to you now, that there is no prospect, much as I love Donna Teresa, of my changing my religion," I said, firmly.

"Even if you do not, is there any necessity of sending a crier around the streets proclaiming that you are a Protestant, and will die in the faith? If you marry the lady, you will consult your own interest and safety by speaking as little of your religion as possible, and let the opinion gradually gain ground that your wife is converting you. This I shall ask for appearances, for not an assassin in Manila would dare raise his hand against a man whom the holy church hoped to convert. Ask questions of the reverend fathers, and listen in silence to their discourses, and if you must argue, do so with the firm intention of being vanquished. Do but this, and many years of happiness will be your portion."

"But I shall have to play the part of a rank hypocrite to do all that," I said.

"Does not the merchant dissemble when he desires to dispose of his goods, or the sea captain when he promises good food to his passengers, or even the lover when he swears that he will be faithful to his mistress, yet violates his vows every time that an opportunity occurs. Hypocrisy, my son, is a sin, but the world is full of it, and even when we avoid speaking our minds, we are guilty of the crime. Let not so common a thing influence you, for there is not a priest, Roman or Protestant, but will absolve you from the charge."

"Now, one question more," I said, fixing my eyes upon the priest; and he met my gaze without flinching. "How shall I account for the interest that you take in my proposed happiness?"

The priest laughed silently, and helped himself liberally to wine before he replied, —

"Through your advancement must I thrive."

"How so?"

"I told you that Father Juan would be made a bishop, if he persuaded Donna Teresa to enter the convent of Sebastian. I am more liberal than he, and know the wants of a pretty woman better. I desire that she shall re-marry, and, through such means I expect to be a bishop."

I started and gazed long and earnestly at the man to see if he was not joking; but I could see no trace of humor on his broad countenance.

"You wish to be a bishop?" I inquired.

"That position I am aiming at, and hope to gain it in preference to Father Juan, who is my rival, and has been for years. If you but aid me, it is within my grasp, for a vacancy exists and will shortly be filled."

"I possess no influence with the archbishop, or with the pope," I said.

"I know that as well as you," replied the holy man, quickly. "I don't require your personal influence, but I do want your money."

I could only stare at the priest in astonishment, while he continued: —

"I want to make a fair and candid bargain with you, and one that shall be binding. You say that you love Donna Teresa. I don't doubt it, and I am glad to see that she loves you. Of the latter I am certain, for I have heard of you and the lady long before I had the pleasure of an introduction. You have saved her life. That she will never forget as long as she lives, for Spanish ladies are grateful, and sometimes prodigal in the expression of their gratitude. You are young and active, and therefore just the sort of man to please a woman as romantic as Donna Teresa."

"To the point," I said, hastily.

"I will, without delay. As I said before, the days of Don Arturo are numbered," continued the priest, sinking his voice to a whisper, and fixing his glittering eyes upon me as though he was reading my thoughts. "When he dies, the lady will control one or two million dollars' worth of property, and I need not say that is a handsome sum for a man to take with a pretty wife. Now, I propose to help you to both wife and money, provided, of course, you will help me."

" But how ? " I asked.

" That question is easily asked and easily answered, yet I feel reluctant to speak out as openly as I could wish," the priest said.

I motioned him to go on, and after emptying his glass he did so.

" To conciliate the archbishop I must give him five thousand dollars, and that is not a large amount when you fully understand the danger of marrying a Protestant to a Catholic, and shielding him from harm."

" It is not an unreasonable sum," I remarked.

" I supposed that you would say so," the priest said, dryly, and continued; " but hear me through, and then decide. To obtain the title of bishop, I must have twenty thousand dollars to expend in making presents to influential friends ; and to maintain my position in state after I get my promotion, I must have twenty-five thousand dollars more, making in all fifty thousand dollars. Now you have heard my proposition, and know what to make of it."

" Why did you not say one hundred thousand dollars, instead of fifty ? " I inquired.

" Simply because I shall get the fifty thousand, and I could not the one hundred thousand," answered the priest, regardless of my sarcasm.

" When you do you will be much older than you are now," I replied ; and I was about to rise from the table, when the holy man gently detained me.

" Let us drink one glass together, to show our friendship," he urged.

While I hesitated he poured out the wine, and I swallowed it; the next instant I found that I was sitting at the table with feelings entirely different from those I possessed two minutes before. I could not account for the change, and I have never been able to since ; but I am inclined to the opinion that the Jesuit was more than a match for the American, and that, for one moment while I was off my guard, a powder was emptied into my wine-glass, which subdued my stubborn nature, and moulded me to the plans of the ambitious priest, so that I could not recede when my senses returned unclouded.

"Remember, I ask no advance of money until the lady is yours by marriage," the priest said; when he saw that I had emptied my glass; "I assist you to a fortune of nearly two million dollars, and only ask a trifling percentage. What man in his senses would refuse such an offer? Without my aid you get nothing, and will even lose the lady whom you love more than you do the money."

"I consent," was my reply.

"Then lay your hand upon this cross, and swear before God and me that in three months after Donna Teresa is a widow you will marry her, and in three more you will convey to me the money which you have promised."

I placed my hand upon the cross and swore the required oath, and just as I had concluded, the door was thrown violently open, and before us stood Don Arturo, looking wild and haggard, and gasping as though for breath.

CHAPTER IV.

DON ARTURO'S DREAMS. — A MOMENT'S ABSENCE. — AN EXCURSION. — A WONDERFUL SPRING. — THE LADRONES.

EVEN the holy father was startled at the sudden appearance of the old Spaniard, who we supposed was sleeping off the effect of his debauch; and I could not forbear a shudder at the interruption, when I recollected the unholy compact which I had just entered into regarding the man's wife. It seemed to me as though some supernatural means was connected with the visit, and that it was intended as a warning for me to desist from further pursuit. The priest was visibly annoyed, and drowned his confusion in liberal draughts of wine; but I had not the power to do so.

"How now, Don Arturo!" the holy man said, with one of his assumed expressions of jollity. "I thought that you were sleeping soundly."

"I have slept," replied the Spaniard, rubbing his eyes and staring at me and the priest as though uncertain whether we were real flesh and blood, or mere counterfeits; "and I have dreamed most unkind dreams."

"The subject, man — on what subject?" cried the holy father, with a most cheerful smile.

"I thought that my wife —"

"Your wife," repeated Benventuro, with a laugh; "why, may the saints bless me if I didn't think you had dreamed that your fortune was swallowed up by an earthquake, or a typhoon, and that there was no insurance. Go back to bed after wetting your lips with wine, and dream something more pleasant."

The Spaniard shook his head, but he didn't decline the wine, and even took a seat at the table, much to the annoyance of the father, who evidently wished him in some other place just at that time.

"And you, my friend," continued the Don, turning to me and grasping my hand, "were strangely mixed up in my dream. I thought that I was dead, and that before my body was cold you espoused Teresa, and squandered my fortune. I awoke with a fright, and intended to rush to my wife's room to see if it was a reality or indeed a dream, when I mistook the door and entered here. The saints be praised that I did so, for I should have sadly alarmed my wife at this unseasonable hour."

"Thus do I put to flight all horrid dreams and unkind suspicions," cried the priest, rising in his chair and dashing a few drops of water over the Spaniard's head. "*Diablo vencer!* Give yourself no more uneasiness, my friend, for the saints have you in their keeping."

"Then to the saints do I return praise," replied the Don, with a feeling of relief which was charming to behold. "Guillermo, forgive me, for I spoke without thought."

"Of course he forgives you, for the Americans are not a revengeful people," chimed in the priest, with a touch of his foot to mine as a hint to be as cheerful as possible. "Come, let us drink and forget the cares of yesterday, for we find enough to-day to engross our thoughts."

Whether the Spaniard was thirsty, or really miserable, I know not; but he drank deeply, and was plied with liquor so skilfully by the priest that in half an hour's time he was no longer cognizant of earthly things, even if he was of heavenly ones, and down went his head upon the table, and he again slept.

"Go and whisper a few words of love to Donna Teresa," the priest said, in a tone not above his breath, for he was Jesuit enough to suspect that the Spaniard might be feigning slumber for the purpose of listening to our conversation, and finding out whether we were really plotting against his welfare or not.

I glanced at the sleeping husband, and declined the command.

"I will attend to him if he should stir during your absence," the priest said, with a smile that looked malicious, it was so entirely different from his usual jovial one.

"Remember," I said, as low and deliberately as I could, "that there are to be no unfair means resorted to to hasten the approach of the events we have spoken of. If I have reason to suspect that my friend is likely to be tampered with, I shall annul our contract and quit the island, even if I should never exchange a word with Donna Teresa again."

The priest gazed long and earnestly at me, as though he was satisfying himself that I meant it, and then he rose from the table and led me to the window, where he continued to speak in whispers.

"I am neither a poisoner nor an assassin," he said; "and were it not for the purpose of defeating the plans of Father Juan, I would instantly renounce the cause which I have taken up, and let you lose the great happiness that is in store for you. I supposed that you understood me to refer to natural events, and not unnatural ones."

"A thousand pardons for my unjust suspicions," I said, hastily. "I did not so interpret you, and it was to prevent any misunderstanding that I renewed the conversation."

"To prove that I mean honestly by you, and by the Spaniard, I shall give you but five minutes for a few whispered words to the lady. Now go, and return in that time, or I will no longer aid you."

He spoke like a man who meant what he said, and although I pleaded for an extension of time, it was not granted me. He returned to the table, and again drew the bottles towards him.

"I drink a glass of wine a minute," he said, filling his tumbler; "by the time I have drank five, let me see you return."

As he raised his glass to his lips I left the room and entered the lady's apartment, which was lighted by a wax candle that stood near the Virgin and her Child, and before which Donna

Teresa never failed to perform her devotions upon retiring to rest.

I remained for a moment at the door, and could hear her low, regular breathing, and with a half-muttered prayer for her safety, turned and fled from the room like a coward. I was not base enough to steal the kiss I wanted.

"You are within time by two glasses," said Benventuro, looking up in astonishment. "What is the matter?"

"She sleeps," I whispered;-" and not to save my soul would I disturb her."

"*Bueno*," muttered the father; "if you will be as considerate for three months to come, I shall die a bishop, for no one can withstand such delicacy."

"You will forgive me if I retire," I said, after a few minutes' silence. "I have had a hard day's work, and feel the need of sleep. You know where your room is, and don't need my assistance in finding it. If you can drink more wine, pray do so, for there is an abundance."

The priest laughed and excused me, but gave as a reason for not retiring just then, that he had a few pious meditations which he desired to indulge in undisturbed, so that he could be ready to assume his high station when called upon.

As I passed the lady's chamber, I saw that the key of the door was on the outside. I know not what prompted me, but I turned the key and then withdrew it from the lock, and slipped it under the door, so that Teresa could find it when she arose at daylight, or when she desired to leave the room. Perhaps I had a faint suspicion that the holy man might seek, during his drunken hallucination, an interview with her, and conduct himself in an unpriestly manner, or, at least, explain the infernal compact, which he had bound me to perform by a solemn oath, while I was laboring under some strange aberration of mind, produced, I was almost confident, by a powder or drug. Yet, strange to say, confident as I was that my wine had been tampered with, I could not muster sufficient resolution to repudiate the scheme, and thus lose all chance of obtaining the lady in case her husband should die and leave her free. I had gone too far to recede without great danger to myself and her, and I knew that if I breathed to the holy father my intention of not complying with the obligations I had assumed, my life would not be worth the value of a bag of paddy, for sometimes, in the Eastern world, blows fall heavily, but secretly; and when a blow fails, drugs are resorted to with great dexterity and despatch.

My thoughts, as I threw myself upon my bed, in a room where Allen was snoring, were none of the most pleasing, and for many hours I lay tossing to and fro like a stout ship in a heavy sea. At one time I half resolved to confide all to my friend Allen; but recollected that he would involve himself in the affair as eagerly as though I was a brother, and that he would scorn all danger for the sake of extricating me from the position in which I stood; so I concluded to keep him in ignorance of the designs of the priest, and let the secret remain in my own breast, even if it consumed me.

With this resolution I fell asleep, and did not awaken until I heard the factory bell tolling the hour for breakfast; and when I looked up, Allen was in the room with a strong cup of tea, which he imagined I needed to quiet my nerves after the night's debauch.

"How's your head?" my friend asked, while I was endeavoring to collect my scattered senses.

"The wine was too pure to leave an ache; but still I feel like a man whose sins are unrepented of," I replied.

"Well, drink this tea, and go with me to the river for a bath; and then I'll warrant you will no longer think of sin, but happiness. Come, Father Benventuro is already astir, and calling loudly for his breakfast, and Donna Teresa looks often towards the door of your room, for the purpose of getting a view of your pale face. Come, will you have a bath this glorious morning, or must I swim alone?"

"I'm with you," was my response; and in a few minutes we were bathing in the cool, clear river.

When we were gathered around the table, the priest looked as fresh and as full of life as though he had passed the night in repose, instead of a wild drinking bout; and even the Spaniard did not dare complain that he felt languid, for fear that his wife, who graced the board with her presence, looking as lovely as a full-blown rose, should find some fault at his absence from her chamber during the night. Once or twice she looked at me as though she would like an explanation in regard to the interruption which we had experienced on the corridor; but I was careful no-to speak to her unless a third party was near, for I felt that the eyes of the priest, and even of Don Arturo, were on me; and once let suspicion enter the mind of a jealous Spaniard, and the work of years is required to eradicate it.

"How are we to pass the day?" demanded Don Arturo, as he leisurely sipped his chocolate; "shall we hunt or ride?"

"I have arranged the whole of it," interrupted the priest, hastily; "we will visit St. Marco's Spring, which is about two miles from the convent. The waters of which act like magic upon the system, and even old men are rejuvenated by drinking therefrom, while young ones obtain a new lease of life by merely visiting the spot. The scenery is the handsomest on the island, and is well worthy the attention of lovers of nature."

"But we have no time to make preparations," Allen said.

"There is no occasion to make them, for I sent word to the convent to have a collation at the spring by noon; and be assured that it will be there. Thus I propose to repay the kindness, in some measure, which I have received at your hands."

"But the heat of the sun will be an objection," suggested Allen.

"There is not to be found so cool a spot this side of Greenland," cried the priest. I saw that he was determined to carry his point so listened in silence.

"But how is Donna Teresa to go? or do you mean that she shall pass her time in solitude?" the Spaniard asked.

"Of course she must go with us, or else our pleasure would be so mixed with selfishness that we should cease to enjoy it. You will find saddled horses for the party, and a palfrey for the lady, awaiting us; and now let us despatch our breakfast and be off."

Donna Teresa had no objections to the excursion, and her husband was delighted when he found that we proposed to carry rifles in hope of meeting with some game during our stay. The old gentleman helped himself to a gun, and talked loudly of his former exploits, while we were getting ready, and his wife was dressing in a costume suitable for travelling and horseback exercise; but when she did appear, with a charming straw hat, trimmed to suit her rich complexion, there was a universal expression of admiration at her wondrous beauty, and even Allen condescended to compliment her on her good looks — something that he had not done before during our acquaintance.

A large banco was waiting for us at the factory landing, manned by four of the convent servants, who received the holy father Benventuro with many expressions of reverence and esteem, and which he repaid with the utmost indifference.

"Drive those dogs on shore!" shouted the priest, as soon as he stepped on board and saw two of our best dogs had determined to follow us; "this is no place for dogs, for we go on a party of pleasure; besides, I think that one of them looks hydrophobish."

This suggestion was sufficient to excite the alarm of Don Arturo and his wife, and the poor brutes, which had not the slightest idea of going mad, were ruthlessly driven on shore in spite of my remonstrances.

"Hush!" whispered the priest, while I was endeavoring to overcome his foolish fears; "I never do anything without a motive."

I looked for an explanation; but the priest declined to give one, and even avoided speaking with me when I whispered and asked what was intended.

We pushed up the stream slowly, and chatted on almost every subject, until we reached the bridle path that led to St. Marco's Spring, where we found horses from the convent awaiting us, and one that seemed worthy to carry even Donna Teresa, with a lady's saddle upon its back, blazing with gilt and ornaments.

"The unmarried portion of the party must wish most fervently, and if with sincerity, they will be gratified with a sight of the faces of their future wives," the holy father said, while the party were disembarking.

Of course the gentlemen of the company scouted the notion, but the lady looked thoughtful, as though she had some confidence in the spring, and would need but little urging to test its truthfulness.

"All ready, senor," said Antonio to the priest.

"Then forward, in the name of St. Peter, who never travelled without carrying refreshments, and therefore should be honored in preference to those good men who depended upon the wayside. Antonio, see that the mule with the hamper is carefully guided, for I famish for a drink of wine and a sandwich, and anything more substantial that you may possess. Senor Allen, will you ride after the knaves and overlook their proceedings, for I have important state matters to talk over with Don Arturo."

"But what shall I do?" I asked.

"You may ride by the side of Donna Teresa, and guide her palfrey's head, for the road is rough in places, and she will need a stout arm. Don't keep close to me, for I have privacy to communicate."

The Spaniard was too inquisitive to object to the programme, and I saw by the expression of Donna Teresa's face, that she liked the arrangement. I lifted her to her saddle, and in a few moments the cavalcade had started.

For the first few rods our course was beside the Pasig, and through a deep valley that was filled with orange trees in their bloom, resembling a field of snow, so white and clean did they look. After crossing the valley, however, we left the river and commenced ascending the small hills which we had often noticed before, and determined to explore for game, but something had prevented.

The morning was delicious, for the sun was not high enough to be felt, and the air that swept over the hills was laden with the perfume of the orange and mango groves, and was almost intoxicating to the senses.

For the first half mile of our journey we were compelled to keep within sight of our companions; but when the bridle path grew more unequal and rugged, Donna Teresa suffered her palfrey to lag behind, and I was too gallant to suffer her to be alone. I checked my horse, and we rode side by side, so near that I could touch her hand when she was careless in guiding her animal.

"You did not return to me last night, Guillermo," she said at length; and I knew by her face that she had long been desirous of asking an explanation, but her modesty had prevented her.

"I returned," I answered, "but you slept, and I dared not disturb you."

She blushed deeply, and seemed to admire the windings of the river, for she turned her head and was silent for some moments.

"You have not told me," she said at length, "why you were absent so long, and whether you discovered the person who played the spy upon our movements."

"I was absent longer than I intended, because interesting topics were discussed by Father Benventuro and myself, and found that the priest had forgotten his ghostly duties, and had turned eavesdropper."

"Then we are lost, Guillermo," she cried, with every indication of alarm, dropping her bridle and clasping my arm, as though she feared a separation.

"I trust not," I replied, kissing her hand, and stealing an arm around her slight waist; and although the position was not a comfortable one, it was too tempting to be relinquished readily.

"It was to disclose our secret that the priest sought the interview with Don Arturo," she said. "Alas! all our happiness will soon be at an end."

"May it never end, Teresa," I whispered; and as her dark, mournful eyes were raised to mine, I could not resist the temptation, but was compelled to kiss her red lips in spite of her faint entreaties to desist.

The horses, as though aware that some mischief was going on, began prancing and arching their necks, and, confound them, compelled me to relinquish my clasp upon the best proportioned waist to be found in Manila.

"Tell me all that passed between you and the priest," she said, as soon as our animals were quiet.

"That I cannot do at present, but I will tell you that the holy father smiles upon my suit, and will help me to obtain your hand, if Heaven, in its mercies, should direct that you become a widow within a reasonable length of time."

"Do not jest, Guillermo," she said, with a face so sorrowful that I regretted my levity. "Although I do not love my husband, yet should I weep bitterly at his death; and I think you would love me none the less for doing so."

"Heaven knows that I love you, Teresa, and I think that you are well aware of the fact; but if I thought that you were heartless and merciless, I should avoid you as though death lay in my path. I desire your hand as an honorable man, and will use only honorable means to secure it."

She pressed my arm in token of her acknowledgment of the course which I had taken, and then I related the long conversation which I had had with the priest, and the designs of Father Juan to force her entrance to a convent for the sake of her fortune.

I did not think it was prudent to mention the amount of money that I had bound myself to pay for the sake of obtaining her hand, for I reasoned that, as a general thing, women know but little about business, and I calculated that perhaps she would think she was valued too highly, and so object to the transaction, although I was resolved, that if ever she became my wife, I would sacrifice my interest in the commercial house of which I was a member, and, with my private funds, make up the amount claimed by the priest, so that her fortune should not be encroached upon.

"Tell me, Guillermo, why the Father Benventuro is so interested in our love?" Teresa asked, at length.

"Simply to defeat the designs of Father Juan, and prevent him from reaching the rank of bishop by means of your fortune."

"If they think to induce me to enter a convent, they know not how much they are mistaken," she said, with one of her resolute expressions, which I seldom saw upon her fair face; but before I had time to further allude to the subject, we came upon the rest of our company, who were reclining beneath the shade of mango trees, smoking cheroots, while Antonio and the other servants were spreading a collation upon the rich grass.

"Well, you have loitered by the way, or else strayed from the path, for we have been here for half an hour," Allen said, as we appeared in the vicinity of the spring.

"Ah, I feared that palfrey would give you trouble," interrupted the priest, before I had an opportunity to speak. "The beast resolutely persists in refusing to travel in this direction, although no objection is made in returning home. You now know, Don Arturo, why I placed a stout arm at your wife's bridle rein."

The Spaniard, I thought, did not appear as profoundly grateful as I could wish under the circumstances; but he did find voice to mutter a few words of thanks for my gallantry in confining myself to his wife, and even advanced to assist her from the saddle; but in this I was before him, for I doubted if he was strong enough to sustain her stately form.

"I must change the palfrey, or else sell her, for she is restless with ladies," the priest said, patting the sleek sides of the brute, and speaking so that Don Arturo could hear him; and I think that the holy father at length lulled all suspicions that our loitering by the way was one of design.

"The collation is ready, senor," cried Antonio; and the priest rubbed his hands with satisfaction at the news.

We repaired to the spot where were spread cold chicken, sandwiches, tongue, jellies, game, pies, and several kinds of fruit, while for liquors we had an excellent brand of champagne, cooled in the icy water of the spring; and I noticed that Antonio, with a full knowledge of his master's weakness, had provided an abundant supply of the generous wine — more, in fact, than I thought becoming for the character of the party.

Beuventuro played the host to perfection, and saw that each one was helped liberally before he would undertake to satisfy his own wants; but when the first bottle of champagne was uncorked, his usual flow of animal spirits commenced, and continued until the conversation was confined to the miraculous virtues of the holy spring, which was within a few rods of us, and, but for the coldness of its waters, presented no great attraction, although the grove in which it was situated was beautiful as fairyland is represented to be.

"I want all to promise me that there shall be no looking into the spring, and repeating prayers to the blessed St. Marco, for the purpose of obtaining a view of the faces of expectant wives. Those present who are married, of course, will have no such desire, and it is to caution the young folks that I speak."

Now, if the priest was really in earnest in his remonstrance, it was a good plan to excite our curiosity; and when I saw that Donoa Teresa looked at me as though advising that I should test the power of the spring, I declared that I would never leave the grove until I had seen my future wife's face, provided, of course, the good St. Marco was disposed to gratify me. Allen also insisted that his rights were inviolate, and that he had good reason to believe that his future wife was somewhere in the world, and that she was as eager to see him as he was her; therefore it was but right that an interview should take place, and as speedily as possible; "for perhaps," Allen said, "I may change my mind after a fair view of the lady's face, and it is only right that I should give her warning, so that she can get a more congenial mate."

I strongly suspect that the priest was desirous that I should test the water, although he pretended that he was not; but after he had drank his second bottle of wine, he gave his consent, and volunteered to do the praying while the rest of us were to take our chances at wife-seeing.

Benventuro led the way to the spring, followed by the company, all in good spirits, and laughing at the absurdity of the test which we proposed to indulge in. It was decided that Allen should have the first look, while I followed as second, and then if Donna Teresa and her husband were curious, they should come last.

"I wish to impress upon your minds," the priest said, in a whisper, "there must be no levity connected with this ceremony; if there is, we fail of our object."

"If you had said there must be no intoxication, I should have despaired of seeing my wife this afternoon," Allen muttered; and even the priest, who was endeavoring to look grim and mysterious, was compelled to smile as he remembered how rapidly the champagne had disappeared but a few minutes before.

"Senor Allen," the holy father said, "I'm astonished at your want of reverence, and I fear that the result will not be very flattering to your wishes. But form a circle around me, and join hands while I repeat the words which must be used to cause the saint to gratify our desires."

We gravely extended our hands, and I had the satisfaction of once more touching the warm flesh of Donna Teresa; and as long as we stood in that position I did not care how many prayers the priest made, or whether they were ever answered by the gentleman to whom they were addressed.

"Now, then," said Allen, encouragingly, "fire away, and put in some strong licks when you tell him to send me a pretty wife, and a rich one withal, for a man who marries a young and pretty woman needs the revenue of a gold mine to support her extravagance."

The priest frowned the scoffer into silence, and began to chant, —

"The good St. Marco will preserve us and bless us, and grant all our prayers, for we have travelled many miles for the purpose of worshipping at his spring — "

"He'll know that's a lie," muttered Allen; "better tell him the truth, and see how he likes it, instead of fiction."

"You'd better leave the circle, and apply your talent to emptying the wine bottles," Father Benventuro said, stopping short in his incantation, and trying to look solemn; but the effort was a failure.

"I would do so willingly," answered Allen; "but you emptied the last bottle before you were in a proper condition to chant the praises of the great St. Marco."

"Then remain quiet, or not a drop of wine shall you have when we visit the convent," was the threat of the priest.

"All right — I'm dumb," said Allen; and thus favored, the priest recommenced his prayer, and at its conclusion we were requested to take long and earnest gazes at the bottom of the spring, and tell what we saw.

No one desired to be first; for although we all looked upon the matter in the light of a farce, yet there was a little superstition in our composition, which prompted us to hesitate when the real test of the truth of the priest's predictions was to be verified.

At length Allen broke from the circle, much to my regret, for I was compelled to relinquish the soft hand of the woman I loved, and vowed he would have the first look, whether St. Marco was willing or not.

He rushed to the well, and for a long time gazed at the clear water, which was fed by innumerable springs, that hardly disturbed the white sand at the bottom; and while we watched him, we saw, to our surprise, a wonderful change come over his face, and at length, with an imprecation, he turned away from the quiet water, apparently dissatisfied with his vision; for there was a frown upon his brow, and more color in his face than I had seen for many months.

"Did you see anything?" we asked, eagerly; but Allen forced a smile, and turned from us without reply.

"Your visions were not pleasant, Senor Allen," Donna Teresa said, with all a woman's curiosity to know whether the face he saw was fair or otherwise.

He muttered something that I could not understand, and walked back to the spot where the collation was spread, in search of a glass of wine.

"Guillermo, you will bear me in your mind when you look at the water?" whispered Donna Teresa, with a sly touch of her delicate hand, that thrilled through my body like an electric shock.

"Do I not always think of you?" I answered. "Be assured, that if constant prayers, and an intense desire to have you ever near me can induce the saint to favor me with your sweet face, I shall see that or none."

She seemed satisfied, but I noticed that she watched me with eager eyes while I stepped towards the spring, and I thought that the priest appeared uneasy.

"Drink a pint of the water before you look, or the saint will think that you are not sincere!" cried Benventuro, who seemed determined that I should go through the most minute form of the ceremony.

The task was a hard one, for the spring was strongly impregnated with sulphur and other substances, and the waters would have been pronounced mineral by the most impartial critics.

"I suppose, if I had drank the water, I should have had a vision of a different character," Allen said, watching the struggle which I was attempting with considerable interest, and smiling grimly when he saw that I had performed my task; but I don't recollect of having smiled, for the taste of the water was awful.

After the last drop had been drained from the goblet, a feeling of supreme happiness took possession of me, and I could only compare it to the effect of smoking a pipe of opium — a feat which I had been guilty of two or three times during my residence in China, when I gained the heart of a mandarin by accepting of his hospitality and strong tea at the same time, not to mention the various strange compounds of cookery which he had served up in honor of my visit to his home. I felt as though I was light enough to fly, and that the earth was too quiet a place for one with such an excitable temperament as I possessed.

With no feeling of fear, therefore, I looked at the quiet water, and thought that it represented beautiful visions of gardens filled with flowers, rich landscapes studded with waving trees, and then those gave place to pictures of rare art; and at length I saw one that pleased me more than the rest, and while I watched it the scene changed, and before me were the beautiful features of Donna Teresa, smiling as I had seen her smile but a few moments before, and apparently inviting me to join her. For only a few seconds did this delightful vision last, and then the picture vanished, and I saw nothing but the clear water and white sand.

"Well, what luck?" I heard a voice inquire; and turning, I saw the priest by my side, with an anxious face.

"Where is Donna Teresa?" I asked, forgetting that she was not free, and that her husband was near me.

"The saints be praised, he has seen the right face," muttered the priest; and then led me a few steps one side, so that the company would not hear my ravings, if I was disposed to indulge in them.

Don Arturo followed us, and seemed as much interested as his wife in my explanations.

"Guillermo, tell me what you saw," the old Spaniard said, laying his hand upon my shoulder in a fatherly manner.

"He has seen nothing but a vision of the blessed St. Marco, who will damn you forever, unless you donate a hundred ounces to my convent!" cried the priest, half in jest and half serious.

"The holy saint I supposed meddled more with hearts than souls," Don Arturo replied, "and until he makes a personal request, I shall decline the petition."

The Spaniard, fearful of further importuning, retired precipitately to a distant part of the grove, and seemed to meditate an attack upon the liquors in case he should find any amidst the wreck.

"Did you see the face of your love in the spring, Guillermo?" whispered the priest, eagerly.

"I know not the trickery that was resorted to," I replied, "but I saw the face of Donna Teresa in the water, as plainly as I see it now."

"Then all is safe," my companion muttered; and he threw his arms wildly about his head, as though he was combating a legion of troublesome hornets.

A sharp report was heard, and turning, I saw a small cloud of smoke ascending on our left, and at the same instant I heard the peculiar whiz of a musket bullet as it flew through the air, carrying, for some distance, Don Arturo's hat in its progress.

The Spaniard, for a second or two, was as much astonished as myself at the suddenness of the attack; and while I was undecided what to do, the Don threw his arms up, and yelled, to the extent of his lungs, —

"Murder! assassin! I'm a dead man!" and down upon the ground he fell, and rolled over and over, as though in the agony of death.

"The ladrones!" shouted the priest, with startling energy. "Fly for your lives, for the ladrones are upon us."

He set the example, and waddled towards the horses as fast as his short, fat legs could carry him, and I must confess that I intended to follow his example; but caught sight of the pale, terrified face of Donna Teresa, who had fallen upon her knees, and was praying to the saints with all the volubility of a Spanish woman, sometimes confounding my name with that of her husband; and I am inclined to think that the saints were requested to preserve me at every risk, and her husband if convenient.

I had just caught her in my arms, and was about to bear her to the palfrey, when Allen called upon me to stop.

"The ladrones be cursed!" he shouted; "I don't care for a dozen of them! They will take care to keep beyond the range of our rifles. Come with me and help explore the woods, and find the assassin. The priest and the servants will care for the Spaniard."

"No, no!" thundered the priest; "save your lives at every cost, for the woods are filled with ladrones. I have seen a dozen of them already. The only safety is to remain with me and claim the protection of the holy church. Mount the horses and reach the banco without delay."

I must confess that I was staggered by this appeal, and that I hardly knew whether to run or to remain; but Allen reassured me.

"Drop the woman," he said in English, in his usual blunt manner, "and lend me a hand to find out the assassin, or I will go alone. Making love is all very well sometimes, but it is out of place here, as you ought to know."

Thus rebuked, I seated the lady upon the ground, and, in spite of her remonstrances, was about to hasten to Allen, when the priest interfered.

"You are mad!" he exclaimed. "There is no occasion for your interference here, and I tell you distinctly that I wish you and Donna Teresa to escape without a moment's delay. I will join you at the banco. Do not trouble yourself about anything that has taken place."

"But you would not leave her husband here, mortally wounded — would you?" I asked, in astonishment.

"Even if he dies you have no cause for regret," the priest muttered, sarcastically.

I stopped to hear no more. I turned from the lady in spite of her tears, and in a few moments was by the side of Allen, who was examining his rifle.

"Ah, I thought you would not desert your old friend at this

time," he remarked, " although, to be sure, there is but little to fear; for I suppose the assassin aimed at Don Arturo, and meant to have picked him off if possible."

"At any rate he has succeeded in his object," I replied.

"Bah! In spite of all that kicking, the Spaniard is not injured in the least, except by fear, although I pledge you my word that the ball was well aimed, for his head was missed by an inch or two only. Did you ever know a wounded man to make so much noise, or did you ever know me to remain inactive when suffering could be alleviated?"

As I couldn't call any such case to mind, I wisely held my tongue, and went towards the still prostrate Spaniard for the purpose of satisfying myself that he was uninjured.

"Come, Don Arturo, you have made noise enough, and have showed that you care but little for bullets or ladrones. Get up, and take care of your wife until we return."

Allen seconded the appeal with a slight punch in the prostrate man's ribs which caused him to howl with renewed agony; but in spite of his protestations that he could never survive his wounds, and that he should die blessing and forgiving his enemies, we lifted him to his feet, and his astonishment at finding that he could stand without assistance was great.

"I bleed somewhere internally," he muttered, looking at his limbs and then rubbing his head.

"Not a bleed," returned Allen; "you are as well as ever, and could lick a dozen ladrones, if they would only give you a fair chance. Come, go to your wife, who is half distracted at your supposed injuries, and requires the constant prayers of the priest to prevent her having fits. We are going in search of the man who attempted your life."

"Had I better go?" timidly inquired the Don.

"Not with us," promptly responded Allen. "Your wife needs you more than we."

The Spaniard was only too happy to escape the duty, and while we started towards the spot from whence the shot was fired, the Don hastened in an opposite direction; and when I glanced towards the priest and wife to watch the meeting, I thought that neither was overpowered with joy to find that the aged gentleman was more frightened than hurt.

We reached the thicket from whence the shot had been fired

at the Spaniard; we saw the tracks of a Mestizo's shoes, and found the very limb upon which the fellow had rested his gun while he took aim, which no doubt he intended should be a fatal one.

"It is useless for us to proceed farther," Allen said, after a a careful examination of the footsteps. "We should not be able to overtake the fellow, and even if we did, we should hardly dare to execute the law of retaliation upon him, for we could prove nothing, but should excite the utmost indignation of the priesthood."

"Why so?"

"Because the fellow is connected with the convent of San Pedro; and think you that Father Benventuro would suffer any harm to happen to his man of all work, — his tool and confidant, — his friend and companion — the supple Antonio?"

"How do you know that the person who fired the gun is Antonio?" I asked.

"For two very good reasons. First, I noticed that the left shoe which he wore had a peculiar formed patch, and you observe in the clay that there is a fair impression of the shoe, patch and all. Second, I saw the fellow leave our select society just after you had made a fool of yourself by looking in the spring, in the hope of seeing your future wife."

"Thank you," I replied. "I believe that I am not far from another fool who was guilty of the same folly."

Allen looked confused for a moment, and then laughed; but I thought he was rather forcing the matter.

"Well, to tell the truth," he said, "there is something wonderful in that confounded spring; and whether the sights that can be seen there are the effects of over doses of champagne, or some trick of that priest, I don't pretend to say; but I will admit that I saw something that resembled a face in the water, but what kind of a face it was I don't know."

"Why do you suppose the priest cared what we saw or what we did not?" I asked.

"The holy father is a Jesuit, and may have some aim in view. Things that we would pass without notice he would study over and investigate. By some confounded mechanical trickery, or by a potent drug, mixed with the water which he proposed we should drink before testing the efficacy of the spring, a strong control may have been exerted over us, and we imagined that we saw things which had no reality. All is a mystery to me so far; but I shall take an early opportunity of getting the holy father drunk, and then learning his secrets."

"A good plan," I replied, dryly, "if it can be carried into effect, of which I have some doubt, for I have felt of his head, and it is like a cannon ball."

"I own that the task would be a frightful one, and that I should have to resort to some of his priestly tricks to accomplish the job; but that it can be done I have no doubt. But after all, we have no cause to be at enmity with the holy man, for I know that he would do much to assist either you or me, and I am certain that I have heard him speak of you in grateful terms."

It was my turn to blush, and I managed to do so after an effort.

"Then it is useless for us to remain here, I suppose," I said, after a few moments' pause. "If Antonio is the man who fired the gun, he is miles from us by this time, and pursuit would be useless. Besides, he might have discharged the piece accidentally."

Allen shook his head.

"There was too much powder in the gun," he said, "or Don Arturo would not now be in the land of the living."

"How do you know that?" I asked.

"You observe that the gun was rested on the limb of this tree, and that it must have kicked badly, or it would not have scraped the bark of the limb, and even knocked Antonio backwards three or four feet, as you can see by his steps. Depend upon it, too great a charge of powder saved the Spaniard's life, and he should be thankful to his saints for the accident."

"But what ill feeling can Antonio have treasured against the Don?" I asked.

"Who knows?" Allen answered, with the energetic shrug of a Spaniard. "The Don may have excited his passions and enmity by a word or look — he may have refused to lend him a dollar some time to bet on a cock-fight; he may have declined to drink a glass of wine with him, or to give him one; or may have charged him too much for a bale of cigars for the convent, so that he could not make a certain percentage. Either one of these causes would be sufficient to make him thirst for revenge, and he will not rest entirely satisfied until he has accomplished it. We must talk to Benventuro in regard to the matter, and have this difficulty removed."

I thought the affair a most singular one, but I preferred to keep my thoughts to myself, instead of intrusting them with Allen, for I feared that, with his usual independence, he would refer to me as having spoken words which I did not care the priest should find fault with. The more I pondered on the shooting affair, the more mystified I became; and even when we debouched from the bushes, and saw that the holy father, entirely recovered from his alarm respecting ladrones, was seated near the Don and his wife, quietly smoking a cigar, I had no suspicions that he was the originator of the plot, and that it was through his orders that Antonio had acted as he had done.

"Did you find the base assassin?" asked the priest, as we approached; but he spoke as though he knew we had not.

"We did not overtake him, but we know the man, and shall mark him hereafter," Allen replied, carelessly.

"Ah, who dared to attempt murder almost within sight of the convent walls? Give me a description of the man, that I may punish him without delay," father Benventuro exclaimed, with every appearance of passion.

"Well, as near as I can calculate," Allen said, with Yankee emphasis and drawl, "the scamp is Antonio, your servant."

The priest was too well drilled to manifest surprise, and not a particle of emotion was visible on his fat face as he heard the name.

"Did you stop to take a drink of the spring water as you came along?" the priest asked, with a loud laugh.

"No. Why?"

"Because I didn't believe that any man in his sober senses would make such a charge against one of the most faithful servants that priest was ever blessed with. An hour since I sent him to the convent to make preparations for your visit there. It is time he should return; and faith, here he comes;" and as the holy father ceased speaking, the fellow approached us, his brow covered with perspiration, and his face flushed with running.

"Have you been to the convent?" the priest asked, even without looking at him.

"Yes, sir," was the prompt answer.

"Are they making preparations for our arrival?"

"I gave your orders and then hurried back, sir."

"You have done well," the holy father replied; and then after a moment's pause he continued: "Our esteemed friend, Don Arturo, has been fired at by some lurking ladrone. Do you know anything of the circumstance?"

"Nothing, holy father."

The fellow was as cool and self-possessed as the most inveterate liar could desire, and he told his story so calmly that even I began to doubt whether Allen had not made a mistake.

"Let us no longer talk upon such a disagreeble topic," the Spaniard exclaimed, speaking for the first time. "See, my wife is all agitation, because she feared that I was fatally injured when I was simply knocked down by the mere proximity of the ball to my head. It was a narrow escape, but nothing, after all, compared to a soldier's danger. However, if you have no objections, I should prefer to leave this spot without delay, as a second shot might be better aimed."

The priest readily complied with the request, and in a few minutes we were mounted on our horses, and on our way towards the convent, whose towers we could just get a glimpse of, as we left the vicinity of the spring, and wound our way by the bridle path towards the river.

"What say you to supping at the convent, and sleeping there to-night?" the priest asked.

"On one condition I'll consent to that," Allen replied.

"You may make as many conditions as you please. Name the first one."

"That but one bottle of wine shall be drank by each of your guests, and that we be allowed to retire at an early hour."

"Is that all?" cried the holy father, with a hoarse chuckle; "by the saints, I thought you were intending to stipulate for a dozen bottles per man, and a tipple until daylight. I accept the first offer with gratitude, for my wine cellar is not overstocked at the present time. Make your own terms, senors, for I shall do the same when I visit you."

The conditions were duly accepted, much to my delight, for I had no desire to pass a second night in a drinking bout; and I thought, from the glance which I received from the dark eyes of Donna Teresa, that she approved of our course in that respect; for although much more wine is drank in Manila than water, and

8

to be slightly exhilarated is considered no disgrace, yet I found that Spanish ladies, as a general thing, preferred the society of men of temperate habits to those of intemperate, and were rather sorrowful than otherwise when their loving spouses were brought home in hackney coaches, or on the shoulders of a cargadora.

None of us were very lively on our way to the convent, for the attempted assassination of Don Arturo, although not of common occurrence, was far from being an uncommon one, so we did not look upon the matter in that amicable light in which East Indians were accustomed to regard such things.

"Guillermo," said the Spaniard, "there must be deer in these woods, and it is a pity that hunters like us should remain idle, when our friends suffer for the want of venison. We must hunt, and why not to-morrow?"

"Ay," echoed the priest, "why not to-morrow?"

There was something in the man's voice that attracted my attention, and made me think that more was meant than appeared upon the surface; yet the holy man's face was calm, and his eyes sincere.

"We can start from the convent at an early hour, first sending for the dogs," the Don continued.

"An admirable plan," the priest replied, "and one that I should recommend. At what hour do you propose to start?"

I thought that I detected the slightest possible sneer on the part of the questioner, and yet I might have been mistaken.

"At any hour that suits your convenience, holy father," the Spaniard replied, with meek humility.

"Then we will settle the preliminaries to-night;" and without another word on the subject, we rode on until the walls of the convent were gained, and the heavy gates were opened to admit us.

We filed in, more like a funeral procession than a gay party who had returned from a pleasant picnic; and when the gates closed with a crash, it seemed to me as though we were cut off from the outer world for life. The cheeks of Donna Teresa were blanched, and I read her thoughts well enough to know that she was far from feeling pleased with her visit or her quarters. Allen was the only one who seemed indifferent, or treated the priest with the same independence inside of the walls he showed outside; and I accounted for it on the ground that he had visited the convent often, and felt more at home than the rest of us.

"Had we better remain all night, as we contemplated?" asked the Don, nervously, not relishing the prison-like aspect of the place.

"Remain here?" repeated the priest, who had overheard the question; "of course you will, for no one departs from these walls to-night without my permission. You are my guests, and I have too few not to appreciate my friends, when I once get hold of them. Ho, Pedro!" the holy man shouted to the porter; "let no one out without my consent."

The dark, sinister-looking porter nodded his head in token of assent, and forthwith locked the gates and deposited the key in his pocket.

"We seem more like prisoners than friends," whispered the Spaniard in my ear, watching his chance when the priest was not observing him. "I hope you don't feel concerned, because I don't; but I will tell you, truly, I had much rather be at home, and surrounded by my servants."

The poor man confessed his alarm, even while endeavoring to convince me that he was unconcerned.

I did not reply, but I could not help thinking that there was much design in what the priest was doing, and that perhaps it would have been better if we had not accepted his invitation.

"Here, Antonio!" shouted Benventuro; "show the lady and gentlemen to the reception-room, and then come to my study."

The servant led us through a narrow passage-way, and then up a flight of steps, at the end of which we found the room indicated. The floor was polished with wax, and contained a few easy-chairs made of bamboo, a few coarse engravings of saints and sinners, a portrait of the Archbishop of Manila, and another of the Governor General. The view from the windows of the apartment was splendid, however, and made us for a time forget our unpleasant feelings.

The room was high enough from the ground to overlook the walls, and we could see the River Pasig winding through rich valleys of rice and sugar-cane, while on our left were the high mountains, which, tradition has reported, contain rich gold mines and precious stones; yet Spaniards nor Mestizos dare venture to the mines, for fear of the natives who inhabit the region, and who, to this late day, have not acknowledged the sway of Spain; and, strange to say, every expedition that has been directed against them has failed, until the Spaniards have lost heart, and let the savages remain in peaceable possession of their lands.

"You look melancholy, Teresa," I said, as we stood at a window, gazing at the landscape.

"My looks then reflect my thoughts; for, Guillermo, I feel very sad, and it seems as though some great misfortune was about to happen to me. Were I alone, I should offer up my prayers to the Virgin to keep me from harm, and protect all those I love."

"Pray here, Teresa, for your prayer will be answered as readily as though alone and before the image of the Virgin."

She shook her head, and seemed incredulous and somewhat shocked that I should advance such an opinion. I knew her superstitious nature too well to continue the conversation.

"I wonder if the priest will let us look at the lady inmates of his convent?" Teresa asked after a moment's pause.

"He will answer for himself, for here he is," I replied, as the holy father entered the room, looking as smiling and pleased as though the high office to which he aspired was already in his grasp.

"The lady was just asking if you permitted visitors to speak with the nuns," I said, turning to Benventuro.

"Were she less beautiful I should willingly comply with her request, but if those under my spiritual charge should once see her face, there would no longer be that peace and happiness in the flock which now prevails. Envy would take the place of humility; and there is enough of that without the walls of the convent."

Donna Teresa turned away, hardly pleased with the compliment, yet not knowing how to resent it.

"Gentlemen, I suppose, receive the same answer," I said.

"No, not the same; because the nuns study mischief enough already, without having additional temptations thrust before them, which would naturally tend to make them unhappy and discontented. Let the nuns converse with a good-looking man three or four times, and there would be a revolt within these walls which low diet and sleepless nights alone could suppress. For these reasons, my friends, I don't think that it is safe for you to visit my chickens."

Father Benventuro was perfectly good-natured while thus explaining why visitors were not permitted to converse with his great family; so I asked him why the ladies were not affected by his presence.

"Me?" he said, with a shrug of his shoulders. "O, I am looked upon in the light of a father, and no one would think of making love to me."

"Perhaps that is the only position in which they can look upon you," Allen said, in his usual blunt way.

The lady colored and looked from the window, while her husband was too much under the influence of fear to notice the joke, and therefore did not understand the meaning of Allen's laughter, loud and hearty as it was.

The priest attempted to look displeased, but when he found that it was thrown away upon my friend, his broad face relaxed, and he suffered a smile to mantle his features.

"No jokes with the clergy, *amigo*, on so serious a subject, and especially in the presence of a lady."

"Dinner is on the table, senor," cried Antonio, throwing open a door which I had not noticed, and revealing a large, well-furnished room, and a table covered with delicacies; and we were hungry enough not to be displeased with the sight.

CHAPTER V.

A NIGHT IN THE CONVENT. — A SUDDEN DEATH. — SURPRISE AND CONSTERNATION. — FATHER JUAN. — SUSPICIONS, AND WHAT THEY AMOUNTED TO.

"GUILLERMO, give your arm to Donna Teresa. Don Arturo, I wish you to sit by my side and temper me in my temporal wants by your grave demeanor. Senor Allen, you will lend me all the assistance in your power in talking and making the dinner party a success. And mind that you do not let the bottles rest when they reach you. I have but a poor dinner to-day, for I fear that my cook has lost his skill, or is growing neglectful of his profession."

There was no occasion for the priest to apologize, for there was an abundance on the table, not only of luxuries, but of the substantial things of this life; and rarely had I seen cookery carried to such a state of perfection as witnessed on that day. Roast, baked, and boiled followed in rapid succession, and as the wine circulated, the holy father threw off all restraint, and charmed his guests with wit and humor.

But this time we were not permitted to drink to repletion, for the holy father, as though anxious to improve in the estimation of Donna Teresa and her husband, gave the signal to rise from the table just at dusk, and soon after the candles were lighted, in heavy sticks of silver, of old Spanish style, that would have charmed the heart of an antiquarian.

We found coffee awaiting us in the drawing-room, and while we sipped the fragrant beverage, the priest chatted on politics and pleasure, arts and the drama, and was familiar with every topic that he broached, and could talk most interestingly upon themes we were unacquainted with.

The evening glided off rapidly, and by nine we all expressed surprise, and thought that the hour could not be later than eight.

"I don't wish to hurry you to your couches, my friends," the priest said, "but my servants are drilled to exact hours, and in fifteen minutes will retire to their blankets. Remember that they have to be stirring long before daylight."

"I suppose that is a hint for us to retire," Allen said; "but it seems to me that you have altered your rules since the time I drank glass for glass with you, and conquered."

The priest did not choose to hear, for some reason or other, and left the room for a few moments.

"Guillermo," cried the Spaniard, "I seem lonely in this huge building, and know not why I feel reluctant to retire. I would give an ounce of gold if I was in my house in Manila."

"Morning will soon come," I replied, "and by sunrise we can be on our way to the factory, where a warm welcome will be extended to us. There is no reason, as I see, why you should feel thus melancholy."

"Do you think, Guillermo, that you could persuade the priest to let us return to-night? I should feel so much better at Santa Mesa, and so would my wife."

"We are not prisoners," I said, "but guests, and the holy father would think but poorly of us if we slighted his hospitality by leaving him as soon as we had concluded dinner. Believe me, I would do all that I could for you, but I dare not offend Benventuro with such a request."

"Then you will sleep near me — I want you to promise that," the Spaniard said, hurriedly; but before I could accede to his extraordinary proposition the priest returned, looking as smiling and amiable as a host should look when he has company that pleases him.

"Before we separate for the night, let us drink one glass of wine to the honor of Spain and its fair women," Benventuro said; and we could not refuse compliance, for at that time there was much ill feeling against Americans on the part of Spaniards, on account of filibustering talk in regard to Cuba.

"I have some rare wine, gentlemen, which was sent me by a friend in Spain, and I desire your judgment before retiring. Antonio, bring the wine here."

We had no objections to test the liquor which the priest so extolled, but it struck me as somewhat singular that we had not seen it upon the dinner table.

The priest clapped his hands, and Antonio and a servant, who looked equally as dark and suspicious as the former, entered the room, bearing salvers of solid silver, together with cut glasses and a bottle of singular shape, covered with cobwebs.

"Serve the guests, Antonio," was the brief command; yet brief as it was, I thought that I detected a tremor in the priest's voice that was unusual.

I looked at him, but he encountered my gaze without flinching; and when the servants served me, I took the glass of wine from Antonio's hand without a suspicion that foul play was intended.

"Honor to Spain and its fair women," cried the priest, when he saw that we awaited his toast.

We repeated the sentiment, and the glasses were emptied. The wine was really excellent, and even Don Arturo commended it, and smacked his thin lips as though he would have no objection to another sip. But he was denied the pleasure, for the servants left the room, but immediately returned with candles, and awaited to conduct us to our apartments.

"Your rooms are near, gentlemen; a sweet night's sleep, and may the saints have you in their keeping. We breakfast at ten, you know;" and with these words the holy father escorted us to the door, and bade us good night.

A glance, quick as lightning, was exchanged between the priest and Antonio, and I wondered what it meant; but there was no time to ask questions, and I had no desire to excite alarm in the breasts of Don Arturo and his lady, by communicating suspicions, which, after all, might be groundless.

We passed up the broad staircase, the steps of which were waxed and polished like marble; and near the head of the stairs, on a broad corridor, were our rooms, to which our obsequious but grim attendants pointed, and held high the candles, while Allen and myself entered the apartment allotted to us.

Directly opposite our room was the one which Don Arturo and his wife occupied, and as we bade them good night and dismissed our attendants, I thought that the face of the old Spaniard looked ghastly in the flickering light, as though he had a presentiment that something terrible was to happen.

"We must be stirring early, Guillermo," he said, "for we must not miss the hunt on the morrow."

He spoke like a person who hoped that no great misfortune was to happen, yet hoped against conviction.

We found a cocoa-nut oil lamp burning in our room, with sufficient oil to last all night; for the priest wisely calculated that candles were too expensive for more than show, and that guests could sleep as well with one as the other.

I sat down upon one of the hard beds, which consisted of a blanket spread over a hide tacked to rude pieces of timber hewn from a tree by some native carpenter, and lighting a cigar, began to ruminate upon the events of the day. Allen followed my example, and for a few minutes we smoked our weeds in silence.

"What are you thinking of?" he asked, after a while.

"I am thinking that if ever I get back to Santa Mesa, I will never exchange its comfortable quarters for the rooms of a convent," I said.

"Hush!" he replied; "even walls sometimes have ears, and I

would not have the priest cherish a prejudice against me for a small stock of ready money."

He lowered his voice to a whisper, and continued, —

"I don't like the appearance of affairs here, and have not all the afternoon; but I have acted a part, and imposed upon the priest the idea that I was content. I have stopped here over night on several occasions, but never saw the ceremony that has been used this evening, which leads me to suspect that something is about to happen."

"Have you any idea what that something is?" I asked.

"Not the remotest; but I tell you I shall not sleep to-night, or, if I do, it will be only for a moment," Allen said.

"Do you suspect that any attempt is to be made upon our lives?" I asked.

"No, no; we are safe enough; never fear; for the priest likes us too well to think of ill-treating us. Besides, I carry a revolver in my pocket, and Benventuro and his servants know it, and they would rather face the devil than a six-shooter. We are not the ones mischief is aimed at; that you may be assured of."

He nodded his head in the direction of the opposite room, and I found that his suspicions coincided with my own.

"If Don Arturo is a live man in the morning, he may well return his thanks to the saints, for they will have had him in their keeping. The priest has an enmity against the old man, and he is Jesuit enough to strike deep when he does strike. In what manner Don Arturo has offended, I don't know; but his death is resolved upon, for I could see it in Antonio's eyes when he lighted us to our rooms. The shot to-day was intended as a finisher, but the fellow put in too much powder and missed, for which I warrant you he got a comfortable damning."

"Can we do nothing to save him?" I asked.

"What can we do? We are only suspecting foul play, and have no proof that it is intended. If we should make a noise, and kick up a fuss generally, the holy father would find means to repay us some way before we were many days older. The best that we can do is to watch and listen, and for this purpose I shall keep awake all night."

I agreed to do the same; and extinguishing the light, we smoked our cigars in silence, having taken the precaution to open the door of our room, so that we could hear if any one stirred in the corridor during the night. For three or four hours we continued to consume cigars until our stock ran low, and then, for the want of something to do, and to rest my tired form, I lay down, thinking that under no circumstances I should drop to sleep; but, like all who make the same resolve, I forgot my resolution and slept soundly; how long I didn't know, for I was awakened by feeling a hand upon my shoulder; and as I started up I heard Allen whisper, —

"Don't make the least noise, or you will spoil all — there's some one in the corridor."

I was wide awake enough then, and listening with all my power; and while I did so I could hear some person moving in the corridor with stealthy steps, as though fearful of attracting attention.

"What shall we do?" I whispered, in so low a tone that the sounds were almost inaudible.

"We can do nothing but watch; but if violence is attempted we can act our part like men."

We slipped off our shoes and crawled on our hands and knees to the door, and then entered on the corridor, where we waited for a long time before we again heard the cat-like tread of some person, who seemed to have just ascended the broad stairs, and was listening for a repetition of a slight noise that we made.

We remained as quiet as mice, close to the wall, and by the light of a window, at the end of the corridor, we could see two forms, stealing along, treading so softly that not even a board creaked. When they got opposite to our room they stopped, apparently surprised at finding the door open, and I could hear them whisper to each other as though asking what it meant. They seemed to be satisfied that we were sleeping soundly, however, for in a moment they passed to the door of Don Arturo's room, and listened attentively.

"I can hear her breathe well enough, but the old man is silent,". I heard Antonio whisper to his companion.

"Hush!" was the reply of the other person; "don't talk about what you can hear so near to the American's room, or we shall get a shot from their pistols, and they fire very close, as I know for a certainty. If they suspected we were up to any trick, it's very short our lives would be."

"I think that the old man has gone to a better world, but I'm not sure of it. Had we not better open the door and go in, and be certain about the thing?"

"And wake the lady up, and have her screaming for half an hour, and those American *diablos* grasping our throats? No, no; that would not do."

"But we have our knives," Antonio's companion said.

"And if we dared to use them upon the holy father's friends, we should be cursed forever. He has a strange love for both men, although they are heretics. Come, let us return and report that all has gone as expected."

They crept to the staircase and disappeared, and just at that moment we heard the nuns, at the other end of the convent, chanting an early mass; and as their voices blended, and the harmony arose, it sounded melancholy enough to be a requiem for the dead. We listened until the chant ceased, and then stole noiselessly to our room, closed the door, and waited for daylight. We did not have to wait long, for the murky gloom was gradually dispelled by the bright glow in the east; but long before the sun rose, the singing of the birds and the shrill call of the parrots, as they flew from tree to tree in the garden, had tempted us to the window, upon which we leaned, delighted with the cool, fresh atmosphere, and wondered why we were usually sluggards enough to prefer spending the best portion of the day in bed, instead of rising and gaining health and appetite, by inhaling the fragrance of the morning air.

"It is time that Donna Teresa was stirring," I remarked, listening for the sound of her footsteps.

"Always thinking of her," Allen said, lighting a cigar, the last that he possessed.

"Not always," I replied, in a tone that contradicted my denial.

"Answer me a question," my friend said, laying his hand upon my shoulder; "do you really think that you could live happily with Donna Teresa, even if you should marry her upon the decease of her husband? Spanish women are not like American or English women. They wither at the age of twenty-five, and that clear, fresh skin, which you now admire so much, will become rough and full of furrows; the bright eyes will become dim, and the plump form lank and bony; her white teeth will decay, and —"

"For mercy sake, forbear!" I cried, appalled at the picture that he was drawing, and yet, lover-like, believing that Donna Teresa would form an exception to the generality of womankind.

"Well, as you are my friend, I won't be too hard on you; but you must think of these things, or —"

He was interrupted by a shrill scream, which proceeded from Don Arturo's chamber. I knew the voice, and it stirred my blood like the sound of a trumpet.

"Donna Teresa is in distress!" I cried, starting for the door.

"Nonsense," replied Allen; "she is only scolding her husband. If she was in distress she would hang out a signal."

Almost before he had completed the words, there was another shriek, louder and more shrill than the first. I broke away from Allen, and rushed across the corridor.

"Blast it, man, you ain't going into her room — are you?" Allen cried, stopping me before I reached the door.

"To be sure I am," I replied, struggling to get away.

"But she may not be dressed. Ask her first. Have a little delicacy in the matter."

"Don't talk of delicacy, when she is in danger," I replied, breaking away from him.

"Well, if you are satisfied, I suppose I must be," I heard Allen say, but I did not stop to reply.

I tried the door of her room, and found that it was fastened. I knocked, but no attention was paid to me. I called Donna Teresa by her name, but received no reply.

"Curse it, man, she was only dreaming. Come away, and let her sleep," Allen muttered.

I made no reply, but I put my shoulder to the door and pressed hard, and the bolt yielded. I rushed into the room, and saw Donna Teresa, partly dressed, bending over her husband, and sobbing bitterly.

"For Heaven's sake, what has happened?" I demanded; and two or three times I repeated the question before the lady answered.

"Ah, Guillermo," she cried, raising her head, with her long black hair hanging over her shoulders, "the saints must protect me now."

THE DEATH OF DON ARTURO. Page 125.

"What is the meaning of your cries?" I asked, tearing the mosquito bars aside which covered the bed.

She covered her face with one hand, and pointed to her husband with the other.

I started back when I saw the face of my old friend, stern, cold, and ten shades whiter than usual.

"He is sick," I said, taking his hand, and finding it cold as ice.

"He is dead," she replied; and a fresh torrent of tears burst from her eyes, and stole through her closed hands, which covered her face.

"Dead!" I repeated; and Allen echoed the cry.

"Alas! I know not how long he has been dead; but a few minutes since I awoke, and spoke to him, and received no answer; and when I looked at his face, I saw that the saints had him in their keeping. O, Guillermo, I now have but you!"

She threw her arms around my neck, and buried her head on my bosom, and for a moment I held her, and tried to soothe her anguish; but I was too horrified to offer much consolation, or to speak. But Allen recovered his senses, and spoke some words of advice, which aroused me.

"We must send for a physician without delay — perhaps the Don is suffering from the effects of a fit; or, if he is really dead, we must know what has killed him. Let us see Father Benventuro, and while we are absent let the lady dress herself."

Even Donna Teresa, much as she grieved, saw the force of Allen's reasoning and advice, and proceeded to array herself in the garments which she had worn the preceding day; but when I offered to vacate the room, she begged of me, in piteous tones, not to leave her with the dead, but to remain and console her; and as there was no impropriety in so doing, I consented. The reader must not suppose that the lady's modesty was not very acute, by her allowing two men to enter and remain in her chamber while she was dressing; but you will please to remember that there are different customs in different places, and that a Spanish girl, confident of her own purity, can look with an eye of unconcern upon the half-nude form of a man, as he staggers through the streets, bearing a heavy burden, as most of the cargadors, anxious to save their clothing, do, and that, in all warm climates, the ladies consider it not indelicate, or out of place, to wear as little clothing as possible, while the children, until five or six years of age, dispense with dress, much to their gratification, and roll about the floor, and between the legs of visitors, without the least embarrassment. Washerwomen, without but a single garment upon their brown bodies, stand deep in the water on the river's banks, and beat their clothes over a rock or log, and shout a joyous melange of blackguardism and fun; and yet some would resent it as an insult, if familiarities were offered. A Spanish maiden, even if surrounded with wealth, cannot escape the prevailing custom; and hence she grows up, and is taught that modesty does not consist in thinking of evil, and blushing at her thoughts.

While Teresa was dressing herself as well as she could under her agitation, I turned my attention to the Spaniard, and after a brief examination was satisfied that vitality had fled, probably some hours before his wife had made the discovery. I can hardly tell what my thoughts were while I gazed at the dead, and recollected all the kindness which I had received at his hands. His faults were forgotten, his petty jealousy and braggadocio were banished from my mind; and if I could have restored him to life, I should have done so, despite my love for his beautiful widow. Even while gazing at the closed eyes and swarthy face, I thought of the compact which I had made with the priest hardly twenty-four hours before; and I asked myself, Could he have had a hand in producing the Don's death for the sake of obtaining the important position which he had determined to reach in spite of obstacles? I knew the man too well to think that it would be of any use to charge him with murder, or to accuse him of violating the contract, and I also knew the man well enough to know that if I did not carry out the whole programme which he had promised I should carry out, that his creatures would be only too happy to snuff out a heretic, and that no official investigation would ever reveal the cause of my death. These were some of the thoughts which passed through my brain, and I asked myself whether it would be better for me to brave his fury, and leave the woman I loved, or to attempt to marry and fly from the island without delay. There were many reasons why the latter course would have been impracticable; and had I attempted to escape, the whole of the lady's fortune would have been confiscated by the crown, or eaten up by greedy lawyers. This was something I had no desire to see realized, because I knew that Teresa had been accustomed to more of the luxuries of life than my funds would permit, without a succession of fortunate mercantile speculations, which our firm were too cautious to enter upon. While I ruminated I felt a hand laid upon my shoulder, and turning saw the tearful eyes of Teresa.

"He spoke of you, Guillermo, last night, after we had retired, and he said that he loved you as a son. Your name was the last one that he pronounced."

I dried her tears and led her from the chamber, and on our way to the reception-room met the priest, his countenance well made up for the occasion.

"May the saints preserve us and have us in their keeping!" he exclaimed, placing his fat hand upon the glossy hair of the lady's head; "but this instant have I heard that my friend died with disease of the heart during the night. I am so shocked that I have no words to convey to you my anguish. Courage, my poor child, for though you are now alone in the world, I'll be a father to you. I have already sent for a physician from Manila, and when he arrives, I wish a thorough examination made as to the cause of his death. I want no suspicion to rest upon the fair fame of my convent."

"Why do you think suspicion will rest on it?" I asked.

"Because the world is full of vice and slander; and why should I escape more than others?" he answered, with a face so full of frankness that Donna Teresa gave him her hand, and received a blessing in return for her confidence.

"Here comes Father Juan!" cried Allen, from the bottom of the stairs.

For a moment the priest started, and was inclined to mutter an oath; but he recollected himself, and his face assumed a graveness worthy of the occasion, as he advanced to meet his crafty rival.

At the sound of Father Juan's name, Donna Teresa clung more closely to me, as though desirous of protection from the wiles of this son of the church.

"Ah, Guillermo," she said, "I fear to meet that man, for my heart tells me he has come for no good, and that he will endeavor to separate us. Let me avoid him, for his looks are evil."

"You must meet him, Teresa; but be firm, and refuse all his

offers of assistance, and his machinations will fail. On you will depend our future happiness, and to you I intrust it, with confidence that you will suffer no trifling cause to interfere with our welfare. Meet him boldly, and receive him as a friend."

She pressed my hand in token of assent, and we reached the reception-room just as the door was thrown open to admit Father Juan, whose thin face, keen, restless eyes, spare body, and precise dress, was in striking contrast with the fat, comfortable-looking form of Father Benventuro, who thought more of a good bottle of wine and a good dinner than he did of his outward appearance.

"The saints have all here in their keeping," was the exclamation of the thin priest, as he stood upon the threshold and waved the sign of the cross with his finger, while his glittering eyes took in the whole party present at a glance.

"May the saints give long life and much happiness to Father Juan, who has deigned to honor my poor place with his presence. A thousand thanks for this visit, and may you relish it so well that hereafter I shall gladden my eyes with a sight of your face once a week."

Father Juan bowed low to the compliments of his brother priest, and looked so grave and sedate that I should have supposed he believed what he heard, had not I seen by the twinkle of his eyes that he did not.

"I am sorry to intrude upon your party, and should not have done so had I not heard some strange news this morning as I was about to land at Santa Mesa, in search of my pupil, my friend, my companion, Don Arturo, whose long absence from his house had rendered me somewhat anxious, although I did not doubt that he was in good company."

"Truer friends a Spaniard never possessed," cried the holy Benventuro, apparently as candid and honest as man could be.

"But what strange rumor is this I heard at Santa Mesa? I was told by some servants of the convent, that Don Arturo had died suddenly during the night. It cannot be, for I knew him to be hale and hearty, and likely to bless the church with rich gifts for many years. Let me hear the report contradicted. No, not from you," as Benventuro was about to speak; "but from the lips of his wife, whom he loved so dearly, and who is so attached to him that the presence of other men is distasteful. Let her tell me in joyful tones that the Don is well and happy."

The sneer was well aimed, but luckily Donna Teresa was unconscious of it, for she was weeping, with her handkerchief to her eyes.

The priest stole across the room, and took the lady's hand and pressed it more warmly than I thought he was entitled to; but the hand was withdrawn hastily, and I saw by the swelling bosom that anger was taking the place of grief.

"Tell me, daughter," the priest said, "is the news true? Is your beloved husband in the keeping of the saints?"

"He is dead," she answered.

"Alas! that all flesh should be mortal. He must have died suddenly, and no doubt it will be a great consolation to you to know the cause of his death. A most rigid examination shall be made, and the first physicians of Manila will be called upon to decide."

"I have already sent for one, brother Juan, and he will probably be here in the course of the forenoon," Benveuturo said, with a sweet smile.

"One physician is not enough. As the confessor of the deceased, I must assume a little authority in this matter, as I have often talked with him in regard to his last wishes. We must have five of the best physicians in the city to investigate the case. For your own reputation, for the reputation of your convent, for the reputation of these young men, whose company the deceased has sought so often, it is necessary that a strict examination should be had, so that all suspicion shall be put at rest."

Benventuro did not wince in the least. On the contrary, he seemed to grow more cheerful as his brother became severe and vindictive.

"I shall cheerfully second you in the work, not because my little retreat will be in any danger from unjust suspicions, but simply to satisfy the wife of our friend, whose anguish at the event only equals my own," replied Benventuro.

The thin priest bowed, and a peculiar smile passed over his pale face. The smile might betoken doubt — it might mean satisfaction.

"The lady will readily acknowledge that this is no place for her since she has become a widow," Father Juan said, after a short pause, as mild as he could possibly speak; "and as she has known me for many years, and is aware that I possessed her husband's confidence in an eminent degree, she will have no hesitation to place herself under my care for a while, until her business affairs are settled. This plan is one that met the approbation of Don Arturo, not many weeks before his sudden death.

Father Benventuro cast a rapid glance at me, which seemed to say, "You see that he is already at work."

"She could not be under the charge of a better man," was his reply.

"I am glad to think that you approve of my course. At the convent of San Sebastian she will not want for attentions and sympathy, and will there meet with friends whose whole thoughts will be devoted to her interest. The world is full of snares, and one so young and good should not be suffered to encounter them. Lady, when shall you be ready to accompany me?"

I trembled for fear that Teresa would suffer herself to be led away by his insidious approaches, but I was mistaken. She withdrew her handkerchief from her eyes, and there were no longer tears to be seen in those flashing orbs, nor was there timidity in her look as she started to her feet.

"If I have remained silent," she said, "during your conversation, it is because I paid but little attention to it, and was unaware of its import. But now I wish you to understand me distinctly — that I am free to do as I please, and shall do so regardless of church, my husband's last wishes, or all the priests in existence. I shall not enter your convent. I shall not request your advice and assistance in my business affairs. My lawyer will attend to all concerns of that kind, and when I leave this place my residence in Manila will be open to receive me. Now, sir, let me hear no more of convents, or of priestly interference."

I had never seen her so excited before during my acquaintance, and I little thought that she possessed such a strong will of her own beneath an appearance of indifference.

A smile of triumph mantled the face of Benventuro, but it vanished in an instant.

"Lady," he said, "have you thought well of the course which you propose to take? Perhaps in the solitary gloom of my brother's convent you would find many attractions that you know not of."

"I have determined, and shall adhere to my plan," she answered, full of dignity.

"But your husband's wishes," suggested Father Juan, in a voice trembling with rage.

"Are not binding upon me. I have been secluded from the world long enough, and have no desire to end my days in a convent," Teresa replied.

"But we have no desire that you should. We simply ask you to find shelter at our holy house, until your period of mourning has passed away. Then you may depart if you wish."

Father Juan could hardly conceal his indignation, it was so great, while speaking. He saw the prize that he had long angled for about to slip from his hook, and he was impotent to secure it. He cast a vindictive glance at Father Benventuro; but that skilful general was looking upon the polished floor, as though he was entirely indifferent in regard to the matter.

"You have had my answer to your proposition," Teresa replied, with a wave of her jewelled hand. "If your advice were meant for my good, I'm thankful; but hereafter I shall seek for assistance from those who know more of the world and less of saints."

The rage of the priest could no longer be restrained. His little eyes snapped as though emitting sparks of fire, and his pallid face became flushed and white by turns. When he looked at me he seemed desirous of annihilating me in the most summary manner; but I appeared entirely indifferent to his rage, and remained on the defensive, still maintaining my position by the side of Donna Teresa.

"I see how it is — love for a heretic has caused you to forget the memory of your husband, and your duty to the church," Father Juan said, with ill-concealed rage. "You know the will of his excellency the archbishop, and be assured it shall be enforced to the letter. No Protestant can marry a rich Catholic lady without abjuring his religion, and giving proof of his conversion to the true faith. This is the law, and I call upon Father Benventuro to confirm my assertions."

"Father Juan is right. He has quoted the custom of our holy church; but he has forgotten to mention that an indulgence can be purchased on the payment of a heavy sum, and on the solemn promise of the bridegroom that his wife shall go to confessionals, and exercise her own right in regard to her fortune, and that her children shall be educated Catholics."

The fair face of Teresa flushed as she heard the priests, and her eyes sparkled with passion.

"Have I fallen so low that I am thus lectured by a man who pretends to be devoted to the memory of my husband, and anxious for my welfare? Am I to be told what I shall do and what I shall not do, simply because I possess wealth in my own right, when it is well known that every Mestiza girl on the island can marry whom she pleases, if she is fortunate enough to own a *peso?* By the saints, I should think that I was a school-girl, and you a guardian, to be thus advised. Go, sir, and when I want your advice I will send for you, and not before."

She pointed to the door, but Father Juan was not disposed to thus give up the contest. His look of rage was dropped, and one of humility assumed; and so quick was the transition, that even I was astonished, and Father Benventuro troubled, for we both knew that kindness was more apt to win with Teresa than harshness.

"If I have said ought that could wound, I pray that you and the saints may pardon me," cried Father Juan, in a tone so mild, that I should have forgiven him on the spot if I had not known that he was acting a part, and for very selfish reasons.

"Guillermo," he continued, " I meant no disrespect to you, for I have always loved you like a father, and would gladly welcome you to the true faith, and hope that the time is not far distant when I shall have an opportunity to do so. But until that time I presume no marriage will unite you with one I love so well as I do Donna Teresa."

"Presume nothing that has reference to myself, sir," I said, speaking for the first time; " you have, this morning, mentioned me in connection with the lady, and hinted at a state of things that neither you nor any other person has a right to allude to. If I love the lady, or the lady loves me, it is none of your business, provided, of course, we do not make you the repository of our secrets, as we certainly shall not."

"That's the talk," cried Allen, who had been industriously engaged in smoking a cigar during the conference, and jerked out his words at the same time that he jerked his cigar out of the window. "It appears to me that there's a cussed sight more talk than is necessary, and that some of you are counting your chickens before they are hatched, as we say in Massachusetts — a state that is of some importance when the raising of schoolmasters and ministers is taken into consideration. Let everything drop until the lady is over her trouble, and then, if she is desirous of marrying, why, let her do so, no matter who he is if she is satisfied. She is more interested than any one else, and should have her way this time. That's my opinion; you have it for what it is worth; and now I should like some breakfast."

It was refreshing to see how quick Father Benventuro walked across the room and shook hands with Allen, after the latter had delivered his speech; and it was funny to see Father Juan put the best face that he could upon the matter, and do the same.

"I think that your suggestions are the best that can be made," said the latter, speaking in a low tone, so that Donna Teresa could not overhear him; "if she wishes to marry a second time, I certainly shall offer no objections, provided, of course, she makes choice of the man who I think would make a good husband."

Father Benventuro looked at me and winked, as much as to say, "Humbug," although he was careful not to let his brother priest see him.

"Coffee and chocolate are on the table," cried Antonio, as he threw open the door and surveyed the party with a malicious grin.

"And we are ready for it," cried the jolly-looking Benventuro, offering his fat hand to the lady, and leading her towards the door; but just as I was about to follow, Father Juan touched me on the shoulder.

"One word, my son," he said, in a tone so significant that I could not help listening to him. "I wish to speak to you confidentially; can I do so?" he asked.

"Certainly. Proceed."

"I wish to be your friend, my son," he continued, laying his thin hand upon my shoulder, and studying the expression of my face with his little black, twinkling eyes.

"I am glad to hear it, although I was not aware that we had ever been enemies," I replied, wondering what he was driving at, and feeling somewhat anxious, for I saw the face of Father Benventuro thrust cautiously into the door, two or three times, watching our conference.

"Not exactly enemies, my son; but still, not friends, although I have always regarded you as a most promising young man, and I think that if you were a native of Spain, we should feel proud of you."

I bowed low at the compliment, and looked for more explicit details.

"This sudden death of Don Arturo weighs heavily on my heart. It was very sudden — was it not?"

"The poor man did not complain last night when he retired," I answered.

"Ah!"

The holy man said no more for a few seconds, and seemed to be thinking deeply; but I noticed that his black eyes were fixed upon my face as though he was struck by the paleness of my complexion.

"He has left a widow of surpassing loveliness, and over a million of dollars," my companion remarked at length.

I pretended to be indifferent; but I was not, for I felt the warm blood rush to my face, and fill the veins as though about to burst them.

"Over a million dollars," repeated the priest, taking a pinch of snuff.

"Don Arturo was fortunate during his long life," I remarked.

"He was; but I know a man who can be more so, if he is willing."

I looked at the priest for a few moments without speaking. He was indifferent, and took snuff with avidity.

"Go on," I said at length.

"I say that I know a man who can be more fortunate, provided my counsels are listened to."

"Let me hear them, and then I can best judge what you mean," was my answer, and looking up saw Benventuro standing at the door, holding up a finger as a warning to me how I unbosomed myself.

"I will be candid with you, and shall expect the same thing in return. May I be so bold as to require it?"

I made no answer, and the priest continued: —

"I see that I may, and thank you for your generosity. Let us work together, and I shall have the happiness of seeing Donna Teresa united to the man she long has loved, and you joined to a lady for whom you entertain the most profound affection. Don't interrupt me, for I know what I say to be the truth. You are not ambitious, but I am, and to rise I must have your assistance. This you will grant me if I help you?"

"How?"

"I will explain. With the immense amount of money that you have at command after your marriage, you can well afford to spare a portion for the use of the church. I am the church that desires it, and I suppose we can arrange the matter to our mutual satisfaction. What say you to my proposition? I will help you, and you help me."

"What position do you desire?" I asked.

"A bishopric," was the prompt reply.

"The devil!" I thought; but I did not utter my thoughts aloud; "here are two priests struggling for the same office, and both hope to gain it by my marriage. Shall I temporize and deceive them both, or shall I be faithful to my first proposition?"

"Your answer?" demanded Father Juan, quite confident that it would be a favorable one.

"I cannot listen to you on that subject, for the hand of Donna Teresa is not to be bought and sold like merchandise. This is not the time to talk of her marriage, and even if it was, I should have to decline your bargain."

"Better think twice before you decide," he said, "for without me you will never espouse the widow."

"Then she will have to remain a widow. I have done as you requested, answered you fairly and candidly, and I hope you are satisfied. Still, as I do not wish your enmity, I will pledge my word to make you a handsome present the very day that unites me to the lady."

"He has been before me," I heard the priest mutter through his teeth; but if he was angry he did not manifest it, for he was too good a manager for that. He applied his thumb and forefinger to his snuff-box with renewed vigor, and seemed refreshed by the fragrance and exhilarating effect of the tobacco. Then he smiled most sweetly, and taking my arm, led me into the room where the rest of the company were sipping coffee and chocolate, none of them, excepting the priest, noting our absence.

Teresa soon left the room, for our conversation was not interesting to her, and she wished to commune with her own thoughts regarding her present condition. Father Juan and Benventuro were unusually gracious to each other, but I noticed that the feeling did not extend to their hearts, and that they hated each other as cordially as ever, but uselessly tried to conceal that sentiment, in which line I think Benventuro had the advantage.

The latter soon made an excuse for quitting the table, and as he did so he made a sign that he wished a short conversation with me as soon as possible. Leaving Allen and Father Juan discussing the merits of Spain and her great men, as represented in the government of Manila, I left the table, lighted a cigar, and strolled into the court-yard, keeping out of sight of those who might look from the window and witness the meeting which the priest was eager to obtain. I had scarcely walked a dozen steps, when I heard Benventuro waddling after me, his face showing the anxiety which he felt to know the result of Father Juan's conversation.

"Well," he said, "fortune is on our side at last. The coast is clear; now lay siege and be happy."

"There is time enough for all that," I replied, with an indifference I did not feel.

"There is not time enough," my companion repeated with energy; "a woman's heart is like a tinder-box full of tinder. It catches at a spark, and is easily extinguished. The women of my country like to be wooed and won in a hurry, and the more love that you show, and the hotter you press your suit, the quicker they yield. Strike now, while away from all her friends, and extort from her a full confession, and if possible, an oath, that she will wed you in three months' time, or even sooner."

"Delicacy forbids me to do so," I answered, not over pleased at the advice.

"To the devil with your delicacy," roared the priest, and then desirous of retrieving his reputation, he went on to say, "We have too much at stake to be over-scrupulous; so let us urge this affair forward, and I'll warrant you will both thank me when united. Be a lover, and an impetuous one, and the lady will not resent it. I am anxious for your happiness."

"And your advancement," I suggested.

"*Diablo!* yes; why shouldn't I? We must work together, *amigo*, or all will fail."

"So Father Juan says," I answered.

"May the blessed saints soon call Father Juan to their keeping, for he is too good for this world," was the pious ejaculation of the priest; and then he was eager to have me repeat the conversation which I had held with the priest.

I complied with the request, and Benventuro was furious at the thought of his brother priest attempting so mean a snare; and not until I had repeatedly informed him that I had declined his offer, did my friend allow his passion to subside.

"We must fight carefully, or that man will spoil our plans," the priest said, and I thought so; but without coming to any definite conclusion, we separated and rejoined the company.

In the course of the forenoon a physician arrived from Manila, talked with Father Benventuro, looked at the body of Don Arturo, shrugged his shoulders, and said that it was a "visitation of Providence," and that the body had better be buried as quickly as possible. Father Juan made no objections, and the corpse was removed to Manila; and in a few hours Donna Teresa, Allen, and myself followed in a banco, and saw her installed in her house, and surrounded by friends and servants.

Eight weeks had passed since the death of Don Arturo, and the period for mourning had expired. Donna Teresa was the toast and admiration of the capital, for she had emerged from her seclusion, thrown aside her habiliments of woe, and mingled with the gay and most fashionable company in Manila. Her spacious mansion received guests once a week, and every night she was not confined to her house to receive them she was absent at a ball or party, with the single exception of Sunday evenings, when the theatre was opened to the lovers of the drama, and where I was certain to find her surrounded by officers in the Spanish army, government officials, men with titles and little fortune, and men with fortune who would have given half their worldly wealth for titles. Catholics and Protestants, Chinese and Malays, Americans and English, all flocked to the theatre on Sunday evenings, for the purpose of gossiping, listening to the military bands which formed the orchestra, talking about trade, and finally laughing at the actors and actresses when too tame, and condemning them when too ranting.

Since the death of Donna Teresa's husband, I had seen her often; but I had forborne to press my visit, or to refer to marriage, simply because I thought that she avoided the subject on purpose, and I did not wish to give her pain, or to make her think that I was eager to conclude a bargain so advantageous to myself. I sometimes met her at the house of a friend, where we had both been invited to a party; but I never went with her, or accompanied her home, and Donna Teresa never intimated that she desired me to do so. She went and returned in her carriage, and was safe in the protection of her servants.

Perhaps there was a feeling of coldness growing up between us, and I thought I could perceive it more perceptibly at every interview. I knew where to trace it as plainly as though I had not seen the thin face and twinkling eyes of Father Juan leaving her house with a thoughtful brow. I was too proud to ask for an explanation, and I think that Teresa labored under the delusion that it was my place to follow her from ball to ball, and be content to pick up her fan or handkerchief, if either should chance to fall while she was dancing with a cavalry officer or a lieutenant of foot; but if she did entertain such ideas, she found out her mistake, and pouted accordingly.

Yet I loved her dearly — better, perhaps, than I had ever loved; and sleeping or waking she was ever before me. But we had not talked of love for many weeks. Our conversation, when we met, was confined to gossip, or an inquiry as to whether such and such a party was pleasant; yet when I mentioned Santa Mesa, and the friends I neglected there, and expressed an intention of seeing them, I could see a look of displeasure upon the face of Teresa, and it would not vanish until I had promised to forego my visit for the present. I had not hunted since the Don's death; I had neglected all the exciting sports, which had made my residence upon the island so pleasant; and I seldom rode upon the Calzarda at sunset for fear of having my jealousy excited by seeing the lady surrounded by a crowd of admirers, upon whom she smiled most sweetly, while I, perhaps, received a nod, or a slight wave of her hand.

Father Benventuro's letters to me, constantly urging expedition and inquiring why I delayed my marriage, remained unanswered; for I could write no good news, and I did not wish to excite the padre by stating the true facts of the case. Thus day after day passed, and the three months were on the wane, and there was no prospect of a wedding.

It was Sunday night, and the theatre was open, and receiving its crowd of votaries, who were landed at the door in carriages, driven between lines of mounted lancers, stationed there to preserve order, and watch over the safety of the governor general, who always attended the theatre when it was open, for the purpose of encouraging the drama, and showing himself to his loyal subjects. I knew that Teresa would be there, and I had resolved all day that I would remain at home and peruse a pile of American newspapers which I had received from the mails the day before; but as the time drew near for the performances to commence, I repented of my resolution, and thought that I could at least have the satisfaction of gazing at my idol from an obscure part of the building, and not let my presence be known. The more I thought of the matter, the more restless I grew, until at length love conquered.

"Ho, *muchacho!*" I shouted to my servant, who was busily engaged in the hall, painting huge eyes upon a kite which he was to fly the next day for a wager with a Mestizo, who lived near us.

"*Si, senor*," he answered promptly, bringing a coal of fire upon a plate, supposing that I wanted a light for my cigar.

"The carriage, *presto!*" I shouted; and he vanished in an instant to inform the coachman of my wishes.

I must confess that for a lover who intended to look at his mistress from a distance, I was a most particular man in regard to my dress that night, and before I had completed my toilet I heard the carriage rumble from the court-yard, and stop in front of my bachelor quarters. My clothes, not made by the bungling tailors of Manila, fitted me admirably, and I could not help nodding my head approvingly, as I surveyed them in the glass just before I started for the theatre.

It wanted half an hour of the time the performances were to commence; yet the theatre was already well filled, and the ladies were flirting their fans and chatting gayly in their boxes, criticising the dresses of their neighbors with a freedom only equalled by the Americans. I glanced at the numerous handsome faces, but did not see Teresa, and I began to fear that she would not be present; but while I was hoping most sincerely that she would come, I noticed an unusual stir in the lobby, and then, proud as a duchess, with diamonds upon her neck and arms, in glided the lady of my thoughts, looking more beautiful than ever, and seeming unconscious of the sensation which she created. She cast her large, dark eyes around the theatre rapidly, and then I thought I saw a shade of disappointment upon her brow; but it was not allowed to rest there long, for half a dozen gentlemen entered the box, and paid their respects to the lady, chatted for a moment, and then retired to give place to others.

Yet still I could see that those large black eyes were often cast over the faces of the audience, and I felt a little pang of jealousy, as I thought that she was watching for a rival, whom she loved more than myself.

At length a dark, heavy-bearded officer, a captain in the army, sat by her side, and laughed and talked with considerable freedom. He seemed determined that the audience should understand that he was on a friendly footing with the lady, and that she was disposed to feel flattered at his attentions.

I had resolved, when I left the house, not to approach her box, or to speak to her; but after the officer's assurance I could no longer contain myself, and determined to convince the lady that I could be as indifferent as herself.

With as much coolness as I could command, I entered the box, and in an instant every glass and every eye in the house were levelled at me. Even the officer turned half round to see who was to disturb his tête-à-tête, and a scowl passed over his face when he saw me. Teresa did not turn her head, or heed me, until I spoke, and then she started and dropped her fan, which the captain hastened to pick up and restore.

"*Buenas noches*, Donna Teresa," I said, as calmly as though I had been speaking to an ordinary friend.

The military man looked as though I was taking great liberties, and even seemed inclined to stare me into a feeling of defiance; but I paid no more attention to him than if he had been a servant waiting with refreshments.

"Ah, Guillermo!" Teresa exclaimed, a slight blush mantling her face; "I am glad to see you. Are you well?"

She extended but the tips of her fingers to me, and I was as sparing of my hand as herself, and had no sooner touched her fingers than I let them drop as though fearful of contagion. I saw a slight pout upon her red lips, and then she renewed her conversation with the captain, much to his delight.

For only a moment did I listen to it, and then, with a low bow and an unconcerned air, I turned to leave the box; but the demon of jealousy was in my heart, and I almost resolved not to speak to the fair coquette again.

"Are you going, Senor Guillermo?" she asked; and I fancied that there was a slight tremor in her voice, but I might have been mistaken.

"I have a few friends whom I wish to speak with," I replied.

"Shall I see you again this evening?" she asked.

"*Quien sabe?*" I replied, with a smile. "I may remain all the evening, or leave shortly. It will depend upon the interest of the play."

I bowed low, and passed out; but when I looked back I saw that she was flirting her fan before her face, and that she seemed not so much interested in the officer's conversation as before my visit. How I boiled with rage and jealousy, and blamed myself for thinking of the lady at all! but the more I tried to banish her from my mind, the oftener she returned to make me wretched. I went to a distant part of the house, and wished for the performance to commence, so that I could relieve my thoughts of Teresa's image. I leaned over a box, with my hand over my eyes; yet even there I was obliged to hear Teresa's name mentioned, for a party of ladies were discussing her merits and demerits quite frankly.

At length the overture commenced, and all talking ceased; for the Spanish people love music, and are capable of appreciating what they hear. The band played very finely, and then up went the curtain, and the representation of a domestic drama commenced. Before the first act was finished, I tired of the dull plot, and was making my way to the saloon for the purpose of smoking a cigar, when whom should I run against but a young fellow named Tom Baker, who was connected with a house in China, and who had run over to Manila for the purpose of having some fun and recruiting his health. The latter was but a second consideration in comparison with the first; and although he had been in the city but a month, yet he had learned more of what was going on than I had known during my residence.

"By thunder!" was Tom's exclamation, as we shook hands, "I am glad to see you, for it's devilish dull here to-night. The idea of putting such a play as that on the stage is ridiculous, and the manager should be told so. Why don't they take pattern from New York theatres, and bring out stars and novelties? Horse pieces would be good. Only get up something startling, and put about half a hundred of those black devils, with their muskets, upon the stage to do the supes," pointing to a soldier, who stood near by, totally unconscious of the compliment, " and I'll warrant that the piece would take, and run three weeks at least. You don't know the manager — do you?"

I replied that I had been introduced to him.

" He don't amount to much, I should think, although I wish I was acquainted with him. I'd put him up to a thing or two, you'd better believe. I wouldn't mind going on and fighting a broadsword combat, with the American flag in one hand and a pair of top boots on my feet to give effect to the scene, and let these Spaniards know that there's one feller ready to defend the honor of his country at all hazards. Or, if that wouldn't do, let's get up " Tom and Jerry," with you and me in the boxing scene, and give 'em a specimen of the " manly art." You can box, I know, for I have seen you do some neat things with your mawlers at Hong Kong. We could kinder be easy with each other, and astonish the folks in this part of the world with the kind of stuff the Yankees are made of."

" I don't think that it would succeed, Tom, for the manager is shy of amateurs," I replied, amused at his rattling, off-hand manner, and forgetting my misery in listening to him.

" Then we must try something else that will carry the town by storm," Tom exclaimed. " Suppose I should get up a ballet, drill the girls myself, and learn 'em all the peritropal movements; see that their skirts are short enough, and that they are graceful while dancing. In a week's time I think that I could give a good representation, and that the girls would do credit to my training."

" It wouldn't do, Tom; the ladies would be scandalized, and refuse to visit the house, if they knew that a *roué* like you was engaged in the matter."

" Then the men would be more fierce to see the ballet, and I believe that it would pay. If the manager refuses to get up my piece, I'll hire his theatre, and open it for the gratification of my friends. I can do it, and I will."

" Where will you find the girls, Tom?" I asked.

" A man with money can always find enough of them. But

speaking of women, my friend, I have observed that you don't look quite like yourself recently; I don't find any of that hail fellow you used to exhibit at Hong Kong, and which was the delight of our club. What is the matter? any trouble? Confide in me, my boy, and I'll give you some good advice. If money matters are not all right, name the sum, and you are welcome to it."

I assured my friend that money was not required to make me enjoy life, and endeavored to give his thoughts another turn, but it was in vain.

"Something is the matter, I know, for I can see that you are growing thin. 'Tain't a woman affair — is it? If it is, just take my advice, and get out of it as fast as possible. I've been there, I have, and I know all about it. Two years ago I had to leave New York to get cured of the heart complaint, or I should have married and settled for life afore this; and then what chance for fun should I have had? There is fun enough without your giving up your life for one woman. Ride, flirt, and have a good time, and the handsomest woman in the country will no longer have a turn upon your heart. I tell you I ain't very old, but I have had a darned lot of experience in this world, and if a feller will only follow my directions, I can bring him out as whole as —"

"Yourself?" I suggested, seeing that he hesitated for a word.

"Precisely; I can do what I promise, you had better believe. Now we are of the same ages, but I'll wager a supper that I've seen more of life than you, 'cos I always lived in New York, and the governor always kept me well supplied with money, and I went it with a rush, until he sent me as junior partner to that blasted Hong Kong, where there's no life, nor fun, nor handsome women. Dust and sand, high winds and naked Chinamen, are all that a feller sees there; and when I want fun, I say I'm sick, and come over here and have it; there's some life here, if you only look for it."

I smiled at his eagerness to convince me that he was up to the tricks of the world, and he continued: —

"Now I don't want you to tell me the secret of your heart, 'cos that is none of my business, but I want to see you cheerful and all right; and to do so I want you to put yourself under my directions for a few days, and if you don't call me a good doctor, then I will resign my position, and give you up as incurable. What do you say?"

"What remedies do you propose to use?"

"That is my secret. I shall use agreeable ones; but to do so, I must have the use of your house for a few nights. Here, just call your coachman, and send him home with orders to have a first-class supper for four all ready at twelve to-night, while I write an order to my landlord to send to your residence a dozen bottles of Mum's green seal. It is wine that I brought over with me; I know what it is."

"But who is to compose our party?" I demanded.

"No matter. Two of them will be gentlemen, and two of them —"

At this moment the thin face of Father Juan was turned towards me, and I saw a malicious smile upon his countenance. He had overheard every word of our conversation, and seemed rejoiced at it. I had gone too far to recede, for I knew that what had been said would be related to Donna Teresa in a few minutes; and perhaps I took a malicious joy in having her hear that I was growing wild under her cold treatment.

"Invite whom you please," I said to Tom; "the supper will be ready, and I pledge the reputation of my cook that it shall be a good one."

"That's the talk — spoken like a man. We will make a night of it, and through the influence of champagne, and as pretty eyes as can be found in Manila, I pledge my word that you will be a different man in a week's time."

I called my coachman, who was not far from the theatre, smoking a cigar on his box, gave him the necessary orders, and directions to return to the theatre as soon as he had executed them, and then once more joined Tom.

CHAPTER VI.

A WARNING. — FATHER JUAN ON THE TRAIL. — TOM AND DONNA TERESA. — THE SUPPER, AND WHAT COME OF IT.

On my return to the theatre I encountered the dark, piercing eyes of Father Juan, who seemed to be hovering around me that night as though I were upon some treasonable errand, and he was determined to secure a reward for my apprehension. I passed him without remark, but I did not fail to detect the sneer of triumph which his thin lips expressed, although he did make an effort to hide it.

While I stood watching the retreating form of the priest, I felt a hand upon my shoulder, and turning, saw Tom Baker.

"I say, old feller," cried Tom, "what are you looking after that old codger for? Don't owe him anything — do you? He has just been telling me what a good friend he is of yours, and so I had to shake hands with him on that, and ask him to drink; but he declined in such a way that I think he would take a drop behind the door. Who is the old cock? He acts like a gentleman."

"That is Father Juan, of the couvent of Sebastian," I replied.

"I knew that he was a priest, but I wish I had known that he was connected with a convent. I'm blessed if I wouldn't have asked him to let me see his girls, and I wouldn't mind giving a pretty sum for the privilege. The old cock seemed kinder gracious, although I didn't talk but a few minutes with him, for he was in a hurry."

"You had better keep your money, and not ask for such privileges as you desire, if you wish to keep a whole skin," I said, walking slowly towards the theatre, arm in arm with Tom.

"Whole skin? What do you mean?" he asked in surprise.

"Simply that the priests of Manila would not let the governor general look at the girls whom they have in charge; so you can imagine what show of success a heretic like you would have. Make no offers of money to such men, unless for church purposes, for they can command a hundred knives."

"That for their knives," cried Tom, snapping his fingers with all the bravado of an American. "I've got a six-shooter in my pocket that would frighten a dozen natives."

"Provided, of course, it was pointed at them, which they would take precious good care should not be the case. The men I speak of strike when you least expect the blow, and in the dark. Be careful, Tom, for your life is precious to your country."

The fellow laughed, and said no more about being introduced to convent girls; but when we entered the theatre he surveyed the house through his opera-glass, one of the relics of his fast days, a splendid instrument, mounted with gold and pearl, and well calculated to catch the eyes of Spanish ladies.

"Who in thunder is that?" cried Tom, regardless of the play, directing his glass towards the box of Donna Teresa. "I thought that I had seen some handsome women in my day, but she knocks 'em all higher than a kite. What eyes! and what a face! Tell me who she is, or I shall go and —"

"Commit suicide," I suggested.

"No, sir, not for a woman. I meant that I should go and take a gin cocktail. And while I am speaking of that strange but extremely palatable mixture, would you credit the assertion when I state that not a man in the city seems to know the meaning of the words, and I am actually obliged to concoct the drink with my own hands? But see, the lady is looking this way, and as I live she is bowing and smiling. Blast it, it can't be possible that I have made a conquest so soon. Yet it must be so, for now the smile is changed to a look of extreme melancholy. What shall I do! Shall I go to her box, and introduce myself? or shall I send her a note, declaring that I love her to distraction?"

"I should not recommend either course," I answered, dryly.

"Why not? I'm not afraid of that black devil in uniform, who talks with her every few minutes, 'cos I believe that I've got more science than he has, and could knock him out of time in a couple of rounds."

"Perhaps the officer would prefer steel to fists," I remarked.

"Even then I should give him a fair show, for I had two quarters with Professor Sharpedge, the best small-sword man in York, and he used to boast of my performances. But joking aside, how shall I make the acquaintance of the lady? for she has lighted a fire in my heart that all cocktails ever concocted could not extinguish.

Is she married or single, rich or poor? But she don't look as though she was short of cash, for, by Jove, she has got lots of diamonds on her person, and they are of the first water, too; for let me alone for knowing paste."

"She is a widow," I answered, "and very rich. She has more admirers than she knows by name; is as good as she is handsome; but I don't think you would stand any chance for her affections."

"Don't believe that," replied Tom, with commendable assurance. "I know how to deal with women better than most men, 'cos I've had such a deuced lot of experience in York. Give me an introduction, and then let me alone for working my way into her heart as a rabbit burrows in a bank of earth."

"The comparison is too strong to be resisted," I replied. "You shall have an introduction, and much good may it do you."

Tom was so overjoyed that he insisted upon repairing to the saloon of the theatre, and imbibing a glass of wine; and as there was nothing upon the stage that was worth seeing, I readily consented.

Tom smoked his cigar and sipped his wine in silence for a few minutes, but at length said, —

"Speaking of the pretty widow with the millions, why the deuce has it never occurred to you that it would be a great stroke of policy to marry her? hey?"

"What chance could I stand with a lively woman, like her, fond of bull-fights and kindred sports?" I replied, evasively.

"That's so," cried Tom, energetically. "A woman likes a man that has got some dash and go-ahead in him — one that is a favorite with her own sex, and gives her a little cause for jealousy."

"Say some such a man as yourself," I suggested, with a smile.

"Well, joking aside, I rather flatter myself that I am calculated to make some woman happy and miserable at the same time; and with your recommendation, I'd marry the widow this night, with all ceremony."

"Provided, of course, she would have you," I replied, with a laugh at his assurance.

"If she knew me she would have me fast enough. But don't let us sit here discussing improbabilities all night, when better things await us. Let us take a look at the theatre, and then for our company and supper."

We locked arms and sauntered back to the theater, and once more surveyed the audience and the stage. On the latter a young peasant was telling a high-born lady that he would die for her, if it was necessary; and the lady didn't seem to know whether it was best to be grateful or indignant, and finally split the difference, and began to cry, which act made Tom sarcastic, for he said it was a weapon that they always used upon all occasions and in all places.

In the box with Teresa was Father Juan, who seemed to be communicating some news to the lady, for she was listening attentively to all that he said; and I saw that, as he proceeded, a frown gathered upon his brow, and she looked as I had seen her but once before.

"Hallo! what is the matter with the handsome widow?" asked Tom, surveying her through his glass. "She looks as cross as a girl that has lost her lover. She's got a bit of temper, I'll warrant, and I'd like her all the better for it. Hang it, I can't bear a woman that's too insipid to quarrel, and always has an amiable expression of face, as though prepared for heaven at any moment. When I was in New York, I used to pay attention to the girls who had the most temper, just for the purpose of getting them mad and jealous at times; but once I carried the joke too far, and got this cut on my forehead, to pay for my trouble."

He showed a scar, an inch long, near his left temple; and the wound had evidently been a severe one.

"The she-devil threw a tumbler at me," Tom continued; "and it struck with some force, you had better believe; and for a few weeks I was incapable of joking. But would you think it, the girl was the first one to offer me assistance, and to express sorrow for the occurrence. What unaccountable beings women are—ain't they? At one moment they are ready to kill us, and the next breath to love us; and hang me if you know when they are ready for either."

Tom continued railing until the priest had finished the communication he was charged with, and then I saw him leave the lady's box in the same cat-like manner which was so characteristic of the man. He passed near us, but did not raise his eyes from the floor, where they were fixed, as though searching for lost pocket-books.

"Come, introduce me to-night to the widow," cried Tom, who

had hardly removed his glass from the face of the lady. "The more I see of her, the more love and admiration I feel. Now is as good a time as any other, and I should so enjoy a chat with her in the face of the whole house!"

The proposition did not suit my convenience; so I found no difficulty in making Tom consent to a postponement until a more favorable opportunity, and by the time his thoughts took another turn, I looked at my watch, and found that it was past ten.

"Come along, for we have seen enough of this for one night," my companion exclaimed. "I'm getting supperish, and must be off to keep my appointment. You take your carriage and drive home, and I'll be there 'fore half an hour's time. Tell the cook to have supper at twelve, precisely, and to cool the champagne by exposure in water in the open air. You be ready to receive me and my company, and then you shall have your choice, and we'll make a night of it."

I promised compliance with his wishes, and we parted just as the curtain fell upon the close of the last piece. He rolled off in his carriage at a rapid speed, and I took my course homeward, dissatisfied with myself, with Donna Teresa, and with Tom, for I began to think that I had consented most too readily to have my house turned into a den of revelry, although I knew that my neighbors would think none the less of me for it, for but few prudish people exist in Manila, and it's one of the best cities for turning deaf ears to little faults I ever lived in.

I found my cook hard at work at his supper, which he assured me should be worthy of his skill, and after seeing that everything was prepared for the reception of my company, I recommenced on my pile of newspapers, and was busy over a long article on the landing of filibusters at Cuba, when my boy-of-all-work entered the room, looking as though he had something important to communicate.

"Senor, the holy Father Juan has been here this evening," he said.

"Indeed! for what?" I asked, somewhat astonished.

"He asked if you were at home, senor, and when I said that you were at the theatre, he left immediately."

"Did he say nothing more?" I inquired.

"Nothing, senor; only he remarked, that by the smell of the food he should suppose you intended to have company to-night."

"And your answer?" I demanded, somewhat sternly.

"I said, senor, that I did not know your business, and that you would inform him if he would visit the theatre."

I ruminated for some time respecting the visit of the priest, for it was to me very evident that Father Juan was tracking my steps, and was determined to see whom I entertained, for the purpose of informing Teresa, and if possible breaking off the alliance which he still seemed to think existed between us.

"I will defeat him yet," I muttered; and summoning the boy, I gave special orders that if Father Juan called a second time, he was not to be admitted to the house, and no answers returned to his questions.

I had hardly given the directions when a carriage drove up, and I heard Tom's voice directing his coachman to return home, as he should have no further use for his services that night. Then I heard my friend talk half in English and the other portion Spanish, with an immense amount of laughing, and up stairs he rushed, leading two young girls, whose black eyes and dark hair would have captured less susceptible hearts than his own.

"Here we are, old boy," he exclaimed; "just on time, as I told you. I've trotted 'em out, and now what do you think of 'em? hey? Pretty — ain't they? Create a sensation in New York — would they? Can't speak a word of English, except to say Blast you, and they don't know the meaning of it. I learned it to 'em as we came along. In a week's time we can make them swear like pirates, and they won't know what it's all about. Capital fun it will be — won't it?"

The girls, apparently about sixteen years of age, had not the remotest idea what he was saying; but as he laughed they felt bound to do the same, and for a few minutes we had a very merry time of it.

"I say, don't it do you good to see the girls laugh?" cried Tom, throwing his arms around one of them in the exuberance of his joy, and kissing her right heartily, for which he got a little pat upon his cheek which would not have injured a mosquito.

"You have not introduced me, Tom," I said, almost envious of the sport which he was appropriating to himself so readily.

"Don't need one, my boy; go in and enjoy yourself as well as you can. Don't you see that I have set the example? But as you are one of the scrupulous kind, here goes for their names

This one with the pink *piney* dress is Catalina, and the one with the white dress is Margarita. Both are pretty, as you can see for yourself, and both can scold or sing, as the humor takes them. Catalina goes with me to Hong Kong, when I leave this city, and if you desire, Margarita will remain to bless your lonely hours."

The girls seemed to be aware that Tom was introducing them, for they took possession of chairs, and then laughed to such an extent, that my boy-servant rushed in with a tray of paper-cigars, thinking that where there was so much mirth, smoking would be of the first importance.

"Now, Tom," I said, as soon as I had made my guests at home, "where did you get acquainted with these ladies? Let me have the whole history."

"I'll do that, and no mistake," he replied, lighting a cigar, and throwing an arm around the waist of Catalina,— a freedom which she permitted without the least reluctance. "A week ago I saw the girls leaving a church, and as I thought they liked my personal appearance, I just followed them to their residence, was asked in, told to make myself at home; and faith I did. I had money, which they wanted; so no questions have been asked on either side. They admire me, and I'm sure I do them. I told them to get ready and come to supper, and they are here. You see they are not of pure blood, but they are just as interesting as though they were. I only wish I had one in New York, promenading down Broadway. I'll bet I would make the boys stare."

"*No habla Ingles mas,*" cried Catalina, with a pout of her pretty lips.

"And we won't, my darling," exclaimed Tom, with overpowering tenderness; "we will speak Spanish if it kills us. What a sweet language it is, to be sure, when heard issuing from a pair of pretty lips! I've learned more of it in the last week than I could by studying grammar a twelvemonth, thanks to Catalina's teaching."

And thus Tom ran on, struggling desperately with his bad Spanish, and laughing heartily as the girls and myself, when he committed a bad blunder, which I think he often did on purpose.

"By the way," said Tom, all at once looking serious, "I met that old cock of a priest just as I was entering the house, and he looked at me as though I was eloping with some of his lambs. What is the old fool doing at this hour ot the night, wandering around streets and theatres, instead of attending to his flock and drinking punch at home?"

"And he stared at me," said Catalina, with a toss of her pretty head, "as though I had no right to visit the house of a friend and partake of a supper."

"I will twist his neck," Tom shouted, "if he dares to look at you again."

"O, no," cried both girls in a breath; "he is a padre, and therefore sacred. You must not strike him; if you do there will be no chance of your salvation, and we love the Americans, and want them all to be saved."

"Angelic simplicity!" exclaimed Tom, with a vigorous laugh; "since you want him unmolested, consider him safe. But come, Guillermo; you still look unhappy. Is not this better than remaining in the house, moping over books and papers, and not knowing what to do with yourself?"

"I am quite contented," I replied; but I must confess I did not feel so, for I had a foreboding that something was about to happen, and that the espionage of the priest Juan had much to do with it. I tried to assume an appearance of gayety that was forced; but I could not help it.

"Go, Margarita," said Tom, "and salute our host with a kiss. If that don't cheer him, nothing will."

The girl hesitated for a moment; but seeing that I did not forbid her, she rose, with burning cheeks, and glided across the room. Then she threw her bare arms around my neck, and pressed her red lips to mine. From that moment all melancholy fled.

"Will the American love the Mestiza girl?" she whispered, as she took a seat by my side, and leaned her head upon my shoulder, while her black eyes were raised to mine as though she would read my thoughts.

"I will try to do so," I answered, smoothing her soft, luxuriant hair, and feeling that I was on treacherous ground, if I intended to preserve my fidelity to Donna Teresa.

"Is it so very hard, then, for you to love me?" she asked, with a slight pout.

"Not hard, for you are very beautiful," I answered; "but you must know that the Americans are reputed to be a cold race.

and only love after repeated interviews. You would not have me assume a passion I did not feel?"

"O, no," she murmured, using her eyes with all the skill of a coquette; "only try and love me, and I don't fear but you will succeed."

I felt the truth of her remark, and I knew that I should prove unworthy the love of Donna Teresa, unless I steeled myself against such insidious advances. I strove to break away from her fascinations; but she knew her power, and exercised it with the skill of a master; and had not the *muchacho* just at that moment informed us that supper was on the table, I fear that I should have forgotten myself, and so lost my self-respect and caution.

"Supper," cried Tom, springing from his seat; "I'm glad to hear it — ain't you, ladies?"

Of course they were; and when they saw how luxuriantly the table was spread, they were in raptures; for be it known, O reader, that even Spanish beauties are as fond of the products of the *cuisine* as American belles after a five hours' sleigh-ride.

"Splendid!" cried Tom, rubbing his hands with satisfaction; and we were just about to take seats, when a loud rapping was heard upon the door of the court-yard.

"Who, in the devil's name, has called at this hour of the night?" demanded Tom, listening for a repetition of the sounds which had so startled us.

I could return no answer, for the knocks were as mysterious to me as spiritual manifestations. My boy looked at me with an inquiring glance for orders, and at length I made him a sign, and he disappeared down the broad staircase which led to the court-yard.

"I hope no one is about to interrupt us with our supper, for we have a very pleasant party already, and additions would only spoil it," Tom grumbled; and hardly had he concluded when I heard a voice in angry altercation with my servant, which made my heart quake with terror, and I would have given thousands to have seen my friend and his two companions spirited through the window by the old gentleman whose name had been invoked but a few seconds before. I was caught in a trap, and the only thing that could save me was tact and assurance.

"Silence, for Heaven's sake!" I pleaded, as Tom was about

to roar out an oath. "Let us hear how the boy deals with the visitors."

My friend saw that I was really in earnest, although for what reason he could not divine; but he left off grumbling, and behaved quite peaceably.

"I tell you, senora, Don Guillermo is not at home," cried my boy, earnestly; and I heard him try to shut the door, but he could not succeed.

"Then what is the meaning of so many lights in the house?" was the inquiry, in tones that made me tremble.

"The servants have a party to-night, senora, during the absence of our master. You will probably find him at the hotel, playing billiards with the English naval officers," was the reply; and I mentally resolved to increase that boy's wages, if his falsehood succeeded.

"Miserable ladrone," was the quick rejoinder, "I know that your master is within, for I saw him at the window not ten minutes since. Stand one side, and admit us, or it will be the worse for you."

"You cannot enter," the lad said, with firmness; and for a moment I heard a scuffle; but it was of short duration. The resistance grew more feeble, and at length ceased; and I thought that I could distinguish the chink of gold, which accounted for the cessation.

Up the broad steps I heard two persons advancing, and I knew the sound of their footfalls as well as though I had seen them.

"For God's sake, what is the matter?" demanded Tom, noticing my tremor and pallor.

"Open a bottle of champagne, and give me a glass as quick as possible," I whispered, for I felt the need of spiritual consolation when I was about to face and lose one I loved better than life itself.

Quicker than thought Tom had filled my glass, and I drained it just as the nocturnal visitors reached the door of the room where my company was assembled. I looked up, and saw a lady covered with a heavy black veil, so that not a particle of her face was visible, and behind her, with gloating eyes, stood the hateful form of Father Juan, the worst enemy I had in Manila.

Truly had his hour of triumph arrived, as he had prophesied it would, at the convent of San Pedro, two months before, when I had refused to sanction the scheme for his advancement at my expense.

"*Buenas noches, senores,*" said the lady, in a voice that was tremulous with passion. "Perhaps we are intruding upon such select company. If we are, say so, and we will retire. I have seen enough to convince me that there is no honesty in the world, and that a man's word is like a rope of sand."

I could not speak if I had attempted the task; but Tom was not so embarrassed, and answered for me.

"Intrusion, lady?" he repeated; "why, you must be a stranger here, or you would know that everything that wears a petticoat is welcome in this house. To be sure we ordered supper for four, but Guillermo's liberality is great, and there's enough for six. So off with your veil, and sit down with us."

"For God's sake, Tom!" I pleaded; but he paid but little attention to me.

"His infamy is worse than I expected; but I thank God that I have discovered his wickedness before it is too late," cried the veiled female, although I thought that I detected something like a sob with the exclamation.

"Did I not tell you, senora;" the priest said, advancing a step forward.

"And I wish that your tongue had been blistered before you spoke a word of his falsehoods," cried the lady, fiercely.

"Senora, have I deserved this?" the priest asked, in a humble tone.

"You have opened my eyes to this man's baseness," she said, pointing to me; and I could see the angry glare of her eyes although covered by a veil; "and I thank you for it; but do not presume too much on that, for perhaps it would have been better for both of us if I had remained in ignorance of this night's doings."

"I sought to prevent you from giving your hand to this heretic, for he is unworthy of your love," returned Father Juan, still maintaining his composure.

"Of that I am the best judge," she replied, so proudly that the priest did not venture another suggestion.

"Madam," cried Tom, rising with a full glass of champagne, "we drink to your health, and a speedy reconciliation to the man you love, for you must love some one; but I hope I'm not the man."

"Silence, sirrah!" cried the priest, fiercely; "you know not whom you speak to so lightly."

"Hallo, old convent; are you there? Come and sit down by the side of me, and I'll drink you blind in an hour's time."

"Let us retire from this scene of vice," the priest cried, laying his hand upon the lady's arm; but she shook him off as though he had been contamination.

"Guillermo," the veiled lady asked, with an evident softening of anger, "have you nothing to say before we part never to meet again?"

"I have much to say to you," I answered; "but this is not the time nor place."

"Then farewell, for I leave the cares of this world, and this life of anxiety and disappointment, for the seclusion of a convent. For your unkindness I pardon you. Think of me sometimes, and I will pray for you."

I could see a gleam of devilish triumph in the eyes of the priest as he listened to this declaration.

"Let us leave these sinful wretches to their worldly pleasures," he said. "For us there are purer joys and better rewards."

She turned to go, but hesitated, as though she would like to speak a few more words of parting advice.

"Guillermo," she said, "did you ever love me truly and sincerely?"

She threw aside her dark veil as she spoke, as though to give me a full view of her glorious beauty, and let me contrast it with the faces of Catalina and Margarita, who, poor girls, had withdrawn to a corner of the room at the first intrusion, and remained there silent and motionless, fearful of the penance which Father Juan sometimes inflicted, or caused to be done through his influence.

"By thunder!" was Tom's roaring exclamation, when he saw the face of Donna Teresa, "it's the beauty I saw at the theatre. Who is she in love with, you or me?"

"Teresa," I said, "I have loved you for many months, and do you think that a passion like mine can be extinguished in a few days? As I loved you months since, so do I love you now, and never better than at this moment."

I could see that her heart was changing from its terrible anger to a feeling more in accordance with woman's nature. The priest saw it, too, and he grew restive and anxious.

"Let us leave, senora," he whispered, "or we may be suspected of partaking in their orgies. We have no time to lose, for I know that the air is tainted with vice."

Poor Tom had sat in a mist of wonderment from the time that Teresa had withdrawn her veil; but at length a light began to dawn upon his mind. He saw at once that there was a lover's quarrel between Teresa and myself, and that the priest was at the bottom of it. His knowledge of Spanish was not extensive, but he could understand enough to know that Father Juan was endeavoring to urge the lady to leave the house before a reconciliation was effected; and Tom's generous nature was opposed to any such arrangement, for the instant he saw that Teresa and myself had been lovers, and were only separated by a slight misunderstanding, he resolved to forget his half-developed passion for the lady, and do me all the service in his power. He considered that the most important duty he could perform, just at that moment, would be to get the priest out of the way; for he knew enough of the world to understand that a lover can act his part to some advantage, if a few moments' private conversation is granted him.

Therefore, when the priest urged a retreat, all of my friend's New York qualities were brought out in an instant.

"Leave the room, padre!" he shouted, laying hold of a champagne bottle, and taking aim at Juan's head.

The holy father dodged behind the lady in visible alarm, but not a step did he stir towards the staircase.

"Gently, Tom," I exclaimed, laying a hand upon his arm, and restraining his anger. "It won't do to kill priests in Manila."

"Well, some of them ought to be killed for interfering in love affairs. But I won't kill the man — I'll only maim him a little, and see how he likes it."

"Be quiet, or you will spoil the advantage that we have already gained;" and Tom sat down, muttering that he could knock the "old buffer" heels over head at the first round.

Teresa had remained standing, undecided whether to retreat or still listen to my explanations; and to my surprise she chose to do the latter, and although she still looked indignant, her anger was not so excessive as when she first surprised us in our revels.

"What explanation do you wish to make before I leave you forever?" she asked, haughtily.

"He can make none," cried the priest, hastily. "He has been caught in the act of committing a sin, which true love should have warned him against. He is not to be trusted. Let us leave him."

Once more Tom's hand sought the bottle, and again did the priest dodge behind Teresa to keep from harm's way; but I interposed and saved the head of the holy father from broken glass.

"Let me talk with you, Teresa," I said, "for a few minutes alone, and with that confidence which I enjoyed some months since, when I was happy — happy because I believed that I possessed your love, and that I returned it tenfold; for when did a day pass that I did not think or dream of you? Was I not always by your side to protect you and console you? and not until you grew cold in your affection did I cease to do so. I still love you most dearly, and always shall; but it breaks my heart to be thus suspected by one to whom I have never been untrue."

"That's the talk," muttered Tom; "pile on the agony, and she can't withstand it. I couldn't do better myself. Fire another shot, and she will strike, or I'm no judge of women."

"I should think there was little need of explanation with these two women in the room," Teresa said, bitterly, pointing to Catalina and Margarita.

"An explanation should not be received," muttered the priest, glancing at Tom as he spoke, and evidently fearful of the effect of his words. "Let us leave, senora, and then they can recommence their carousals without restriction. You swore to cast him off; now remember your oath, and do so at once."

"I swore to forget him," she answered, with dignity, "if he had ceased to love me. If I thought that he had — "

"But he has not, senora," cried Tom, starting up; "for I assure you on my word as an American gentleman, and one who has resided for many years in New York, the Empire City of the new world, that I invited these two excellent ladies here this evening on my own responsibility, and that my friend Guillermo never saw them before to-night."

The priest stepped forward to whisper a word in her ear, for he didn't care about trusting his voice in the hearing of Tom; but the latter gentleman was on the alert, and on his first motion the bottle was raised, and the holy father made a dodge backward.

"Can I believe him?" she asked, earnestly, her voice trembling with emotion.

"He has told the truth," I answered; "and under such circumstances is it too much to ask for a moment's private conversation? Think, Teresa, what I have suffered the past few weeks by your coldness, and how eager I am to learn why you have been so distant. Five minutes is all that I require, and then, if you wish me to leave you, I will do so with as sorrowful a heart as ever man carried away from the presence of his mistress."

"He has been the most unhappy man that I ever saw, the past few weeks," Tom said, thinking he had remained silent long enough. "He is reduced to a skeleton, and moans in his sleep; but for all that, senora, he has always mentioned your name in his daily prayers, and uttered no complaint. I couldn't see my best friend dying by inches without doing something to save him; so I introduced these two ladies, daughters of highly respectable parents, I assure you, to him. I'm engaged to one of them, and the marriage will take place when I'm ready, and not before."

The three last words were uttered in English, and with as grave a face as was ever assumed by a Chinese merchant when about to make a good bargain.

The cloud passed from Teresa's brow, but she didn't wish to be convinced too soon.

"I thought you told me that the girls were *malo*," she said, looking at the priest.

"And so they — "

Before the priest could finish his *exposé*, Tom had sprung to his feet, and interrupted him.

"I demand," he said, "that that man leave the room while this conference is going on. He has no right here, and he is continually interrupting business. Such a thing would not be tolerated in New York for a moment. Even the Empire Club would kick against such a state of things."

"I am the champion of this lady," the holy father replied.

"Then you are a cursed bad champion, and I'm going to vanquish you with a bottle. I'll battle you with a basket of champagne, and the loser shall pay for it." •

Teresa did not understand my friend's meaning, and supposing that he was hurling a challenge at the priest's head, she became eager to prevent trouble.

"Go, father," she said, "and remain in the street until I call you; or you had better return to your convent, and I will trust to the kindness of Guillermo to see me home."

"Blast me, if things ain't working all right!" exclaimed Tom, draining his glass of champagne, and winking at the girls, who still remained in a corner, to keep quiet, and he would make it all smooth with them at some future time, not very definitely stated.

"I cannot leave you here, daughter, without incurring a great responsibility. This is not the place for one like you to remain in, at such an hour of the night. Go with me, and let the senor call upon you in the morning, at your residence, and there offer such excuses as he may invent."

For a moment I feared that she would accept this reasonable proposition; and if she had, the priest would have brought such influence to bear, that I should never have had the satisfaction of speaking with her a second time. For only a moment she hesitated, and then her wilful look returned, and the priest was vanquished in a fight where I had such tremendous odds against me as two good-looking girls. Had they both been plain and old, she would not have cared near as much, for a handsome woman is seldom jealous of homely girls.

"I have said that I would speak with Guillermo, and I will," she cried, angrily; and the padre saw, with rage, that any further urging on his part would be useless, for he knew that Teresa had a will of her own, and knew how to use it.

Father Juan cast a look of malignant hatred upon me as he crept towards the stairs, and his anger was not decreased when he saw that Tom was standing up, and drinking his health with mock solemnity.

"Good by, old Daddy Longlegs," shouted Tom; "call again when you happen this way, say a year or two hence."

"I don't understand you," said the priest, willing to delay his departure as long as possible, turning to Tom, who had spoken in English.

"No; I suspect you don't want to understand some wholesome truths; but I am glad that I've had the opportunity to tell you what I think about your conduct. A feller like you would be rode on a rail by the Bowery Boys of New York, if he 'should attempt to separate true lovers. Now you may go, and the devil go with you for company. Catalina and Margarita, will you come and join me in drinking to the confusion of the holy father?"

The poor girls hung their heads with some show of terror, for they knew what would be their penance if they insulted the padre.

Father Juan smiled savagely for a moment; but when he saw that the girls had too much respect for his office to insult him, he turned from them to Donna Teresa.

"Do you still insist upon remaining here, senora, with libertines and wantons for companions?" he asked.

"I have told you that I think Guillermo entitled to a hearing, and that he shall have one. The subject needs no further discussion."

"Then I go, senora — "

"Well, why in thunder don't you go, and not stand there talking about the matter all night?"

Tom had paid such repeated attentions to the bottle, that he began to grow jocose, and perhaps the padre thought quarrelsome; for the latter, after one more look about the room, stole quietly down stairs, and in a moment afterwards I heard the boy let him into the street.

"Teresa," said I, taking her hand, which she as quickly withdrew, "will you now allow me to speak to you alone, and with the same confidence that I enjoyed a few weeks since? Perhaps your coldness can be explained and remedied."

She bowed her stately head, and I led her to my sitting-room, leaving Tom and his young ladies to whisper and talk of love as much as they pleased.

"To enable us to understand each other, it is necessary that a confession should be made," I said, placing chairs so that I could throw my arms around her waist, if I thought there was a prospect of her fainting, or forgiving me.

"I am ready to listen to all that you may have to offer," she replied; and I saw by her face that she was determined I should define my position before she was ready to answer my questions.

"Have you ceased to love me?" I asked, in tones so sad that I knew words would have commanded the unbounded admiration of my friend Tom.

"No, no," she replied; "I still love you, Guillermo, but do you deserve it?"

Of course I said that I thought I did, and wondered why not.

"Have you been true to me since we exchanged vows at Santa Mesa?" she asked.

I thought of her jealous disposition and quick temper, and therefore boldly answered that she alone possessed my thoughts night and day.

"Guillermo," she said, laying her hand upon mine, and speaking so feelingly that all thoughts of levity vanished from my heart, "I have been told many disagreeable things respecting your course of life, and although I tried hard to steel my mind against the many insinuations, yet still they made an impression; and perhaps I showed my thoughts too plainly by manifesting a coldness that I hoped you would endeavor to overcome by explanations. To my surprise you did not do so, and therefore I felt the more confirmed in what was told me."

"For which I am to thank the holy Father Juan," I said, bitterly.

She made no reply to my charge, but sat for a few minutes in deep meditation. I stole an arm around her waist, and pressed her gently to my side, and to my great joy she did not resist or offer any objections.

"Reports were brought to me," she continued, "by people whom I thought most disinterested. They told me that you were a spendthrift, a gambler, and a libertine; but O, worst of all, they said that you professed a passion that you did not feel, simply for the purpose of securing my fortune."

"They lied, Teresa!" I exclaimed, warmly, for with all my sins I must confess that I loved the lady for herself alone.

"I now begin to see that I was deceived, and acknowledge my error. Forgive me, Guillermo, as I forgive you."

Her head was on my shoulder and her lips near at hand. Need I say that I sealed our reconciliation in a manner that provoked no angry response, but before I could repeat the operation, Tom, after knocking at the door, threw it open.

"That old humbug has come back again," cried he.

We listened for a moment, and sure enough we heard noise sufficient to answer for a moderate earthquake. The huge gate which opened on the court-yard was shaken as though all the people in the house were deaf or dead, and those on the outside were anxious to break in without a moment's delay.

I was about to step to the window for the purpose of interrogating the priest in regard to his intentions, when Tom begged me to desist, and leave the matter entirely to him.

"I know how to treat those kind of fellers," he said.

I readily gave my consent, for I began to fear that the knocking would attract some attention, and lead to inquiries which would not be likely to raise the reputation of Donna Teresa in the estimation of the thoughtless.

Tom, with an expression of intense delight upon his face, went to the table, drank a huge glass of champagne, and then made the girls, Catalina and Margarita, do the same, after which operation he began to look around the room, and at length lighted upon an earthen jar, that would hold about two pails of water. This he directed the boy to fill, and then to carry it down stairs.

"Remember, Tom," I said; "no violence to the priest. He is most powerful here in Manila."

"I wouldn't hurt a hair of his head for a thousand dollars," my friend answered. "That row, however, must be stopped, and I'm the boy to do it. Peaceably if I can, forcibly if I must, as some celebrated New Yorker once said; but when, or where, I don't know."

With these words Tom went down stairs.

"Why in the devil's name don't you open the door," some one roared in the street. I thought that I knew the voice, for it didn't sound like Father Juan's; but I was somewhat nervous and confused, and didn't pay that attention I should have done, had I been calm, and not beneath the roof with Donna Teresa, and two ladies whom I wished away.

"All right!" shouted Tom, in reply, laughing so heartily at some freak that entered his head, he was compelled to hold on to the boy to support himself.

"You shall be attended to in a minute; never fear," Tom continued, motioning for the boy to withdraw the bar of the door.

The lad did as he was directed, and just as the bar was raised I saw Tom grasp the huge stone jar that contained the water.

"What are you going to do?" I demanded, somewhat alarmed at his proceedings.

Before he could answer me there was a vigorous push against the door. It flew open, and a burly form darkened the entrance.

"Watch, O! watch, and heave!" Tom shouted, adopting the language of sailors when about to try the soundings by a deep-sea lead.

By a vigorous jerk the water was shot out of the jar and dashed upon the person of the intruder, covering him from head to foot.

"Now, old cock," roared Tom, "how do you like the fashion of rousing people up at this time of night?"

There was an immense amount of blowing, and spluttering, and grunting; and at length I could hear a loud laugh, which I should have recognized in any part of the world.

"By the Lord Harry, Benventuro; but this is a reception with a vengeance. Thank Heaven, you got the worst of it."

"Allen!" I shouted; "is that you?"

"Well, I should think that it was," he replied, with another laugh, more loud than the first.

"Don't ask if this is me; may the devil confound you and the house too," cried my old fat friend, Father Benventuro. "Santa Barbara! What have I done that I should be treated like a rat? What was water ever made for except to drown people in. It seems as though the whole of the Rio Pasig had been emptied over me."

"Why, this isn't the old convent cock," cried Tom, completely sobered by the mistake he had made. "I thought that it was Father Juan."

"Father Juan be cussed," roared Benventuro. "I look no more like him than the man in the moon. "If you are a Catholic you shall do penance for this."

"My dear friend," I said, hastening down stairs, and interposing, "this shower-bath was not intended for you, but for your worst enemy, Father Juan, who has bothered us greatly to-night by his presence. You will forgive this gentleman, when I tell you that he has a great respect for you, and that he is the owner of a dozen bottles of champagne of the green seal."

"Are the bottles in this house?" demanded the priest, eagerly.

"Yes; and three of them are already opened, and waiting to be drank."

"The Lord be praised, for I am as dry inside as I am wet outside. Young man, I forgive you, and take back the curse I bestowed upon your head, although, faith, I hadn't ought to, for the showering that you gave me was none of the most pleasant. Ugh! I'm wet to my skin, and not a change of clothes in the city."

"Come up stairs and I'll make you comfortable," I said; and as my guests followed me, I asked how it happened that they had reached Manila at so late an hour.

"Because," cried Father Benventuro, "we thought that you were dead, or had left the city, for we haven't heard from you for two weeks. This afternoon I could wait no longer, and after I had finished a few games of cock-fighting, by which I won a couple of ounces,— the saints be praised for my luck, for my birds have acted confounded bad lately,— I left Santa Mesa for the purpose of seeing Allen, and making him accompany me. He did so, but it was long past dark before we got started, and we had one or two miserable sinners to talk with after we landed."

"Pretty girls, he means," muttered Allen.

"You are both welcome," I said, once more shaking hands with them, and introducing Tom in due form, and after another hearty laugh at the drenching which the priest had received, the latter's eyes suddenly rested upon Catalina and Margarita.

"May the saints preserve us — but what have we here? Two live women, and handsome at that. What would Donna Teresa say if she should hear of this?"

"She has already heard of it, and has expressed her disapprobation," cried Teresa, suddenly making her appearance.

"Donna Teresa!" exclaimed the priest, in astonishment, hardly able to believe the evidence of his senses.

"Donna Teresa!" re-echoed Allen, grasping a bottle of champagne for support, and in a moment of abstraction, filling his glass and emptying it at a breath.

"Yes, gentlemen," the lady replied, "I am Donna Teresa, and came here to-night to show your friend that his duplicity is exposed, and that he cannot deceive me with false vows."

"O, d—," muttered the priest, with a furious look at me; "you have ruined everything by your imprudence."

"Now you are in for it, sure enough," was the consoling remark of Allen, handing the priest a glass of wine, and helping himself at the same time.

The holy father gulped down his wine without a groan, and its flavor was so good that it restored the equanimity of his temper immediately. He did not smile, but he held out his glass for more of the sparkling beverage, and it was promptly supplied.

"Senora," he said, "I have seen so much of life that I have resolved not to condemn a man without a hearing. The practice is a good one, and I recommend all to follow it. No doubt Guillermo can explain a few things, which now look dark, to your satisfaction. Speak, Guillermo, and put the hearts of your friends at rest."

"I am but entertaining Senor Baker, and two respectable ladies of his acquaintance," I replied, bold as brass.

A cloud passed from the fat face of Benventuro, and he seemed to comprehend the position of affairs immediately.

"Why did you not mention in your letter of invitation that you were to have ladies for company?" the priest demanded, turning to me.

"My letter?" I stammered.

"Yes, sir; your letter inviting me to supper. Stay; I have it here."

He searched his pockets without success.

"Ah, I recollect. I left it at the convent. But it's no matter. Had it not been for a sick man whom I was called upon to visit, I should have been here earlier, and this scene would have been avoided. Senora, banish all jealousy, for Guillermo is an injured man, and I believe a pure one."

"What a story!" muttered Allen, in English, with another attack upon the champagne, which Tom joined in most heartily.

"I have already forgiven Guillermo," Teresa said, extending her hand, which I seized upon with avidity; "but still I should like a few bad impressions removed."

The priest's eyes sparkled with joy and champagne. He saw that his ambitious hopes were still within the bounds of possibility, and that there was a prospect of triumphing over his rival, Father Juan. He paused a moment to recover his composure, and then exclaimed, —

"Let me be the peace-maker, and it's lucky that I am here to render assistance to those I love, and who love me. Guillermo invited his friend here to supper; the latter invited his betrothed and her friend. There is no harm in that, surely; but my brother priest, the most suspicious man in the world, and I will say the best" (perhaps the speaker remembered that there were servants in the house, and that they had ears and tongues), "thought that something awful was to take place; therefore he considered that it was his duty to inform your ladyship. That was both right and proper, and I should have done the same, if I had known my friend was likely to forget himself as a gentleman and a lover. Here are the young girls, who feel hurt at your suspicions; and here is the young gentleman who is to marry one of them. Ask him if what I have stated is not correct. I have but your happiness at heart, and" (the priest glanced towards the table, and saw that Allen and Tom were imbibing wine at a rapid rate, and he feared that he would lose his share. He scowled at them in a frightful manner, and then continued to speak to Donna Teresa, who was perfectly willing to listen as long as my faults were being glossed over) " would die to secure it. As long as I have known Guillermo, I am sure that you alone have possessed his thoughts."

I felt a slight pressure from the hand which I held, and rejoiced that the battle was nearly over. I did not approve of the course which the priest had taken to reinstate me in Teresa's affection; but if I had contradicted or interrupted him, I should have lost his support, and gained a powerful enemy.

"They tell me," said Teresa, gliding across the room to where Tom sat, "that I have wronged you. I pray you to forgive me, and believe it was done unintentionally."

Poor Tom, with all his New York experience, was not prepared for the apology, so he could only struggle to his feet and stammer out a few words.

"Don't say a word about it, I beg of you," he exclaimed. "I am sorry that there's been any misunderstanding, and think that the best thing you can do is to make it up the way that we do in York."

As Tom's remarks were made in English, — for he was too agitated to speak Spanish, — it is supposed that the lady was not much enlightened until an interpretation took place. Teresa smiled most sweetly upon the New Yorker, and that simple act almost turned his brain.

"I understand that one of these ladies is betrothed to you. Will you present me to her, so that I can explain why I am here?"

"Why, the fact of it is," Tom stammered, "I think some of marriage. All men do, you know; but I have —"

"He means, senora," interrupted the priest, "that he has not yet decided on the day, and that he will let you know when he has."

Allen hit Tom a powerful kick on his shin, under the table, and while he was rubbing his foot the priest stepped in and resumed the conversation.

"Perhaps the lady will be more communicative," Teresa said, glancing towards the two girls, who evidently wished that they were some distance from the house. "Let the one who is to marry this gentleman be presented to me. I should be pleased to know her."

"Marry me!" echoed Tom, regardless of the priest's secret signs. "Blast it, we don't do things in that way in York, I can tell you."

"Will you be silent?" asked Allen, lifting Tom's glass.

"Silent as you please; but a fellow can't be married in a moment, you know, even to oblige a friend."

"There is no occasion, if you will remain quiet for a moment. Things are working all right. Drink, and pay no attention whatever to what is passing."

Tom accepted Allen's advice; but he did it rather reluctantly, for every few minutes he would mutter, "What would the governor say, if I should carry home a Spanish wife?"

Donna Teresa, who had now assumed one of her most amiable moods, was about to advance towards Catalina and Margarita, when the priest interposed.

"Gently, daughter, gently. Remember that you are a highborn Spanish lady, of wealth and position, and that these girls have mixed blood in their veins. You cannot associate with a Mestiza, for they are an inferior race. They do not expect it. On the day of her wedding send her a present, and that will be a sufficient acknowledgment of your good will."

Teresa stopped and looked at me for advice. I saw that the

words of the priest had roused her Spanish pride, and therefore I adopted his suggestions.

"You are right, Guillermo; but I will no longer embarrass them with my presence. Let us retire to the next room, so they can eat their supper with your friends without restraint."

"But what are we to do for something to eat?" cried the priest, in the greatest alarm for his inner man.

"Why, we three can sup together in the sitting-room. There is enough for all, and it shall be divided. Thanks to the hot climate, the food is as warm as when put upon the table," I said, hastily; and before Donna Teresa could offer any serious objections, the priest had escorted her to the apartment designated.

I explained to Allen and Tom the nature of the bargain, and then called the servants to carry it into effect, and in an incredibly short time the priest had spread his legs beneath the mahogany; an expression of extreme satisfaction passed over his visage, which a few glasses of wine helped to improve.

"Guillermo," he said, "let the *muchacho* open another bottle. For all the favors we receive in this world, the saints be praised. While we live life is worth enjoying. You have both seen trouble, and will be better suited to each other for the little afflictions cast in your path. The saints be praised that you have withstood persecution. Give me another glass of wine, and the breast of a chicken, unless the senora wants it."

The lady disclaimed any inclination for the dainty morsel, and the holy father viewed it with a sigh of satisfaction.

"Another spoonful of the curry, if you please, and a portion of the calabash. That is sufficient. My feelings have been so excited this evening, that I have not the slightest appetite; besides, I ate supper at Senor Allen's, and a most bountiful one it was. Don't let my abstinence, senora, prevent you from picking a wing, however, for the hour is late, and an empty stomach is an evil in this climate. The saints be praised, my digestion is still good."

Teresa felt like myself, and was too busy with her thoughts to care for the pleasures of the table; but our abstinence had no effect on the priest. He drank, ate, and talked with a freedom which only long practice could have enabled him to do.

"Guillermo," asked Teresa, "why didn't you remain in my box

longer this evening, when you must have known that I visited the theatre solely for the purpose of seeing you?"

"Simply because I had no desire to share the pleasure of your conversation with Captain Francisco, who, I thought, was too attentive for a mere acquaintance."

"I have known him for a number of years," she said; "but he is only an acquaintance, and not a friend. Of him you have no need of a particle of jealousy."

"Jealousy!" echoed the priest; "why, jealousy is one of the best passions in the human heart, because it makes men more attentive to their wives, and women more constant to their husbands. Without jealousy there is no love; and were I a girl I would banish from my presence a lover who could look on unmoved, and see me flirt with every good-looking man who chose to devote a portion of his time for my entertainment. Yes, senora; let Guillermo cultivate his jealousy, for 'tis a plant that will keep his passion alive, and prevent you pining for his society. Be jealous, both of you. It may cause a few angry words and looks, but will also cause many pleasant ones. When you cease to be jealous, you have reason to fear your love has departed."

"I feared that Guillermo's had gone many weeks since," Teresa said, in a hesitating tone, and with a blush.

I was about to utter a hundred protestations to the contrary when the priest interrupted me.

"You don't half understand his nature," the padre said. "The hearts of the North Americans are not as inflammable as our own; but when once the tinder has caught, the fire is not easily extinguished. It will smoulder for years, but not entirely die out. Guillermo loves you now with as much devotion as ever, and will love you ten years hence equally well. That surely should content you."

"I am content," she whispered, laying her hand upon mine, and giving me one of her old trusting looks, which set my heart fluttering like a ship's colors on a gala day.

"Did I not tell you," the priest continued, still addressing Teresa, "the very last day that you were at the convent, and every time that I have seen you since, that you must beware of traducers, who would seek to prejudice your mind against your lover. Of course I told you so, and my predictions have come true."

"I could not help feeling as I did," Teresa whispered, still retaining her hold of my hand.

"Neither could Guillermo. You both felt jealous. That was natural enough, but you should have asked for an explanation. Hand me that other bottle of wine, for I feel as thirsty as though I had said mass, and attended a dozen or more cock-fights."

The boy who was in attendance hastened to comply with the order, and after the padre had emptied his glass, he again spoke:—

"After you are married (here Teresa blushed — women always blush when you talk to them of marriage), you must have more confidence in each other, or the result will be unhappiness. Be true to each other, my children, and the saints will provide for you."

"You speak," I said, laughing, "as though we were really to be married; yet I have not heard the first word from Teresa on that important subject for the past two months."

"And I can safely say that during that period Guillermo has been equally as silent as myself," Teresa exclaimed.

"Ah, I see," muttered the priest; "he has been standing on his dignity, and for that would sacrifice his happiness and interest, and the welfare of those connected with him. That won't do. You love each other dearly, and no reverse of fortune should interfere to separate you. I will imagine that I was called upon to unite you," the priest continued, stepping to the door and speaking so that those in the other apartment could hear him; "I should tell you to kneel before me."

To my surprise Teresa knelt upon the floor, still retaining my hand as though she desired me to take my place beside her. I did so, and when I looked up saw Tom, Allen, and the girls gazing at us from the door with sedate faces. I heard the padre mutter a hurried prayer in Latin, and then he spoke in Spanish:—

"In the name of God and the holy saints, I, Benventuro, priest of the convent of St. Pedro, by the power invested in me by the Archbishop of Manila, do hereby pronounce you, Guillermo ——, and you, Teresa Arturo Engracio, both being of lawful ages, and free to act, man and wife; and may the saints have you in their keeping, and your days be happy."

"*Amen!*" cried the crowd at the door, with wonderful unanimity.

CHAPTER VII.

A SURPRISED HUSBAND. — A COOL PRIEST. — AN EXPLANATION.

SCARCELY had the priest concluded the last words of his ceremony, when I began to suspect the trick which he had played us, and sprang to my feet, indignant at his duplicity, and anxious to show my friends that the wedding was not by my connivance.

"Priest," I said, " was the ceremony which you just performed a farce or a reality?"

"As real as I could make it in the absence of an altar, lights, and assistants," he answered, quite coolly, extending his hand to congratulate me.

"And am I really married?" I demanded, my blood boiling, and my senses in a whirl at the novelty of my situation.

"All the lawyers in the country cannot prove that you are not married," was the reply.

"Teresa," I exclaimed, throwing myself at her feet, "I love you dearly, but I did not suspect that we were to be made the victims of a trick, or I should have scorned to obtain your hand in this manner. Will you acquit me of all connivance in the matter?"

Her hands were before her face, and I could see tears stealing from between her fingers. Gently I removed her hands, and kissed the tears from her long eyelashes; and then her head fell upon my shoulder, and she whispered, —

"Perhaps you never desired to marry me, Guillermo."

"May the saints pardon you for that thought, darling," I exclaimed, beginning to think that the priest had not made such a great mistake, after all, and that, if the lady was satisfied, there was but little reason why I should complain.

"And you imagine that you love me just as much now as ever you did?" Teresa asked, hesitatingly.

"More than ever," I whispered.

"Then why should we complain, except for the absence of friends to congratulate us?"

"Don't be foolish and ruin the best day's work that you ever saw performed. If you love the lady, be satisfied, for I am sure that she seems to love you," Allen whispered in English; and even Tom came forward and offered congratulations for the surprise which we had afforded him.

"It was the suddenest thing that I ever saw," Tom cried, wringing my hand until it ached. "I don't believe that it could have been done better even in New York. And what a difference between this old feller and the other old vinegar cock! Why, this one can put a glass of wine out of sight in less than no time, and it seems to do him good. Wine like mine is not thrown away upon him, for I can tell by the smack of his lips that he knows what is what."

"Teresa," I said, leading her to a distant part of the room, "I will not take advantage of the trick which united us, for I love you too well to see you wronged. I offer you your freedom again, and never by word or look shall you know from me that we have been married. This I must do as a man of honor; and if you accept of the offer, I shall still cherish the hope of one day calling you mine, but in the presence of a more brilliant company than we see to-night."

"Guillermo," she said, laying her hand upon mine, and bringing her sweet lips in close proximity to my face, " if I thought that my happiness was not sure in your keeping, I should repudiate the ceremony that has just been performed, and renounce you. But I know," she continued with all the candor of a Spanish girl, "that I love you, and that you love me; and as we expected to be married some day, I don't feel much grieved at what has passed. Do you, my husband?"

How could I reply except to fold her in my arms, and to kiss her again and again, and to vow that I would remain true and loving until death.

"Well," cried the priest, who had been quieting his conscience by repeated attacks upon the 'green seal,' "what conclusion have you come to, senor? Do you intend to introduce us to your wife, or to Donna Teresa Arturo?"

"My wife, senors," I said, as proud of her beauty and accomplishments as bridegroom could well be.

I led her forward, blushing and clinging to my arm, happy, yet embarrassed at the novelty of her situation, and looking so very beautiful that Tom gave vent to a groan of envy as he surveyed her features.

"What a sensation she would make in York!" he exclaimed; and then found consolation in the wine; but his generosity overpowered his envy, and he rushed back and shook my hand, and bowed to the lady with all the grace of a man of the world.

He was about to leave us, when he suddenly stopped, and looked around the apartment with ludicrous surprise. Even the priest released the bottle which he held in his hand, and listened with pallid face, while my wife clung to me with terror, and rested her head upon my breast, as though sure of finding protection within my arms.

There was a roaring sound in the street, and I could hear a rush as though torrents of water were sweeping by the house; and then came a tremendous shock, that nearly threw us to the floor, while huge pieces of plastering and wood-work fell around us, barely clearing our heads. The glasses upon the table danced to and fro as though enjoying a quadrille or polka. For about fifteen seconds the commotion continued, during which time not a word was spoken by those present, although there were many cries in the street, and a dozen voices in the houses opposite uttered shrill yells of —

"*El terremoto! El terremoto!* May the saints preserve us."

"What in the devil's name is *el terremoto?*" demanded Tom, drawing a long breath.

"Earthquake," replied Allen, with admirable composure; "and unless we get out of this confounded city, we shall be fifty feet under water before daylight."

"I've never seen the operations of an earthquake," Tom said, quite coolly, "although I've run to fires in New York; and they ain't slow for fun and destruction. Let's drink to the '*terremoto*,' as you call it, and pray that we shall have another shock."

"You had better pray to Heaven to forgive your sins, for you may not have an opportunity presently," replied Allen, grimly; but Tom was unacquainted with the danger, and therefore scorned it.

"Let her rip!" he shouted, cracking the neck of a bottle of champagne, and drinking the foaming liquor as unconcerned as though all danger was passed. "I suppose that the earthquake wants a drink of this good liquor, but it must gape amazing quick, or it will all be gone. Who will join me?"

"May the saints forgive me," was the muttered ejaculation of the priest, who seemed to have lost his usual presence of mind in consequence of the midnight visitor.

Had I been alone, I should not have feared for the result, uncertain as it was; but I had a wife to save, and I felt that I would sooner perish than aught should happen to her. I remembered that once before, when I first made her acquaintance, I had saved her life and her husband's also; but now that she belonged to me, and her warm love was all my own, I felt my arms strengthened, and my heart, which had first trembled at the shock, grew firm and resolute, as I held the lady in my arms, and pressed her to my breast.

"Guillermo, my husband," she exclaimed, in low tones, "save your own life by instant flight. Do not think of me, for I shall only encumber your movements. Go while you can, and before the waters of the bay and river cut off all retreat. One kiss, and then leave me."

She got a kiss and a stronger embrace than she ever had received in her life; but I scorned her self-sacrificing proposal, and it's probable that she knew I would, for a glad smile passed over her face, and she returned kiss for kiss, and her arms grew tighter around my neck, as though she intended they should remain there, even if the building fell and crushed us.

"We will be saved together, or perish together," I whispered.

"Well," asked Allen, "what are we to do? Stand and look at each other, and await another shock, or escape?"

"Escape by all means," I replied.

"That is the first sensible word that you have said this hour," was the complimentary response. Of course he had not heard one half the endearing expressions I had addressed to my wife; therefore I didn't consider that he was a judge.

"How shall we go? by banco or carriage? for of course we must travel to Santa Mesa for safety," Allen asked.

"By carriage, if we can procure one. My horses are in the stable."

"And my carriage stands at the door," cried Donna Teresa; "we can take that."

Allen rushed to the window, and looked into the street. The coachman had taken advantage of the first alarm, and driven off, although Allen did not seem discouraged at the information.

"We shall have to take your carriage and horses, if we can get them out in time," he said, mildly.

"Will they go in two-forty?" asked Tom, who stuck as close to the table as possible, and who had succeeded in getting Father Benventuro to join him; and the way they were making wine disappear would have delighted a wholesale liquor dealer.

Allen sprang to the stairs leading to the court-yard, for the purpose of finding the servants, and giving directions to the coachman; but he speedily returned.

"The outer doors are open, and not a servant is to be seen," he said.

The cowards had fled at the first intimation of the earthquake, and cared not whether we perished or survived.

"Save yourself, and leave me," my wife said; but I stopped her mouth with a kiss.

"What is to be done?" Allen asked.

"We must harness the animals ourselves," I replied.

"Let me drive!" exclaimed Tom, suddenly starting from the table, and spreading his hands as though urging a fast horse at a killing pace.

"You can help us if you will," I replied, as I led Teresa towards the staircase, close upon the heels of Allen.

"You shall have all the help that I can give you," was my friend's response, grasping the priest by his arm, and accompanying him to the stairs; at the same time he uttered a few encouraging remarks well calculated to steady the nerves of the padre.

"If you can't get up a better specimen of an earthquake than this," said Tom, "I shall call 'em humbugs, and won't patronize 'em again. Why, this feller don't begin to shake as bad as some western fellers do with the fever and ague, and I don't know but I would give a Hoosier odds over this last Manila earthquake. I'd like to see one regular cracking feller, just for the fun of the thing, so I could spin a yarn to the boys in York when I get home."

The priest paid but little attention to Tom's jargon, for his thoughts seemed to be upon his own safety, although, to do him justice, he did beg of me to take good care of Teresa, as though I would not have protected her life at the sacrifice of my own.

When we reached the foot of the steps which led to the courtyard, Tom suddenly recollected that Catalina and Margarita were not of our party, so he bounded up the steps in search of the girls, but found, to his disgust, that they had fled at the first shock; for they cared more for their lives than they did for Tom's, although it was a long time before he could be convinced that such was the case.

"Them's the women," he muttered, "who said they would die for me; and yet, after eating supper and drinking wine, they clear out without a word of thanks. That's Manila gratitude, I suppose. Girls wouldn't serve a feller that way in New York, I know."

He paused a moment as though overcome with the reflection; but just at that moment the bell of St. Pedro Church rang a mournful peal, and no sooner did the crowds, who were hurrying through the streets, hear it than a wild yell of fear was uttered by them, and many, instead of continuing their flight, threw themselves upon their knees, and began praying with all the energy they had left in their bodies.

"We are soon to have another shock," cried Father Benventuro; "save yourselves as well as you can; but as for me, I must go forth and succor the maimed and the dying."

He rushed through the doorway and disappeared; and at that instant the water from the bay rolled through the street a foot deep, and loud above its roaring we could hear the shrieks of children deserted by parents, and wives deserted by husbands.

"This begins to look something like an earthquake," cried Tom, who was still standing by me on the steps, while I held my wife in my arms. "If we can only get a few shocks like the first, I don't know but I shall feel satisfied. Devilish lucky we got that priest out of the way — wasn't it? He would have taken up all the room in the carriage with his fat carcass, and I don't believe that he would have prayed enough to pay for his passage.

"One of you will have to come and lend me a hand with these horses," cried Allen from the stable, where he had been hard at work. "They are wild with fright, and it's doubtful if they can be harnessed."

I was about to consign Teresa to the care of Tom, when the latter volunteered to go and assist.

"I don't know that I ever attempted to harness a horse but I succeeded," he said; "so I guess I'll give your animals a trial."

He cast one regretful look at his patent-leather boots, and then waded through the water to the stable, where Allen was at work.

Again did the bell of St. Pedro peal forth its warning, and again was there a rush of water through the streets; and now I could hear the voices of people in bancos as they sought to escape by their boats to high land, or where falling buildings would not crush them to death.

"These blasted horses won't stand still," shouted Tom from the stable. "They do nothing but snuff at us and kick. Come and help us."

"Go, my husband," Teresa urged; "I will remain here until you return."

I hesitated a moment, and then seated Teresa upon the steps, and dashed through the water to the stable.

"What kind of cussed horses do you call these?" asked Tom; but hardly had he spoken the words, when the buildings began to rock back and forth, the earth to tremble and groan, and the wind sighed as it swept through the court.

"Let her rip," yelled Tom, releasing the horses, and plunging into the water.

I heard a scream, and thought that it sounded like Teresa's voice. For a few minutes I was so mixed up with the horses, that I could not leave the stable without danger of broken limbs; but the instant that I could escape I rushed past Tom and Allen to the spot where I had left my wife, but she was no longer there.

The shock of the earthquake had passed away by the time that I reached the steps, so that I had no longer any fear of being crushed by falling walls and timbers; yet when I found that my wife was absent, I thought for a moment that she had taken refuge in the house through fright at hearing the earth groan, and the water dash wildly about the court-yard. I called her by name, but she returned no answer; and at length I sprang up the steps and reached the dining-room. The table still stood there, but half the dishes which were upon it when we left the revel, were scattered about the floor in wild confusion. The lamps alone remained undisturbed, owing to their peculiar flat shape and weight.

I glanced hastily around the room in hope of seeing my wife; but no such agreeable sight met my eyes, and I passed to the next apartment, fronting the street. Still I did not find the one I sought, and I began to have sad fancies respecting her disappearance. My voice trembled as I called her name, but there was no response. There were but three other rooms in the house, my bed-chamber and a spare chamber next to it, and the room used by the servants. For a moment I thought that she might be in my apartment, and my heart grew light at the idea; but a moment was sufficient to dispel the illusion. The rooms were not destined to shelter so much loveliness on that eventful night; and sick at heart, and with a feeling that some dreadful calamity had happened to Teresa, I retraced my steps to the court-yard, where Allen and Tom were standing, the water dripping from their clothes, and their whole appearance not very inviting, after their bath in front of the stable.

"Where's Donna Teresa?" asked Allen, who saw that I was in search of some one, and that I was unusually excited.

"I left her but a moment since to assist you with the horses, and when I returned she had disappeared. Help me in my search, for she may still be in the court-yard, half dead with terror," I replied.

"You should not have left her for a moment," was the consoling respose of Allen; but although he grumbled at what he considered my carelessness, he nevertheless was alive to my great loss, and did not waste a moment in joining me in the search.

We procured lights and looked through the court-yard most thoroughly, and in every building; but still we found no trace of the lady, and I began to feel all the despair of a man and a lover at my loss. I sat down on the steps, and could have shed tears, but I feared to let my companions witness my grief and weakness.

"This is devilish mysterious," Tom said, at length; "and I began to think that Manila ain't such a slow place, after all, and in some respects can equal New York."

I started towards the street without any definite plan, but before I could reach the gate Allen had overtaken me.

"What do you propose to do, and where do you think of searching at this hour of the night?" he asked.

"I know not; the saints will direct my steps," I answered.

"I don't believe but his mind is wandering," I heard Tom whisper to Allen; "and I think a good proof of it is shown by his calling upon the saints. I never heard him mention them before."

"Hush!" Allen replied, in the same low tone; "don't make sport of his grief, for the poor fellow will suffer enough before he ever sees his wife again."

"You must not commence the search now, my dear friend," Allen continued addressing me in the most soothing manner, "because the streets are filled with water, and there is not a banco to be seen. They have all gone up the river with passengers, and will not return until danger is past."

I saw that it was madness to think of searching through the dark streets; but still I was reluctant to yield, and only by Allen's persuasion did I consent to return to the house, and wait until the water subsided, and daylight appeared.

The first thing that Tom looked after was the wine, which was uninjured, while some half dozen bottles still reposed on the balcony, wrapped in wet cloths for the purpose of cooling their contents. One of the bottles was quickly opened, the broken dishes pushed one side, and goblets filled to the brim.

"Here," said Tom, handing me a glass of the sparkling beverage, "is something that will cheer your heart, and make you forget your great misfortune. Drink, and hope for better days."

I felt so entirely depressed in spirit, that I did not refuse the invitation, and the wine inspired me with hope and confidence that all would yet end well.

"I can't say that this resembles a very happy wedding," Tom continued, "but still I think that things might be worse. For instance, if the grumbling old earthquake had rattled the house down about our ears, and buried us twenty feet deep with rubbish, our friends wouldn't have known us when a party of Mestiza's dug us out in the morning, and picked our pockets in the bargain. Cheer up, old fellow, and have another drink of wine. Always look at the brightest side of human life, 'cos the other part is black enough, I expect, to suit the most-fastidious lover of the sombre."

Allen and myself remained in deep thought while Tom rattled off his homilies, and perhaps he imagined that we were complimenting him for his flow of words, for he talked on every subject that he thought was interesting; nor did he forget to express his private opinion respecting the conduct of Catalina and Margarita in deserting him without saying good night — an omission that he took very much to heart.

"I've hit it!" said Allen, suddenly, starting up.

"Hit what?" demanded Tom, in astonishment, looking round the room for an enemy with a broken head.

"Why, the manner in which Donna Teresa has disappeared."

"Then I should advise you to hit the parties who carried her off. But let us hear what you have to say on the subject, and if one bottle of champagne can throw light on the matter, what may we not expect by the time two are drank?"

I motioned to Allen to continue his remarks, for I knew his ability for investigation, and had confidence in his judgment.

"The lady never left those steps willingly," said Allen, after a pause; "and to speak candidly, I thought I heard a female scream while we were busy with the horses; but I supposed that the sound came from the street, and that some woman was calling upon the saints to save her from a violent death. Screams are so common during the continuance of a shock, that they excite but little attention; but you will never make me believe that Donna Teresa would have been so alarmed as to forget her husband and rush into the street, and take refuge on board a passing banco. There was force used, and quick work they made of it, or I'm much mistaken."

"But who are the parties who would dare to commit such an outrage?" I demanded.

"That question time will answer, but at present I cannot. She may have been kidnapped by Mestizas, anxious for a large reward, or her late husband's relatives, fearful that she was about to bestow her hand and fortune upon a foreigner and a heretic, or, worse than all, the holy Father Juan may have had a hand in the matter, and if he did, our work will be long and arduous before we ever see the light of her handsome face again. Of one thing, however, we must be careful."

"Well, what is it?" asked Tom, cutting the wire of a champagne bottle.

Before he had time to reply, we heard a footstep on the stairs. Not a light, elastic step, like a lady's, but a heavy one, as though the body which it bore was wearied with toil. Thinking that some one had arrived with news from my wife, I rushed to the staircase, and saw Father Benventuro toiling up the steps, his robes covered with mud and water, and his peculiar-shaped hat looking as though it had been used for a paddle to guide a banco through the streets.

"Father Benventuro!" I exclaimed in astonishment.

"Yes, son, what there is of me — a mixture of mud, water, and a little weak flesh. The saints forgive me, and all here; but had I not heard that cork fly from the champagne bottle, I should have dropped in the court-yard from weariness. You have not emptied the bottle, I hope. If you have, my curse shall be upon you."

Tom snatched a full goblet of the wine from the table, and held it to the padre's mouth. He drained the glass at a breath, and then sighed because it was empty.

"A thousand thanks," he said. "The curse shall be changed to a blessing, and prayers for your welfare, provided, of course, you can find me a bit to eat, and a few more drops of something to drink."

"Water, of course, you mean," Allen said, pretending to pour some of that fluid from a decanter.

"Avaunt, thou scoffer!" cried the padre, in melodramatic style. "Look at me and see if I have not had water enough to last me a lifetime. What was it ever made for except to drown unbelievers? and I tell you that one of the faithful came near sharing a heretic's fate this night."

"Have you seen—"

At my emotion the priest looked up astonished.

"You're a smart bridegroom," he said. "Why in the name of the saints ain't you abed and asleep, as every well-conducted husband should be, on his wedding night? You didn't let the shock of a petty earthquake destroy your nuptial happiness? or, have you and your wife quarrelled so soon? and did she turn you out of the room to feast with these revellers?"

I gave the padre a brief account of the disappearance of Teresa, and he listened to the recital in breathless astonishment.

"More of that cussed Jesuit's work, he muttered," as I con-eluded; and then he began to ponder on what had been told him, his meditations only interrupted by sighs.

"Well," said Allen, "do you intend sitting there like a blessed old elephant, and do nothing but mumble and groan, and shake your head as though there was something in it. If you can enlighten us, do so, for you look as mysterious as a Chinaman in a Joss house, or a woman possessed of a secret."

"My dear children," Benventuro replied, "I think that I can account for the disappearance of Donna Teresa in a most satisfactory manner; for did you not tell me that the holy Father Juan, whose devotion to his own interests is unparalleled in the annals of the church, has hovered around here this night, and even accompanied the lady to this house for the sake of breaking off a match that was sure to lessen his influence, and destroy a project that he has long cherished? Now, if Father Juan has been here, and was compelled to leave the premises contrary to his will, you may rest assured that Father Juan was concerned in the lady's disappearance."

"Impossible!" I cried; "the priest would not have dared commit such an outrage."

"My son," replied the padre, with the faintest possible smile of contempt, "you little know what a Jesuit is capable of doing, when prompted by malice and a desire for revenge. Father Juan is a good man, but he sometimes acts hastily."

"If he has dared to lay violent hands upon Teresa," I exclaimed, "he shall suffer for it most dearly, even if I have to penetrate the walls of his convent, and tear him from an altar."

"Hear the man!" cried the priest, with a contemptuous laugh, which instantly disappeared when he thought how closely we were bound together. "That is a fair specimen of American braggadocio, and I suppose, if I was not here to guide and direct you, that you would butt your head against every stone wall in Manila, and then cry at the wounds inflicted. It is not the way we people in Manila conduct business, because we have a more sure and perfect method of accomplishing our ends."

"And pray how is that?" I asked, with a slight sneer, as a recompense for his smile of contempt.

"You will have to wait for events, that's certain," replied the padre; "but I don't counsel idleness. You must work, but in secret. Let me have a glass of wine, and I'll explain a little more fully."

The wine was passed to him, and the good man was careful to help himself largely, and then to forget to return the bottle.

He continued: —

"If you complained to the captain general that you were married to the richest heiress in the city, and without his consent, it's quite probable that he would rejoice at the disappearance of the lady; for the count is jealous of his power, and would fear that you might take occasion to remove your wife's wealth from the island as soon as possible. That, I need not tell you, is a matter which concerus him deeply. Again, if you should hint that I performed the ceremony, it's probable that your friend would be stripped of his robe of office, and pass a few of his days in a place where a man has to diet or starve. That portion of the programme I should object to decidedly, because I am not calculated to live on bread and water, and fresh air and sunshine are so very pleasant. The only thing that I have to rely upon is the favor of the archbishop, and he must have weighty reasons for standing between me and executive wrath. You understand me, I suppose, for I can't be very explicit, under the circumstances. We must make the best of the affair, and find out where the lady is concealed, and then use craft to recover her. This I am confident we can do if we are careful, and use our mother wit to advantage. But there must be no outcry and coufusion, or our search will be delayed."

"But why can't we present ourselves at the convent of St. Sebastian, and demand the lady?" I asked.

"Because she is not there, and indeed we don't know that Father Juan was concerned in her removal. If he has her, he has her safe under lock and key; but I don't think he would be likely to take her to the convent. It don't seem to me to be Jesuitish enough. He is as cunning as a fox, and knows how to work with but little noise. It's quite probable that he waited near the house, after he was excluded, watched the whole of your operations, and when he saw that Donna Teresa was left alone, he hailed a passing banco, and hired the Mestizo to assist him to remove her as speedily as possible. While the earthquake lasted, she would be half dead with fright, and be incapable of offering much resistance. And while I am speaking on the subject, I am inclined to think the very banco that brought me here carried Teresa away; for the fellows grumbled when I recompensed them with my blessing, and said that a priest had paid them liberally for half an hour's work. Men who are incapable of appreciating my blessing must be bad, and capable of committing any act."

" Then our best plan is to find the banco men, who brought you here, and see if your surmises are correct. A bribe will open their mouths, even if Father Juan has ordered them closed. An ounce of gold possesses rare attractions for a Mestizo," Allen said.

Before there was a chance for further remarks, my cook, looking as though he had been ducked in a horse-pond, made his appearance, and close behind him followed my boy.

"The saints be praised," exclaimed the cook; "our master and his friends are alive and well. Our prayers were of some avail."

"Why, you impudent knaves," cried Allen, "do you mean to say that you stopped running long enough to repeat a prayer for any one excepting yourself?"

"*Si, senor*," returned the fellow, with a look that was intended to be quite convincing; "we thought of but you and your safety, and tried to hire a carriage to return to the house, but we could not offer money enough."

"Now, the truth of the matter is," the priest exclaimed, "these vagabonds left the house at the first shock, and they thought of none but themselves, and I doubt if they stopped running until they reached the road leading to Santa Mesa. I should discharge them for lying."

"In the name of the saints, don't do that," exclaimed the servants in alarm; "we have been very faithful to our master, and stolen nothing. The next time that an earthquake occurs, we will remain in the house until we get permission to leave."

As I knew that the rascals were as honest as they could afford to be, and remain Mestizos, I told them to stay, and prepare some strong coffee without delay — an order that they obeyed with alacrity. While this was under way, the priest took me one side.

"Guillermo," he said, "we have been defeated in our schemes, but we shall yet prove a match for the enemy. Our bargain holds good, you know; but owing to the expense which I shall incur, you couldn't increase your donation to me about five thou sand dollars — could you? Of course I don't demand it; but think of the dangers I shall be exposed to in working for your good. Five thousand dollars is not much for one like you, who will be worth more than a million."

"Find my wife, and you shall have no cause to grumble," I said, evading the main question; but the priest seemed satisfied, and shook my hand with renewed good feeling. I was about to turn away, when my companion detained me.

"You must go to the residence of Donna Teresa this morning, and make inquiries regarding her. She has an aunt, you know, who takes charge of her house and affairs while absent. Ask the old lady if she has heard of her niece, and pretend that Donna Teresa disappeared in a mysterious manner; but don't mention Father Juan's name on any account, for we know not whom to trust. Be as unconcerned as possible, and appear as though it was merely a whim of the lady to be thus absent. You understand me?"

I nodded an affirmative answer.

"Then go and take your morning bath while the coffee is preparing, and be sure to erase those lines of care which I see upon your face. Dress gayly, and report to us the result as soon as possible."

I followed the priest's advice, and by the time I had bathed and dressed, the coffee was ready, and its strength and exhilarating qualities were quite acceptable, after the night of agitation and distress which I had undergone.

While Allen, Tom, and the padre threw their forms upon lounges, for the purpose of obtaining a little repose, I left the house, and wended my way towards the splendid residence of Donna Teresa. It was situated upon the left bank of the Pasig, just above the bridge, and on the Birondo side; for her husband, when alive, had an eye to money, and as he was largely engaged in commerce, he could not carry on his contracts very readily without free access to his agents at all hours, day and night. For that reason he had built and furnished a house on the trading side of the city, some distance from the aristocratic part of Manila, which is surrounded by walls and draw-bridges, and is strongly fortified. In Manila proper no foreigner can reside, or even sleep, without permission of the governor general; and at eleven at night up go the draw-bridges, and all communication with the outer world is cut off until sunrise the next day. Of course such restrictions would interfere with the avocations of a merchant, and Don Arturo had wisely turned his back upon the aristocracy for the sake of adding to his wealth; and by the act he had not lost caste, as might have been expected, but had retained his position up to the time of his death. Much of his influence, however, was due to his wife, whose pure blood was acknowledged even by the titled rulers of the island.

The house of Donna Teresa was surrounded by a high wall, which also enclosed a garden beautifully laid out with walks and arbors. All the fruit trees indigenous to the country were to be found in the garden, bearing their rich burdens every month in the year; and as fast as one variety of fruit was plucked from a tree, a fresh supply of blossoms would appear, and quickly arrive at maturity. The mango, one of the most delicious fruits that grow in the East, was there found in profusion, and in a state of perfection; oranges were more famous for quality than their quantity, and grew to an enormous size, and were the envy of every gardener in Manila. In fact, the garden was more like a miniature paradise, in beauty, than any earthly abode; and so I used to regard it when I had my Eve, in the person of Donna Teresa, by my side.

I reached the court-yard leading to Donna Teresa's house. The old porter was standing at the entrance, smoking his paper cigar with an air of unconcern that led me to hope the lady was safe within her castle.

"Good morning, senor," the old man said, raising his hat with great respect; for I was a favorite of his by virtue of certain pieces of gold which I had given him at various times, and therefore he entertained an affection for me because it was for his interest to do so; "the saints have you in their keeping."

"Is Donna Teresa at home?" I asked, with as firm a voice as possible.

"She is not, senor. She left the house last evening for the theatre, and has not returned. Neither has her carriage. It is probable that she drove to her country-seat at the conclusion of the performance. We have had a wretched night, senor; I have had no sleep, and one of my game cocks is dead. By the mass, I would not have taken two *pesos* for him."

"Is Senora Raquel at home?" I asked, meaning Teresa's aunt.

"She is at home, but it is because she could not get away By the saints, senor, it was as much as I could do to hold her, she kicked so when the earth shook. But the saints defend me Here she comes, for I hear her voice."

CHAPTER VIII.

TERESA'S AUNT. — HER IDEAS AND CONFESSIONS. — HOW THE SEARCH PROCEEDED, AND WHAT WAS THE RESULT.

"Pedro! Pedro!" I heard the old duenna exclaim from the top of the first stairs.

"I am here, senora," Pedro found heart to reply; but he didn't seem very eager to face the lady.

"I don't see what good there is in earthquakes, when they don't swallow up those who make themselves generally disagreeable," the old man muttered, throwing away his cigar, and beginning to sweep the dirt from the front of the yard.

"O, you are here — are you?" the old lady asked, as she came in sight. "I suppose I might have screamed myself to death, and you would take care to answer only at the last moment. If you can get a man to talk with, and listen to your stories, it's little work that you will perform night or day; the saints preserve us, but you seem to prefer the conversation of the ungodly to that of the good. Out upon you for a lazy drone, not worth the food that you eat."

"Ah, senora, did I not run to your assistance last night, at the first shock of the earthquake?" asked Pedro.

"You ran for the wine-vault, thou consumer of good liquor; and had I not called you, ay, and a number of times at that, it's little you would have thought of attending to me, you coward."

"Yes, but I remained with you, senora, until all danger was passed, although my body will bear witness that I was badly used while the earth shook," replied Pedro, somewhat bluntly.

"What does the varlet mean?" she demanded, turning to me, as though I had a hand in the matter.

I could not reply, but nodded to Pedro to continue his defence. The fellow grew more confident, and retorted.

"Why, senora, when you lay upon your back, and kicked worse than the new carriage horse, I feared that you would injure or kill yourself; so I attempted to raise your body from the floor; but the saints pardon me, it was impossible, for your feet struck the pit of my stomach ten times in a minute, and knocked the wind out of my body faster than it could enter. God be praised that I am alive at the present time."

"Why, thou impudent varlet, I have a great desire to turn you into the street and have you beaten for falsehoods. This comes from associating with heretics. The saints deliver us; but no wonder we have earthquakes and sickness. I'll speak to my niece of your boldness, and then we will see how you will deport yourself."

"That is what I have made my appearance so early for," I said, breaking in upon her volubility. "I desire also to speak with Donna Teresa."

"Well, so do I, but I can't," the old lady rejoined, rather tartly.

"She is not at home, then," I said.

"No, she is not at home, and has not been here all night. There's pretty goings on nowadays. I wonder what Don Arturo would say if he was alive. The poor man is dead and buried, and happy enough he ought to be when he thinks of his blessed condition. I am sure that I sometimes wish I was with the saints."

Old Pedro took occasion to turn his back, and to express by his face, that he really wished the saints were encumbered with her.

"What women want to run after men for, and heretics at that, I can't see. You needn't tell me, I ain't blind; although I pretend to be sometimes. I can see what's going on as well as other folks, and let me tell you, I think it's a mean piece of business."

Having thus emphatically delivered her opinion, she looked me full in the face to see if I was annihilated; but finding that I was not, she prepared for another outburst, but I interrupted her.

"Pardon me, senora," I said, quite calmly; "but I did not come here to argue with you on subjects of marriage or religion. I came in search of Donna Teresa."

"And dare you tell me that you don't want her to marry you?" the old lady exclaimed.

"That question I am not bound to answer," I replied, with perfect good nature.

"But I know your motives; and let me tell you that sooner than marry a Protestant, I'd dig my eyes out."

"My dear senora," I asked, "has any one been tampering with your virgin affections that you are so bitter?"

"I am told, senor," cried Pedro, with a malicious grin, "that thirty years since a gay young Protestant laid siege to the senora's heart, and captured it, and that both were the envy of the young people in Manila, for their grace and beauty. It's but three days since my uncle was speaking of the matter, and wondering whether Senora Raquel could dance the Bolero as gracefully as in former times."

The change that came over the withered and sour face of the lady was wonderful to behold. Pedro had awakened recollections of her youthful days, when her heart was sought by the young and brave, and when a wave of her hand was sufficient to drive away or collect a crowd of admirers. There was truth in the old porter's words. She had loved an American, thirty years before, and if report spoke not false, he had loved her most devotedly. He proposed marriage, but she did not care to listen to the subject from one whose religion she had been taught to despise. But love was more powerful than prejudice, and after a long suit the American obtained her solemn promise that she would consent to a secret union, and that both should then make efforts to get some priest to solemnize the nuptials, as well as the American consul, who was willing to do his part.

Before the project was carried out, the American was attacked with that awful scourge in a warm climate, the small-pox, and died after a week's sickness. He was buried near Santa Mesa, at the senora's particular request, and regularly once a week for many years she visited his grave, for her grief was terrible at his sudden death, and many months elapsed before she made her appearance in society. That, of course, happened long before Teresa was born, and when her first husband was comparatively a young man.

She never married, although she had many brilliant offers before her beauty began to wither, and her temper grow harsh. There were times, however, when she liked to talk of her young days, and express regret for the happiness that she had lost; and by Pedro's forethought he had struck the auspicious moment for opening the fountains of her memory, and altering her humor to a conciliatory one.

"I am changed, Pedro, I am changed," she said, with a smile; "and for many years I have not danced. There was a time when I could excel the belles of Manila, but that was many years since. The last time that I danced the Bolero was at the governor's palace, and his excellency was pleased to say that never in Spain did he see anything to equal it. I was young, then, Pedro; I was quite young."

"You speak as though you were old at the present time," I said, feeling that she expected me to say something agreeable. "I know of many ladies who do not possess your elastic step and bright eyes, although they claim to have seen but sixteen summers."

"It's quite probable, senor, for the girls are degenerating every year; and even my niece, Teresa, fair as you think her, will not possess my good looks by the time she's twenty years older. Beauty withers. Beauty withers. More's the pity."

I had my private opinion on the subject, but I did not express it, for I desired the friendship of the lady, and was anxious to have her assistance in the matter which I had in hand.

"I love young people," Raquel continued, "and love to see them happy; but they think that I'm cross and obstinate, and take no pains to secure my good will. They call me an old maid, as though that was something criminal or laughable, and when I lose my temper all smile. You have done so frequently," she added, addressing me; and I could not deny the soft impeachment.

"I will never do it again," I said, most sincerely.

"Then we will be friends henceforth, even if you are a Protestant. The saints forgive me; I never loved but one man, and he was a foreigner and a heretic."

She extended her thin, wrinkled hand, and I did not disdain to bend my head and imprint a kiss upon it, and when I looked up saw that her eyes were filled with tears, and that her face had lost its austere expression.

"I think that you are a good young man," she said, with a smile; "and I know that you will make Teresa a nice husband. She loves you, or she would not torment you as she does, and you must love her, or I have lost all faith in men's eyes. Let not your religion stand in each other's way, for toleration will overcome that objection."

"Alas, senora! you talk to one who does not hesitate to acknowledge his love; but I fear that Teresa is lost to me forever."

"How?" demanded the old lady, in astonishment. "Has any accident happened to her? She was away from home last night, but I supposed that she had gone to her country-seat, fearing the earthquake."

I saw that Pedro was listening with greedy ears to the conversation, and I was not disposed to enlighten him in regard to the doings of the preceding night. With all the grace of a modern cavalier, I begged for a few moments' private conversation, and the lady willingly signified her consent. She extended her hand, and I led her up the broad staircase to the sitting-room where I had passed so many days in the society of Don Arturo and Teresa, listless and unambitious of everything except a smile from the latter.

"You are a stranger to the house," she said, as she motioned me to a seat, "and I began to fear that we had lost you forever. A lover's quarrel, I suppose. They frequently happen before marriage. Be careful that they seldom occur afterwards."

"You said you approved of my passion for your niece," I remarked, with a close scrutiny of her face, to see if it was possible for her to put on a semblance of friendship that she did not feel. I remembered the warning that Father Benventuro had given me, and determined to be cautious.

"I will answer you frankly," she returned, "my feelings have undergone a great change within a few weeks, and I no longer look upon you as a fortune-hunter. Marry my niece by all means, and I think that much happiness will spring from the union."

I could but bow to the compliment. She looked honest and sincere, and I determined to trust her. Before I could touch upon the subject nearest my heart, the senora continued,—

"Thirty years since I was engaged to be married to a countryman of yours, and a Protestant. He was a noble-looking man, handsome, and generous to a fault, so there is but little cause to wonder why I loved him dearly, and that he loved me. We should have been married in spite of the prejudices of friends, had he not sickened and died. Our plans were well laid, and Father Juan, who was then poor and in want of money, agreed to perform the ceremony for a certain consideration. This fact has bound me to the father for many years, even knowing, as I do, that he is not favorably disposed towards you, for reasons that are purely mercenary and selfish. He is powerless, however, for Teresa is wilful, and will have her own way."

I no longer hesitated to reveal to Donna Raquel the proceedings of the night, even to the visit of the strange ladies, although I took good care to say that they were friends of Tom, and in no way connected with me. I told her of the marriage by Father Benventuro, of the earthquake, and the disappearance, and then I pictured my unhappiness and anxiety. The old lady heard me without interruption, although she did manifest some surprise when I alluded to the matrimonial part of the story; but I thought that she rather approved of it than otherwise, as it reminded her of the adventurous days of her youth.

"You are really married, then, the saints be praised?" she asked.

"Father Benventuro tells me so, although I have no cause to rejoice thereat, for the little that I have seen of married life has been far from pleasant."

"Poor child!" the old lady said, soothingly, "I hope that there are better days in store for you, and that the great happiness which you so much desire may soon be within your reach. I should have preferred a priest a little different from Benventuro's principles, for he is reputed unscrupulous and cunning, and I was never wholly satisfied with the investigation of Don Arturo's death, which occurred at his convent of San Pedro. Still, as I know that he hates Father Juan, and that Father Juan detests him, he may have lent you his assistance out of spite. Time will reveal the workings of their hearts; but I tell you, sincerely, that neither of them is as pure in mind and principle as I hope you are."

Of course I could only blush and murmur some indistinct expressions, which were not noticed.

"Now, in this matter I intend to stand your friend, for, the saints be praised, I have still a feeling at my heart that warms at the sight of youth and domestic happiness. But my opinions I must keep to myself, for we must meet craft by craft, and if Father Juan has Teresa in his power, we must discover her place of residence by stratagem, for we cannot obtain it by force or kindness. I shall have to pretend for him sentiments of friendship that I do not feel, for I now know what his plans are and his expectations. My poor niece is not fit for a convent, for she is impulsive and headstrong, and would soon break her heart fretting for liberty. Poor child! poor child! I wish that I was able to see her before me now."

The old lady was so deeply affected, that she was obliged to call a servant to bring a glass of cordial, which she was very fond of, and which she contended was a certain specific against the jungle fever. Of course I was compelled to join her, and praise the liquor, as it really deserved to be; and by such a course did not lose ground in her heart.

"Father Juan loves this cordial dearly, and always asks for a glass if we forget our usual hospitality. I shall see him before many hours, and perhaps by the influence of the wine his heart may expand sufficiently to enlighten me in relation to his secrets. I have no doubt in my mind that he has Teresa in his power; but I fear that he won't be ready to acknowledge it. We must hope for the best, however, and keep him in ignorance of the marriage. Now go, and the saints be with you. Call and see me to-morrow, in the evening if possible, and report progress. Keep your stout heart pure and strong, and God will aid you."

She extended her thin, wrinkled hand, and I kissed it, and left the house as heavy hearted as when I entered. Even Pedro, the porter, seemed to pay me more respect on account of the grief which he could not help noticing upon my face; and as he removed his hat, he hoped the saints would shower any quantity of blessings upon my head, give me long life and perfect health for the four-real piece which I tossed him. A piece of silver is a cheap way of obtaining blessings, and I wondered sometimes if the Mestiza's prayers, which seemed so sincere, were ever heard.

There was one place which I still desired to visit, and yet I dreaded to do so. It was the Morgue house of Manila; that common receptacle, where Catholic and Protestant, Mestizo and Chinaman, soldier and sailor, were conveyed to await recognition in case of sudden or violent death in the streets, or at the numerous drinking houses, where sometimes bloody fights occurred, and which only terminated by the arrival of armed soldiers, the police of the city.

The house of the dead was usually the scene of considerable excitement after an earthquake, as those who had lost friends were always fearful of the worst, and rushed in crowds towards it, for the purpose of satisfying their fears, and sometimes hopes. The building was situated near the cigar factory, and was not a substantial brick or stone house, but built of bamboo, one story high, and thatched with leaves like common huts.

To this melancholy place I determined to go, for the purpose of being assured that my wife's body was not there; for I still had a fear that she might have been drowned while attempting to escape, and while bewildered at the earthquake. The distance was not great; so I determined to walk to the house and not call a carriage, many of which stood in the street waiting for fares, while their drivers or postilions smoked or slept upon the boxes.

I found the house of the dead, as I expected, surrounded by an excited crowd of people, males and females, children and old men, and all kept at a distance from the place by a line of bayonets, which sometimes were made to prick the flesh if the excited rabble pressed forward too rapidly, or were not respectful to their masters. Only a few people at a time were allowed within the enclosure, and even these were closely questioned by a fierce-looking orderly sergeant, before permission was granted, for the man knew that two thirds of those present were attracted to the spot by mere curiosity, and that to get sight of the dead they would lie, and even steal, if the latter crime was necessary.

For a few minutes I remained standing in front of the men, almost determined not to enter, yet anxious to satisfy myself that Teresa was not there. I saw a few Mestizas pass in and out with the most stoical indifference, so it was impossible to tell by their looks whether they had lost a relative or an enemy.

"I beg your pardon, senor," said the sergeant, touching his cap, "for disturbing your reflections; but if you fear to enter alone, and see the dead, I will go with you."

The man supposed that I was timid, and that the sight of death would alarm me.

"Has the senor lost a friend?" he asked, before I could convince him that I was not so timid as he supposed me.

"I have," I replied.

"Was it a male or female?" he demanded.

"A lady," I answered.

"There are several Mestiza girls in the house, but only one that was handsome and worthy to be a cavalier's companion. Will you go with me, and see the corpse?"

I consented to do so, when the soldier rapped the shins and backs of half a dozen natives who stood in his way and didn't move quick enough, and entered the building. The fellow supposed that I was looking for the remains of a mistress, who was killed during the earthquake, and the circumstance of a European living with a Mestiza girl was too common to excite comment or particular notice. In fact, most foreigners who reside there form a *Maison* with native women, and they preside over the household as though regularly married. There are a few exceptions to the rule, to be sure; but humanity shows itself in the East Indies as well as in the Atlantic cities.

"Here is a fellow," said the sergeant, touching, with his rattan, a body, "who got jammed in between two canoes, and so died. His body floated to the shore, and was landed in a court-yard. Examine him, and you will see that his ribs are bruised and his back broken."

I declined the office, and the soldier passed on.

"There is the Mestiza girl that I spoke to you about. She was found drowned in the court-yard of an English merchant's house. She lived with him as his mistress for one year, and proud enough she was of her position. It's a little singular that she should have drowned in two feet of water, for I have seen her swim like a deer; and many a time has she crossed the Pasig with a strong current running down stream, sufficient to tax the arms of a stout boatman to make headway in his banco. I wonder if the arrival of the Englishman's wife had anything to do with the girl's death."

We passed the lifeless form of the girl, and then took a quick survey of the remaining bodies; but Teresa was not there, and I turned to depart.

The sergeant touched his cap, and was about to move away, when I slipped a dollar into his hand, which called forth expressions of good will, so that he accompanied me to the entrance of the square.

I turned to leave the spot, when a Mestiza girl, not more than fifteen years of age, appeared as though desirous of speaking to me.

" What do you desire?" I asked, calling the girl to me; the more readily, I believe, because she was remarkable for her good looks, and fine, plump form.

" Has the senor visited the house of the dead?" she asked.

I replied in the affirmative.

" I have waited here all the morning, senor, for the purpose of visiting the Morgue, to see if my sister was there; but the crowd is so great, and the soldiers so cross, that I can't get in. Will the senor tell me if there is a girl there who resembled me, when living?"

I compared the features of the Mestiza with the Englishman's late mistress, and was compelled to confess that there was a strong resemblance between them.

" There is no doubt but it is Sara," she said, after I had given her the information. " I was told that her body was there, but I wished to be certain. The saints be praised; she will have Christian burial."

I started towards my house; but to my surprise the girl continued to walk by my side, as though she had no thoughts of parting company so soon.

" Why do you not return to the house of the dead, and claim the body of your sister?" I inquired.

" Why should I?" she asked, with a look of surprise; " the priests will see that she has Christian burial, and what more could I ask?"

" Have you no money to pay for burial?" I asked.

" No, senor, not a medio."

" But where are your parents?"

" My mother is dead, and my father is a bancario. I seldom see him, senor, for he spends his time upon the water and in the wine shops," she answered, with charming simplicity.

" Suppose I should give you money to bury the body of your sister — would you do so?"

" Of what use would it be, senor? The priests will attend to her, and give her the benefit of their prayers."

"Your sister did not live at home?" I said, finding that the girl was determined to walk by my side through the streets.

"No, senor," she answered, without the least confusion; "she lived with a rich merchant, who gave my father ten dollars for her two years since. She had many dresses, plenty to eat, and smoked nice paper cigars. She was very happy at her good fortune in attracting the attention of the Ingles. I hope that the saints will permit me to be as successful."

Here was a confession with a vengeance, and made to a young man supposed to be susceptible to female influences. But I thought of my lost wife, and determined to resist temptation for her sake.

"Do you mean that you would be willing to live with a foreigner, in case he should ask you?" I demanded.

"Why not, senor? The girls are petted and well dressed, and don't have to work for a little rice and a few plantains for food. If we should marry we would be ill treated, and have to support our husbands by washing from morning till night on the banks of the river. Besides, I like the Ingles — they are brave and rich."

I saw that, like her more refined sisters of other climes, she was willing to sell all for gold; and there were plenty of foreigners in Manila who would not have scrupled to accept the barter, but I did not know how I could prevent it.

"Don't the priests reprove you for having such thoughts?" I asked.

"I don't know, senor, because I never confessed my thoughts to them. I only tell them just as little as possible, so that I shan't get a severe penance. When my sister went to the merchant's house, she gave the priest a dollar, and he pardoned her for the wrong she had done. Couldn't I do the same?"

I returned no answer, but walked by her side in silence, thinking of her strong desire to lead a life of shame, and wondering if I could not save her.

"Senor," she said, looking timidly in my face, "don't you want me?"

I shook my head in the negative.

"I am so sorry," she answered with a sigh; "I have no home, and no one to care for me. If you will give me shelter I will love you dearly."

"But I am married," I replied.

"Then let me wash your clothes and mend them, or I will embroider your shirts and make new ones, for I have done such things. If you don't like me, I will leave any time that you desire. Besides I can help your wife dress, and take care of the children."

"But my wife is away now, and I have no children."

"But she will return, and the saints will bless her with a little one."

There was no withstanding the appeal. She had touched me with a random shot, and I was compelled to surrender without a struggle.

"You may go home with me," I said, "and stay there until my wife returns; but remember, I shall keep a strict watch over you, and if I see any signs of wickedness I shall send you away. Your duties will be light, and I shall pay you a certain sum per week for attending to them. But you must understand me that you are to occupy one part of the house at night, while I occupy another."

She readily agreed to the proposition, and I thought, as she walked by my side, what an acquisition she would be to Teresa's household, if I could preserve her purity and good looks until my wife's return. At any rate, it was worth something to take her from the reach of the tempters who thronged the city, and were ever ready to pounce upon the young and thoughtless; and I knew that Teresa would thank me for it, after she fully understood my motives.

I reached the house about eleven o'clock in the forenoon, just in time for breakfast, which was all ready for me. Father Benventuro had made his toilet, and put on his robes, cleared of their stains by my servants, who had labored while the padre slept, while Allen and Tom both looked the better for a change of clothing, which the latter had supplied by sending to his hotel during my absence.

"We have been waiting nearly an hour for you," cried the priest, as soon as he saw us coming up the stairway; "I'm half starved, for I've eaten nothing of any consequence since yesterday."

At this instant Gracia, the new servant, made her appearance, and was saluted with a roar of astonishment from the graceless scamps.

"Here's a model husband for you! He starts to look for his wife, and not finding her, brings home a substitute. And faith, she isn't bad looking, either, for a Mestiza. Come here and kiss me."

The girl looked at me and then at the priest, as though uncertain how to act.

"Do you wish to salute the holy father?" I asked.

"No, senor; I had rather kiss you. He is too fat."

"He has trained her well for so short a time," Benventuro said. "Who would have thought that he was such a sly young dog? Where did you pick her up? What did you pay for her?" and other questions were propounded, until I thought that it was about time to relieve their minds.

"Gentlemen," I said, "this girl I have taken to my house for the purpose of preserving her purity, and because she is friendless and homeless. I know your thoughts, and believe me, they are ill-founded. The respect and love which I entertain for my wife will enable me to be a safe guardian to this girl."

"O, gammon! that's all wasted on us," was Tom's exclamation; and as I knew that any assertion of mine would be regarded with suspicion, in case I was too eager to refute all that was hinted at, I said no more to the company, but called my boy, and gave him directions to prepare Gracia a room, and to look to her for assistance in taking care of the house, not only during my absence, but while I was at home.

The orders rather astonished my friends, and they began to comprehend me, although they often wondered how a man could remain pure in a country where immorality is not regarded as a crime, and where wife and mistress often reside under the same roof, and fathers barter for a daughter's virtue.

"Gentlemen," I said, "if you have finished your interrogations, we will eat breakfast."

"We have not a word to say in opposition to that project," said the priest, delighted at the sight of the well-loaded table, my cook having done his best. "For these blessings," cried the padre, as he tucked a napkin under his chin, "let us be thankful, and wish for more. Amen. May the saints give us good appetites and strong digestion. Hand me the bottle, for I am parched with thirst."

The bottle was passed without delay, and the holy father was then in his element. He forgot all earthly care while feeding, and nothing but an earthquake could have shaken him from the table.

But all pleasures must terminate, and at length the priest was compelled to lean back in his chair, and acknowledged that even his stomach was incapable of receiving more solids; but for liquids he professed himself competent to drink all night, if any one was disposed to keep him company.

"You talk of drinking all day and night, and yet you know that we have an engagement at San Pedro Macati, to witness a cock-fight to-morrow," said Allen, who was disposed to be light with the bottle.

"Ah, curse it! I forgot that," was the rather irreverent response; "I have two ounces bet upon my favorite cock, and if I should lose, I'll curse the whole Mestizo race. I have lost all the revenue of the convent the past two weeks, and unless I win, the nuns will have to suck their fingers for nourishment, for food they'll not get from me."

"Then it is necessary that you should keep sober, for you are a reckless better after dinner," Allen said. "Come, my banco is at the landing by this time, waiting to carry us to Santa Mesa. I invite all present to go with me, and promise that you shall have a good dinner, and a bottle of excellent wine."

"Hurrah!" cried the priest; "that last consideration is entitled to much weight; I go with Senor Allen, and will never leave him until his wine turns sour, or he becomes a good Catholic."

"I go with you!" cried Tom.

"And you, Guillermo?"

"Alas! I must remain, and search for my wife. I am in no mood for revels, and should mar your enjoyment."

"Nonsense!" cried the priest; "you do no good here, and might do much harm. Go with us, and I'll see that your interests are looked after while absent."

"Perhaps the Mestiza girl might object," suggested Tom, with a wink.

"O, if he prefers her society to ours, we have nothing to say," they shouted in chorus.

I could no longer refuse, for if I had remained at home, a bad interpretation of my conduct would have ensued. So, for the sake of my reputation and that of the young and handsome girl whose protector I had suddenly become, I was obliged to leave the city with my guests. Not every one would have acted as I did; but a pure conscience is now my reward.

The resolution, which I had formed for the purpose of leaving Manila for a few days, cost me a bitter pang; for I thought that the time could be much more usefully employed in searching for my wife. The assurances of the priest and Allen that it was useless for me to stir in the matter at present, as I was doubtless surrounded by spies who would report to Father Juan and his satellites every movement that I made, at length had the effect of restoring me to a feeling of composure which I had not enjoyed for some time. I hastily put a few articles that I should need into a carpet-bag, locked up my private room, and was giving instructions to the boy regarding his conduct during my absence, when Gracia interposed.

"Will the senor be gone long?" she asked, with every appearance of sorrow at my contemplated absence.

"I shall return to the city to-morrow night, but only for a few hours," I replied.

"I shall be very unhappy during your absence," she said; and her words produced a shout from the priest and Tom which amazed me exceedingly.

"By the saints," muttered the priest, "it's quite refreshing to hear such innocence and simplicity in these selfish days. Bring her along, Guillermo, if you think that she can't survive your loss for a few days."

"My dear child," I said, regardless of the shouts of my companions, "I did not bring you here for the purpose of winning your love; so you must not mention such a subject in future. Stay here in the house and conduct yourself in a proper manner, and you are sure of my protection as long as you do so. If you want work while I am absent from the house, the boy will show you what to do."

She held down her head, and I thought that she only restrained herself from weeping by a violent effort.

"Unless I had seen the exhibition with my own eyes, I would not have believed it. Hereafter I am astonished at nothing. An American, twenty-three years of age, refuses the advances of a damsel of fifteen. Senors, we must drink a glass of wine in honor of the miracle!" shouted the priest.

The wretches solemnly pledged each other, and even had the impudence to ask me to join them.

"Come," cried Allen, "let us hurry to the river, or Guillermo will alter his opinion, and then there will no longer be a miracle. Come, gentlemen, it's time we were on board."

We left the house in a body, and reached the banco by three o'clock, just the hour when the sun pours down the hardest, and the principal portion of the inhabitants are taking their siesta, preparatory to a good dinner, and a life of enjoyment in the evening.

The banco was large and comfortable, and while we settled our forms upon the mats which lined the bottom of the boat, while wet ones screened us overhead from the fierce rays of the sun, Allen passed around his cigar-case, and ordered his crew to shove off and commence the slow ascent of the stream, against a strong current.

"This," cried the padre, producing a bottle of wine from a pocket of his robes, and exhaling a mouthful of smoke, "is what I call comfort. Show me a finer scene than the one we are gazing at. Here is commerce, which brings us wealth; here is industry, which brings us prosperity; here is religion, which brings us happiness (pointing to the numerous churches to be seen on both sides of the river); and here is the juice of the grape, which brings us contentment."

He reached his hand out to touch the bottle, but it eluded his grasp. He turned his head a little to look for it, and saw that Allen had raised it to his mouth, and was making sad havoc with its contents.

"Avast, Satan!" shouted Benventuro; "I took that from the table for my own especial benefit, to cheer me on my way, and to sustain me in case of sickness or shipwreck. Wretch, you will be cursed in this world and the next for thus trifling with the church."

"Now, by St. Peter, but you shall not have a single drop of the wine until you give me your blessing!" cried Allen, making a motion as though to pass it to Tom.

"Heretic! why will you thus torment one of the faithful?

There is but a pint within the flask, and what is a pint compared to my appetite?"

"The blessing, or none," repeated Allen.

"You shall have it, my child — may the devil confound you;" and with this rather equivocal assurance, the bottle was handed to the priest, who clutched it with pretended eagerness, and stowed it away under his robe. "Not a sup shall one of you have from this, to pay you for the unpardonable crime of stealing from the church. Thirst, sinners, or else drink river water."

"We shall do neither, holy father. Antonio, pass the basket."

One of the crew, a young fellow with a ready smile, stopped his rowing, and from the bows passed aft a basket filled with half a dozen bottles of choice claret. The eyes of the priest brightened, and he made a sudden movement that was the means of producing his flask from beneath his robe.

"I will share with you, my children," he said; "no man should be selfish to friends, or even to his fellow-man. I contribute what I have to the common stock."

"You see, most holy father, that I was more thoughtful than you," Allen exclaimed; "I told the men, when they came after me, to put a few bottles of wine in the boat, for I suspected that I should have company. Now, not a drop do you get, unless you spin us a yarn while we are on our way to Santa Mesa."

"Is that your firm resolution?" demanded the padre.

"Unalterable as destiny," was the reply.

"But you will allow me a drop before I begin?"

"Not a drop until the yarn is commenced."

"Will you have a serious or mirthful story?"

"Mirthful, if possible; for, see, Guillermo looks as though he had lost his friends in addition to his wife."

The holy father refreshed his mouth with a long pull at his private bottle, and then commenced: —

"Were either of you ever in Cadiz, a seaport city in Spain? You were not. Then I shall not tell you what beautiful women are there, nor what excellent wine can be obtained for two reals — two articles which should always be taken into consideration, when a permanent residence is thought of by a gentleman of means and leisure. I was born in Cadiz, and in that city I first obtained my ideas of religion and pleasure. It was there I spent my boyish days; it was there I learned to love or hate, as suited my notions of independence or passion.

"When I was fifteen, I was sent to the college of St. Salvador for an education, and for the purpose of being initiated in the secrets of priesthood. It was a Jesuit college, and in its days of pride was rich; but the French, may the saints confound them, during the Peninsular war, nearly ruined its resources, and crippled its usefulness in more ways than one.

"I was no more fit to become a priest than my friend Allen, here, who would require years of probation before he could confess a person in a manner not to scandalize the church. But my parents were firm believers in my wonderful talents, and always prophesied that I would die a bishop, or something higher — what the higher meant I am unable to say. Perhaps they imagined that, as I was rather a desperate young fellow, the gallows would ultimately fall in my way. The saints forbid that such a death should happen to me, for I know of a dozen more deserving than myself of the honor. Of course I except all in the banco but the crew, and I don't care what becomes of them.

"For the first few days of my imprisonment in the college — for I thought that I might as well be in a dungeon — I passed my time lonely enough. I could look from the grated windows, and see the crowds of ladies and gentlemen passing, on horseback and in their carriages; and I thought a seat by the side of a pretty senorita, or on the back of a spirited animal, a much more pleasant place than pondering over dry books and listening to musty precepts.

"Leave of absence was only granted us once in three months, and then we were compelled to see our parents in the presence of a priest, who listened to what we said, and reported the unfavorable words that we used, if we were imprudent enough to do so. Then followed punishment in the shape of bread and water, a hard bed, and frequent application of the rod to shoulders which were tender and unused to severity.

"All of this galled my spirit; but of what use were my complaints? They were unheeded by the superior, a stern man, accustomed to bend men's minds to his own mould, and who looked upon us boys as fitting instruments to experiment with. I would have run away, but I knew that I should be brought back and punished with terrible severity; so I concluded to make the best of my situation, and repay myself for the privations when I took orders and emerged from my seclusion."

" And faithfully have you kept your word," interrupted Allen, passing a bottle of claret for the purpose of refreshing his stomach, and stimulating the padre during the recital of his story.

The priest smiled, and continued: —

" While I was pondering on the subject of my captivity, one day, a student, about my own age, named Antonio, accosted me as follows.

" ' Benventuro,' he said, ' you are thinking of the world and its follies; its wine shops and its flirting women; its vanities and its pleasures. Give up such thoughts, and consider how you can obtain the order of sanctity.'

" ' It's an order that suits me not,' I replied. ' I had much rather be a sinner than a saint.'

" ' I'm fearful that you were not intended for the church,' Antonio said, with a sigh, casting his eyes upon the floor of the chapel where we stood, waiting the arrival of a priest to give us instructions in prayers.

" ' I have been of the same opinion for many months,' I answered; ' but I dare not hint as much to the superior.'

" ' In that you show your sense, for the holy father is a man of few words, and has no patience with youth who cling to recollections of the flesh. But, after all, of what use would a free communication with the world be to us, when we have not a *peso* we can call our own?'

" ' In that you are mistaken,' I replied, sinking my voice and speaking in a whisper: " when I left my home my parents gave me twelve doubloons, and requested the amount to be expended in prayers for my success in the world. I have the money in a belt around my body, and shall keep it there until I can find a priest willing to pray for my restoration to life and its pleasures.'

" My companion's face assumed a look that betokened great interest.

" ' Would you like to expend the money?' he demanded.

" ' Yes, but not for charity or religion,' I replied; ' I have enough of both, every day, to last me a lifetime.'

" ' Bah!' he answered; ' I don't mean that the money should be given to these spying priests, or the cold-blooded superior. What say you to a glorious spree in the city, where we can revel in wine, and flirt with handsome women — dance at the masked balls, and drive jealous husbands crazy?"

"'Can this be done?' I demanded, in astonishment.

"'To be sure it can, and a glorious time we can have of it, if we are only cautious, and keep from drinking too much wine.'

"'Show me the way, for my gold is burning my flesh, and I long to get rid of it,' I answered.

"'And you will share with me in everything?' Antonio whispered.

"'Six of the doubloons are yours, if you will only lead the way to expend it.'

"'Agreed. This night you shall taste of pleasure, and know the first principles of a Jesuit's life. But you must also use a Jesuit's circumspection, and keep your tongue and thoughts under discipline. Not by word or sign must you let the priests comprehend the conversation that has passed between us. If you do, a deep cell and a damp one will receive us. Be ready, after the nine o'clock vespers, to start.'

"We separated, for just at that moment the priest entered the chapel, and had he seen us speaking together, it is quite within the limits of probability that he would have required a knowledge of our discussion; and if he could have wormed it from us, the superior might have paid us a visit in our cells — I can't call them chambers, for the doors were locked upon us at night, and iron bars were before the windows.

"I heard but little of the good man's exhortation that day, and I learned but little from the volumes put before me. The priests appeared to my eyes like huge goblets of wine, or men and women dancing. Four or five times I looked up, and saw the suspicious gaze of the superior fixed upon my countenance, and I had no means of allaying his doubts of my goodness but by counting my beads, and raising my eyes in rapt devotion to a picture of the first grand general of the order, which hung in the school-room."

"Then it appears to me," interrupted Allen, "that you were acting the hypocrite most admirably."

"Not so, my son," Benventuro replied; "I was acting the Jesuit, and very successfully, too, for one so young. I don't mind making the confession here, for I know that I am with friends — that neither of you will ever be converted to Catholicity, for your bumps of sinnership are too largely developed to believe in the true faith, and all the money that I get from you for the benefit of the church, of course must be in the way of cock-fighting — more shame for you."

"Take another pull at the bottle and a fresh cigar," Allen said, with a laugh at the confession.

"Thank you, I will indulge in both, because the tobacco calms the nerves, and the wine stimulates the brain. But to continue. I managed to contain my secret, although I thought that I should burst with the effort; and when at sundown we partook of our humble supper, a piece of bread and a cup of water, I cleverly avoided eating for fear that I should have no room for the soup, and eggs, and chicken, which I fancied I saw before me. The saints knew I was hungry enough, and had been ever since I became an inmate of the college; but I had eaten so much coarse bread that the sight of it sickened me, especially when we poor devils of students could smell the savory messes, cooked in oil and seasoned with garlic, which were being prepared for the superior after the duties of the day were over. Another reason why I refused to eat the bread was because I noticed that Antonio didn't do so, and that he made me an almost imperceptible sign to favor my appetite.

"After supper we were allowed to work in the garden attached to the college until the nine o'clock vespers; and when we had listened to a few prayers and a short address concerning the beauties of Jesuitism, we were marched to our cells and locked in, where we were generally left unmolested until four o'clock in the morning, at which time we were compelled to rise, summer and winter.

"I did not lie down to sleep that night, you may be assured, for I was all anticipation of a visit from Antonio. His cell was next to mine, and I knew he was awake from the fact that he was praying loud enough to be heard through the corridor, and if his words were a criterion, he was the most devout boy in the college. What blessings he hoped would be showered upon the superior's head! and how he roared concerning the priesthood! It would have done your heart good to have heard him. At length the spies, who were stationed in the corridor for the purpose of listening to the conversation of the students, got tired of such stuff, and left us to our fate; for you know a man can't stand everything, and they had heard enough to satisfy themselves that

Antonio was a most promising young man; and indeed he was. I have rarely seen his equal.

"About ten o'clock Antonio's prayers ceased for the want of fuel to keep them up; and in consequence of the silence that prevailed, every boy went to sleep excepting Antonio and myself. While the snoring was raging all around us, I heard some one at my door, and in a few seconds it opened, and my friend entered my cell.

"'Don't speak a loud word,' he whispered; 'if you do you will bring some of the watchers down on us, and that we shouldn't like. Take hold of my hand, and follow me.'

"'But how did you get my door open, and your own?' I asked.

"'I merely picked the locks, and when we come back I shall lock you in, and then do the same for myself. But don't stop to ask questions. We have a night of eating and drinking before us, and time is precious. You have got the money safe?'

"I had taken good care not to leave that behind.

"'Then follow me,' Antonio said, 'and mind that you tread as lightly as a cat.'

"We crept through the gloomy corridor, until we reached a small gate, that was quickly unlocked, and as quickly secured again; and in a few seconds we were in the chapel, and standing before the altar lights, which burned night and day in front of the virgin and her child. For a moment I stopped to cross myself and mutter a *pater noster;* but before the latter was finished I was pushed towards the altar by Antonio, and told to remove a piece of carpet that covered the floor where the priests were in the habit of standing when saying mass. I did as he directed, but nothing but the floor met my view.

"While I was wondering what he could mean, he motioned me back a few paces, and touched a secret spring. A panel slid back, and a flight of steps met my gaze. My companion intimated that I was expected to go down, and I obeyed him, he following and closing the panel noiselessly. We found ourselves in the most intense darkness, without a single ray of light to tell us which way to turn; but Antonio seemed familiar with the place, and no longer confined his remarks to whispers.

"'Stand where you are without moving, and I'll find a light,' he said.

"'But where are we, and what is the cause of this humid, sickening smell?' I asked.

"'We are under the chapel,' Antonio replied, 'and the smell which you complain of is not very agreeable, I must confess, because it is occasioned by the decomposition of a dozen or two priests, whose bones have been deposited here at different times within the last fifty years. I wish that the blessed saints would take them all in the course of a year, and leave us to begin the world as we please. Spain would lose nothing, while I think we should be gainers by the arrangement.'

"I didn't like the idea of standing there in the dark, surrounded by dead priests; so I begged Antonio to hurry with the light. He laughed at my timidity, and rattled at some boards until I thought the priests were struggling to life to punish us for the desecration.

"At length I heard the sound of flint and steel, and in a second afterwards a pale, flickering light, hardly relieving the gloom and darkness, appeared.

"'Here's where I keep the tools for a light, in case you should come here alone,' my companion said, raising the lid of a coffin that rested on a huge stone slab near the steps which we had descended. 'You can always find them in the coffin, because I don't think that any one would be likely to disturb them. You can see that only a few bones remain of a priest, who at one time must have been of some importance, for I see a silver plate on the wood-work; and faith I have a good mind to take it, and dispose of it to the first broker we may meet. The money would do me more good than the dead, and I have no doubt that the fellow, if alive, would thank me for my forethought.'

"As I was unused to such things, I begged Antonio to let the plate alone, promising him all the wine he could drink if he would oblige me. I think that my liberal offer had the desired effect, for he gave up his purpose, then wanted me to examine the coffins, and see how I liked their arrangement. I declined the tempting offer, and expressed a wish to get clear of such scenes as fast as possible; but my companion laughed at me for a simpleton who was afraid of the dead, when the dead were incapable of inflicting any harm.

"'The fact of it is,' said Antonio, — seating himself upon one of the stone slabs, and resting his light upon a coffin that had been covered with black velvet; but the moths and mice had made terrible work with the sombre cloth, and but little of the original material remained,—' I rather like this place. There is no restraint here. If one wishes to laugh, there is no stern-looking priest here to rebuke you for levity, and inflict penance — from malice. A man can learn more here in an hour, than from all the teachings of the superior in a year.'

" ' That may be true,' I replied; ' but all people are not constituted alike. I expect every moment to feel the cold hand of a skeleton upon my neck, and don't see any pleasure staying in a damp vault, when the wine shops are open and invite us.'

" 'By the saints, you speak truly,' Antonio said, rising and leading the way to the other end of the vault. ' Let us be moving, for my mouth is watering for a glass of Madeira and a mouthful of chicken. Keep close to me, and bend your head, or it may come in contact with a beam occasionally. Step carefully, and don't mind the rats. They won't trouble us; at least they never have showed fight to me, and I think that they are disposed to be friends.' "

"If you could, without much inconvenience to yourself and friend, get out of that vault, I should be much obliged to you, as I think you have been there long enough," Allen remarked, as the priest stopped to take another pull at the bottle, and to light a fresh cigar.

"I have no objection to that, I assure you," replied Benventuro, " for I am not one who likes to hover around the dead, unless they have left me and the church good legacies. Let me see — where was I ? "

" The rats were chasing you from the vault, I think," Allen said, with a yawn.

" O, yes; there were many disagreeable associations connected with that vault, and I afterwards learned that before the Peninsular war the place was filled with racks and thumb-screws, shower-baths and penances, and other delightful inventions for converting Pagans, Jews, and Protestants to Christianity. I suppose I could tell you reminiscences of that place, which would make your blood run cold."

" Do so then, for Heaven's sake, for I'm roasting with heat," Allen said.

The priest disdained to notice the interruption, and continued : —

"When we gained a wall, Antonio showed me a small door which would have escaped notice unless a close examination was made. The hinges were rusty, and creaked most discordantly when the door was opened; and had my companion not shaded the light with his hand, the strong draft of air would have extinguished the flame. I looked into the dark passage, but could see nothing but mould and darkness, and I drew back somewhat alarmed."

"'There is nothing to fear,' Antonio said. 'I have traversed the passage many times, and never met anything worse than a bat or a toad. But you are not to go out yet, for it would be rather inconvenient to meet with a priest belonging to the college, and have him take us before the superior. Explanations are so unpleasant at certain times!'

"'Then we are not to show ourselves in our college costume?' I asked.

"'Of course not. I should be a poor pupil to a Jesuit society, if I did not guard against such an unnecessary display of our robes. We visit the city as cavaliers, and very good looking ones we shall make, I have no doubt.'"

"How you must have changed since your youth!" Allen suggested; but the padre merely shook his fat fist at the speaker, and continued his narrative:—

"Antonio paid a second visit to a coffin that reposed in solitary grandeur near the door, and produced two tight-fitting jackets, with bell buttons and velvet trimmings, and trousers of the same material, open at the legs, and about the right size. We threw off our robes and put on the clothes without waste of time; and after I had adjusted a red sash around my waist, my companion thrust a hat upon my head, placed all of our clothing in the coffin, covered it with the lid, and gave the signal to start.

"'How did you ever discover this passage?' I asked, as we groped our way along, starting bats from their slumbers and toads from their apathy.

"'By keeping my eyes open, instead of sleeping, as many young men would have done. But to let you into the secret, I don't mind saying that a year ago I was ordered to do penance in the chapel all night. You may recollect what I was punished for. It was for throwing a loaf of bread at Pedro's head, because he said that he could write better Latin than myself. The fool, he knew no more about the dead languages than I did, and I was not intimately acquainted with verbs. However, I had violated a rule of the college, and I was punished by being locked in the chapel all night, and I was expected to repeat one hundred prayers before morning. I managed to get through with one by way of pastime, and while I was practising a new dance before the altar, I thought I heard a noise underneath the chapel; and although I have but little belief in the devil, I didn't know but there might be such an individual, and that he was in want of me. I considered that the best thing that I could do would be to get out of the way as fast as possible, for I had no notion of visiting the regions of the damned, where all but good Jesuits go.

"'I thought that the nearer to the altar I got, the safer I should be, and with a brief prayer, only extorted from me on account of fear, I hid under a lounge, and lay there with a quaking heart. In a short time, to my intense horror, I saw the floor move, then open, and a rush of cold air, laden with sickening effluvia, which, to my imagination, smelt like brimstone, filled the chapel, and convinced me that I was really to receive a visit from the devil.

"'First a head was thrust through the opening, and then a body followed slowly, as though tired with exertion. I shut my eyes to hide the dreadful sight, but for fear of consequences I remained quite still, and waited the moment when the forked tail was to be stuck into my side, and I was to be borne to other regions, where prayers and masses are of little avail. At length I found that I was unharmed, and I ventured to look up. You may imagine my surprise, Benventuro, when I saw that, instead of the devil, it was only his friend, the superior, changing his clothes; and from a cavalier's suit he gradually assumed the plain robes of the priest. He did the work very deliberately, too, as though he had been through the same operation before, and could do so again.

"'I was slightly astonished, you may well imagine, and as all fear had left me when I found that I was dealing with a natural body instead of a supernatural one, I watched the old man's motions with considerable interest. I saw him close the trap door, and cover the same with the carpet; and once when he bent his body near mine, I detected the smell of wine, and I jumped at a conclusion at once. I supposed that our respected superior was only common clay, after all, and that he liked the society of the world and a sup of wine as well as the rest of us, and that, to enjoy himself without restraint, it was necessary he should visit the city in disguise. I reasoned that if he could leave the college by the way of the vault, what was to prevent me from doing the same?

"'I resolved to act, and when the superior had left the chapel for his bed, I took a candle that stood on the altar, and commenced my discoveries. I raised the trap door, and made the descent; but I was almost inclined to abandon the search, when I saw before me the remains of the dead. But I reasoned myself out of all fear, and continued my investigations until the door was found, and I stood where we now stand.'

"Antonio extinguished his light as he uttered those words, and a few more steps led us to what I supposed was a door; but the darkness was so intense that I could distinguish nothing. I heard my companion slip a bolt, and then we stepped out into the open air, outside the college walls, and free from observation. The outlet of the passage-way was so contrived that a person might make a strict search for the door, and yet be unable to find it unless he had passed out that way and knew its exact locality.

"Antonio deposited his lamp where he could find it when we returned, and then we started on our adventures, the college clock tolling the hour of ten just as we arrived outside of the grounds.

"'What a joke it would be to set fire to the whole concern!' suggested my friend, as we stopped and looked at the college silent and dark like its old superior.

"'It would be much better to run away and become soldiers,' I replied.

"'And be returned bound like cattle,' sneered Antonio. 'No, no; before we were gone a week we should be overtaken and brought back, and then the treatment we should receive would be none of the mildest. No, no; I don't run away as long as I can raise money and enjoy myself outside. I think that I can manage to pass away the three years of my probation in an agreeable manner, and after I am a priest, an ordained one, I can do pretty near as I please, especially if I am placed beyond the reach of superiors. No, Beuventuro; don't run away, because such an act would be disgraceful, not only to yourself, but to the great society which we have sworn to support.'

"I had my private opinion respecting the theory of his disgraceful acts, but I did not state it, as I was too overjoyed to breathe the free air of heaven to argue with him. I was intoxicated with delight at the novelty of my position, and I could hardly refrain from shouting my joy, and bringing upon us the wrath of the sentinels stationed at the corners of the streets. Our first course was steered directly for a *fonda*, where we could satisfy our appetites and quench our thirst. We entered the place, and found that it was thronged with visitors — senoritas and senors of every age and description in life; virtuous women, and those not quite so prudish; libertines and impotent rakes, coxcombs and cuckolds, all mixed together, and sipping their coffee and wine with a freedom that was charming to behold.

" I would have preferred a seat where I could have watched the company and remained unseen, but Antonio was not one of the retiring sort. He swaggered into the grand saloon with the air of a general, and shouted out his orders to the waiter in such a manner that he soon had half a dozen of them standing around our table, waiting in respectful silence for orders. And the orders were not slow in being issued. One was told to bring eggs fried in butter, another chickens cooked in oil and covered with grated garlic, a third was started for two bottles of wine, while a fourth was despatched for fruit and vegetables. O, we had a rare feast that night, and I have often looked back upon my exploits in the gastronomic line that eventful evening with envy, for everything was relished; I had digestion and good appetite — two things which I am sorry to say are somewhat impaired at this late day; and now if I worry down a piece of chicken and drink a glass of wine, I think that I am doing very well."

Allen exploded with laughter, and even Tom and myself were forced to join him, the idea was so preposterous; for had we not seen the padre an hour before eat to repletion, and drink wine enough to float a small banco? Benventuro, apparently, did not expect us to believe him, for he smiled freely as he emptied a bottle of claret and lighted a fresh cigar.

" Go on with the yarn," Allen said; " but please to confine yourself to facts, not fancies. This is not the age of romances."

The holy father took not the slightest notice of the interruption. He puffed out volumes of smoke from his sensual-looking mouth, and continued: —

" Of course all eyes were upon us, for it was something unusual for two youths to expend so much money upon a single entertainment; but Antonio's *sang froid* never for an instant deserted him. He inspected the wine by the light of the chandeliers, and after sipping it, condescended to call it good, much to the relief of an old servant, who stood at his elbow; and after we had satisfied the first pangs of our hunger, we began to look around and admire the female faces present. Presently Antonio sent two glasses of wine, with our respects, to two young ladies who seemed desirous of obtaining protectors. The wine was accepted, and thanks returned. Then my friend proffered a present of fruit, and that was likewise gratefully received. Then we sent an invitation for them to partake of coffee at our table, and they did not reject the overture. We found them to be very intelligent girls, fond of company and show, and we readily offered them our protection home, which was accepted without much maidenly diffidence.

"We paid our bill and left, but not until the proprietor had informed us that a masked ball was to be held at the *fonda* in two weeks' time, and that our patronage was solicited. Of course we promised to come, and then, giving the girls our arms, we sallied out for their homes, laughing and joking on the way; but at three o'clock in the morning we entered the secret passage and gained our rooms unperceived, and without a soul in the building suspecting that we had been absent.

"The next day we rather drooped over our studies, but we attributed it to a slight indisposition; so no notice was taken of our sleepy looks. I was anxious to make another attempt the very next night, but Antonio refused to consent, and persuaded me to save my money until the night of the masked ball, when he promised that I should see fun enough to last me for a month. I could hardly contain myself to wait so long; but Antonio found a ready argument when he said that our money would soon be exhausted by going out twice a week, and that we should attract suspicion by writing to friends for more.

"I counted the days impatiently until the time arrived when we were once more to go forth into the world, and mingle in its pleasures and avoid its pains. At length the night did arrive, and with a heart swelling with promised rapture, we stole through the chapel and sought the hidden door; but to our surprise we found that some one had been before us, and had evidently passed through the vault to the outer world. For a moment we hesitated whether we should venture; but a love of the good things of this life conquered all fear of detection, and in another moment we were with the dead, and our pale light flickered in the humid air. We found the vault door open, as we expected; but Antonio took a skeleton key with him, which he declared would open the lock, even if the priest, who had gone before us, should return first to the college.

"I must confess that I felt a little uncomfortable with the thought of detection before me; but Antonio strove to banish all apprehensions, and by the time we reached the *fonda*, he had nearly succeeded. A few glasses of wine did more than his words, and after a hearty supper I felt as though I could encounter the superior and all his aids single-handed."

"You must have been quite drunk by the time you arrived at that conclusion," remarked Allen, interrupting the good man.

"Exhilarated, my son, nothing more," Benventuro replied; "there is quite a distinction between the two words, and I beg that you will remember them when conversing with a member of the church. Let me see — where was I?"

"Drunk, or exhilarated," promptly responded Allen, "whichever you choose."

"The music was sounding overhead," the padre continued, "and we could hear the feet of the waltzers as they whirled around the hall, shaking the building and starting the rafters — stirring our young blood with the thought of scenes which our teachers had endeavored to convince us were vain and sinful, but which had intruded upon our minds, during our wakeful hours, as the most profitable pleasure of the world — until we could no longer remain idle. To join the dance it was necessary that we should have costumes; so Antonio called the head waiter for a conference.

"'Ah, senors,' the old man said, 'you have spoken just in time. Never since I have been connected with the *fonda* was there such a demand for costumes as to-night. All the beauty and fashion of the city are at the ball, and the costumes are as varied as the ages of the ladies. I have but two dresses left, and they are sweet things for a ball-room. They are just suitable for gentlemen of spirit.'

"'Produce them,' was Antonio's command.

"The old servant, who had grown fat upon the good fare of the *fonda,* waddled off, and returned with two costumes and masks, which he proceeded to display.

"'Why, these dresses are intended to represent young devils, with horns partly grown,' shouted Antonio.

"'Yes, senor, and capital counterfeits they are. But have no fear. A priest has blessed them, and showered them with holy water, so that the Evil One can have no control over the wearers. They will create a sensation, senors, among the ladies.'

"What were we to do? Refuse the costumes and thus lose the ball, or buy them and have a fine night's enjoyment, frightening old women and nervous young ones. We determined to invest, and I had the satisfaction of paying away one of my doubloons in exchange for dresses which were ugly enough to cause hysterics with the innocent and convulsions with the wicked.

"We were shown to a private room, and soon donned our new robes, and then marched solemnly and majestically to the ball-room. Our appearance was hailed with roars of laughter from the men and looks of terror from the women. Way was made for us wherever we went, for none seemed disposed to come in contact with us, however much they might admire us. If any accosted us, we answered with all the wit that we could command, and sent joke for joke flying to the right or left without regard to age or personage.

"'Senors,' said a tall mask, dressed like a troubadour, 'your father is anxious to find you. See, he has just entered the ball-room.'

"We looked in the direction indicated, and, sure enough, we saw an old devil more ugly and more fantastically dressed than either of us. His horns were near a foot long, and his tail was trailed upon the floor, except when he whisked it around his body or over his shoulder. Our hearts died with envy at the sight, for it seemed as though our glory was gone for the evening. The vast audience applauded the old devil, and left us young ones entirely unnoticed. In this, however, it was but following the custom of all nations, which is to run after novelties.

"'Senors,' said a young and beautiful girl, whose beauty had melted my heart, 'why don't you salute your parent?'

"'Because, senora,' I replied, 'he is the father of liars; but when I tell you that I love you, I wish to forget my relationship, and speak but the truth.'

"'O, is that the reason?' she asked, with a laugh. 'I have been loved many times and by many men, whom I knew to be devils, but this is the first time that one ever had the courage to appear in his true character. When your horns have grown to a sufficient length, I'll consider of your passion. Till then, adieu.'

" She waved her fan and swept towards the old devil, who was gamboling and attracting much attention in another part of the hall. Antonio and myself followed her, and when we reached the spot where our respected parent stood, the crowd opened to the right and left for the purpose of enclosing us in a circle. We found ourselves, by these means, face to face with the object of our envy.

"'Children,' cried the people, 'advance and salute your father, and ask the news from Hades.'

"To my surprise Antonio obeyed. He threw his arms around the neck of the old devil, and embraced him in spite of his opposition to that kind of treatment. The crowd saw the reluctance, and shouted with joy, and urged me to follow the example of my brother; and even the young lady, whose eyes had made so serious an impression upon my heart, accused me of ingratitude in not testifying more affection. I did not stir, however, until Antonio made me a signal to come to his assistance.

"'Our father,' he said, 'has not danced for many years, but he is so pleased at meeting his sons, that he desires us to waltz with him. Let us give him a turn around the hall.'

"In vain the old devil pleaded that he had no taste for such display. We refused to listen to him, and when the music struck up, we each seized an arm and capered around the room to the intense delight of the spectators, and the great disgust of the person who had robbed us of our glory.

"'In the name of the saints,' he muttered, 'let me go, or I'll curse you. Brats that you are, what mean you by this treatment?'

"'Our father is old,' cried Antonio, ' and needs new blood. Let us emulate the pelican by giving liberally from ours. Another turn around the room will fire his veins with renewed ardor for enjoyment on earth. . Now, then, away with him!'

"' Wretches that you are, I shall die from suffocation!' moaned the old fellow; and faith, there was some fear that he would, for he staggered and it required all our strength to keep him on his feet.

"'Supper and wine for both if you will let me alone,' the elderly devil managed to gasp; and as the proposition was a fair one, and our appetites quite good, we consented.

"We escorted our parent, as we called him, to the dining-room of the *fonda*, threw aside our masks, and called for all the good things that we could think of, and prepared to make merry.

"'Come, good devil,' Antonio said, 'doff your mask and enjoy yourself; we are friends now, and on an equality.'

"'That I am forbidden to do by a vow which is sacred,' our new friend replied; 'but let not my refusal have any effect upon your appetites. The young devils rule to-night; to-morrow the old one will have his turn.'

"The words were uttered so sarcastically that they attracted my attention, and I looked to the old man for an explanation."

"Most holy father," interrupted Allen, "we are within a mile of Santa Mesa. Already I can see the smoke issuing from the engine chimney; yet you are so mixed up with the devil and handsome women, that I sadly fear we shall never hear the termination of your wonderful adventures. Cut some of the devils, and drown the women in a generous draught of claret, and then get out of the maze which surrounds you like a veil of brimstone."

"Your advice relating to the wine is sound," Benventuro replied, "and I approve of it; but do you think that a man can cut a story short, or reel it off like one of your ropes, manufactured to order? You stick to your hemp, which you will reap the benefit of one day, and leave me to deal with the — "

"Devil, who will have you at no distant time," Allen exclaimed.

"The saints forbid," was the pious exclamation. "Because I associate with profligates and libertines in the hope of saving them, is it a reason why I should be condemned? The saints never intended that I should labor for such a bad reward."

"Well," replied Allen, lighting a fresh cigar, "we are even on personalities. Now go on with the yarn, and pay out at a rapid rate until the whole is completed."

The priest nodded, and continued his story: —

"The remark of the old devil was certainly suspicious; for what did he mean by saying that, if we triumphed to-day he would tomorrow? I asked for an explanation, but our father in sin did not seem disposed to give one, and rather treated our offers of friendship in a disdainful manner."

" ' Senor Devil,' Antonio said, raising a decanter with one hand in a menacing manner, ' if you don't treat us with more respect, I'll brain you with this bottle of wine, and make you pay the damages. We are gentlemen, and must be honored by respect.'

" ' Carefully, senors,' the old devil replied. ' Don't be violent until there is occasion. I have no doubt that you are gentlemen; but how long is it since you left the Jesuit college of St. Salvador, where you are pupils?'

" Had an earthquake occurred, we could not have been more startled. We began to suspect that we were dealing with a bona fide devil, after all, for how else could he have been aware that we were connected with the college?

" ' How do you know that?' I asked.

" ' Why, one of my imps told me. Is not that information sufficient?'

" While we were staring with astonishment at the old fellow's horns, and wondering how we could get a view of his face, our evil genius arose, saluted us with fantastic courtesy, and walked towards the desk where the proprietor was seated, paid his bill for the supper, turned, and took another good look at us, and then left the *fonda* without speaking a word.

" We drew a long breath, expressive of great relief, when his form was no longer in sight; but the old devil had dashed our spirits, and we were in no mood for revelry just then. We emptied the bottles of wine before us, but they failed to inspire confidence or courage; for we feared that we should be punished the next day for our truancy.

" ' What is to be done?' I asked, after we had sat drinking in silence for half an hour.

" ' I know not, unless we make the best of our way to the college, and try and sleep off this disagreeable feeling which now oppresses us,' Antonio said, after a few minutes' hesitation.

" I was willing to listen to such advice, for I knew the cruelties which we should be exposed to, if our flight was discovered by the superior.

"We seized our clothes, tied in bundles, and started for the college, walking rapidly to escape the jeers of those whom we passed in the street; but after we reached the entrance to the subterranean passage, we felt somewhat relieved to find that the door had not been disturbed in our absence; or at least it was not bolted on the inside, as we feared it would be. With eager hands Antonio lighted our lamp, secured the door, and then we started for the vault where the dead reposed, and which I never ventured near without trembling and fear.

"We gained the vault, and bolted the door after us; and then for the first time Antonio spoke.

"'The saints be praised for this lucky escape,' he said. 'Who, in the name of Satan, was the old devil?'

"'I!' was the answer; and, to our horror and consternation, from behind one of the coffins rose the form of the devil, whose name we had just invoked.

"There he stood, grinning at us, with horns and tail as large as when we romped with him in the ball-room, an hour or two before. I never flattered myself at praying; but if I did not repeat a *pater noster* that moment quicker than I ever did before or since, it is because my memory is treacherous. As for my companion, Antonio, I don't think that he was much less frightened than myself, although he tried to seem composed; but the effort was a failure, for the lamp which he held in his hand shook so, that a portion of the oil was spilled upon the ground, and the flame danced around the vault until every coffin in it was lighted up.

"'Who are you?' demanded Antonio, with chattering teeth, at length mustering courage to speak.

"'Don't you see? I'm the devil,' was the answer.

"'I don't believe you are any more of a devil than we are,' my companion continued, gaining courage every moment.

"'Would you like to see a specimen of my skill?' the devil asked. 'Shall I cause these dead priests to be alive again, and walk the earth with flesh and blood upon their bones? or do you prefer that I should show you the mysteries of hell?'

"'I had rather view the latter than the former, for we see enough live priests every day without awakening the dead. Let the old fellows sleep, for they need all the rest they can get,' was Antonio's answer.

"'But suppose I should chain you here until the breath left your bodies, for the insults you have heaped upon me to-night?' the devil demanded, seriously.

"'Why, then you would lose two good servants, and the college two promising students,' was the response.

"'Explain yourself,' the devil demanded again, more grave than ever.

"'Why, you know that a man can't be a Jesuit unless he serves a master, and I know that you have none too many friends to thus quarrel with them.'

"I thought that Satan smothered a laugh, and it gave me courage to hope that Antonio and his tact would yet save us.

"'Do you know me?' the devil inquired.

"'Not if you wish to remain unknown,' was the prompt answer.

"'And you think that even if I should punish you as you deserve for this night's exploits, you would never mention my name?' our questioner continued.

"'Your secret will not be known, and we shall escape punishment,' Antonio said, promptly.

"'How so?'

"'Because your life is in our hands. We are young, active, and armed, while you are old and weak, and none to heed your cries within hearing. We have learned enough of Jesuitism to understand that the first law of the institution is self-preservation. We shall obey that law, sure.'

"'Why, you young devils! would you murder me in cold blood?' demanded our new acquaintance, more in surprise than alarm.

"'We should dislike the task; but if forced to save ourselves by that act, we should do so, and none in the college would be the wiser. A Jesuit can keep a secret, as you well know.'

"'You know me, then?' the masquerader asked.

"'I do — you are Father Vider, the superior of the college,' was Antonio's reply.

"I was astonished, and well I might be, for the superior was nearly sixty years of age, and the last man in Cadiz whom I should have suspected of visiting balls, and playing the pranks of youth and hot blood.

"'You have guessed rightly — I am the superior;' and off

tumbled the hideous head, horns, and mask, and revealed the thin, wrinkled, and dark features of Father Vider. I could hardly refrain from falling upon my knees, and begging for forgiveness; for I had become so accustomed to his rule that I dreaded his rebuke.

"'Are we to be treated as children, or as rebellious students?' demanded Antonio, as bold as a bishop.

"'As children, with my forgiveness, if nothing is said regarding this night's adventures,' the superior replied.

"'Then swear it upon the cross which you wear around your neck, and which has been blessed by the pope.'

"The superior hesitated for a moment, to see if he could not avoid the oath; but finding that Antonio was resolute, he consented; and then we knew that we could trust him.

"'Throw off your dresses,' he said, 'and go to bed, for it's near the hour of early mass, and I would not have the inmates of the college know of this adventure. To prevent such scenes in future, I shall have the entrance to the vault secured, and thus stop ingress or egress by this route.'

"'But how will you manage when you wish to visit the city during the hours of night?' asked Antonio, with bold audacity.

"'That is none of your business,' was the tart answer.

"'But how shall we manage?' demanded my friend.

"'If you are discreet, I shall give you a day's liberty once a fortnight. Now to bed, and remember the scenes of this night as though they were a dream.'

"We obeyed without a murmur; still I had some misgivings that the superior would punish us some way or other; and he did, but a little different from what we expected; for in the course of three months Antonio and myself were pronounced competent to receive priests' orders, and we were duly ordained, and then despatched in different directions. Antonio was sent to Rome, where he is engaged to keep watch upon the pope and cardinals, while I was provided for at Manila; and here I have remained ever since, doing as little as possible, except in the eating and drinking line; but I believe that is all the archbishop cares for, and if he is satisfied, I am."

"Did the superior ever allude to the adventures of that night?" Allen asked.

"Never, in word or deed. Even when he parted from me, and

gave me his blessing, I expected that he would say something; but he did not. I never saw him afterwards. He lived until over seventy years of age, and his name is revered as that of a saint in Cadiz. He had his faults, like the rest of us, and like us was anxious to conceal them from the public eye."

Just as the padre concluded his story, the banco reached the side of the river opposite the factory, at Santa Mesa, and we landed.

"Can you spare the men half an hour, Senor Allen?" Benventuro asked.

"Certainly."

"I want to send word to my steward to join me here on business, immediately."

"What, the fellow with the black beard and hang-dog expression to his face?" Allen asked.

"I must confess that you have drawn his portrait, although it is not a flattering one. He is the one I mean, and a useful man he is sometimes," replied Benventuro.

"Especially for a sudden death," whispered Allen to me; but the priest did not hear the remark or see the movement of my friend's lips.

We left the priest giving orders to the crew of the boat while we walked slowly towards the house and factory, situated about twenty rods from the landing.

At the gate we saw Mr. Huckford, and shook hands with him, presenting Tom in due form. No matter how much company arrived, Mr. Huckford was never disturbed from his accustomed serenity, provided his guests were Americans, or could speak the English language. He gave every one a hearty welcome, and the best that his house afforded was always freely offered.

"It is still two hours from dinner-time," Mr. Huckford said, looking at his watch. "How will you manage until that hour arrives?"

Tom decided upon visiting the factory, and learning the mysteries of rope-making, while I concluded to take a little rest, which I very much needed after my night of labor and anxiety; and for that purpose I went to my old quarters, where a net hammock was always kept for me, and where I could lie and read, or else watch the river and the many burdens which it bore upon its surface. I had not been alone more than five minutes when Allen entered.

"Excuse me for disturbing you," he said; "but I want to tell you the reason of Benventuro's sending for his steward. He intends to despatch him to Manila in search of your wife, and I think that the movement is a good one. The fellow is a precious scoundrel, I know; but the holy father has him in complete subjection, and I am sure that he will not dare to work except for his master's advantage. Some good may come of the visit, and at any rate, no harm can take place unless Father Juan takes a hint that his steps are watched."

"Let him go, by all means," I said, "and any expenses that he incurs I will cheerfully meet."

"I have a young fellow at work in the factory, who was born in Manila, and is well acquainted there. He will serve us faithfully for money, although I think that he would sell his father for an ounce of gold. In this matter we can trust him, for it will be for his interest to be honest. Besides, he knows your wife by sight, having often seen her here while visiting. If you think it expedient, I will engage his services for a week, and send him off this very afternoon to commence the search."

I had no objections to the course which Allen suggested; and we concluded to start both men for Manila that afternoon, with instructions to send us information, if there was any of importance, twice a day, or to report themselves at my city residence in the evening, between the hours of seven and nine o'clock, when they could enter without observation, and talk at leisure.

Allen left me to complete his arrangements, and I fell asleep, during which I dreamed that my wife had quarrelled with my protégée, Gracia, and swallowed her whole as easily as though she had the flexible muscles and good digestion of a boa constrictor. I imagined that I attempted to prevent the gluttonous act, and that I even seized Gracia by her feet and tried to prevent her disappearing from sight; but while I was pulling first one way and then the other, Teresa kicked me with such force that I was compelled to cry aloud for assistance.

"Hallo! what is the matter with you?" some one asked, shaking me most violently by the shoulder.

I started up, rubbed my eyes, and saw that Father Benventuro was standing over me.

"I have been in the room for three minutes," he said, "watching your struggles while asleep. What is the matter with you? Have you been dreaming of earthquakes or snakes?"

"Pardon me," I replied; "I was dreaming of anacondas, and I thought that one had got hold of me."

"That is not very complimentary to me, for I never show such snake-like propensities except at the dinner table. And speaking of dinner reminds me that I was sent to inform you that that important meal is on the table, and we are waiting for you. Come, dip your face in this bowl of cool water, and take some of the fever out of it, and be sure that you retire early to-night. They may urge you to drink stoutly; but it is a vile habit, so you can conscientiously refuse. Imitate me in that respect if you can. I know that it is difficult, but be firm and refuse."

With this advice the priest left me, and I dressed for dinner, considerably refreshed by my sleep, yet feeling far from easy in my mind, when I thought of my wife, and considered where she was hidden by the treacherous Father Juan.

The dinner passed off as all dinners usually do, where a portion of the company is disposed to talk, and other portions remain quiet listeners. The priest was profuse in his remarks, and told some wonderful and startling adventures concerning himself the night before; and I think that on the whole he actually believed what he said. The deeper he drank the more astonishing were the sacrifices which he had made while saving some imaginary person from being crushed by a falling wall, or drowned by the rushing tide. Those present listened to him highly amused, and only ventured to contradict when he went beyond all reason.

"Come," said Allen, addressing me, "let us take a few hours' ride on horseback this evening, while the rest of the company can remain at the table, or follow our example. We shall have a full moon at eight o'clock, and the cool air will be delicious as it sweeps down from the mountains and crosses the river. Who will go with us?"

"Not I," said the padre, "as long as I can find a companion to drink with."

"And I prefer to increase my knowledge of Spanish to being skinned on a hard-trotting horse," Tom answered.

Mr. Huckford agreed to remain at home and attend to business, and in a few minutes Allen and myself were supplied with horses, and trotting leisurely in the direction of a village which is about five miles from Santa Mesa. The place is much frequented by merchants, who do business in Manila, on account of the cool, clear water which flows through the village, affording unrivalled facilities for bathing, and because the nights are unusually cool, and the air free of insects — two things which invite slumber and comfort, and which cannot he had in the city.

"It is now seven o'clock," said Allen, consulting his watch. "We can visit the village, bathe in the clear, cold waters of the river, and back again to the factory by nine. Touch your horse with the whip, and let's see which has got the most speed."

In a few seconds our slow pace was changed to a gallop, and as the animals were fresh and eager for the fun, we went over the ground at a rapid rate, and did not draw rein until we were in the heart of the village, and every one in town was tagging at our heels, as though they had not seen a stranger for a twelvemonth. The noise brought many of the natives to their doors; but after one stoical stare they retreated to their hammocks, and commenced chewing betel-nut with renewed vigor.

We rode to the bathing-pool; but before we could dismount, a little girl, whose costume was fashioned after that of Mother Eve, excepting the fig leaf, came towards us with her arms filled with grass-cloth towels, and begged our acceptance of the same; and after we alighted, a Mestiza took the bridles of our horses, loosened the girts, and rubbed them down with wisps of grass and the husks of cocoa-nuts.

"What a polite part of the country we have reached!" I said to Allen; but he only laughed, and made preparations for the swim.

The little girl squatted down upon the bank of the river, and seemed to watch our movements with some curiosity; so I thought that I would give her notice that her company was not wanted, until our bathing was completed.

To my surprise, however, the little wretch took no notice of my hints, and I was compelled to suspend operations, although Allen did not.

"Go away, little girl," I said; "and don't come again for half an hour."

"What for, senor?" she asked.

"Because I am about to swim," I answered.

"I know it, senor," she replied, with composure.

"And you won't move?" I asked.

"No, senor; I must stay and watch the towels."

Here was the cause of the difficulty; and while I was somewhat mortified that our honesty should be questioned, Allen laughed so heartily that he was compelled to suspend operations until he grew more composed.

"Why, I thought the girl was too honest to suspect dishonesty," I said.

"Then, to prevent you from judging hastily hereafter, study the motives of people;" and with this sage advice Allen dove from a rock like a duck, and rolled over and over in the cool water like a mermaid.

"Come on," he shouted; "the water is perfectly delicious."

"But this girl; what shall I do with her?" I asked.

"Why, give her a real, and she will show how much better she can dive than either of us, and how much faster she can swim."

I declined the proposition, and as nothing that I could say would induce the girl to move, I thanked Heaven that the moon was not up, and that the sun had set; so in a moment I cast my clothes aside, and modestly plunged into the water. As far as I could tell, the girl did not seem much shocked at the outrage, and occupied her time, while we were swimming, in sucking the sweet milk from a cocoa-nut.

For half an hour we sported in the water, and then judiciously used the grass-cloth towels belonging to the girl. By the time we had concluded, she had finished her nut, gathered up the napkins, and then led the way slowly towards the house.

"Where are we going now?" I asked of Allen.

"For coffee and cigars," he replied.

"This, then, is a hotel?" I said, pointing to the bamboo hut before us.

"It is what they call a hotel in this part of the country, and a very good one they think it is, too. All foreigners who come here to bathe, stop at the hut for towels and coffee, and if it don't have anything else that is good, you can always be sure of a strong, clear cup of coffee, the berry of which was grown within a few rods of us, and towels of their own manufacture. But come and contrast this watering-place hotel with the houses at Newport and Fort Henry."

We entered the hut, and found the owner, with his wife and several children, squatted around a huge wooden dish filled with rice; and the rapid manner in which they made it disappear was wonderful to behold.

CHAPTER IX.

THE INN. — OUR COFFEE. — THE AMBUSH. — THE ATTACK. — ITS FAILURE. — THE EXAMINATION. — THE RESULT.

"THE saints have you in their keeping, senors," cried the landlord, as we entered the rather dimly-lighted room, which was too modest to even boast of a floor, for the hard earth had been levelled and beaten into service, and had the advantage of not requiring washing or repairing.

"May the saints protect you and yours," was the rejoinder of Allen, as we took seats upon a bamboo bench, and watched the progress of the meal.

"Will the senors partake?" cried the husband, opening his mouth to receive a ball of rice which he had skilfully collected with three fingers.

He threw back his head as he spoke, and the rice, about the size of a grape shot, was hurled into his mouth with wonderful precision.

"Heaven forbid," I cried hastily, with a look of disgust at the numerous black and dirty paws which were thrust into the mess; and every one of which was imitating the older to the best of its ability.

"We thank you, we have already dined," Allen hastened to add; and then he spoke in English to me.

"It is not always policy to show the disgust that you feel at an invitation to dine with a Mestizo. He asks us to eat from motives of the purest courtesy, and you must, in this country, decline with the same grace with which an invitation is extended. These people have never eaten or been taught to eat with spoons, or knives and forks, and they consider them as useless as some of our countrymen seem to think butter-knives are. Some Americans, you well know, are none too clean at the table, or at their work; so don't despise these natives for doing what their grandfathers did before them.

I felt rebuked, and no longer regarded the group with disgust, but with interest. All were fair and impartial at the bowl. Even the smallest children had as free a chance at the rice as the largest boy, and an infant was only rebuked when it attempted to crawl into the vessel, and cover itself with the food. And the rebuke was received without a murmur from the little one. There was no yelling with passion, and compromises by allowing even a foot to remain in the bowl to keep the young one quiet. The Mestizos are too sensible for that, and I don't think that during my whole stay on the island I ever heard a child indulge in a protracted cry, or give way to such gusts of passion as are common with European or American children. Yet they receive not half the attention, and are allowed to herd with the dogs and chase the chickens at leisure. Their life, until they are ten years of age, is one of freedom from medicine and schools. Once or twice a day they are taken to the river, washed, and taught to swim; and they take to the water as readily as ducks. Their fondness for it they never forget, and even the workmen, who toil from daylight till dark, will seek the river after the fatigues of the day, and refresh their bodies with a swim.

"Where is the coffee you promised me?" I asked of Allen, tiring at length of seeing the family devour their rice.

"That will be here when the landlord has completed his meal, and not before," replied my friend. "The hosts of this country are as independent as in America; although here they are to be seen occasionally, while at home they are not known except to newspaper correspondents. Have patience, for I see that my friend begins to falter, as though he is nearly filled. A few more balls, and he will be finished and ready to serve us."

The result proved that Allen's surmises were correct. The head of the family sighed, then watched his young ones for a few minutes, as they continued to throw the rice into their mouths with renewed ardor, and at length arose and stood before us.

"Senors," he said, "what shall I serve you with?"

"Are you sure that you have done eating?" Allen asked.

"Quite sure, senors; I am as full now as a sugar-sack."

"Then bring us coffee and cigars; and mind that the former is strong and the latter mild. You understand?"

"Of course I do; have I not kept a hotel from my youth, and did not my father keep one before me?"

The Mestizo looked as dignified in his shirt and loose trousers, and feet hardened by constant contact with the earth, as American landlords, dressed in fine cloth, patent-leather boots, and diamond pin. Our host clapped his hands, and one of his numerous daughters awaited his commands.

"Coffee and cigars for my friends," he repeated.

In a few minutes the fragrant beverage made its appearance in large brown-ware cups, manufactured in the country, and used in all the native houses.

"There," said Allen, "taste and drink coffee for the first time."

I did so, and although the coffee was destitute of milk, and was sweetened with coarse brown sugar, yet I never tasted anything more delicious. As we drank, a dreaming, half-forgetful feeling took possession of us, and we leaned back and gave full play to the fancies which crowded upon our brains. I thought that my wife was present, and smiling through the clouds of tobacco smoke which filled the room from our cigars, and more than once I was on the point of speaking to her; yet felt that the sound of my voice would dispel the illusion, and she would vanish. I could see our host moving about the room, and once he replenished our cups when he found that they were empty, and would have done so again had not Allen spoke, and thus roused me from my stupor.

"It is time that we were on our way home," he said.

I looked at my watch, and found that it was within a few minutes of eight.

"Is it possible that we have been here an hour and a half?" I asked.

"Ah, senor," cried the Mestizo, "that is but a short time to devote to my coffee. Some gentlemen stay here for hours, and swallow many cups, and yet go away unsatisfied. You have done very well for new beginners, but I hope to see you both here often."

Allen slipped a four-real piece in his hand, and the landlord gave vent to many expressions of gratitude. He escorted us to our horses, and wished the saints would have us in their keeping on our ride home; and even the young girl who witnessed our bathing exploits hoped that we would soon return for another swim.

The night was magnificent. Not a cloud was to be seen in the heavens, and the moon looked down upon us with tropical brightness. A cool breeze came from the mountains, and the air was so pure and clear that the barking of a village dog could be heard for miles. We were so enchanted with the scene that we suffered our horses' bridles to fall upon their necks, and plodded along at as slow a pace as they pleased.

For a few miles we jogged on in silence.

"Hark!" cried Allen, suddenly, stopping his horse; "I thought that I heard a shrill whistle."

"And I heard the same; but it is not an uncommon event. The only thing that would surprise me would be to hear some one whistle Yankee Doodle at this time of night. I should certainly think that we were within hailing distance of a countryman."

Allen paid no attention to my remarks, for while I was speaking, directly ahead of us, in a small clump of trees and underbrush a shrill whistle was sounded, and then all was still.

"There is a meaning to that," my friend said.

"Of course there is," I replied, with a laugh at his serious face.

"A Mestizo has lost his dog or his buffalo, and is searching for them."

"Your theory is a good one, but I can't believe it. Natives never whistle when looking for cattle, and dogs don't desert their masters. Let us turn from this road, strike across the paddy fields, and leave that cluster of suspicious-looking trees far in the rear. The hour is late, and few travellers of respectability are abroad at this time."

"Still thinking of native treachery and assassination," I said, laughing. "Do you suspect that there is a Mestizo within ten miles of us who would dare to come within range of our revolvers this bright night? Let us keep the road, and only leave it after our pistols are empty."

"O, if you have your pistol with you, that is a different thing," remarked Allen. "I left mine at the house by accident, and I thought you were as bad off as myself. Come on, but be careful how you aim."

He started his horse, but the aspect of affairs had undergone a sudden change, and I began to feel a doubt of our security.

"Wait one moment," I said; "while I was speaking so boldly I imagined that you were the person who was armed, and to your valor I was willing to trust myself. It seems that you have been as careless as I, and ventured out unarmed. Now, I am not naturally of a suspicious disposition, but if you have no objections we will adopt your suggestions and cut across the paddy fields. By that means we may save our throats from close contact with a knife."

To my surprise Allen did not seem to heed me. In fact he allowed his horse to trot slowly towards the brush, and as I did not want to be left alone, I struck my animal a light blow with my heavy riding-whip, one end of which was loaded with lead, and in three seconds was alongside of him.

"I thought that you were in favor of the paddy fields," I remarked.

"So I was until my curiosity got aroused, and now I am determined to see if there is design in that whistle. If a party of ladrones is around, they will keep at a respectful distance. But if others —"

He did not have time to say more, for just at that moment we entered the wood, and before our animals were concealed by the trees, I heard a rustling noise in the bushes, and forth sprang two tall Mestizos with long knives in their hands. The natives jumped towards my horse's head, and one laid a hand upon my bridle. The animal, surprised at the movement, reared and swerved, and, luckily for me, in the direction of the Mestizo who had not touched my bridle; for the latter, with as good will as I ever saw depicted upon the face of mortal, aimed a blow at me with his knife, that just grazed my left leg, and struck the pommel of the saddle. The villain intended the cut for my heart, and nothing but the movement of the horse disarranged his well-meant plans.

I was somewhat surprised, but did not lose all my presence of mind. I had seen the gleam of the knife in the moonlight, and tried to avoid the blow, but the Mestizo was too quick for me.

Hardly, however, had his knife touched the saddle than I had raised my riding-whip, and with a full swing I let the loaded part fall upon the ruffian's shoulder. The blow fell heavily, and I heard a crushing sound, that told of broken bones and bruised flesh. The fellow uttered a furious oath, and called to his companion to stab quick and fly; to do him justice, the latter's intentions were good enough, for he flourished his knife most wickedly, and then directed it towards me with a swing that told of much practice in that particular line; but I had no notion of making my body a target; and, as I found that my horse could not move quick enough, I vacated my saddle by slipping off; and hardly had I touched the ground before the animal made a sudden spring, snorted wildly, and then I heard a sound like running water, and with a quiver the beast fell to the ground. The blow that was aimed at my head had pierced the horse.

"Vamose!" shouted the fellow whose shoulder I had disabled, turning his back, and starting to run towards the paddy fields.

"Not till I have had a clip at you," I heard Allen shout; and looking up saw that he had dismounted, and was swinging his riding-whip, similar to mine, over his head.

Then I heard a blow that seemed to have crushed as it fell, and one of the midnight assassins dropped and groaned as though he was badly hurt.

"Don't let the other escape!" shouted Allen, starting after him on the full run, followed by myself.

We dashed through a quantity of underbrush, and then caught sight of the fugitive running at good speed over the paddy fields, in the direction of the river, where he undoubtedly had a banco concealed.

"We are gaining on him," shouted Allen, putting on more speed, and jumping over the small ridges which mark all paddy fields for the purpose of holding the water; and then for ten minutes we continued the pursuit, until we could hear the wretch pant as he labored along, and struggled for breath.

"Ho, ladrone! stop, or we will kill you as you run," my friend exclaimed; but the Mestizo was cunning enough to know that if we had had pistols we should have used them before; so he merely glanced over his shoulder to see how near we were to him, and was about to redouble his exertions, when his foot caught a vine, and down he went, falling heavily. He sprang to his feet in an instant; but by this time we were upon him, and a cut across the face that started drops of blood, and left a livid ridge upon his cheeks, once more caused him to fall upon the ground, where he lay and prayed for mercy, as only a Mestizo defeated in his infernal plans can.

"Dog! what prompted you to attempt our assassination?" shouted Allen, plying his whip with hearty good will upon the form of the fallen man.

"Mercy, senor, and I will tell you all!" the wretch exclaimed, seeking to avoid the blows.

Allen suspended his punishment, and allowed the Mestizo to stand upon his feet, first taking the precaution to see that his knife was gone.

"What was your object in thus seeking our lives?" Allen asked, as we led the way to the scene of the outrage, having tied the fellow's hands behind him, with our pocket handkerchiefs, to prevent his escape.

"Ah, senor, we were directed not to molest you unless you interfered in our work," was the answer.

"And did you suppose that I should stand by and see you butcher my friend without offering my aid?" demanded Allen, indignantly.

"We were told that such would be the case, senor," answered the fellow, meekly.

"Ladrone, you are not speaking the truth," said Allen, fiercely.

"By the saints I am, senor," answered the fellow, with apparent sincerity.

"And you expected to kill my friend — did you?" Allen asked.

"We were in hopes that we should, senor," answered the fellow, with a degree of candor that surpassed all belief.

"What harm have I done that you should seek my life?" I asked, scanning the man's features to see if I had ever met with him before. His countenance was not familiar, and I was compelled to entertain an impression that Father Juan had set the men upon my track for the purpose of carrying out the great scheme, which he had long entertained, of inducing my wife to resign her property and enter his convent.

"You have never injured us, senor; but there is a person in Manila who thirsts for your blood; you have crossed him in some way, and he never forgets an injury."

"His name?" demanded Allen, confronting the fellow.

"That, senor, I can't divulge."

"Then you have your choice of a speedy death by pistol or hanging from the limb of a tree. Think quick, and give us an answer."

"You don't think of carrying your threats into execution?" I asked in English; "let us surrender them to the law, and let the law deal with them."

"The law is a humbug, and you will think so if you ever have occasion to invoke its aid," Allen answered. "I intend to make this fellow reveal all that he knows, and yet I shan't harm him a great deal, as you will confess. I think that I know who set them on, and if my suspicions are realized, we shall hold a trump card."

The Mestizo looked first at Allen and then at myself, while we were talking, as if he were endeavoring to comprehend the meaning of our words. He seemed to think that we were in earnest with our threats, for he answered in a resigned tone, —

"I can die; but I will not reveal the name of the person who engaged us."

"Then die you shall," was the only answer that Allen made, and we walked on in stern silence till we reached the scene of the struggle, where lay the dead horse, and the uninjured one standing over him, as though grieving for his loss.

Allen secured the animal, and then we looked for the body of the villain whose shoulder I had smashed with my whip. To our surprise he had vanished, and this elicited a chuckle from the prisoner.

"Ah, Antonio is tough, senors, and the arm must be strong that can make an impression upon him. He has escaped, but I can find him if paid for it."

The wretch was all ready to sell his comrade for gold, and a small sum at that.

"He can't be far off," Allen remarked. "Take a portion of the bridle from your horse, and tie this fellow, and then we will search for the missing one. He is probably concealed in the underbrush, for no man could travel far after receiving such blows, unless his frame is made of cast iron."

We secured our prisoner to a tree, disbelieving his protestations that he would not attempt to escape; then we examined the place where the ladrone had fallen. We saw that he had made several attempts to get on his feet, but he had not succeeded; for we found a trail in the dust where he had crawled on his hands and feet towards the brush by the side of the road, and a few steps brought us upon the fellow, his face covered with blood, and a large gash upon his head, that did not look promising for his speedy recovery. He was nearly insensible, and as there was not the slightest danger of his leaving the place in a hurry, we left him and returned to the other prisoner, who had suffered no harm beyond smashing the bones of his right shoulder

"My comrade has escaped," the prisoner, still bound to the tree, exclaimed, when he saw us return so soon. "I told you that his head was hard, and that no impression could be made upon it."

"You are mistaken," Allen answered, quite composedly, without even looking at the man. "Your brother assassin is nearly dead, and probably before morning he will cease to live."

"Dead — dying!" echoed the fellow, apparently astonished at the intelligence.

He remained silent for a few moments, and then spoke:—

"If he is dying money can be of no use to him. Won't you just search his pockets, and bring me the doubloon that you will find there. It is mine by right, for he lost that amount of money to me by betting on a cock-fight yesterday."

"You can see how much love one Mestizo has for another," Allen remarked in English, while busily arranging some portions of the bridles by knotting them together.

We paid no attention to the request of our prisoner, although two or three times he repeated his demand that we would be kind enough to hand him the money found in the pockets of his comrade. At length our silence and proceedings seemed to strike the Mestizo with a mysterious feeling, which he tried to banish by humming a song that was very popular, in those days, with all classes of the community; but his eyes followed our movements, nevertheless.

"Senors," he asked, "what do you intend to do with me?"

We returned no answer, but threw one end of the bridles over the limb of a tree, and made a slip-noose with the other.

"Senors," continued our prisoner, his assurance gradually deserting him, "if you let me escape, I will never raise a hand against you again."

"We don't intend you shall," Allen remarked. "In a short

time you will be in the other world; so, if you have any prayers to address to the saints, you had better begin them."

"You will not dare to kill me?" asked the fellow.

"Why should we not serve you in the same manner that you attempted to serve us? We must learn who paid you for thus assaulting us, or we must have your life," was the quiet answer; and Allen tested the strength of the gallows by swinging on it for a moment.

"Why, senors, would you have me damned for revealing my secret?"

"We care not whether you are damned or blessed; we will know who hired you," I remarked.

"Senors, I cannot tell," was the decided answer.

"I am fearful that we shall have to pinch his throat a little," Allen said in English. "But don't be alarmed," he continued, "even if you see him strangle; he won't die without giving us the information that we seek."

Allen untied his horse, and led him in front of the Mestizo.

"Cast off all his bonds excepting those which confine his hands," my friend said.

I did as directed. The prisoner looked wild, and stared first at my friend and then at myself.

"Now mount the horse," Allen ordered; but the Mestizo was unable to do so, owing to his hands being tied. I stepped behind him, and lifted him upon the animal's back.

"Ah! you intend to carry me to the city — do you?" the fellow asked, his confidence returning.

We did not venture an answer, but backed the horse until the bridle, suspended from the tree, touched the man's head. He looked up, and saw the noose dangling over him; but even then he had some thought that we were only frightening him. He tried to smile, but the attempt was a wretched one.

"Senors," he said, "you had better take me to the city; or give me your horse, and I'll go alone. I know the way by land as well as by water."

Allen made no answer. He merely took the noose and dropped it over the man's head, and then pulled it tight around his neck. The fellow's eyes for the first time began to express the terror which he felt.

"What do you intend to do?" he gasped, struggling to withdraw his hands from the bandages.

"Only hang you. Keep perfectly quiet, and you will experience an unknown sensation in a few seconds. I don't think it will hurt you much," Allen remarked, lighting a cigar and handing me one, for the purpose of making the fellow think that we were remarkably cool about the execution.

"Senors," cried the Mestizo, after a moment's pause, "I am not fond of sensations. Why won't you let my comrade, who is half dead, hang instead of me. He is of no use to the world, while I have two daughters in Manila. They will mourn for me."

"What are their names?" I demanded, prompted to ask the question by a feeling which I could not control.

"Sara and Gracia," was the answer.

Here was a confession. We were about to hang, in jest, the father of my new protégée, whom I had picked up near the Morgue. It was evident that he did not know that his eldest daughter was dead, and I was not disposed to enlighten him in relation to the matter.

"We are very sorry to be compelled to hang you," Allen remarked, after I had explained in English the true position of affairs; "but our future safety requires that you should die, or disclose the names of the parties who incited you to commit the crime of murder. You have but a minute to live. Call upon the saints in season, for it's the last time that you can address them."

"I can't reveal, senors," was the answer.

Allen touched the horse, and the animal stepped forward a few feet, sufficient to bring the noose tight around the neck of the Mestizo.

"Hold on," he gasped; "I'll tell all, if you will save my life."

"Go on with your confession, then," Allen remarked.

"But remove the rope first," the Mestizo pleaded.

"No; what you have to confess must be said as you are. We have gone to considerable trouble for the purpose of hanging you comfortably, and we had little rather do it than save your life at this late hour. But even now, if you don't tell the truth, your neck is not worth the price of a betel nut."

"Then swear, senors, that my life shall be spared, and I'll tell all," the Mestizo cried, glad to make terms when he really supposed that we preferred his life to a confession.

"You have the word of two gentlemen. We do not bind ourselves with oaths," was Allen's reply.

"Well, then, please give me a cigar," the Mestizo said, with characteristic impudence.

I handed the fellow a cigar, when he lighted it and adjusted it to his mouth with considerable precision, and then commenced his confession.

"This forenoon, senors, a man applied to us, and wanted to know if we desired a good job. We were lying in our banco at the time, opposite the European Hotel, waiting for passengers. I answered that we were always ready to earn money, provided we could do it honestly. Our visitor did not seem pleased with the reply, and at length my comrade said that he never refused a job of any kind. The stranger smiled at this, and asked us to follow him a short distance, so we could talk without fear of being overheard. He led the way to a wine shop, and called for drink, and we did not hesitate to swallow all that he set before us. Why should we, as long as he paid for it? and he seemed to have plenty of money. At length the stranger handed to us a doubloon, and said that two more would be given us if we obeyed his orders. We took the money eagerly, and then asked what the job was. We were told that it was necessary for the good of the church that a heretic should die, and that, if we committed the deed, the saints would not only pardon, but bless us. I asked who the person was, and the stranger said that he was an American, endeavoring to damn people's souls by converting them to Protestantism. Then I felt that we should be justified in killing, and my comrade seemed to be of my way of thinking. We asked to see the one we were to despatch, and the stranger said that he would point him out to us when the time arrived. Then we drank more wine, and swore that we would kill not only the person whom the stranger desired we should kill, but everybody else who had offended him, and yet retain his secret. You see, senors, we were not thinking of the ropes around our necks, or the heavy blows which you deal out with whip-handles. *Caramba!* you have broken the bone in my shoulder, and my comrade's head — two things we did not expect."

"Go on with your confession," Allen said, sternly.

"*Si, senor,*" the fellow answered, more humbly, and continued: —

"We were told to go on board of our banco again, and push up the river a short distance and wait there, concealed from observation by some bushes. The stranger went with us, and this afternoon a banco passed us, on board of which were a priest and three gentlemen. You, senor (pointing to Allen), we knew by sight, but the other two were strangers to us. You (nodding to me) was the one we were to kill, and we were strictly charged not to fail, even if we had to wait a week to accomplish the job. The saints be praised," the hypocrite continued, "we failed in our designs."

"Then you followed us to the factory — did you?" Allen asked.

"Of course — we never lost sight of you except for a few minutes, although you did not see us, for the very good reason that we kept in the background. When you started for the ride, we followed on the same road, certain you would have to return that way; but you came near getting clear, after all."

"How so?" I asked.

"Why, when you first appeared in sight, my comrade was some distance from me, looking for stray travellers, and trying a little robbing on his own account. He is a man never satisfied with doing well, but wants to do better. I had to repeat the signal several times before he would attend me. If he had not come, you might have gone clear, for I don't like attacking Europeans alone."

"Now for another question," Allen said. "Who was the man who paid you for attempting to kill my friend?"

The Mestizo hesitated, but the horse moved a little and brought the halter tighter around the fellow's throat.

"For the saints' sake, don't," he gasped, struggling so violently that he but tightened the band, and tortured himself.

"The name," demanded Allen, quite cool, and deaf to all his sufferings.

"Let me but breathe, then," the Mestizo gasped.

I touched the horse, and he stepped back a few inches, sufficient to allow the man to move his head.

"The saints forbid that I should ever die by hanging," was the fervent prayer. "There are other deaths which are much more to be preferred. The knife, for instance, only inflicts one pang, in the hands of a skilful artist, and then life ebbs away so quietly that it resembles sleep. Poison is very good in difficult cases, where the victim can't be got at easily; but it ain't sure, like the knife, since those English and Dutch doctors have settled in Manila. The knife never fails, if a man will only take the trouble of carrying a whetstone in his pocket. I even prefer it to a pistol."

"Why, you wretch, we did not spare your life to listen to a long dissertation on murder," I said, although I must confess that I was somewhat amused at the philosophical manner in which he treated the subject; but I had no doubt he was competent to judge, if the number of his crimes was taken into consideration.

Allen looked at his watch, and found that it was near nine o'clock.

"We shall be missed at the factory, and they will feel anxious regarding us unless we are home in a short time," he said. "We can no longer play with this man. He must reveal his secret at once, for at any time we are liable to be surprised by a band of prowling ladrones, and they will certainly rescue this fellow, and make a stand against us; and what could we do without revolvers?"

As I didn't know, I made no answer.

"Come," said Allen, turning to the Mestizo, "we want the name of the party who hired you to assassinate my friend."

The scamp was just about to answer and give us the information, when from the direction of the river was heard a peculiar cry which resembled the "craw" of a parrot. Our prisoner pricked up his ears and listened eagerly, and to my surprise Allen did the same.

"The name," demanded my friend.

Instead of replying, the Mestizo opened his mouth and uttered a shrill "craw" which could have been heard, in that calm, moonlight night, for half a mile or more.

"Dog!" thundered Allen; "if you make another signal you shall hang by your neck, even if the ladrones are in sight. You can't escape giving us the information. Let us have it at once."

The Mestizo seemed to be paying more attention to the signals from the river than to us. Again we heard the peculiar cry, and this time much nearer to us. The prisoner raised his head, and was about to answer, when Allen suddenly started the horse, and the halter was brought tight around the fellow's neck; and instead of producing a craw, he found it somewhat difficult to obtain breath. He struggled fearfully to free his arms, but, as before, was unsuccessful.

"The name," cried Allen, making a motion to start the horse, and leave the man dangling in the air.

I saw that we had conquered. I could tell by the expression of his face that his stock of fortitude was exhausted, and that he was willing to submit to our wishes. The horse, which performed a very important part that night, was backed a few steps, and the halter loosed around the man's neck.

"Now, then, what is his name?" demanded Allen, hurriedly.

"Father Juan, of the convent of San Sebastian," was the answer.

"Did he give any reason for wishing for my friend's death?" Allen asked.

"Only the reasons which I have stated," was the answer. "He said that you were not only his enemies, but enemies of the church; that the saints would thank us for killing you, and that for so doing he would grant us full absolution."

"Did he mention the name of a lady, during the conversation?" I asked, eagerly.

"He did not, senor; but the night before —"

He stopped suddenly, for at that moment, within a few rods of us, arose the doleful "hoots" which we had noticed before.

"We must make our escape while we can," whispered Allen. "A gang of river ladrones are prowling around, and if they find us so far from the factory, and unarmed, our watches and probably our lives will not be safe. With a couple of revolvers we could scatter them like chaff; but alas! those are safe, like the Dutchman's anchor, at home."

Our prisoner was inclined to be jolly at the prospect of a sudden liberation, for although he did not dare to speak a loud word, yet he hummed his favorite tune, and seemed to flatter himself that we should soon change places.

There was no time to lose, if we meant to escape, for the ladrones must have heard our prisoner's signal, and knew that it proceeded from the only clump of bushes and trees to be seen for two or three miles, the rest of the ground being covered with

OBTAINING INFORMATION. Page 244.

paddy fields and grazing tracts. They also knew that there was occasion for their services, or the peculiar signal by which they called each other would never have been given. As the river thieves were all bound together by ties of dishonest brotherhood, it was to be expected that they would help each other from disagreeable positions, and revenge ill treatment if in their power. I did not feel much alarmed at our position, for I knew that the scamps seldom carried fire-arms, and that they would be very careful how they approached us, until they found out that we were destitute of those very useful articles; and even if they did make the discovery, I was in hopes of keeping them and their knives at a distance by the use of our legs, or our heavy whips. It's no disgrace to run away from a fight, when the enemy muster four or five to one.

"What are we to do?" I asked of Allen, who seemed to be deliberating on the matter.

"I don't know, unless we hang the fellow, and escape on horseback. If we leave him here alive, he will tell in which direction we have gone, and join them in pursuit, like a blood-hound that he is. I don't want to kill the man, and yet I see no other way of leaving this position," my friend remarked.

"I have it!" I cried. "Let us tie the fellow upon the horse's back, and start the animal towards the factory at its best speed. The ladrones will give chase, and by that means we may escape."

"Admirable!" cried Allen. "We could not hit upon a wiser plan. Hold the horse while I tie the fellow's legs under the animal's belly."

He took a portion of a bridle, and in a few seconds the Mestizo was secured, although much against his will, and it required a few energetic threats of punishment to keep him still.

"Now," cried Allen, "let go of the horse, and apply your whip to his hind quarters. Don't be afraid to strike hard, for on his speed depends our safety."

He raised his whip as he spoke, and showered down a number of blows; and I think that, from the yell which I heard, a few of them fell upon the legs of the Mestizo.

The horse, unaccustomed to such treatment, reared wildly; but the rider kept his seat, and the next instant the animal dashed along the road leading to the factory at pretty good speed. We watched his course but for a moment, and then Allen touched me on the shoulder, and whispered, —

"Follow me."

I did not wait for a second invitation. With a bound I cleared the road, and alighted in a clump of bushes; and just as I alighted, half a dozen men came in sight, and looked eagerly for the person whose signals they had answered.

"Don't stir for your life," whispered Allen. "The best of the gang has gone in pursuit of the horse, and the rest are searching for booty. They are old hands, or we should be clear of them."

It was even as my friend had said, for we could hear the voices of those in pursuit of the horse, away in the distance, and they seemed to be communicating to the men who were near us, that a ruse had been employed to send them off.

The ladrones passed within six feet of us, their black, suspicious eyes glancing to the right and left as they scanned the bushes, apparently in expectation of finding a foe or plunder. They were too cowardly to search the bushes immediately, fearing treachery; but every moment they seemed to gather more courage, and how long before they would pounce upon us, was a question that was not settled to our minds satisfactorily. Had we but carried our revolvers, we could have frightened them, and pursued our way to the factory unmolested.

Suddenly the party stopped in front of the dead horse, and a short conversation ensued, in the Mestizo tongue, which but few Spaniards understand; therefore the natives have great advantages for the concocting of plots, and planning little acts of rascality. I could not understand a word of the lingo; but Allen was somewhat acquainted with it, and listened eagerly to the discussion.

"This is a factory horse," said the fellow, whom we supposed to be the chief of the party. "I know it by the brand upon its right flank. How came it here, and dead at that?"

"Perhaps one of our gang stole the animal, and being pursued, was compelled to kill it to save himself from capture," was the answer.

"That is not a likely story," was the contemptuous rejoinder; and he was about to offer a further solution of the mystery, when the wretch whose head Allen had smashed uttered a deep groan, as though life was a burden to him.

The gang were all ready to run, for fear that the sound was a signal for attack; but the chief cursed them in set terms for their cowardice, and after a moment's delay he boldly ventured alone to the spot where the wounded man was lying, and dragged him to the middle of the road..

"There, you fools," he said; "is that an object to run for?"

He dropped the body suddenly, and the rough treatment produced another groan, which caused the gang to gather around in search of his injuries.

"He has been robbed," cried one.

"No such thing," returned the chief, slipping his hands into the man's pockets, and rifling them with wonderful dexterity. "Whoever heard of a man being robbed, and left with money in his pockets? Look and see if any of you know him."

They stood one side, so that the moon would strike upon the face, and reveal his features more distinctly.

"I know him," cried one; "he is a barcario, and a bold man. Many a *fat* one has he plucked, and many a *weak* one pinched."

"Then he belongs with us, and we must find those who injured him. Search the bush in couples, and do the work thoroughly."

The men scattered in obedience to the orders of their chief, and a portion of them came towards us.

"Now, then," said Allen, "we must run for it, or lose our lives. Put your best foot forward, and let us keep together."

For a few steps we moved without breaking a twig, and if we could have continued on in that manner, our escape would have been assured; but unfortunately Allen caught his foot in a vine and fell, and the accident, slight as it was, caused him to give vent to an imprecation that was heard by the ladrones, although they could not see us.

"They are here," was shouted, not daring to advance until the whole gang was together, for they knew they had to deal with Americans or Englishmen, and that if we had pistols we would scorn to run.

"On them, then, with your knives," cried the chief. "They have no pistols, or they would have used them long since. A fair division of plunder shall be made if they have money."

"Now, then," said Allen, "let her slide. Strike out and do your best."

We had gradually increased our distance from the ladrones while they were waiting for each other, and by the time they were ready for the rush we were clear of the brush and trees, and upon the paddy fields. The latter are not favorable for running, owing to the low ridges, generally about a rod apart, and which I have already spoken of; but the ground was as fair for us as the ladrones, so that we had no cause to grumble on that account. The only thing we could complain of was because so many were after us, thus offering large odds that we should be overtaken and lanced by a short knife before we could reach a place of safety.

The devils uttered a shrill cry when they caught sight of us, and then started in pursuit, probably with the expectation of running us down in a few minutes, for they put on their best speed, and tore away at a tremendous rate.

"Don't run as fast as you can yet a while," Allen said, seeing that I was drawing ahead of him. "We have got over a mile to go before we can reach the factory, and must have some breath for the home stretch. Govern your pace by mine."

I did so, but he soon found that more steam was required, for the Mestizos can run when trained, as they are thin and destitute of surplus fat, as a general thing. I glanced over my shoulder, and saw that the scoundrels were bounding over the ridges like deer, and, what was worse, were actually gaining upon us.

The devils even had their knives in their hands ready for use when within striking distance. I could see them flash in the moonlight as they were waved in the air. What would I not have given for my revolver at that moment? Even as shaken as my nerves were, I could have put four of the seven, who were in pursuit, *hors de combat*, as fast as I could take aim. I even muttered my thoughts, and Allen overheard them.

"Blast your wishes," he said, rather unkindly. "What's the use of wishing now? If wishing was any good, I'd wish for a pair of seven-leagued boots, and be thankful for the favor. Cuss their pictures, how they do run! Let out more speed, for I see that one of the rascals is not far from us."

I did make my feet move a little faster, and for a few seconds we held our own; but the ladrones still crowded us, and came on yelling like so many hounds.

"Ah, blast you; yell and expand your breath, if you will. I wish that you would burst a blood-vessel, or break your necks, I shouldn't care much which."

"No use wishing," I replied, glancing over my shoulder, and redoubling my exertions, when I saw the foremost scamp was close upon us, and puffing like a locomotive under a full head of steam.

"Let him come," muttered Allen, who had also taken a look at our pursuers; "if I don't sweeten his head for him may I never smoke another cigar."

He shook his heavy riding-whip, which useful articles both of us had retained possession of, and, to my surprise, my friend rather slackened his pace, as though tired.

"For Heaven's sake don't lag," I said, fearful that his strength was yielding. "See, the old factory is in sight. A few minutes more and we shall be safe. We can't make a stand here, and beat them off."

"I know it," was the quiet answer. "Do you keep out of the way of that fellow's knife, and leave him to me. I intend to make his head ache by a few blows, or there's no virtue in lead and a stout arm."

The foremost ladrone was within ten feet of us, while his comrades were as much as twenty feet behind him. The leading robber apparently prided himself upon his speed, for he bounded along as easily as though he was good for two miles. He evidently expected to use his knife to advantage, for he flourished it, and yelled like a demon when he saw that he was gaining on us.

I diverged a little to the right, so that we could bring the fellow between us; and by that means he was compelled to single out one of us for the attack. I won't say that I was pleased when I saw that he decided to try Allen first, because I was not; but I felt as though the fellow would find his match, and I determined to lend my own assistance in teaching him a lesson always to be remembered.

I managed to keep one eye upon the ladrone and one upon Allen, and when I thought that the time had arrived for action, I slackened my pace slightly, so that the Mestiza was brought a little in advance of me, and I had the appearance of pursuing him instead of his pursuing me. The fellow, in his eagerness to strike Allen, overlooked me, or possibly thought his companions would attend to my case. I saw Allen measuring the distance between himself and the ladrone, and it looked to me that with one more leap the ladrone would be up with him. I saw the latter raise his knife, and then uttered a shout of triumph as though sure of his victim; but never was a man more disappointed, for just as the knife was descending, Allen sprang aside, and thus avoided the blow. The Mestizo stumbled forward, but before he could recover himself, the loaded whip was whirling in the air, and down it came with force enough to kill an ox. The Mestizo plunged headlong to the ground, and when I passed him, all ready to give a second edition of what he had received, he was lying perfectly quiet, with his head doubled up under his arm, as though he was asleep.

"You did well," I panted, as I struggled to gain Allen's side. "His skull is broken, certain, and all the surgeons in Manila can't save him."

"Save your breath," grunted Allen, "for I think that you will want it before we get out of this scrape. Blast 'em, how fast they run!"

I expected that the ladrones would certainly stop to pay some attention to their comrade; but with characteristic selfishness they passed the poor devil as though he was unworthy of notice. To be sure they did raise a shout, which betokened a desire for revenge; but we thought nothing of it, as we were pretty certain that they would punish us if they could get hold of us, even without the shout.

"A few steps farther and we shall be out of danger!" I said, to my great joy looking up and observing half a dozen men about a hundred rods ahead of us, apparently waiting with patience to see what the race was all about. I supposed they were servants connected with the factory, and they were attracted outside of the walls by the cries which they had heard.

The ladrones apparently saw the men as soon as myself, for they raised a peculiar yell, and it was answered by those who I supposed were factory people. I expected every moment that the pursuit would be abandoned, but to my extreme surprise, when I glanced over my shoulder, I saw that the Mestizos were running as fast as ever.

"Here they come towards us," I remarked, as well as my breath would permit, pointing to the men in the distance. "A few moments more and we shall be with them."

"I hope not," replied Allen, altering his course and edging

away towards the river, so as to leave those in front of us at a greater distance than those in the rear.

"They are not factory people," he continued, after a moment's pause. "They are the other portion of the gang, who went in chase of the horse. If we are not in luck then, I'll be — "

He did not stop to finish his sentence, for we saw that both parties were coming for us at a tearing rate, and as the men who were fresh were likely to outrun us, our situation was none of the most pleasant. We edged away more towards the river, leaving the house on our right hand, and as we drew past it we could see a light in the dining-room, where, but a few hours before, we were feasting in peace and security. How we were to escape from our foes was a mystery to me, for if we plunged into the river we should be no safer than on land, as a Mestizo can swim from the age of six, or even earlier.

"Can you hold out a few minutes longer?" asked Allen, as we dashed along, stumbling, or jumping over ridges, and using our best exertions to escape.

"I think so," was my answer, although I was not over-confident, for if I had lost my footing, I should have been unable to rise before the ladrones were upon me.

We were heading directly towards the lower end of the ropewalk, which visitors to Santa Mesa will recollect extends along the bank of the Pasig for about a third of a mile. Near the end of the building were quite a number of trees, planted there for the purpose of shading the factory, and for ornament. They were so dense that the moon's rays were entirely excluded from the arbor which they formed by their abundant foliage. Our only hope of escape, I considered, was to take refuge in the grove, and while the ladrones were searching for us, to crawl upon our hands and knees towards the river, and swim across to the other bank. I had but faint hope that the ruse would be successful; yet I considered that it was our only chance for escape from death.

"Now, then," panted Allen, when we were within two rods of the end of the building, — "now, then, for a rush; for every second gained will count."

Spurred on by the hope of life, we increased our speed; and as we turned the corner of the building, we had the satisfaction of seeing the ladrones two rods in the rear,

"Follow me close," Allen said; and as he spoke he applied a key to the lock of a door, the existence of which I was ignorant of.

The door flew open without trouble. I sprang into the building, and fell upon the floor, amidst hemp and rope; and the next moment Allen had closed the door, locked it, and tumbled over me, panting as though his heart would break.

We heard the ladrones, as they reached the end of the building, pause, and we supposed that they were listening to discover the direction which we took. We could hear them pant from the effects of their long race, and perhaps it was well that they were as tired as ourselves, for I certainly feared that they would hear us breathe, although to prevent such a possibility, I stuffed some hemp into my mouth, and liked to have smothered in consequence.

"Which way did they go?" were questions freely asked; but no one was able to answer correctly. Some suggested that we must have kept on direct to the river; but the chief of the gang did not favor that theory, because the distance was so great to the water that he argued we should have been seen. One Mestizo suggested that we must have climbed a tree, and he even swore that he could see our white clothes amid the branches. The thought was not a happy one for the scamp, for the chief very coolly ordered him to shin up a stately bamboo, and investigate. I think the fellow was a little reluctant to undertake the job, for I heard the command issued to him twice before he started, and I could understand the jeers which were uttered at his expense for his reluctance, although I suppose that every one of the gang would have manifested as much modesty had they been ordered separately to hunt us up.

At length the fellow who had been sent up the tree, reported that what he had supposed to be a suit of white clothes was nothing more than the remains of a paper kite.

CHAPTER X.

THE SEARCH OF THE LADRONES. — THE FIRE. — A BAD PREDICAMENT. — LOOKING FOR A WIFE.

"Where could they have gone to?" we heard the chief ask, after the fellow in the tree had reported.

Not a Mestizo among them could tell. They listened for a while in the hopes of hearing our footsteps and deep breathing, but we took care to smother our heads in hemp, and thus defeat the plan for our detection. At length the chief sent his men off in different directions, with orders to give a signal if any trace of us could be obtained.

"Now is our chance," whispered Allen. "We must reach the house while the ruffians are engaged in the search, and if we are spry, we will return and blow the devil out of them."

We crept along the ropewalk, stumbling over spinning jennies, or some other kind of jennies, the names of which I have entirely forgotten, — although I am positive that the articles with female appellations were not females in any sense of the word, — sometimes getting our feet entangled in rope, and uttering an expressive word in consequence, until we gained the upper end of the factory, where we had but to unfasten a door and pass from the building without trouble.

The dogs inside of the wall, which surrounded the house, were growling as though they snuffed danger, and were ready for it. As soon as they heard our footsteps their yelling changed to gambols of joy, and with some trouble we were enabled to force our way through the brutes, and ascend the steps leading to the dining-room, where we heard the voice of the priest talking as freely as when we left, three hours before. We stopped a moment to listen, and found that Father Benventuro and Tom were arguing the probability of our remaining absent all night.

"Don't tell me that those scamps haven't a design in staying away from their friends this night. I know it, I tell you. They are after some fun. It's just like them; may the devil take them for their impudence. But I'll find out all about it, and then will come their punishment."

"But I supposed they would have asked me to accompany them, if such a thing was contemplated," insinuated Tom, in a tone of voice that showed he concluded himself an ill-used man.

"It's because you are too pure — it's because I am too pure for such work," exclaimed the priest. "They knew that you and I would not countenance such proceedings on the part of a newly-married man. There's nothing in our faces that gave them any hope that we should consent to witness their immoral conduct."

In spite of our late extremity we could not help laughing at the idea which the priest had contrived to get into his head. The noise aroused the drinkers, and then we burst in upon them.

"O, you old wretch!" Allen shouted. "We can't leave you for a moment but you must plot and play virtuous. . Where are our pistols? We will not be slandered."

"Bless us, Charley, you ain't going to shoot a fellow for praising you when your back is turned — are you?" demanded Benventuro, although he manifested no alarm.

"Pretty kind of praise you bestow — calling us profligates and wretches," I remarked.

"Why, you stupids, I was only exercising your friend in the Spanish language. There are many words which he don't know the meaning of; so I was instructing him. He will find them very convenient, if he associates long with you."

By the time the priest had finished speaking, we had got hold of our revolvers, and were examining the charges.

"Come," cried Allen, turning to the priest, "a party of ladrones has had the pleasure of chasing us to-night, and now we propose to chase them in return. Will you go with us?"

"Do you expect me to run after the rascals?" demanded Benventuro, surveying his stout proportions with complacency. "Because, if you do, you will find yourself much mistaken. My body is fashioned like a Dutch galiot — made for burden, not speed. If there is anything to carry, I'm your man; but as for racing like a horse, you will have to do that yourselves. But, after all, what use is it to sally forth to-night in quest of the band? It's very probable that they are miles from here by this time. Sit down and make yourselves contented. Brown and myself have emptied six bottles of claret and a bottle of sherry each, and we are good for half a dozen more. Sit down, and I'll tell you some wonderful adventures which I experienced last night, during the shock of the earthquake."

"We have already heard you tell lies enough on that subject," answered Allen, moving towards the door, "and we don't propose to ruin your soul forever by listening to others. You can go with us, or remain and drink until you get asleep. You will have no company, for Tom goes with us."

"If that is the case, I shall go also," was the priest's remark; and in a few seconds he had thrown aside his robes, and donned a short jacket, which did not improve the appearance of his figure.

With many words from the holy father for our obstinacy in refusing to listen to his advice, we led the way down stairs and out through the court-yard, beyond the walls.

"We will return the same way that we came, through the factory, and perhaps we can take the fellows by surprise," Allen suggested; but the priest laughed at the idea of our capturing a gang of ladrones, and offered a basket of champagne for every prisoner.

We entered the factory, closing the door after us, and then, by the aid of a dark lantern which Allen had brought with him, we groped our way through the ropewalk until we reached the door we had entered an hour before, and which was the means of saving our lives. Here we paused and listened, and to the intense delight of the priest, no sound but our own suppressed breathing was to be heard.

"I told you so," he muttered; "ladrones don't stay long in one spot. Better go back to the house and finish a few more bottles of wine, and listen to my adventures. Besides —"

He stopped suddenly, for just at that moment there was a crackling sound outside of the factory, and in an instant a red light was seen through the many cracks of the edifice.

"The scoundrels have set fire to the building," cried Allen, rushing towards the door, followed by the rest of us.

"And blast them, they want to burn me as though I was a Protestant, or a dog," echoed Father Benventuro, knocking down Tom in his eagerness to escape such a fate. "Open that door," he continued, "or I shall curse some of you, and then the devil will have you, certain."

By the time he had finished speaking, the door was thrown open, and we rushed out; and none too soon, for a quantity of dry wood and hemp had been collected and placed under the factory, and then set on fire. The flames were making rapid progress, and in a few minutes the building would have been consumed.

I gave one glance around as I gained the air, and saw four or five ladrones standing near a tree, surveying their devilish work with considerable composure. We had issued from the ropewalk so suddenly, and they were so engrossed by the fire, that they did not see us, and not until they heard the sharp crack of two revolvers did they fully understand that an enemy was near.

I saw two men give sudden springs into the air and fall heavily to the ground, and then the remainder darted amidst the trees like lightning, and were instantly lost to view.

"I'll have one of them!" yelled the priest, forgetting that he was fat and incapable of running, starting towards the spot where the gang had stood but a moment before. He made pretty good time for a second or two, and then his feet caught in the rank grass, and down he went, plunging head first amidst a quantity of bushes, each branch of which bore thorns an inch long, and sharp at that.

I had time to listen to a volley of curses, prayers, and earnest supplications to all of the principal saints, before I turned to assist Allen in tearing the burning brands from beneath the building, and trampling the fire under foot until it was extinguished. The instant that all danger ceased, I could not refrain from giving vent to laughter — a proceeding that caused some astonishment on Allen's part.

"Is this a laughing matter?" he asked.

"The fire is not, I'll admit," I replied; "but look in that thorn bush, and tell me if you ever saw a priest in a worse position."

"Help, you young devils!" came in doleful strains from the priest; and as there was no danger of an attack from the ladrones, we had time to advance towards the padre, and survey his position at leisure.

"Hallo!" cried Allen; "what are you doing there? I supposed you was in pursuit of a ladrone."

"Don't stop to ask questions," Father Benventuro replied, "but help me from this cussed bush, which is as full of thorns as a woman's frock is full of temptation and pins. I'm full of punctures, and my body is pitted as though it had had the small-pox. Give me your hands, that's a good fellow, and assist me, for the more I stir myself the worse I'm off."

"But how came you there?" demanded Allen.

"None of your business, you inquisitive Yankee," was the reply. "Help me, or I'll leave you to do your own fighting another time."

With some trouble and danger to ourselves, we succeeded in extricating Benventuro from his uncomfortable position; but when the priest was fairly released from the embrace of the thorn bush, he abused us in the most hearty manner for leading him from the pleasures of the table to an encounter so much to his disadvantage. In fact, he offered to show us certain portions of his body, to prove that he was a martyr; but we declined the exhibition with much firmness, and laughed at his scars so sincerely that he was compelled to join us, and acknowledge that he might have been injured much worse.

"The way of it was," the padre said, in explanation, "I started for the incendiary, who lighted the fire, and overtook him after a short run. We grappled, and a terrible struggle ensued. He attempted to use his knife on me, but I avoided the blade, and wrenched it from his hand. I was just conquering him, when two of the scamp's friends attacked me, and I was compelled to devote my attention to them; but while I was striking to the right and left, I slipped and fell upon those bushes, which the saints may curse if they please, or they may let it alone."

We had no desire to refute the story which the priest had conjured up; so we let him continue to magnify until I think he really attributed the success of the sortie to his own efforts. When he had concluded, we paid a visit to the two ladrones whom we had seen fall, and found that they were both seriously wounded, and needed immediate attention. The priest conversed with the men for a short time in a low tone, while we stood at a distance waiting for him.

"These men must be cared for," he said at length, calling us to him. "They are hurt — probably fatally; and although they are bad men, and would have killed you if possible, still you are well avenged, and must feel satisfied. As a priest, it is my duty to see that their injuries are attended to. You can have no objections to that, I trust."

Of course we had no objections. Our enmity terminated when the men fell, and we felt thankful to think they were not killed outright.

"If we can be of any assistance, command us," Allen said.

"No, no; go home and go to bed, and leave me to take charge of the wounded," replied the priest, somewhat eagerly. "You can be of no use here, and might do much harm. Leave all to me."

"But the ladrones may make another attempt to fire the factory," Allen said.

"I pledge you my priestly word that your building shall not be molested by these men," the padre cried. "I have some control over them, and they will obey me quicker than a file of soldiers. Now go and leave me alone with them, and be sure that you don't return or send any one to disturb us."

"What do you propose to do?" Allen asked. "You will need help to remove these men, for they are incapable of motion."

"I will find help as soon as you leave the ground. Now go, like good boys that you are, and don't let me have to beg of you to do so again. Moments are precious, for life is ebbing away rapidly."

He spoke so earnestly that we no longer hesitated to leave the spot and retrace our steps towards the factory. When we were about forty yards from the priest, I heard a peculiar cry that sounded like the wail of a wounded monkey. The cry was so singular that we stopped and looked back. Amid the trees we could see the figures of many men moving as though bearing burdens towards the river.

"The priest has called the gang together, and they are removing the wounded to boats," Allen said; and then we turned our backs upon them, and let them work without molestation, confident that the priest was a safeguard against any further attack, for that night at least.

"One would hardly have expected such a display of sympathy on the part of Benventuro," my friend remarked; "yet I, who knew the man well, was not unprepared for it. He likes fun as well as any person outside of the clergy, yet when the rites of the church are required, no man can perform them with more dignity.

THE NEXT MORNING.

He is a strange mixture of sinner and saint — man of the world and minister of the church — always ready for a drinking bout or a feast, a funeral or a marriage. Take him in every respect, I had much rather have his friendship than his enmity."

It was past eleven o'clock when we reached the house, tired and anxious for that rest which we so much ueeded. We drank a few sups of cool claret, and then separated, Tom and myself to swing our hammocks in one room, while Allen did the same in his apartment.

I do not know whether the scenes through which I had passed were conducive to sleep, or whether the long race which I had run had so entirely fatigued my system that all dreams and spells had to give way to slumber; but certain it is that I did not awaken until I heard Tom roar out an inquiry as to my intentions of remaining in bed all day.

The table was already spread when we reached the dining-room, and down we sat without formality.

"By the way, how are your patients, whose carcasses were riddled last night?" Allen asked.

The jolly manner of the priest changed at once. His face looked serious, and his eyes thoughtful.

"My dear young friends," he said, "there are some things which even you must not discuss. Speak no more about the men, and try to forget them. They will never trouble you again; that I can assure you."

"But why this air of mystery?" I asked.

"Your tea is excellent this morning. Was it brought from China by private hands, or did it pay the queen's dues at the custom-house?"

Allen winked, and I knew by the signal and the priest's evasion that it was useless to question further. He had his secrets, and no human being could obtain them; so, whether the men were dead and had made a confession, or whether they were likely to get well, was known only to Benventuro and the other parties interested.

"At what hour shall we leave here for the cock-pit?" Allen asked, after a few seconds' silence.

"About twelve, I think, would be a good hour," the padre replied. "We can then witness the sport and be back by dinner time, if nothing happens to disarrange our plans. I have ordered the convent banco to be in readiness to take us to San Pedro Macati, or if you like we can dine and sleep at the convent."

There was not that willingness to consent to the latter arrangement which one would have expected. Allen and myself remembered the night we had passed there too vividly to desire to visit the place a second time, even knowing, as we did, that the priest was friendly to us. The sudden death of Don Arturo had never been satisfactorily explained to my mind, although I was married to his widow.

Our silence was growing embarrassing, when Tom suddenly relieved us.

"Don't go off there," he said, "'cos the basket of wine that I have sent for will arrive this afternoon in time for dinner."

"If ever there was a sensible man, you are one," cried the padre, in a burst of enthusiasm. "We will return to the factory. I feel my throat parched at the very idea of commencing a contest with twelve gentlemen in black, with silver heads and effervescent stomachs. We will make them yield, or fall in the attempt."

"Where? under the table?" asked Allen.

The priest looked fixedly at the interrogator for a second without speaking. Then he winked one eye rapidly, and smiled as he lighted a cigar, and drew away from the table.

"There is a man in the court-yard who wishes to see the holy father Benventuro," said the servant, entering to clear the table.

"Well, what does he want? To confess his sins, or to be wedded?" demanded the priest.

"He does not look as though he was a candidate for matrimony, senor, for a more villanous face I never saw on man."

"*Santa Marie!* he must mean my steward, the amiable Antonio. I know of no other man whose face is frightful enough to scare women. He has returned from his expedition in season. Show him in. If he brings not good news, I'll have his head shaved as a punishment."

The servant left the room to obey the orders of the priest, and in a few seconds we heard the cat-like tread of his man-of-all-work.

The fellow entered the apartment, and threw a rapid glance around the room; and this time his eye rested upon the servant, as though wondering why he was permitted to be present.

The priest seemed to comprehend the fellow's thoughts, for he ordered the servant to give his steward a glass of gin, and then to leave the room.

"And hark you," the padre said; "if I catch you or your companions listening at the doors, I'll make you do penance that will reduce you to skin and bones in a week's time. Recollect, I shall be as good as my word."

I was dying with anxiety to hear some intelligence respecting my wife; yet I was forced to appear composed, and sat there in solemn silence, while the steward poured down his gin with a gusto that showed he had sent many drinks of the strong liquor on the same journey.

The fellow smacked his lips, and then looked into the bottom of his glass, as though sorry that it had not contained a larger quantity. He deposited the tumbler upon a table, and then stood before the priest to await his interrogations.

"Have you found any trace of the one I sent you in pursuit?" the priest impatiently demanded.

The steward glanced at us and then at the padre in a meaning manner.

"You need not fear to speak before these gentlemen as freely as though I was alone. They know the object of your going to Manila," the padre said.

"I have made a few inquiries," the steward remarked, "and find that the Senora Donna Teresa is in the power of Father Juan, and that he is likely to keep her a prisoner for some months, unless he changes his mind."

"Tell us all that you have learned," the priest said.

"I like to act, not talk," the fellow cried, somewhat sulkily.

"And when I command, you must do both," Benventuro replied, haughtily; and as he spoke he held up one of his fingers, and made a significant motion, which must have meant something, for the man's manners underwent a most miraculous change, and instead of the bold bravo, we saw before us the cringing ruffian, trembling at the frown of his master. "Now that we understand each other, go on with your story, and mind and speak the whole truth," the priest continued.

"I always speak the truth to you, senor," the steward said, hardly daring to lift his humble eyes to those of the holy father.

The priest made a motion of impatience, and the steward commenced an account of his discoveries in Manila.

"As soon as I reached Manila, senor, I visited the Convent of St. Sebastian, where I have a friend, and pretended that I thought some of leaving your service, and that I should like to get an engagement where there was some life and fun going on. I knew the man I was talking with, for we have done some odd jobs together in other days, and I always found him as true as steel. I had to represent that I was disgusted with the peaceful, quiet life which I led at the convent of San Pedro before I could gain my friend's confidence; and even then a bottle of wine was required to open his heart and make him confide in me. But after his head was affected, his feelings underwent a change. He told me that I could engage with Father Juan in a few weeks, if everything worked well, but that I could not make a definite arrangement at present, because the convent was poor."

"May the blessed saints always keep it in that condition," was the fervent prayer of Father Benventuro.

"I asked for an explanation," Antonio continued, "but my friend only laughed and shook his head. At length he did tell me that the convent would become one of the richest in the island, if Father Juan's plans were not interrupted by a number of cursed heretics, who were prowling around the city for the purpose of making their fortunes at the expense of good Catholics. I joined my curses to his, and said that a sharp knife would soon rid the holy father of their presence, and that I should have no objections to perform a certain part, if good inducements were held out to me. This answer had some effect, for my friend then told me that a lady, whose name he did not wish to mention, but she was independently rich, had taken an amorous fancy to an American who was residing in the city, and who was doing a large business, exporting rice to China; that Father Juan had made desperate attempts to break up the connection, but had failed, just as he supposed he was about to be successful, through the wilfulness of the lady; that he was determined to get possession of her person, and hold her a prisoner until she was willing to enter the convent and give all her property to Father Juan. For that purpose the father had lingered around a house which she was visiting, intending to seize her as soon as she attempted to return home."

"The cursed scoundrel!" I cried, no longer able to suppress my rage.

"Peace, my son," the priest said, as gentle a rebuke as he could utter; "let not your passions overpower you. What has been done was the will of —"

"The devil," interrupted Allen, who saw that the priest hesitated for a proper word.

Benventuro made no reply. He waved his hand, and his satellite continued:—

"After my friend spoke thus freely, he no longer sought to conceal anything from me. Perhaps it was because I carried a couple of flasks of wine with me, or because he thought that I was speaking the truth, when I said that I desired to change my masters. If he supposed that I was sincere, I am fearful he has altered for the worse during the past few years, for my friend was seldom guilty of uttering more than one truth for ten lies, and I was always considered much like him. At any rate the wine opened his mouth, and his tongue told me that, on the night of the earthquake, Donna Teresa was brought to the river door of the convent in a banco, and even entered the building, but that Father Juan feared the archbishop would be bribed by you to interfere, senor; so the same bancarios who took her to the convent were further employed to carry her up the river to a house which the priest has full control of; but where that house is, my friend did not know, or refused to divulge. I tried every offer that I could think of, without letting my mission be discovered, to get the desired information, but I failed."

"Tell me," I cried, "did your friend see the lady when she was brought to the convent?"

"He did, senor," answered the steward.

"Did he tell you that she was much affected by her imprisonment?" I demanded.

"She wept sometimes, senor, but oftener uttered threats like a high-born Spanish lady who felt that she was ill treated. She did not supplicate, but many times, in her anguish, she called upon her husband to save and protect her."

"This is monstrous!" I exclaimed; "a lady is suddenly seized and imprisoned, and I must content myself by waiting patiently for her deliverance. If I could but lay one hand upon the neck of that rascally priest, he would never commit another outrage, or cause a tear in Teresa's eyes."

"But as you can't do as you wish, you must be governed by our advice; and that you will find judicious in the end. The search is not yet ended, nor the danger that you are liable to meet at the hands of Father Juan. We have succeeded wonderfully so far; so don't defeat the object of our enterprise by any rash action. Be calm and patient, and your wife will yet repose in your arms, all the happier for her trials."

What argument could I employ against the advice of the priest? I was a stranger in the land, and unaccustomed to the tricks of the Jesuits and Mestizos; and much as I loved my wife, I was compelled to let others work in my behalf, and do that which I would have given all my wealth to have done.

"You have not disappointed me," the priest said, addressing his steward; "the information which you have imparted is important, and is appreciated by us all. But you must do better, even if you go without sleeping or eating for a week. You must discover the house where the lady is imprisoned, and when you have done so, we will take steps to free her. Go back to Manila, and like a shadow track Father Juan's steps; let him not move a dozen yards without your knowledge; night and day keep him in sight, and yet let him not even suspect that he is watched. Now return to Manila, and give us early information."

The fellow bowed as though the priest's word was law, and was about to leave the room, when I stopped him.

"Remember that you are not working for an ungrateful man," I said. "If you discover the lady, a heavy reward will be your portion. What you have done already shall be paid for; but be careful and not purchase too much wine."

I slipped two doubloons into his hand, and the dark face of the man lighted up with such a satisfied look that I did not regret the gold.

"Senor," he said, with more courtesy than I ever saw him exhibit before, "if your wife is in Manila I'll find her."

He turned and left the room suddenly, as though he had some fear that Father Benventuro might request a dividend of what he had received. I watched him until he reached the river, where he had a banco, and had the satisfaction of seeing him paddle towards the city with lusty strokes.

"A trusty fellow," exclaimed Benventuro; "but he requires a steady hand to manage him. He is wilful at times, but I think he means well. He is useful, very useful, 'on occasions.'"

"I will lay a wager that he has committed some crime in the course of his lifetime, and that you keep him in subjection by having a knowledge of it," Allen said.

"Fie, for shame! to suspect so good a fellow," the priest said, smiling; but he did not deny the charge, or make further allusion to it; and as we knew the priest confided to us what he pleased, and no more, we did not press him for an exposure.

The time lagged until the hour for dinner, which was served at twelve o'clock, thus conforming to the usage of sea-life. As soon as the meal was concluded, we left the table, and embarked on board of the convent banco, and were slowly paddled up the river towards San Pedro Macati, where the cock-fighting was announced to take place, and where the priest hoped to make a few ounces on a favorite bird which he had been training for some time past; but his passion for gambling was too deep rooted to care for reverses, and I had no doubt that, if occasion required, he would stake even his black robe for the sake of a little excitement. The fact of a priest being partial to cock-fighting was too universal in Manila to provoke comment. Some would frequently leave the church for the cock-pit, and yet lose none of the odor of Christianity in the estimation of their followers. They staked heavily on the result of a fight, and, if they lost, paid with as indifferent an air as possible. If they won they were glad, but that was the only emotion observable upon their smooth faces. It was only during the excitement of a battle that they lost all control over their passions, and made wagers, which, in their calmer hours, they would have hesitated to take.

By one o'clock we were at San Pedro Macati. Already was the village alive with people, who had flocked to the place from all quarters, with their favorite birds in their hands, and a small stock of money in their pockets, for the purpose of betting. The air was vocal with crowing, each chanticleer endeavoring to drown the noise of his neighbor, but not being successful, grew frantic with rage, and made demonstrations of hostility towards all who approached. These bursts of passion were looked upon with great interest by the natives, as they exhibited the true breed for fighting purposes, and many small bets were made before the cocks were exhibited in the arena, where they were to contend for the supremacy, and kill their antagonist, or suffer themselves to be killed.

Before we had reached the central portion of the village, the individual who exercised the same functions as a mayor, being responsible to the government at Manila for riots, murders, or plottings, and authorized to arrest the actors in such dramas, made his appearance, and greeted the padre with every demonstration of respect. He was an old man, with a grave face, as became his station, and a severe eye, which told how little he would hesitate at ordering a hundred blows with a stick, or make the victim come down handsomely with gold for pardon and escape of punishment. And the Mestizos seemed to stand in awe of his authority, for they did not press around us when they found that he was to take us in charge, and that we were vouched for by such a respectable man.

One of the peculiar laws of the island is that which prevents foreigners from visiting the several villages on the river, unless a passport is obtained. This is for the security of the Spanish authority, which brooks no interference, and is continually haunted by thoughts of revolution, and a general massacre of the soldiers and citizens of Spain. The government is well aware that the country offers great inducements for intrigues; hence in each town is an individual who is called the mayor, whose duties I have defined. In addition to this official are several spies, whose occupation is to watch the mayor, and see that he is faithful to his trust.

If a foreigner, therefore, wishes to land at a village for even a few common necessaries, his arrival is quickly communicated to the mayor, and that worthy pays him a visit, perhaps with his pants under his arm, or minus a shirt. The arrival is questioned. He merely landed for the purpose of buying some milk. Has he a passport? No. Then he will be kind enough to occupy a room under a guard of natives, until the will of the authorities at Manila is known; and as the latter are slow at moving, a week or more elapses before a release is ordered, or a command to bring the prisoner to the city for examination.

It was quite fortunate for us that the mayor was not only acquainted with the padre, but was on terms of intimacy with Allen, Santa Mesa and San Pedro Macati being but a few miles apart.

Under these circumstances, of course, no inquiries were made regarding our visit, although candor compels me to state that we were immediately made captives by the mayor, and marched to his residence, surrounded by a whole body of inquisitive Mestizos.

Our imprisonment was not of the rigorous kind, by any means, for the mayor with great pomp conducted us to the best house in town, and showed us to a room where we could make ourselves comfortable, in huge bamboo chairs, with rests for the feet and pillows for the head; and while we were trying the softness of bamboo, a naked little boy brought us cigars and fire, and when we were in a cloud of smoke our host ushered in a young girl, evidently a daughter, but she bore a huge jar of liquid, the perfume of which seemed very grateful on a warm day. The vessel was deposited on the earthen floor, and then two more girls made their appearance, in costumes which would hardly be considered as appropriate for females in this country, excepting in a ballet or circus.

"O Lord!" muttered Tom, whose susceptible heart began to blaze at the sight of so many charms; "I can't stand this long. If those girls don't cover up their necks, I shall certainly have a fit."

The girls filled pint cups of stone ware from the jar, and then advanced and offered them to us with considerable grace. We were at a loss to understand what the beverage was made of, but a slight sip soon set our minds at rest. It was lemonade of the most delicious quality. Cool and crispy as ice water. Such as I had never drank before, but often drank afterwards, when I could get a native who understood the art to prepare some.

For a few seconds four heads might have been seen thrown back, and then four long sighs, as the cups were emptied, heard, and four voices proclaimed the rapture which was felt as the soothing beverage tickled their palates.

And the mayor stood by, and saw our delight with an expression of intense satisfaction upon his dark face at the admiration with which we hailed his skill.

"Holy father," cried the mayor, "let the girls assist you and your friends to another drink."

"My son," replied the padre, "my senses are in such a whirl

of delight at tasting your cool lemonade, that you shall have my blessing. Kneel, my son, and receive it."

And the mayor did as directed. He dropped upon his knees, and the sign of the cross was made over his head. The man arose, seemed very grateful, while the father looked very commanding and very thirsty.

"Now, my daughters," the kind-hearted padre said, holding out his mug, "fill this, and see that it don't remain empty while I am in the house. If you are attentive, my children, I shall bless you before I go."

The mayor was so pleased at our praise that he sent one of his daughters for fruit, and she returned with a variety; and for an hour we sat in the cool room of the house smoking and quenching our thirst, and occasionally complimenting the ladies, while the longer we staid the better terms we were with them. But a rude native, who considered cock-fighting superior to love-making, entered, and in humble tones announced to Father Benventuro that the battles were about to begin, and that only the presence of the mayor and himself were wanted.

Of course we all arose at this announcement, and began to make preparations to start; but I noticed that Tom seemed indifferent, and was not inclined to move, and I instantly guessed the reason. He preferred the society of girls to cock-fighters, and if I had not been a married man, and a faithful one at that, I should not have blamed him greatly, for the girls were quite fresh-looking, and had very plump, enticing forms.

"Come, Tom, we are about to start," I said. "If you are going with us, you had better put your coat on, and get ready."

"O, I don't care for cock-fighting," he replied. "There'll be a crowd, and I don't like crowds. Better go without me, and call when you return this way."

"Confound him," whispered Allen, "he wants to make love to these girls during our absence. I don't blame him much for it; but, as we shan't stand a fair chance, I'll cheat him of his fun."

He spoke a few words to the mayor in the Mestizo tongue, and that functionary appeared extremely gratified. He gave his daughters an order, and expressions of the most profound delight were instantly observed upon their faces.

"Well, if you will remain here," Allen said, speaking to Tom, "make yourself as contented as possible. You will have the house all to yourself."

"But the girls intend to remain — don't they?" demanded Tom, with some eagerness.

"O, no; they are going with us. Women are too fond of crowds and battles to stay away from them."

"Hang the luck!" muttered the disappointed man; "I won't stay here all alone. I think I'll also go."

We started from the house, sheltering our heads from the sun by means of Chinese umbrellas, which the mayor loaned us, while to Tom's extreme gratification one of the young girls suffered him to hold the screen over her head while on the way to the building where the cocks were to fight.

Our arrival seemed to be the signal for the fights to commence, for two natives brought in two cocks, one white and the other red. After showing the birds to the audience, and proclaiming their owners' names, the cocks were allowed to peck away at each other, while the natives held them in their arms. After their passions were excited to the highest degree, the animals were dropped to the ground, and joined in combat.

Then the betting began with enthusiasm, the priest leading off by shouting, "Two dollars on the red!" Hardly were the words out of his mouth, before his bet was accepted by a native who carried a bag full of dollars in his hand, and shook them to attract attention, and give evidence that he was capable of paying his losses.

From all parts of the building were heard bets, from five dollars down as low as six cents. The audience was not kept long in suspense regarding the battle, however, and it seemed to me that before the bets were all made and accepted the fight was finished, the white cock having received his quietus from a long spur, made of steel, and fastened to the red cock's legs.

"Thank the saints, I have started well," muttered the priest, as he pocketed the native's two silver dollars, and lighted a cigar.

"It's devilish exciting — ain't it?" asked Tom, who was seated by the side of the girls, making desperate work speaking intelligible Spanish.

"The cock-fighting, or love-making?" I asked.

"Why, the fighting, to be sure. I'm too much accustomed to the other sort of thing to mind it much," was Tom's cool reply, but I knew that he was in a flutter of agitation all the time.

The dead and live cocks were carried off, and a black and gray were brought in of more pretensions than the previous ones.

"Bet your money on the black cock," whispered the priest to Allen and myself. "I own the bird, and know his metal. He will whip the gray to a certainty."

"An ounce on the black!" shouted Benventuro.

I supposed that not a man in the whole crowd possessed the sum, but I was mistaken. The fellow with the bag of dollars took the wager up in a second, and several others manifested a strong desire to win the padre's money. For a few minutes the confusion was intense, as all were shouting their bets and their favorite birds.

But after the wagers were all made, silence was instantly restored. The birds were dropped to the ground, and went at each other like human brutes engaged in a prize fight. At every blow exchanged the crowd applauded. The battle was a very good one, for both of the cocks were of the real sporting breed, and were well trained before the steel spurs were buckled on their legs. The blows were fiercely given, but no particular damage was done for the first five minutes.

I saw that the priest was uneasy for the safety of his investments, and I almost hoped that he would lose; but the devil stood his friend that time, at any rate, for the black cock made a sudden movement that the gray one was not prepared for, and through his brain was driven the long steel spur; and so strong was the blow that the victorious cock could not extricate the weapon without assistance.

"The saints be praised for my luck," piously ejaculated the priest. "If I can only keep on as I have begun, I shall make up some of my heavy losses."

In the mean time my attention was attracted towards the girls, who were laughing, and apparently in a great state of excitement.

"Only think!" shouted Tom; "the girls are betting dollars on the fights, and seem anxious to win. It's great fun — isn't it?"

"It's fun for them, but your purse has to suffer," replied Allen; and sure enough, I saw that the foolish fellow was supplying them coin to bet, and that it disappeared into their pockets as soon as a battle was decided. The mayor smiled approvingly upon the sport, and seemed to envy the shrewdness of his daughters. Tom also seemed delighted, and as he was his own master, his proceedings were none of our business."

"How much did you win that time?" I asked of Benventuro.

"Three ounces, and all paid up. I've got one more bird here from the convent, and I shall stake all on him. Here he comes. The red one, with eyes like balls of fire. He'll fight like the devil, and lick anything in the shape of a cock that lives. See him strive to get away. Bet all your money on him, and you will be sure to win."

The convent bird was a magnificent specimen of game cock, being unusually large, and full of fight. His opponent was much smaller, and was nearly black; but he had a wicked look, which induced me to think that he was full as plucky and smart as the priest's pet. For five minutes the betting went on very briskly, and hundreds of dollars were staked on the birds. The holy father bet all of his winnings, and was confident of the result, and the excitement raged so that I forgot my unhappiness, and found myself staking two ounces on the black bird, much to the priest's disgust, for he whispered to me that I should certainly lose my money; but I was not so sure of it, and preferred my judgment to his.

The result was fully equal to my expectations. The convent cock made a rush for his opponent as though he intended to annihilate him, but the black cock was wide awake, and dodged very handsomely. The ruse produced a round of applause, the ladies adding their sweet voices to the general uproar. The priest grew anxious, and pronounced a curse upon cock-fighting generally.

Once more the birds stood face to face, their feathers curling with rage, and their eyes glowing with fire. They made a few feints like prize fighters, but the black cock was evidently waiting for the attack, and rather stood on the defensive. Suddenly the red bird made a rush, and struck like lightning; but the black cock's head was close to the ground, and the blows missed. The priest groaned, and calculated the amount of money which he had staked. The ladies laughed, and doubled their bets, Tom finding the money, of course.

The red cock strutted around the arena like a dandy, and

even attempted to crow; but before the defiance had quitted his throat, the cunning little black fellow dashed towards him, and, with a spiteful blow, drove one of his steel spurs into his opponent's neck. The blood spurted, and the red cock endeavored to keep his feet, and fight the battle to the death. But his strength was not equal to the courage. He staggered first one side and then the other, and at length fell upon his side and died; but even then the black cock was not disposed to let him alone, and had to be plucked from the body and carried away struggling.

"What do you think of the convent cock now?" I asked of the priest.

"Blast the cock, and curse cock-fighting!" he cried. "I have lost the last dollar that I have about me, and if I remain here a second longer, may the saints curse me."

"For shame!" I said; "a priest, and to display so much passion for the loss of a few dollars!"

"O, it's all very well for you, who have won three or four ounces, to cry shame; but how would you feel to have your favorite bird killed, and win nothing on his head? It's all a cursed trick, and I won't bet another real on a cock-fight as long as I live."

"Wait a moment," Allen said, delighted at the opportunity to hector the holy father. "Make another bet, and perhaps you will win. Here come two noble cocks for a fight, and the Mestizos are more anxious than ever for wagers. Take some of them up."

The priest hesitated for a moment, then felt of his pockets; but not finding a dollar there, muttered a curse, and struggled to escape from the building — an example I was only too glad to follow, for I had seen as much as I desired of cock-fighting, for one day at least.

Poor Tom, who seemed destined to be thwarted in his little love adventures, begged of us to wait until the show was ended, but when he found that we would not, he cursed in set terms our obstinacy; the fear of being left in the village all night without company was before his eyes, and he was compelled to tear himself away from his inamoratas, and follow us grumbling.

"If this is not the meanest piece of business that I have experienced since I left York!" he exclaimed. "Just as I was captivating the girls by my unbounded liberality, you must needs be starting off. It's all jealousy of the favor they were showing me. I know it is, and you cannot deny it."

"How many dollars are you out of pocket?" Allen asked, hardly noticing our friend's upbraidings.

"O, I don't mind the money, 'cos I've got a plenty," Tom answered. "They borrowed about ten dollars from me; but I am sure they are welcome to it, and I shall never expect or receive payment. The only thing that I am disposed to find fault with, is coming away and leaving those poor girls inconsolable at my loss."

"This," said Allen, stopping suddenly, and assuming a serious aspect, "is the gratitude we receive for saving this gentleman's life. I saw that you were in danger of having your throat cut, and I hastened to save you. A few minutes more and you would have been past help."

"God bless me! what was the matter?" asked Tom, eagerly.

"Do you mean that you did not see the lovers of the girls glaring at you from the opposite side of the building, and that they worked at the handles of their knives as though desirous of exterminating your flirtation? You must have seen them, and tried to make the fellows believe you cared nothing about the matter."

"No, I pledge you my word I did not; and if such was the case, why, I don't blame you for wishing to get me out of the way of danger, although you know that if I had fair play I should care but little for them. My revolver is worth a dozen knives. How the girls must miss me!"

"And your dollars," I ventured to suggest; but Tom was content to have the hint pass without notice, confident in his own opinion that the girls cared more for his person than his money — a mistake which too many Europeans indulge in, when they confide their affections to a Mestizo girl.

We had proceeded but a few steps on our way, when the mayor came running after us, and in most urgent tones begged us to again visit his house, and have some refreshments; but the padre's temper was soured by his losses, and he refused to touch another drop of lemonade unless there was wine on the table to warm his stomach; and as the mayor never knew the luxury of a glass of champagne, there was no hope of getting anything for our friend short of the factory.

We excused ourselves, therefore, to the mayor as well as we

were able, and once more embarked for home. As soon as we were on the water the priest's spirits rose, and he no longer alluded to his misfortunes. He hinted that the time was not far distant when he should have funds enough to enable him to buy all the game cocks in Manila, and get up fights for his own amusement; and while he was thus congratulating himself, the banco reached the factory.

I was too anxious to obtain information of my wife to care to remain at Santa Mesa for supper, which generally was served at seven o'clock; but all my arguments were overthrown, and I was compelled to wait until Allen could leave his business and accompany me.

Absence from my wife had but increased my love for her; and as I sat by the window which overlooked the Pasig, and saw the sun hide its face behind the hills, I could hardly restrain the deep emotion which I felt when I thought that perhaps Teresa was also gazing at the scene, and wondering why I took no steps for her recovery.

I felt more than ever determined to wage an unceasing war against Father Juan, and in spite of his hired assassins and bravos to gain possession of her I loved so well; and I thought if she was once more clasped in my arms, that I would take care and protect her with a strong heart and an unfaltering hand.

While I was thus indulging in reveries, I felt a hand upon my shoulder, and looking up, saw the holy Father Beuventuro standing over me.

"Why do you look so sober, Guillermo?" he inquired. "Are you still thinking of your wife?"

"Who else should I think of at such an hour?" I demanded.

"There are many things to attract a young man's attention," he replied, "and had you been married and lived with your wife a couple of years, you would think so. But I am glad to see that you feel miserable without her, for it will spur you on to greater exertions for her recovery; and when you have gained possession of her, I shall expect to see such perfect domestic bliss that all the young people in Manila will visit you, for the purpose of learning the history of your happiness. Mourn on, Guillermo, mourn on; but as for me, I must live without a wife, or children to call me father."

"And do you really chafe under the vows that bind you to celibacy?" I asked, somewhat astonished.

"Well, I can't say that I do, for in fact I am not one of the marrying kind. I had much rather unite people in wedlock than to be united myself."

"But do you not like children?"

"I am passionately fond of little pets, and some day I will show you quite a number who call me uncle. That title is a respectable one, and solves a good many questions from people who are fond of asking them. No, I am not a father in the general acceptance of the term, but love my nephews and nieces.

I let the conversation drop, and, acting on Allen's hint, got ready to accompany him to Manila, the Mecca of my hopes and fears.

We took the convent banco, with but two assistants, for the purpose of not attracting attention. The men who paddled the boat were tolerably trustworthy, and were almost strangers in Manila; so we knew that they would be likely to remain by the banco until our return, even if we were gone all night, which we did not expect.

We reached the city about eight o'clock, and the first visit I made after landing was to my wife's house, for the purpose of consulting with Donna Raquel, Teresa's maiden aunt. I left Allen in the street while I entered the house, for my friend stood in wholesome fear of the old lady's tongue, and did not care to encounter its bitterness, if he could avoid it.

The old lady received me with great cordiality, and instantly rang the bell, and ordered me a glass of her bitters, for fear the night air would affect my stomach and disarrange my liver; and after she had watched and satisfied herself that I had swallowed the dose, she prepared herself for a string of questions; but I got the best of her by first inquiring if she had seen my wife, or had any joyful tidings to communicate respecting her whereabouts?

"O, you poor child!" she began, "I have not slept an hour, thinking of you and Teresa, and wondering when we shall see the last of these disagreeable troubles. My appetite, too, is all gone, and were it not for the bitters I should sink into my grave;

and I don't know but that would be the best place for me, for really there's nothing for one to live for."

I stated that I hoped the saints would spare her for many years of happiness, and I have no doubt but that she desired the same thing, but thought it would not look well to acknowledge it. Once more I asked for information concerning my wife, but I rightly judged that she had none to give me.

"I have not heard the first word respecting her, poor child, and sometimes I think I never shall again. I wish hey had taken me instead of my niece; I think that I could have found means to escape, had there been fifty men employed to watch me. But Teresa has not got half the courage that I possess, and I am afraid that but few women have. They are not what they used to be; the saints pardon me for saying so."

I had no hesitation in saying that the abductors knew better than to attempt the capture of so spirited a lady as Donna Raquel — a remark that was considered complimentary; and as a recompense I was made to drink one more glass of her famed cordial, which she warranted would enable me to bear up under my misfortunes, and keep me in good condition until I was enabled to see my wife.

"Have you seen Father Juan?" I asked, after a few moments of silence on my part, but vigorous conversation from my maiden friend.

"He was here this forenoon, and remained but a short time, pleading that he had a pressing engagement. He asked for Teresa, and I told him that she was at her country-seat, I supposed. I manifested no anxiety in regard to her; but watched his face and actions closely, and I am firmly convinced that he has confined Teresa somewhere in the city, and that he is determined to keep her a prisoner until she consents to his demands. I said nothing that would lead him to think I suspected such a thing, and the priest left me after a few hasty inquiries respecting yourself."

"And pray what did he say regarding me?" I asked.

"Simply whether I thought Teresa would marry a heretic, regardless of the wishes of her best friends. That question, I told him, I was unable to answer, for women were wilful when their hearts were touched. He said nothing, but left the house very thoughtful."

I was sorry that Raquel had no better news for me; but the lady promised to work in my behalf, and not even to take a *siesta* until I was righted, and her niece set free. I pleaded business, and left the house, promising to call in every day and give her the result of my doings; and with a recommendation to the saints to have me in their keeping, she bade me good night. Outside of the garden walls I found Allen, smoking a cigar, and waiting with patience my appearance.

"Well, how was Donna Raquel to-night? In a pacific mood, or an argumentative one?" he inquired.

"She was mild and hospitable; full of sympathy and regrets," I answered.

"You have, then, accomplished the greatest triumph that has been witnessed on this island for years," Allen answered. "Donna Raquel I considered untamable by man or woman."

In silence we walked on through the crowded streets, until we reached my residence. We paused at the foot of the staircase, for we heard a female voice singing a Mestizo song, not in the monotonous tones that characterize the Mestizo race, but with much sweetness and power.

"Hallo!" whispered Allen; "your pet bird is pining in your absence. Go and greet her, and I'll return to the house in an hour's time."

He turned to depart with a smile, but I detained him.

"I have once explained matters to you, and was in hopes that I should not have to speak again on the same subject," I said, with as offended an air as I could assume.

"O, so you did. I ask your pardon. Go along, and I'll follow you."

We passed up stairs so quietly that we did not disturb Gracia, who was seated at a table sewing by the light of a candle. For a few moments we stood looking at her, and a very pretty picture she was to look at. Her clothes were neat and clean, but cut too low in the neck for fashion. In her dark hair were numerous flowers, looking as fresh as her full face, beneath the dark skin of which could be seen the red blood dancing through her veins in all its purity.

"Are you lonely, Gracia, that you sing such a mournful song?" I asked.

The girl started at the sound of my voice, and sprang to her feet; but the instant she saw my face, her look of terror changed to one of joy and surprise.

"O, senor, have you returned?" she asked, as though doubting the evidence of her senses; and in the joy of the moment she would have thrown herself into my arms, but I checked her before she could commit such an impropriety. I thought of my wife, and was safe from temptation. I wish all husbands could truthfully say as much. The world would be better, wives happier, and men would not be kept awake nights thinking of their sins.

"Pardon me, senor," the poor girl said; "I forgot, in the joy of seeing you, that I must not love you. I will try and remember your commands."

"Hang me if this isn't most marvellous," muttered Allen, regarding the girl and myself attentively. "If I should tell Tom and Benventuro, they would swear that I had been drinking, and was unworthy of belief. It's better than a play — much better."

"I told you, Gracia," I said, addressing the girl, "that I had a wife living, and to her I should remain faithful."

"Then bring your wife here, and I will love her and her children as well as I now love you," she cried, earnestly.

"As soon as I have found her, Gracia, you shall see her," I remarked, and was about to pass to my private room when she laid her hands upon my arm and detained me.

"Senor, can I aid you in finding her?"

I hardly knew what to say. I did not like to tell the girl that her father, the night before, had made an attack upon me, and nearly succeeded in his designs; yet I thought for how little she had to be grateful to that parent, who had left her to gain her bread the best way she could.

"If I could see your father, Gracia, perhaps he could aid me," I said, at length.

"Then you shall see him," she exclaimed, promptly. "He was here this afternoon, and promised to call this evening. It is time that he arrived. He met with an accident, so he is incapable of working, and that accounts for his visit to me."

I knew what the accident was, but I did not tell her what caused it. I looked at her attentively for a few moments, and determined to trust her.

"You say that you like me, Gracia?"

" Better than any one in the world," was her candid answer.
" And you are willing to serve me?"
" Faithfully, senor."
" Then, when your father visits you this evening, take him to the sitting-room, and give him a glass of wine; be cautious; see if he won't tell you where he carried the lady, whom he took from this house on the night of the earthquake. He was employed by Father Juan, and a hint to that effect may awaken his recollection. If you succeed, you shall be well rewarded."

" I shall be amply repaid," she said, " if I contribute to your happiness. I will do as you direct, and I pray the saints that I may succeed."

I found that the other servants had all gone to the theatre, so there was but little danger of their interrupting our project; and I thought, if I could get the father of Gracia to confess to his daughter his connection with the plot, I should have a card in my hand that was well worth playing.

While I was giving instructions to the girl, an old man, poorly dressed, and with a staff in his hand, entered the house, and stood at the head of the staircase, bowing low, as though desirous of charity. I held a few coins in my hand, for I supposed the fellow was a beggar; but to my surprise he did not seem anxious for money, for he refused to advance and receive it.

" Can you give me a bed to-night, senor?" he asked, in tremulous tones. " I have travelled for many miles, and am weary."

" I will give you money to buy a bed and supper, but you can't stop in the house," I replied, somewhat astonished at the novel request; for but few Mestizos enjoy the luxury of a bed, or even care for one.

" Well, senor, I suppose I must take the money," he said, after a moment's pause, as though deliberating whether it was best to accept it.

I advanced towards the man, keeping my eyes fixed upon his movements, for I had a slight suspicion that he might mean treachery; but when I was within a step of his person, a voice that I remembered whispered, —

" Can the girl be trusted, senor?"

The suspected beggar put his hand to his face, and lifted a long, white beard, and then I saw the villanous features of Benventuro's steward, Antonio, the convent servant.

I was so astonished that I was about to call his name, but he interrupted me by whining out, —

"I must have something to eat, senor, or I shall never be able to leave the city. The saints will bless you for what you do for me — that you may depend upon."

"You shall have something," I answered; and then turning to Gracia, I directed her, somewhat to her astonishment, to get a plate of cold meat and some bread.

"Why don't you turn the old vagabond out of doors?" asked Allen; "he will fill your house with fleas and vermin of another and more troublesome kind, unless you are very fortunate."

Gracia did not seem pleased with her errand, but she was too anxious to stand well in my estimation to refuse. As soon as she left the room, Antonio's bent form became upright, and his air of dejection deserted him.

"Senors," he asked, "can you trust that girl?"

"I am not certain," I replied, "for I have known her but a few days. She seems faithful."

"And I seemed an old man a few seconds since," was the answer; and there was scorn with the words, as though a man was a fool for trusting any one in this world.

"It's that scamp of Benventuro's," muttered Allen in English, as much surprised at his disguise as I had been.

"If you are not sure of the woman, I had better pass into another room, where we can converse privately," Antonio said.

I pointed to the door of my chamber, and he dodged in just a moment before Gracia returned.

"Here are meat and bread on the table, senor," she said.

"The beggar has left the room, and perhaps the food will not be wanted. Let it stand until after your father has gone, or give it to him. We are now about to enter my chamber. Seat your parent near this door, and make him speak loud, so we can overhear all that he says. Remember, my happiness depends upon you."

I held out my hand to her, which she kissed, and looked so kind that I patted her head, and felt tempted to touch her lips; but thoughts of my wife again prevented, for which I should now feel deeply grateful.

"Well, Antonio, what news have you to communicate?" I asked, as soon as we had closed the door.

"None, senor, of importance. I've been on the track of the holy Father Juan all the afternoon; but he has not visited a house where he would dare leave Donna Teresa for an hour. I just left him at the Church of San Marco, repeating masses for the repose of a rich merchant's soul. He will be detained there two hours, and then I shall track him again, and perhaps he may visit the house where your wife is a prisoner—"

The spy stopped while speaking, and listened attentively.

"Some one is coming up the stairs," he said; "and I hear the young girl speak to him."

How he could have heard as much was a mystery, for although Allen and myself listened attentively, we could not distinguish a sound or footstep.

CHAPTER XI.

GRACIA'S FATHER. — A CONFESSION. — ON THE TRAIL, &C., &C.

"Your girl has a visitor, and she is urging him to take a seat in the front room," Antonio said, with a keen glance at my face, as though he was desirous of satisfying himself that I was not engaged in a plot against his welfare.

"I expected him," I replied, with a gesture to keep silent, and the fellow obeyed; but I could see that his ears were open, and that his snake eyes glistened in anticipation of overhearing private conversation.

Gracia and her father entered the sitting-room, and I could hear her say that she was alone, and expected no one until eleven o'clock. I pardoned the deception that she was practising, because it was for my sake, and men will overlook much on that score.

"You have a good house here, child," the father said. "I hope that the master gives you plenty of money and dresses. Take all that he offers, and if you have no use for money I can relieve you of it. Foreigners make gold fast, and don't value it where a woman is concerned. You are young and handsome, and should command a good price, although I am sorry that I was not consulted in the matter. Women have got too much heart to make a trade."

"But I am not engaged as a mistress," Gracia said. "I am employed to sew and do a little washing."

"Then I am not too late. I'll see the senor to-morrow, and talk with him about your price. He shall pay well, Gracia, for I know how to manage foreigners. And then, if you but do your duty, a pension will be secured to you for life. He has money, and shall pay, or I'll set Father Juan on to him."

At the mention of this name, Antonio redoubled his attention. He seemed to comprehend by instinct that important disclosures were to be made. His eyes grew brighter, if possible, than ever.

"Do not speak to the senor," Gracia said, in a tone of voice that showed how much she disliked the subject of conversation. "The senor is a married man, and virtuous; I have known him but for a few days. He has been kind to me, and I love him as a brother."

"Love him as much as you please, but still make money out of him to help your poor old father in his misfortunes. See, I have lost the use of one hand by an accident; may the saints confound the luck, and only think how pleasant it would be if I could come here and get what I want to eat and drink. Your sister Sara was always thinking of me, and many a glass of wine has she given me."

"And I will do the same," Gracia replied. "Sit where you are, and I will bring you wine and food."

The father grumbled out a few thanks, and signified that whatever she brought would be acceptable.

No sooner had she left the apartment, than Antonio quietly arose and noiselessly bolted the door of the room in which we were sitting.

"What is that for?" I asked.

"It's quite probable that the fellow will desire to see what there is worth stealing in the house, so I have taken the precaution to prevent his getting in here and making a discovery. I may be wrong in suspecting him of stealing, but it is always best to be on the safe side."

Hardly had Antonio concluded, before a hand was laid upon the latch of the door, so softly that had I been alone and reading,

I should not have noticed the incident. There was a slight push to force the door open, but not succeeding, all was quiet again. Antonio gave us a look which expressed his satisfaction at the result, and then recommenced listening with renewed-ardor.

I heard the fellow creep back to his chair after his attempt to explore the recesses of my chamber, and from that time until Gracia's return he sat still, as though conjuring up in his brain some scheme by which he could live without work. His cogitations were not of long duration, for his daughter, perhaps, suspected that he might be restive during her absence, and put something in his pockets that she would prefer I should not lose.

"Here, father," she said, " is wine and bread, and meat."

"Give me the wine first, child," he replied; " because, with a bottle of wine a man can be independent of hunger, and happier than if he ate hearty and drank nothing but water. As a general thing I prefer wine to bread."

"I should think that wine would be bad for your wounded hand, father," Gracia said.

"There is where you are wrong again, child. Wine enables me to endure the pain, and think how I can revenge myself for the injury. After all, the thought of revenge is nearly equal to the reality."

"I think that you told me that your hand was injured by an accident," Gracia observed.

"Then I told a lie, for it was smashed by a heretic, whom I shall make pay for it some day with his blood."

"Can I help you, father?" the girl asked, not suspecting that I was the one who committed the act.

"I am not so certain but you can, girl, if you are shrewd enough to get the fellow in your toils, and keep from loving him. He is detested by the church, for he is a heretic, and Father Juan has no cause to love him."

"Why should Father Juan dislike him?" asked Gracia, filling her father's glass for the second time. "I am sure," she continued, "that if the padre hates him, the heretic is unworthy to live much longer."

The parent did not reply to this speech for a few seconds. He was occupied in draining his glass, and thinking how far he should trust the girl.

"He is unworthy to live, girl; but what makes him unworthy

in my estimation? Because I can make money by his death, and enough of it to give you plenty of dresses, and a ride once in a while on the Calsarda."

The girl filled his glass a third time, and I knew that she was waiting impatiently for a full confession. There were three others equally as curious, and if possible more eager, to hear how the money was to be made.

"A few nights since I made an ounce in an hour's time," the Mestizo said, removing his tumbler to take breath.

"That is a large sum of money, father. Let me see the gold."

"O, it is all gone, child; I had to pay off some old scores with it. But more will come from the priest, or I'll tell my secret to one who can afford to pay well for it."

There was a pause of many minutes' duration. I could hear the fellow's teeth at work as they crunched the food which his daughter had offered him; and while eating he seemed to have no disposition to talk. I wanted to rush out and take him by the throat, and make him tell me all that he knew regarding the abduction of my wife; but I feared that he would prove obstinate, and maintain a stern silence.

"Father Juan is a good man — is he not?" Gracia asked, at length.

"He pays well," was the response; as though that was sufficient to establish his claims for goodness or rascality.

"Shall you get more money from him?" the daughter asked.

"That will depend upon his success in an enterprise he is now engaged in," was the answer; and I fancied that I detected a malicious laugh while speaking.

"What is the enterprise, father?" was the next question, yet asked in such a careless manner that the fellow did not got alarmed and refuse to reply.

"Are you sure that no one can overhear us?" the Mestizo asked, and I fancied that his eyes were directed towards the room in which we were concealed.

"Quite sure," was the answer; and I was ready to admit that if my protégée possessed no other merit, she was something of an adept at deception. But that I pardoned, because it is constitutional with the Mestizo race.

"Well, then, I don't mind telling you; but be sure and keep it a secret, because I expect to make money out of it before I have concluded with Father Juan. I said that a heretic stands in the padre's way, and the reason of it is because he has married, or was about to marry, the widow of old Don Arturo, the Spanish merchant, who died some time since, immensely rich. The holy father wanted the lady to enter his convent, but she had no wish for such a life, and to force her to do so he seized her on the night of the earthquake, and hired my comrade and myself to carry her to the convent. That was a bold trick, but it paid us well, and may the saints send me many more just such jobs."

"And the senora is now confined there?" Gracia asked.

That was a most momentous question, and I held my breath for fear that I should lose the answer.

"No, child, the senora is not there at present. The holy Father Juan is too cunning for that. He feared a search and discovery."

There was another long pause. I heard Gracia fill her father's glass, and the old vagabond smacked his lips as though he rather approved of the wine with which the house was supplied.

"Did the senora complain when she was carried off?" Gracia asked, at length.

"*Diablo!* She was indignant, and abused us all like ladrones. Then she cried, and asked for her husband, and Father Juan wanted to know if she meant the dead one."

I made a movement, and if Allen had not restrained me, I should have gone out and throttled the scamp.

"Poor lady," Gracia said; "it was cruel to treat her so harshly."

"But think of the money we made by doing as we did."

"True, I had forgotten that. Then you know where she is imprisoned at the present time?"

"Of course I do, and that I intend to keep a secret."

"But if I am to assist you I must know all your plans," the daughter said.

"True; and as I think that you can keep a secret, I don't mind telling you. After Father Juan decided that it would be dangerous to keep the lady in his convent, we again took her in our banco, and pulled up the river until we passed the bridge, and reached Mother Machit's house, an old building that is near the edge of the water. No one lives there but the old woman and her son; but they know what the business means, for they have had customers like the senora before. They asked no questions when Father Juan carried the lady to the house; but what was said after we were gone is more than I know. We got our money, and left in search of more."

"And you think that the senora is there at the present time?" Gracia asked.

"I saw the holy father leave the house this afternoon. I suppose from that he had been to pay her a visit."

After this information it was with difficulty that I could restrain my impatience, I was so anxious to start for the house, and commence my search for Teresa. It seemed to me that the ruffian would never leave off guzzling wine, and more than once I heard Gracia hint that perhaps the senor would soon return; but he was deaf to such insinuations, and was just drunk enough to be obstinate and quarrelsome, for every few minutes I heard him mutter that his children cared but little for him, and never divided their earnings, as dutiful and loving daughters should do.

The coolest person compelled to listen to the Mestizo's mutterings was Antonio. He did not seem in the least disturbed by being compelled to wait; but I suppose it was a part of his education to bide his time.

At length all conversation and mutterings ceased, and by the Mestizo's deep breathing I judged that he slept. Carefully Antonio opened the door and looked out, and then he motioned Allen to follow him. Gracia was standing at a table, her eyes red with weeping, and in my pet arm-chair was her father reposing, his dirty legs resting upon the bamboo frame, with as much independence and sang froid as if he was the owner of the house and contents. The villain was snoring most unmusically, and we were not disposed to disturb his rest just at that time, for we feared that he might interfere with our designs.

"Gracia," I said, holding out both hands, "I shall never forget the service that you have done me."

"Did you hear all?" she asked.

"Every word that was spoken."

"And you think that you can find your wife from the confession which he made?"

"I hope so; we are about to start for the house."

The poor girl wished to say something, yet feared to give utterance to her thoughts.

"Speak, Gracia," I said, in a kind tone.

"If you should find the senora, you would bring her here?" she asked.

"Perhaps I should. Why?"

"Because I think she might feel a little jealous seeing me here without knowing my position. Perhaps it would be well for me to leave."

I could hardly believe that there was so much consideration for the feelings of others in the heart of a Mestiza girl, and even Allen shook his head as though he did not exactly know what to make of it.

"Stay here, Gracia, until I tell you to go. I hope that my wife — if I am so fortunate as to find her — will put some little confidence in my honor."

"I wouldn't, if I was a woman," Allen muttered; but as he was always inclined to be sarcastic, I took no notice of his remark.

The girl withdrew to a corner of the room, apparently satisfied; and as we did not care about remaining in the presence of her father, in case he should awaken, we quietly left the house, and stopped to deliberate in the court-yard.

"Let us lose no time," Allen said, " in discussing the matter. We must proceed at once to Mother Machit's house, and force an entrance. If Donna Teresa is there we will find her, and if she has been moved, we may gain some intelligence respecting her."

Antonio said nothing. He seemed to place himself under our command, and was ready to act as we directed. Perhaps he had received orders from Benventuro to do our bidding, and he feared that worthy too much to oppose us in anything.

We started towards the banco which we had left some two or three hours before, and were glad to find that the Mestizos were sleeping soundly upon the mats in the bottom of the boat. We roused them up with but little trouble, and in as quiet a manner as possible, for fear of attracting more attention than we desired at that time of night. I was too excited to fear any danger, yet constantly suspected some trick or treacherous movement on the part of the priest Juan, which would deprive me of the treasure sought for so eagerly. But I was armed, and determined that I would fight to the last in defence of my rights.

"Do you know the house where the lady is confined?" I asked of Antonio.

"Si, senor," I replied.

"Then steer the banco to the spot as quick as possible."

He took the paddle that guided the boat, and then we shoved into the stream, and commenced working our way against the strong current that flowed down the river.

There was not another banco stirring when we started, although there were many moored near the bridge, as though waiting for freights upon the closing of the theatre. The night was uncommonly clear, and by the aid of the moon objects could be discerned for many yards distant. Even the sentinel, who stood upon the bridge, pacing too and fro, could be seen as he stopped for a moment to look at our boat as though wondering if he ought not to challenge us, and find out our business. But he altered his mind, if he had any such intention, and resumed his round, his steel and brass accoutrements glistening in the moonlight like diamonds in a ball-room.

"How much farther have we to go?" I inquired of Antonio, as we swept through one of the lofty arches of the bridge.

"Not more than half a mile, senor," was the answer.

"Then pull strong, men, and let us get home in season," Allen said, addressing the Mestizos who were rowing.

The fellows answered with a grunt, and renewed their exertions, and as we hugged the edge of the river to escape the current we made considerable progress, and I was congratulating myself that we should soon know the worst, when Antonio touched my shoulder, and pointed to a banco that was coming down the river at a rapid rate, being urged through the water by four oars and a steersman.

"That banco belongs to a convent," Antonio said.

"How do you know?" I asked.

"Because, instead of its being covered with a mat it is covered with cloth of a dark-green color."

"Can you tell the name of the convent that it belongs to?" I demanded, somewhat eagerly, for I saw white garments in the stern of the boat, and I thought it was barely possible the priest might be changing the prison of Teresa.

"I am not certain, but I think the craft belongs to the convent of Sebastian. A lady is in the stern of the boat. Shall we give chase and see who they have got? We can shoot across the river, take advantage of this tide, and I think run across the banco's bow."

The spy read consent in my eager looks, and even before he had finished speaking altered the course of our boat, and she was gliding along in almost parallel lines with the convent banco.

"Pull, you scamps!" shouted Allen; "we must reach the arch of the bridge first, or we shall lose sight of the banco."

The men stretched to their long, clumsy oars in earnest, and for a few seconds we actually gained on the strange boat; a fact which was quickly noticed; and then we saw, by the hurried strokes which the convent men gave, that they were determined to keep us at a respectful distance, if hard rowing could accomplish it.

"By heavens! there is a woman in the stern of that banco," Allen said suddenly, after he had watched the course of the convent boat for a few moments in silence. "I think that I can see her struggle with a man who sits beside her."

This information almost drove me distracted, for I imagined that it was Teresa who was being carried away to some place that the priest thought more safe than Mother Machit's.

"An ounce to each man if we overtake the boat!" I shouted. "Pull for your lives, men, and you shall never know want hereafter!"

"Keep cool," whispered Allen, fearing I would commit some rash act while in such an excited state; "sit still in the boat, for your movements make it difficult for the men to row. They can hardly hope to escape us, unless a miracle intervenes."

I did manage to control myself sufficiently to sit down; but I drew my revolver, and longed for an opportunity to use it.

"Good God!" cried Allen, seizing the weapon and wrenching it from my hand; "are you mad, to think of firing a shot directly in front of the city, where we can be covered with a thousand muskets in a minute's time, and riddled with balls before a single question is asked? This is not the time nor place for revolvers. If we intend to capture the crew of that banco, it must be done without noise or confusion. Even the sentinel on the bridge must suppose that we are having a little quiet amusement by racing."

The advice, I have no doubt, was good; but it seemed hard not to fire one shot, just to bring the fellows to their senses, and make them wait our coming.

"There *is* a lady in the banco," Antonio said, aiding the boat through the water with his paddle and steering at the same time.

We had made the discovery some time before.

"She is struggling with a man who has his hand over her mouth," the spy continued, as calm as though great results did not depend upon our success.

"Guillermo!" was the cry I heard proceed from the other boat, and then followed a struggle and exclamations as though a man was endeavoring to prevent some one from speaking.

I should have known that voice from a thousand others, for I had heard it too often ever to forget it.

"Teresa!" I replied, struggling to my feet, and once more endeavoring to wrench the pistol from my friend's hands. "Teresa," I continued, "I am near you, and will save you."

"For Heaven's sake keep quiet," cried Allen; "you will overturn the banco and drown us in the river, and it is a fate I am not prepared for."

But I was too excited to pay attention to his caution. I could only see my wife struggling in the arms of a stranger, and calling to me for protection; and the thought that I was only separated from her by a few rods, and yet unable to assist her, was maddening. I cursed the cowards for their treacherous conduct, and even while I was raving, the bows of the bancos came together with a crash that made them tremble like reeds in a gale. With a desperate leap I attempted to reach the boat containing my wife. My feet just touched the gunnel of the convent banco, rested there for a second, and then I was pushed off and fell into the river, yet before I sank I thought that I could hear a mocking laugh, and the voice sounded much like that of Father Juan.

I found that I had passed through one of the arches of the bridge while I was under water, and that I was exactly opposite the town, but travelling towards the light-house at the rate of about four miles an hour, which was much faster than I desired to go. I looked around for the bancos, but could only see those in shore, fastened for the night. The pursuing and pursued were not in sight. I was too good a swimmer to call for help, and have a dozen or twenty bancos start towards me in hope of the rewards which they would receive, and not for the purpose of saving my life, so I struck for the shore, my anger somewhat cooled, but my hatred for Father Juan as vivid as ever.

Five minutes later saw me land at the quay opposite the European hotel, and just as I was crawling up the stone-work, I heard the voice of Captain John Miller, a stout, bluff old fellow, whom I had seen frequently at the American consul's office, and who had invited me to visit his ship, the "Darling Nancy," or some other nautically endearing name, favorite with antique sailors. The captain was reported to have seen all parts of the world; had been upon the ocean ever since he cut his teeth; was reputed wealthy, and the owner of half a dozen daughters, justly entitled to the name of "Salem witches," at which city the captain resided when at home, which remarkable event happened about once in two years; but not oftener if he could help.

The captain was fond of company, — provided the company would listen, and not interrupt him during his long yarns, which he was fond of spinning. He liked his pipe, his grog, his daughters, his ship, and his comfort, and for the purpose of enjoying the latter, he preferred stopping on board of his vessel instead of living on shore.

"Hallo, matey!" was his first salutation; "what ship are you running from? You are blowing like a humpback whale that has been gallied in shoal water."

I made no reply, but held down my head, so that he should not see my face, and endeavored to pass him.

"Avast, there!" he shouted; "you can't run my blockade without showing a signal, so spring your buff and round to."

He laid his hand heavily upon my shoulder, and I found that there was no use in opposing him.

"What are you, French, Dutch, or Spanish?" he asked.

"I am neither. I'm a Yankee, like yourself," I answered, brushing the hair from my forehead, and looking him in the face.

The captain started back in astonishment, and shaded his sharp gray eyes with his rough hand, as though the moonbeams affected his sight.

"Blast it, Mr. ——, you don't mean to tell me that this is you? You don't mean to say that you, a man of respectability and wealth, are swimming round in the river at this time of night with your clothes on?"

"Why, you wouldn't have me swim with them off—would you? What would the women say if they should see me?"

"Don't go through the streets at this late hour," the captain continued; "it's mighty unsafe, for the Mestizos are as handy with their knives as a marine with a musket. Come, go on board my ship and sleep to-night."

Almost before I was aware, the captain had edged me towards the boat, and stepped in. In another instant the Mestizo had shoved off, and we were pulling out of the river, the captain puffing vigorously at a cigar, and chatting confidentially.

"I s'pose, if the truth was known," the captain said, with Yankee curiosity to learn the secrets of others, "that you have had some confounded love scrape to-night, and had to swim or be discovered. Was it an angry parent, or a jealous lover, or a revengeful brother? Don't be afeard to trust me, 'coz I can keep a secret as well as the next man."

"Well, to tell you the truth, captain," I answered, more with a desire to excite his curiosity than anything else, "I was in search of a wife."

"Don't do that out here in this hot quarter of the globe. There ain't any fun in it, I tell you. Don't go and marry one of these black gals, with her skin shining like copal varnish, and her hair greased like a slushed top-mast. Blast it, man, wait till you get home, and marry a Christian, with a white face, clean hands, and who can talk your own lingo; where two thirds of your nights are cold, and mosquito bars ain't known. Take my word for it, if you marry one of these natives you'll regret it afore you've bin spliced a week."

We soon reached the side of the ship. I mounted to the deck, and was received by the mate, who probably had been cursing his captain's late hours, and then was conducted to the cabin, which was handsome enough for a packet-ship, and where a man couldn't help taking comfort if so inclined.

"Here we are at last," cried Captain Miller, seating himself, after putting away a few suspicious-looking packages which he had brought off in his boat. "What do you think of the Nancy? She is as fast as she looks to be, and can knock the spots out of thirteen knots for hours, and not seem to be hard at work either. Steward!"

A colored man made his appearance, rubbing his eyes as though awakened from a sound nap.

"Steward, lay out a suit of my best togs for this gentleman, and then give me the Santa Cruz rum, and a few lemons and sugar. Or, give me the rum first and the clothes afterwards. I can mix the punch while he is changing his clothes. Strike a glim in my state-room, and let him go in there. Mind and don't hit the chronometers. I'd rather you would hit my wife."

I found a neat suit of clothes ready for me, although I must confess they were much too large; but I didn't mind it, as there were no ladies present to witness my exploits — drinking punch or listening to the captain's yarns; which I must confess did much towards relieving the sadness of my heart, when I thought how near I had been to my wife, and yet was compelled to leave her.

"Come, don't stop to titivate yourself, for there's no women here," I heard the captain shout. "The punch is all ready, and I've got the start of you by drinking a glass."

I hurried out and seated myself at the dining-table, at the head of which the captain was installed in all his dignity, a pipe in his mouth, and a glass of punch in his hand.

"Here's cigars and pipes; which do you prefer?" the captain asked, filling my glass.

I lighted my cigar, tasted my grog, found that it was excellent, and I didn't fail to say as much.

"Ah, there's no liquor like old Santa Cruz rum, if you get the pure; and I take care that I don't have anything else."

"Did you ever cruise in the latitude of the West Indies?" asked the captain, after he had paid his devoirs to the punch, and had refilled his pipe, and lighted it to his satisfaction.

I shook my head in the negative.

"'Tain't a very pleasant latitude at certain seasons of the year, for there's arthquakes and hurrycanes, and calms and rains in abundance, and a man can't lay down and be certain that he's not going to wake up with his masts over his side, or his ship on her beam ends, and forked lightning playing round the chain topsail sheets, like dandies round a ball-room belle. Howsomever, that has nothing to do with my yarn, as I knows of, although you knows and I knows, and every sailor knows, that it's awful hard work to spin a yarn and not bring in a petticoat.

"I think that I was one day's sail from Santa Cruz, on the night that I am about to tell you of. The wind was very light, and we were not going through the water faster than two knots an hour. I left the deck at ten o'clock in charge of my mate, a Salem-bred boy, named Cooper, and a smart fellow he was. He afterwards commanded the ship Sarlow, which you might have heard of. She was lost at sea five years ago, and Cooper went down with her, I expect, for he was never heard of. Left a wife and three children, with money enough to get along without trouble, and that's some comfort to a widow. I told Cooper to keep a sharp look out for squalls and suspicious-looking vessels, for we were directly in the track of homeward-bound slavers, and as I had met them a number of times without any good result, I was not anxious to see them again, and preferred giving them a wide birth.

"I hadn't been napping more than two hours, when Mr. Cooper called me.

"'Captain,' he said, 'the moon is just rising through a black cloud, and directly in its wake I can make out a vessel, braced sharp up, and standing across our hawse, as though she wished to speak us.'

"I went on deck and took a squint at the craft that had somewhat alarmed my mate, and I must confess that I didn't feel quite satisfied with her looks, for she was a large topsail schooner, with tremendous hoist to her sails, and they set as though made for her by a master hand. The craft was low in the water, and was as black as the devil is reported to be. I saw that the schooner was jammed tight on the wind, and that she would be likely to pass our bows, at the rate she was going, about half a cable's length distance; but while I was examining her through my glass, I saw her sails were shaking, and that her headway was materially deadened. It seemed to me that her skipper wanted my vessel to draw ahead, in hopes of not being noticed, and possibly he would have succeeded had not Cooper's eyes ferreted him out.

"I examined the stranger for a few seconds, and then I came to the conclusion that the chap was either a slaver — uncertain of our character — or a pirate. But at all events, I determined to be prepared for either, for I thought that I had guns enough to stand something of a tug before consenting to walk the plank.

"'Mr. Cooper,' I said, 'just call all hands in a quiet way, and let's get these guns ready for business. Don't make a fuss, and seem frightened, 'cos there's no occasion for it.'

"'Ay, ay, sir,' he answered, and in a few seconds the men were on deck and casting loose the twelve pounders, all of which had been loaded two days before, with canister and round shot, and all that we had to do was to get up ammunition and place it in the cabin handy, and then load our muskets, and take the boarding pikes out of the racks.

"'We are all ready, captain,' my mate said in less than five minutes after he received the orders; 'the men are all stationed at the guns and ready to fight at command.'

"'I hope that there'll be no occasion for the use of the bulldogs,' I replied; 'but there's no telling what that feller's intentions is. He still keeps his luff, for his sails are shaking, and he don't draw ahead any.'

"'Perhaps he wants us to pass him, and not be noticed,' my mate remarked; and I didn't know but such might be the case, 'cos the brig did look very much like a man-of-war, and to tell the truth, I had no objection to be taken for one of Uncle Sam's vessels, 'cos it rather flattered my pride.

"By the time the stranger was off our beam, and when I began to think that he cared nothing for us, he filled his sails and steered so as to just run under our stern, and I didn't know but the fellow was determined to rake us, and if he had, there wouldn't have been anything left of us. However, I resolved to let him know that we were not asleep, so I sprang into the main rigging and hailed, —

"'Schooner, ahoy!'

"There was no response; but I could hear a bustle on deck, as though there was some confusion at being spoken. I fancied that there was some scuffling on deck, but I could not make out anything distinct. I thought that I would give him another chance to reply, so I hailed again, —

"'Schooner, ahoy!' and this time there was an attempt at an answer.

"'Hallo!' came in gruff tones over the water.

"'What schooner is that?' I demanded.

"'The ——.'

"There was a moment's hesitancy, and then some one in the waist of the schooner shouted in startling tones, —

"'Help! treachery! murder!'

"'Gag the d—n fool!' cried the man who was answering my hail; 'gag him, and throw him overboard.'

"There was another scuffle, and many suppressed mutterings, and then I heard a woman's voice raised in imploring tones.

"'Have mercy, gentlemen,' she cried; 'and spare his life! He will not offend you again! he did not mean anything, I am sure. O, let me entreat of you to spare his life.'

"You see," said the captain, stopping to refill his pipe and tumbler, "there's where the petticoat comes in. I told you I should get hold of one during my yarn."

"Never mind the explanations," I replied, "go on with the story, and let me hear how it terminated."

"I put my glass to my eye, and as the moon had got clear of a black cloud, I was enabled to see what I had to deal with. I could only make out half a dozen men on deck, and I calculated that was all the schooner had on board. There was something wrong going on, and I determined to investigate it, even if I was exposed to some little peril. I determined on a bold stroke, although I had some fear of the result.

"'Schooner, ahoy!' I shouted, just as she was directly astern of us.

"'Well, what is it?' was the answer.

"'Send a boat on board immediately, and let us see who you are,' I commanded.

"'Who in thunder are you?' was the impudent question.

"'The United States brig Perry, bound to Santa Cruz.'

"There was a breathless silence for a moment, when suddenly I heard a shrill whistle on board of my own brig, such as is used by boatswains of a national vessel when the crew are to perform any work. The trick was one of Cooper's, and was intended to aid me in the deception.

"'Brace up the head yards!' I shouted, and the men left their stations and performed the work without the usual accompaniment of noise.

"I put my helm hard starboard, and the brig came quickly to the wind, and remained stationary with her main-topsail to the mast. Then we were heading in the same direction as the schooner; but the latter did not seem in a hurry to obey my orders, and send a boat on board. I could hear some loud talking on the quarter-deck of the stranger, as though the officers and crew were debating the feasibility of attempting to escape or fight. I sincerely hoped that we should be spared the latter alternative, 'cos I knew that at the very first broadside they would discover our imposition, and rage like devils for revenge.

"In the mean time the schooner continued to draw ahead slowly, as though to get beyond the reach of our guns; but I determined to prevent that by bracing up and maintaining my position. The instant, however, that we had boarded the main tack, and were making some headway through the water, I hailed the schooner again.

"'Hallo!' was the gruff answer.

"'Do you intend to send a boat on board, and give some account of yourself?' I demanded.

"'Ay, ay, sir, as soon as we can make her tight.'

The answer I did not deem satisfactory, for it seemed to me as though the crew were attempting some dodge that was dangerous to our welfare, and I determined to prevent it if possible, by taking them by surprise.

"'Mr. Cooper,' I said, 'bring one of the larboard guns to bear upon the fellow's bow, and see how near you can come to him. Don't miss if you can help it.'

"That was a job the mate liked, for his soft heart was all of a tumult when he heard a woman's voice, and thought that a female was in distress.

"'We are all ready,' Mr. Cooper said, blowing a Josh stick which we used to touch off our guns.

"I looked towards the schooner and saw that there was no movement for lowering a boat, and after listening quietly for a moment, became satisfied that a desperate quarrel was raging on board, but what it was all about I could not tell.

"'Give them the gun, Cooper,' I said; and I had not much more than spoken, before there was a stunning report, and the brig shook from truck to kelson.

"I heard a crashing sound as the iron hail struck the schooner, cutting the halyards of the jib, and letting that sail down by the run, and I could see numerous rents in the foresail through which the grape shot had passed.

"'Get the other gun ready, Cooper,' I said; 'you have done very well with the first one. Keep the brig well to the wind, so that the stranger shan't get away from us,' I continued to the man at the wheel.

"'The gun is all ready, sir,' my mate replied.

"'Well, don't fire until I give the word. I don't want to kill the poor devils, if I can help it. I'll try 'em with another hail, and see if they have found their senses.'

"'Schooner, ahoy!' I shouted; 'do you intend to send your boat on board, or must I sink you with a broadside?'

"Again I could hear the angry discussion going on, for we were just abeam of the schooner, and were holding our own with her, no attempt having been made to hoist their jib. Suddenly I saw a man spring upon the bulwarks.

"'There is treachery and murder on board; don't desert'—'

"His speech was cut short by a blow on his head, and with a loud splash he fell into the water. But the poor fellow had strength to swim, for I saw him strike out towards our brig, although we were moving about three knots an hour.

"'Clear away the boat, Mr. Cooper, and pick that man up. Mind and do it ship-shape fashion. No confusion or fear, for we should have had a gun from the schooner if she had been armed.'

"It was the work of a few minutes to clear away the starboard-quarter boat, and to send four men in it for the swimmer. I could see that the crew of the schooner was watching the proceeding from their vessel, and I managed to count twelve men, which I supposed was all that they could muster. The boat soon reached the swimmer, and took him on board, and then returned to the brig. The stranger was helped over the rail, for he was quite weak from the effects of a cut upon his head, which bled profusely.

"'Sir,' he said, grasping my hand, and speaking with a Spanish accent, 'you have saved my life, and I owe you a thousand thanks. My gratitude, however, shall be more substantial than words. I have a brother and sister on board, prisoners, and in the power of a desperate man. Save them, and we are your debtors for life.'

"'I'll do what I can for you,' I replied; 'but my force is small as you can see.'

"'Is this not a United States vessel?' he demanded looking over the deck in astonishment.

"'I'ts a United States vessel, but not a naval one,' I answered.

"'Then, for Heaven's sake, don't destroy the deception, for the schooner is armed, and the crew will fight desperately. They suppose that you are a brig of war, and the reason that I hailed was because one half of the ruffians were advising a surrender, and the other half wanted to fight you at all hazards.'

"Here was a pretty kettle of fish, and no mistake. I had supposed all along that the schooner was unarmed, and that a few discharges from our guns would be sufficient to compel a surrender. If the scamps should discover the deception that we had practised before we secure them our lives and property would pay for it. Impudence was the only thing to carry us through, and I determined to exercise a little of that which sometimes answers as well as courage.

"'Schooner, ahoy!' I once more shouted; 'if you don't send a boat on board, I will blow you out of water. Pipe the men to the guns, Mr. Cooper, and aim so as to sweep the vessel's deck.'

"The latter part of my remark was intended to be heard on board of the schooner, for I spoke loud enough.

"Instantly the mate commenced a series of toots with his whistle, that would have done honor to the oldest boatswain in the navy. The effect was beyond my most sanguine expectations, for I heard the pirates clearing away their boat in sullen silence.

"'For the love of Heaven, sir,' my new passenger pleaded, "order them to bring as passengers my brother and sister, for I fear every minute that they will be murdered by the desperate ruffians. They have already threatened to do so half a dozen times.'

"I saw that the crew of the schooner were piling into the boat, so I just told them to bring the woman and gentleman, and that if they were ill treated I would hang every one of them at the yard-arm. It was loud talk, but you see I had got my hand in, and it kinder came natural to speak big.

"The fellows muttered something that I couldn't understand, but I soon saw white petticoats going over the rail, and it made my heart jump that the lady was soon to be out of danger. I counted seven persons in the boat, including the girl and her brother, and as the boat was pulled by four oars, it didn't take long for it to get alongside. I knew that the instant the yawl touched the brig's side the cheat would be discovered; but I was prepared for the scamps, and allowed them no opportunity to escape. I stationed Mr. Cooper and five of the crew with loaded muskets on the vessel's rail, while another hand held a small grappling-iron for the purpose of throwing it into the boat to prevent the men from shoving off and returning to their vessel to reveal our true character.

"Things worked just as I expected. No sooner had the pirates shipped their oars when they got alongside, than one of them said, —

"'Dis is no man-de-war. It is a d—d merchantmens.'

"'Sacre,' cried a Frenchman.

"'Diablo,' muttered a Spaniard.

"'Nix cumrouse,' said a Dutchman.

"'We are deceived — shove off,' cried a man in the stern sheets.

"'Not as you know of,' cried Cooper. 'The man who offers to lift an oar dies instantly.'

"The six muskets were pointed within a fathom of the pirates' heads, and then down into the boat was dropped the kedge. It caught in the bow thwart, and held the boat firm alongside, and the only way to get clear of it was to cut the rope; but at the first intimation of that we would have blown them to pieces.

"'I'll trouble you to walk over the side, one by one,' Mr. Cooper said, addressing the pirates. 'The least noise or resistance shall cost you dearly. Walk up like men and settle your accounts, 'cos we would like to show the lady some attention, for the poor thing looks as though she was not partial to your company.'

"'It's a mean Yankee trick,' muttered the man in the stern sheets, who I afterwards found out was the captain of the schooner, and an Englishman by birth. 'If I had known for sure that you were nothing but a merchantman, I'd blown your tub out of the water.'

"'But, as you didn't know anything about it, we have saved you some trouble. So just walk up, and quit grumbling, for it won't do you any good;' and Mr. Cooper's advice was followed, for the skipper came slowly over the bulwarks, and as soon as he struck the deck his arms were seized, and a nice pair of handcuffs were thrust upon his wrists.

"Hands were also thrust into his pockets, and a pair of pistols and a huge bowie-knife were found, and after the fellow was disarmed, he was shoved down the after hatch with a gag in his mouth, to prevent his shouting too loud. Every man was served in the same manner, and then I assisted the lady on deck, and very happy was I to do so, for she was a beautiful craft, with the prettiest pair of eyes that ever wrecked a sailor, and I think that I am a judge of beauty.

"'Which is the captain?' she asked, the first thing, as soon as she reached the deck.

"Mr. Cooper and her brother pointed to me, and bless me if she didn't give a little scream and throw herself on my bosom, while her arms went round my neck as tight as a cap fits to a top-mast.

"'O, capitani,' she said, 'you is mine preserver; my angel — my good man — my everything.'

"'Hard up,' I cried, for you see I couldn't stand it. 'Ease off a little, and belay the rest for a while, mum. Don't take on so, 'cos there's much more work to be done afore you is safe.'

"Well, she kissed me three or four times and then her brother took her off; but I didn't feel much obliged to him, I tell you, 'cos her lips was awful sweet and red.

"I told her folks to take her into the cabin, and give her something to eat if she desired it, 'cos I wanted to be perlite, and show her some attention; but she said that she wasn't hungry, and should have no appetite until the rest of the pirates was secured; but how to get 'em was a question that I had asked my own mind half a dozen times, and no satisfactory answer had been returned. I had the skipper and half of his crew; but there were six more that I wanted, or my work would be incomplete, for it was plain that the schooner was faster than the brig, and that she could fight us running a race I had no relish for, for you know that it don't take many shots between wind and water to send a vessel and crew to Davy Jones's locker.

"'Captain,' said Mr. Cooper, while I was meditating, 'I know what you are thinking about, and the only way that it can be done is to send me on board in the boat, with half a dozen of the crew, and take possession. We can go well armed, and still make 'em think that we are Uncle Sam's men.'

"I didn't like to run the risk, but Cooper was so positive that I consented to let him undertake the job. For the purpose of carrying out the deception, I lent the mate a cap and coat with brass buttons, and put a sword at his waist, while the six men he took with him put on white duck trousers, so as to appear as uniform as possible. Well armed, the crew started in the schooner's boat, although for the sake of seeming all right it was piped away in man-of-war style.

"I watched the course of the boat with considerable anxiety, for I feared that every minute the pirates would let one of their guns fly, and send boat and men all to the bottom; but fortune favors the brave, they say, and in this instance I can swear to it. The boat got alongside without trouble, and the next instant the men had tumbled on deck. There was no sound of fighting or scuffling, but I knew that the mate was at work, and at last I had the satisfaction of hearing him hail, and say, that the schooner's crew were all prisoners and under hatches, where they could do no harm.

"Then I began to breathe freer; I told the mate to stick close to the brig until daylight, when we would see what could be done, for I didn't know, as yet, on what ground we had taken the schooner. I axed the brothers to reel me off an account of their adventures, and they did so in a ship-shape fashion. They belonged to Santa Cruz, where they owned a large plantation, and were looked upon as A No. 1 in rank. They had bought the schooner for the purpose of trading among the islands, and I guess for running a few cargoes of niggers; but that they said nothing about. They had hired a man, who called himself Smith, an Englishman, as skipper, and he shipped his crew, and a bad lot he got hold of. One day, when the vessel was all ready for sea, the brothers and sister were invited on board, and while they were enjoying themselves in the cabin the cable was slipped, and the schooner put to sea, and before the owners knew where they were, or what was going on, they were out of the bay, and the mask was thrown off. The skipper made no secret of his intentions to visit the coast of Africa, and by way of making things pleasant, offered to make the lady his mistress or his wife, he was not particular which, and if we had not fallen in with him just as we did, I don't think that he would have waited for a priest to perform the ceremony.

"However, we took the schooner into port and she was condemned, and the crew imprisoned, and I made ten thousand dollars by the job. And now drink one more glass of grog, and then to bed, for four bells has struck, and it's time I was asleep."

There was no other course but compliance, and in a few minutes I was dreaming of Teresa, priests, and pirates.

"Come, rouse and shine," I heard some one say, while dreaming of my wife and happiness. "It's near seven bells, and breakfast is most ready. You sleep as sound as the ground tier, and are about as hard to move. Come, make a stir, and be ready to go on shore with me by at least nine o'clock."

I was too willing to comply, for with morning and rest came the recollection that I had a holy duty to perform, which I had neglected by visiting the Nancy, and listening to the captain's yarns. I sprang from my berth, and after a bath in an original bath-tub, invented by the captain, and which he expected to have patented some day, I dressed and was ready for breakfast.

"I don't expect company," Miller said, as we took our seats at the table, "so I have nothing that is very nice for breakfast. Such as I have you are welcome to, and if you don't find anything to suit your appetite, you must save it till you get on shore. I'm a plain man, and like good plain grub."

In spite of the captain's apologies, I found that his breakfast, as he really intended it should be, was excellent, and consisted of a piece of cold salt beef, — a luxury I had not tasted for many days, — curried rice and chicken, a respectable omelet, light warm biscuit, and butter brought from Boston, and as fresh as the day it was made.

When breakfast was finished, I was ready for the land. The instant the banco struck the quay I leaped on shore, and was about to bid adieu to the captain, when he laid his hand upon my shoulder, and detained me.

"Avast, my hearty, and don't be in such a hurry to claw off as though on a lee shore. I've got a proposition to make to you. Come to an anchor for a minute, and listen to reason. Don't you think of marrying one of these yaller gals — take my advice, and don't do it. If you want a sailing partner through this 'ere voyage of life, and want something nice, I'll let you have the pick of my daughters. That's an offer I wouldn't make to every man, but I do to you 'cos I've taken a fancy to you."

"Captain," I replied, "I feel highly favored by your esteem and confidence, but there's an impediment in the way."

"What in the devil's an impediment?" he growled.

"Why, a wife, to be sure;" and I broke away from him just in time to hear him mutter, —

"By thunder, I thought so all along!"

I did not dare to look back for fear the captain would again make me a prisoner; so pushed on through the crowd of boatmen until I reached a carriage, and gave directions for the driver to take me to my house without delay.

As I entered the court-yard of the house, I was surprised to see there were many signs of neglect on the part of the servants. The horses had not, apparently, received their morning meal, the yard had not been swept, or the sidewalk washed. I passed up the broad staircase without meeting any one, and continued on until I reached the sitting-room, when I was surprised to hear some one weeping. I listened for a moment, and found that the sounds proceeded from my chamber. I entered, and saw Gracia, with her face in her hands, kneeling before a picture of the Virgin and Child, and crying bitterly.

"What is the matter, Gracia?" I asked, laying my hand upon her head.

The girl started to her feet with a scream of delight, and before I was aware of the fact, her arms were around my neck, and her head was resting on my bosom. I was so much surprised that for a minute or two I remained motionless; then the thoughts of my position flashed across my mind, and I remembered that my honor, as a married man, was in danger. Gently I disengaged the young girl's arms, and led her to a seat.

"Pardon me, senor," she said; "I was so rejoiced at your appearance that I forgot my position."

"There is no great harm done," I answered, with a smile; "but pray be a little more careful with your demonstrations of pleasure in future. I understand that you feel grateful to me for a few favors, but don't let the world imagine that we stand upon a false basis."

"I will try and remember in future, senor," she answered, her eyes filling with tears and her face with blushes. "I could not help feeling surprised to see you alive, when I was mourning you as dead."

"And pray who told you I was dead?" I asked, somewhat astonished at the information.

"Your friends, the Senor Allen and the other man, were here last night, and seemed quite anxious regarding you. Their clothes were wet, and they talked in low tones of your mishap, as they thought you must be drowned. Senor Allen was much affected, but your other friend did not appear to mourn much."

"No, I suppose not," I muttered. "It would have been singular if the spy cared enough for any human being to mourn his death. How could they have made such a mistake as to imagine me drowned?"

"Because they searched the river, and saw nothing of you, and then thought you would return home if alive. They waited here until two o'clock, and then gave up all hope of your being in the land of the living."

"Confound the luck," I thought. "I had no business to go on board the Nancy last night. Like a respectable citizen, I should have come home, and gone to bed, and not given my friends so much trouble. I must start for Santa Mesa without delay, and let them see that I am alive and well, barring the effects of that punch. It was confounded good, though."

These thoughts passed through my brain very rapidly. I determined to visit the factory, and let Allen and the priest see that I was not quite dead, and then return to the city and recommence my search with renewed ardor. Just as I arrived at this sage conclusion, one of my servants entered the house, and expressed the utmost astonishment at my visit; but I quickly changed his tone to one of anguish, for I gave him a most unmerciful rating for neglecting his duties, and getting partially intoxicated, under the impression that I was many feet under water. Indeed, to Graeia alone was I indebted for preventing the rascals from stripping the house of everything of value, and selling the same for what they could get. The girl had threatened them so severely that they had desisted from their object, and walked off to celebrate my supposed death by getting drunk if possible.

The boy begged and promised good behavior, and left the house, rubbing his shoulders, in search of the coachman; for I thought I

20

would give the lazy scamp something to do besides drinking weak wine, and wondering whether my soul was in the realms of the blessed, or those of the damned.

It was wonderful how soon the news spread among my domestics that I was alive. By the time I had dressed in habiliments that fitted me better than those of Captain Miller's, the house was looking as neat as ever. The floors were waxed, and the yard swept; the dishes were washed, and put in their proper places; and in each room the furniture had been dusted and arranged. The scamps knew that one of their number had been thrashed, and all felt they deserved a like fate; but my time was too precious to indulge in such amusement, and after a few consoling words to Gracia, I drove off at a gallop for Santa Mesa.

I left my carriage at the corner of the road that leads to the factory, and started alone for the house of my friends. We all feel as though we would like to know what is said of us after death; and as I was supposed to be dead, I considered that I had a right to judge of the estimation in which I was held by those with whom I was associated for so many months. Instead, therefore, of approaching the house in front, I scaled the adobe wall, and entered by the rear; and luckily I did not meet a single servant, although workmen were seen in abundance. I noiselessly ascended the stairs, and looked in at the door. Benventuro, Allen, and Tom were seated at the table, eating dinner; and a very hearty one I judged it was, from the number of dishes before them.

"Poor fellow!" I heard the priest say, holding out his plate for an additional supply of curry and chicken; "his early death has quite spoiled my appetite. I don't feel as though I should enjoy life again. The shock to my nervous system has been too great."

"Who will take care of that pretty little girl of his in Manila?" demanded Tom, his thoughts evidently on the probable result of her falling into his hands.

"She might enter my convent," the priest suggested. "I can provide for her there, I think."

"O, blast your convent! Do you suppose a woman wants to be locked up in a convent all her lifetime?" Tom asked.

"For my part," Allen said, speaking for the first time, "I am of the opinion that he may yet be alive. He was a stout swimmer, and may have been picked up by a banco bound on a cruise in the bay. I shan't give him up for lost for two or three days to come."

"What do you suppose his wife will say?" Tom asked.

"I expect she will act like other women — shed a few tears at first, and then think of somebody else, of course," was the priest's ungallant reply.

"She is the handsomest woman that I ever saw," Tom continued. "She bangs everything I ever saw in York. She'd make a sensation in that city."

I saw the priest glance at Tom's face as though reading his thoughts, but the scrutiny did not appear satisfactory. Could he have already considered whether a bargain with Tom would be advantageous for his convent and himself? At any rate, I had heard as much as I desired; so I stalked slowly into the room.

"Can you give me a dinner?" I asked, in a sulphurous tone.

There were sudden springs from the table; chairs were overturned, glasses were dashed to the floor, and then I found Allen's arms around me, while the priest, with his long garments in both hands, was performing a most ungraceful dance, which I could compare only to the floundering of an elephant. Tom suddenly disappeared from the room after one or two yells, which he used to assure us were exact imitations of the calls of York Bowery boys; and I never had occasion to question the truth of the assertion.

"This day," said the priest, sinking into a chair, and fanning his heated face, "is one of the happiest of my life. The dead has come to life. I knew my son was never intended for such a death. Not two minutes since I said the same thing."

"What an old humbug you are!" cried Allen. "You have done nothing but prophesy the worst things imaginable for the last three hours, and now you have the impudence to speak as one inspired."

"I appeal to Tom," roared the priest; but just at the moment that individual entered the room with a bottle of champagne under each arm.

"This event must be celebrated in due form!" Tom exclaimed. "Here's the articles to do it with, and now let us sit down and finish our breakfast with far better spirits than when we began."

After that I couldn't bear enmity towards a man who had taken the liberty of calling my wife handsome, and wishing that he possessed just such a one.

We sat down to the table, and all were anxious to hear my statement. Feeling a little ashamed of my conduct, I sketched my adventures as briefly as possible, but took care to convey the impression that visiting the ship was not the result of deliberation, but of accident. Without telling a deliberate falsehood I succeeded in extricating myself from the position in which I was placed, and I believe to the satisfaction of my friends.

"You should have remained in the banco," Allen said, after I had concluded. "That jump of yours cost us all pretty dear, for when you left our boat you took care to capsize it, and into the water we went as well as yourself. Instead of going through one of the arches, however, we lodged on the stone-work of the bridge, and remained there until taken off by a passing bauco. As soon as we landed we went to your house, and frightened Gracia out of her seven senses by asking if you had been there, and to our great surprise we learned that you had not. I concluded that you was drowned, although I sincerely hoped not. We lost our prize, and you must alone blame yourself, for you was too eager."

"Eager in a good cause, though," the priest said, encouragingly, touching glasses, and swallowing a bumper of champagne — an example that was so contagious we all followed suit; nor did they stop at two bottles; for, I am sorry to say, when they once commenced they hardly knew where to leave off; and while we were in the midst of our revels, who should enter the room but Antonio, the spy? He surveyed the condition of the party without the least surprise, and when the priest roared out that he was the most dishonest scamp in the country, looked as though he tried to believe it.

"The senor is safe," he said, with a grin that was intended for me.

"And no thanks to you!" thundered the priest. "How dare you, ladrone, let one of my friends fall overboard, and narrowly escape drowning! Have I not learned you better manners?"

"It was the senor's fault alone," Antonio answered; and I backed that opinion so strongly, the priest was obliged to admit that his protégé was not so bad as he might be.

"You shall drink a glass of wine with us, and hope for better luck the next time," I cried, handing the fellow a bumper, which he tossed off with considerable relish.

"Do you bring us news, Antonio?" Benventuro asked.

"I do, senor," was the answer.

"Well, what is it? Speak quickly, and speak plainly."

"The lady, senor, is at the Convent of San Sebastian."

"How know you this?" we all asked in a breath.

"I heard so not two hours since, senors."

"Bah! the report may have been false."

"No, senors; I saw the lady with my own eyes, looking through a grating."

"Tell me," I cried, starting from the table, sobered in a minute, "how she looked and acted, or what she said."

"Senor, I had no time to speak with her, and if I had looked long in one direction, my motives would have been suspected. I saw the lady, however, and mournful enough she seemed."

"Is there any chance for her to escape? Can I see her? Can I speak with her, even for a moment?" I cried, trembling with impatience.

"What madness to ask such a question!" the priest said. "Every avenue to the convent is guarded, and you can't pass in or out without being noticed."

"I have thought of a plan," the spy remarked, after a moment's consideration, "that I think might answer. I found out that Father Juan has gone to Caveta, to be absent two or three days, and the business that called him away was too urgent to be neglected, even for the sake of Donna Teresa. I also learned that he removed her to the convent thinking she would be safer there than at Mother Machit's, although, to tell the truth, I think the padre suspected the old woman might be bribed to give the lady up to her friends."

"Well, well, never mind what you suspect. Let us hear what your plans are, and then we will debate whether they are feasible," the priest said.

"*Si, senor*, that is what I am coming to. I think that if a man could be smuggled into the convent, there would not be much trouble to remove the iron bars, and let the lady escape in the night time."

"But how is a man to enter the convent?" Allen asked.

"He must do it in disguise," was the spy's answer.

"And what kind of disguise do you suppose a man can wear, to deceive the Argus eyes of the convent people?" I demanded.

"He must go disguised as a woman, senor," was the answer.

"Bah!" cried the priest; "Father Juan is too sharp to be caught in that manner. He would detect the imposition at a glance."

"Father Juan would, but the padre is not at the convent, and if things are managed rightly the lady will be free before he returns. I can have an interview with my friend, who acts during his absence, and by the free use of wine I don't think he will be in a condition to tell a woman from a monkey, and before he gets sober Donna Teresa can be at liberty."

"And pray how?" demanded the priest, who, being in the same business that Father Juan was, felt a little interested.

"We must be near the convent at a certain hour, and remain there until daylight, waiting for signals from the one who is within. A rope-ladder must be drawn up, and by that, after the iron bars are wrenched from the window, must the lady escape."

For a few minutes we remained quite silent, astonished at the bold plan that was laid before us. Suddenly Allen spoke.

"You have told us how to get out, now tell us how to get in the convent."

"The matter is quite simple, senor. One of you must act the lady, and the senor (pointing to Tom) must play the part of a lover. He is unknown, and can do so with my friend without detection. He must represent that he wishes to board the lady at the convent for a few days, until his vessel sails. If he pays an ounce in advance, but a very few questions will be asked of him."

"There's something in the fellow's reasoning, after all. Guillermo, can't you take the part of a woman for a few hours?"

I rubbed my mustache as an answer.

"O, it can be shaved off, and your whole face made smooth in ten minutes. If you could look a little modest, I should have no fears for the result."

I had to thank the priest for his good opinion, and after a few more words I agreed to enter the Convent of San Sebastian in the character of a woman, and thus make a bold blow for my wife.

The feat was a perilous one, but the prize was worthy of all the danger incurred.

Tom was the most disgusted man in the party, and he did not conceal it.

"To think that I should ever make love to a man," he said, "is more than I can endure. If he was good-looking, I should not care; but for a smoker of cigars and a drinker of punch to expect me to be overcome with anguish at parting with him, is too ridiculous. However, I will do as well as I can, if I can keep from laughing."

"And if you laugh, you will have the satisfaction of knowing that you have not only ruined me, but perhaps deprived my wife of her liberty for life," I said.

After that I heard no more of levity from Tom. He entered into our arrangements with avidity, and was not at all backward in helping us to the extent of his ability.

We took the factory banco, and rowed to Manila as quick as possible; and then my friends scattered to find a wig that would fit my head, and pass off for a woman's glossy locks. The priest was the most fortunate in this respect, for he borrowed one from a lady friend of his; as she was fat and plump, her false hair fitted me admirably. The next thing was the dress; but even this difficulty was overcome by Allen, who borrowed a very pretty muslin, and all the paraphernalia of a well-conditioned woman, from the wife of an American captain, whose vessel was lying in port.

I was subject to many remarks which a lady would not have listened to in silence; but I was compelled to submit and undergo the tedious operation of trying on the dress and skirts, and practising a fascinating kind of walk, that was so entirely different from my own, I feared my feet would rebel at the treatment they were constrained to undergo. As a last resort we found that it was necessary to send for Gracia, and let her into our secret, for the purpose of giving me a few instructions in woman's department. Very much surprised and grieved the poor girl was when she learned my destination, and it required all my assurance to convince her that I was not rushing upon certain death to thus think of visiting a convent in disguise.

At length I think I learned how to step lighter and more mincing than usual, and after I had suffered the manipulations of a barber, who touched my face so lightly, that not a hair could be seen except upon my eyebrows, I was declared ready for the final dressing. At this stage Antonio left the house for the convent, with four bottles of champagne in a basket — a sight that caused the priest to sigh most dolefully, and to wish that his duty led him to undertake so delicious a job as drinking the best of champagne.

"You will want these few articles in your pockets, in case the bars are obstinate, and refuse to yield," Antonio said, laying upon the table a saw not longer than my finger, yet of such admirable steel, that it was capable of cutting through the most obdurate iron, a small iron "jimmy," such as burglars find very useful in this country, a revolver not larger than a baby's hand, and lastly, a ball of twine.

Luckily, our women are fond of convenience, and therefore have quite a number of pockets in their skirts and dresses; so I had no difficulty in placing all the tools, so kindly loaned me, out of sight; yet I had only to raise my dress and they were at hand.

By three o'clock I was dressed, not in the Spanish style, for my shoulders and bust would not have borne an inspection, but after the manner of a young maiden, chary of her charms, and inclined to modesty; and after I was all ready with an elegant white bonnet, covered with flowers of every hue, and a thick veil to hide my blushes, I ventured to approach the glass and view myself; and I don't fear contradiction, when I boldly state that I have seen worse looking women than the counterfeit which I presented.

"A trifle more stuffing for the chest," said the priest, "would improve the appearance of things in that region. Here, look at Gracia, and see the difference between the two;" and despite the girl's blushes, he compelled her to stand beside me to show the contrast.

The defect was soon remedied, and then they complained that my dress did not have the right swell in the rear, and considerable work was required before that defect was remedied, and I was declared, even by the fastidious Tom, a fit subject for his gallantry.

"Perhaps it would be as well if you understood only the English language, while at the convent. It would save you many questions, if brought in contact with the inmates of the institution," the priest said. "Let Tom represent that his lady is a Catholic, and desirous of remaining at the convent while he is absent from the city on business; and he may represent anything else he pleases, that is not improbable. He is conversant enough with the language to make himself understood, and if he sticks for a word, let him hold out a gold piece. That is a language which is known the world over. None fail to comprehend its magic influence, and but few can withstand its temptation, more is the pity."

The good man sighed, as though he was never guilty of taking a bribe in his life.

Tom listened to his instructions with a greedy ear, and felt quite proud to think that his Spanish was complimented, for he was rather weak on that point.

After a few more lessons a carriage was called, and Tom, hat in hand, assisted me to it. I heard a suppressed exclamation as I passed down the stairs, and, on looking back, saw that little Gracia was crying as though her heart would break.

"We shall remain in the house until night, and will take care of your servant," Allen said.

"But remember she is to be treated like a sister during my absence," I replied.

"Of course, honor bright, you know;" and before I had time to say more, Tom hurried me to the carriage, and we drove off, the priest at an upper window pronouncing a benediction upon us as we started.

While riding through the streets, I began to comprehend the magnitude of the undertaking which I had commenced. I knew there was much danger, but I felt that I was ready to encounter it for the love of my beautiful wife. It seemed to me that if I could only be assured of her escape, I would willingly assume much greater risks. We rattled over the bridge that spans the Pasig at a much faster rate than I thought necessary, and I would willingly have told the driver to use less expedition, if I had not feared to betray my knowledge of the Spanish language by speaking. It struck me also, that Tom had given secret orders for a quick pace; for, confound him, I really believe that he was somewhat ashamed of his company, although I am sure I looked very well, and even commanded the respect of three Spanish officers, who took off their hats and made me a low bow, just as we reached the end of the bridge.

"Well, if they ain't big fools not to know a woman from a man!" my friend muttered.

The Convent of San Sebastian is located in the city proper of Manila, near the border of the bay, and to reach it a gate guarded by soldiers has to be passed. The gate, after eleven o'clock, is closed, and none can pass or repass without a written permit, signed by the captain of the guard, or the governor general. I had not thought of the matter before, till it suddenly occurred to me that, if we could not leave the city at any hour of the night, Teresa's escape would be frustrated.

"Tom," I said, addressing my companion, who was sucking the head of his cane with a diligence that was worthy of all praise, "you must tell Benventuro to get a written pass for our party to leave the city. He is gifted with an imagination sufficient to find an excuse for asking for such a document. Don't forget to remind him of it."

"All right," Tom answered, taking his cane from his mouth a sufficient length of time to speak, and then recommenced sucking it as though dying for nourishment.

In a few minutes the carriage entered the court-yard of the convent, a gloomy-looking building, with a wall extending completely around it, excepting on that portion which faced the street; and that part of the structure had no windows in the first story, for fear the curiosity of the citizens might be provoked and excited. I glanced towards the windows in the second story, and saw that a number of faces were peering at us through the iron bars, but I did not recognize the features of my wife.

The instant the carriage was within the court-yard, the heavy gates were closed as though to cut off all retreat. I glanced at Tom, and saw that his face was pale as ashes, and that he was visibly agitated. I felt my heart beat quick, but by a powerful effort I managed to maintain my composure, and seem indifferent.

"What is your pleasure, senor?" asked the *portero*, an aged man with a face that would not pass for an honest one in any part of the world.

"We wish to see the holy Father Juan," Tom managed to answer.

"He is absent, senor, and will not return until day after tomorrow."

How my heart jumped at these words! I could have embraced the man for joy, and even his face did not look as bad as when I first saw it.

"I have a lady here I wish to board at the convent for a few days," Tom managed to say.

"Ah, Lorenzo can attend to you as well as the padre. I will call him, senor, if you will enter our poor abode."

Tom assisted me to alight, and with as much grace as possible, I entered the reception-room of the convent. The porter disappeared, and left us wondering whether Lorenzo was the person Antonio had spoken of, and whether he was drunk enough to suit our purpose. We did not have to wait more than ten minutes for the steward's appearance, and the instant he entered the room, I was confident that at least one bottle of my champagne was beneath his waist-belt, and that he was anxious to put another there without any unnecessary delay. He cast an impatient glance at me, but my blushes were partly concealed by the lace veil, which I found stood me in good service.

"What are your wishes, senor?" the steward asked of Tom.

"Well, I — you see — going out of town — a few days — this lady feared — don't like to stay alone — pay you well for your trouble — money no object;" and Tom stumbled on in his confusion, until I feared he would spoil all by his conduct.

But luckily for us Lorenzo was about half happy, and was anxious to be wholly happy; so he paid but little attention to my friend. He only knew that an application was made to board a lady for a few days, and as the request was not a singular or unusual one, he only stopped to consider if there was money enough in the pocket of the gentleman to pay for the accommodation desired. I saw what was passing in the man's mind, and I spoke to Tom in English.

"Hand him the ounce, and promise another if I am well accommodated," I said.

Tom thrust his hand in his pocket, and exposed to the glistening eyes of the steward several doubloons.

"Give the lady the best of accommodations and kind treatment, and another ounce shall be yours," he cried.

"She shall be treated like a princess, senor," Lorenzo said, pocketing the money with wonderful dexterity, and then ringing a bell that rested upon the table.

The ringing was instrumental in calling to the room a thin, withered old woman, with a huge bundle of keys attached to her girdle, and a nose that looked snuffy.

"Here is a lady who is to board at the convent for a few days. She is to receive the best of attention, and the best food," the steward said.

"And where am I to find the time to attend to all the women, I should like to know. There's one here now, who keeps me running from morning till night, and I don't get a civil word from her. I wish that she was miles from here, or with her husband she keeps calling for all the time."

"Don't get angry, Barbara, for you will have a spell to rest your weary limbs by and by, when the convent is rich. Show the senora to her room, and introduce her to the sisters, if she desires company."

The old woman didn't refuse to obey the commands of the steward, although she continued to mutter to herself and take snuff with avidity.

"Well," said Tom, rising, "I suppose this is a hint for me to make myself scarce, and I am only too glad to do so. Good by (after an immense struggle), my dear, and don't keep awake nights thinking of me."

He held out his hand as he spoke, but the eyes of the steward were on us, and I determined to save my reputation for affection, even if I lost it afterwards. We were conversing in English, which language I supposed the two listeners knew nothing about.

"Thomas, my beloved," I cried, throwing my arms around his neck, and straining his head to my bosom, "farewell. Avoid bad company and you will be happy. Keep in doors nights, and don't expose yourself more than possible to the blandishments of women."

"O, bother!" cried the lover, with a shade of vexation upon his face. "Don't make a fool of yourself. I can't stand it, and I won't. I suppose you will want to kiss me next."

"And what would be the harm if I did?" I demanded. "Ain't you the idol of my soul? and won't I be true to you during your absence?"

"Go to thunder!" he cried, breaking away from my embrace; and to prevent his disgust from being seen, hid his face in his handkerchief.

"The senor is affected at parting," cried the steward; "but the senor must remember that it is but for a short time."

Tom could not reply. He went out of the room in a hurry, and after the old woman had looked me over a little, she told me to follow her — a command that I obeyed with some readiness.

"But few English women visit our convent," the old woman said, as she hobbled along before me, while mounting a flight of steps.

I pretended not to understand, and my cicerone, after waiting a moment, continued: —

"I wonder if all the English ladies can walk up stairs as fast as she does. May the saints preserve me, she seems capable of taking two steps at a time."

I took the hint instantly, and modulated the length of my strides.

"I wonder if she will be troublesome, and want much attention while here? because she won't get it from me, I can tell her that much. I hope she will give me something when she goes away, because I'm nearly out of snuff and cigars."

"Senora," I managed to say, "me give you this, very good — me."

I put in her hand an ounce of gold, and the stare that she gave the money and me was highly ludicrous.

"For me?" she asked, thumping herself upon her bony breast.

"*Si*," I replied.

"*Muchas gracias, senora*," she cried; and in spite of my resistance, she seized my hand and covered it with kisses. "Only to think," the old woman continued, talking to herself, "a doubloon given me, and Father Juan will never know it. I can buy cigars enough to last ten years, and a drop of wine, too, if need be. Some ladies are liberal, that is a fact, and this one shall fare well for her generosity."

By the time she had finished speaking, we had passed through several doors, which were carefully bolted after us; and then I found that we were in a long corridor, with chambers on each side. The doors stood open, and I was enabled to see that the rooms contained but an apology for a bedstead, and only a blanket and a small pillow for bedding.* No girls were visible, and I rightly conjectured that they were in another part of the building at work, embroidering handkerchiefs and dresses. I saw that one side of the corridor overlooked the street and the other a large garden, and I trembled for fear that I should be given a room on the latter side. But the old woman, after a moment's hesitancy, muttered to herself, —

"I'll give her a room where she can look at the men once in a while, for they say that some women like to be in the company of the brutes, although for what reason is more than I can tell."

I found that I had some trouble to keep my countenance just at that moment, for it occurred to me that the venerable virgin knew but little of the world, and its pleasures and pains.

"Here," she said, pointing to a room of more pretensions than the others, "you may sleep or sit, just as you please. If you want company I will send some of the sisters to attend you, or, if you would like, you can go to the work-rooms and the gardens, and see them."

I don't suppose she had the slightest idea that I understood her; but her gestures and grimaces were so expressive that no one could hardly have helped comprehending some portion of her signs. I thought I would visit the garden, and found a few words to state my wish.

"Our garden does not amount to much, for the convent is poor. But it looks very well. I have no doubt that we shall find a number of the sisters, and perhaps one or two of the boarders there."

I hoped that among them I should see my wife, yet I trembled with agitation at the thought.

"Our rooms don't look so well as usual to-day, for the holy Father Juan is absent, and the sisters and boarders take advantage at such times. Last night, may the saints protect me, they acted like young devils, and all I could do or say was not sufficient to keep them quiet. Their talk was not of saints, but of men and worldly matters."

I thought that they but proved themselves women, whether confined in convents or parlors; and if they had not sometimes exercised their tongues, they would not have been worthy the name of females.

The old woman opened a door and led me down a long flight of stone steps, and when we reached the bottom, I found I was already in the garden, but shut in by such high walls that the surrounding houses could not be seen, and any attempt to scale the walls, without a long ladder, would have been useless. I found that the garden consisted of a number of well-laid-out walks, a few fruit trees, and an arbor, which was at the farther end, and covered with grape vines. Just as we entered the garden, I saw a young girl leave the arbor and advance to meet us. She was very handsome, and but a few years younger than Teresa.

"Well, Sara, is she still the same?" asked my companion.

"There is no change — her husband is the only one who occupies her thoughts for a moment. With him she could live or die. Without him —"

"Well."

"She will die."

My head seemed to swim at the conversation, and I was compelled to lean against a tree for support. It seemed to me that they were speaking of my wife, and I longed to question them, but did not dare to.

"Does she weep?" my companion asked, speaking of some person who appeared to be in the arbor.

"Sometimes she is in tears, and sometimes she is loud in her exclamations of anger, and threatens loudly. Poor lady! I pity her," the gentle-looking nun said.

"Pity her for what?" Barbara demanded, in a shrill tone, and with some asperity. "Because she persists in refusing to be happy and spending her days with us in peace and quietness, instead of being trampled upon by brutal men? I am ashamed of you, Sara."

"I'm sure I didn't mean anything that is wrong," sighed the pretty little nun, her dark eyes cast to the ground, as though she was trying to trace in the sand a picture of one of the detested men mentioned by her antique mentor. "I am sure, Barbara, I like the life of a nun; but I should think it must be very pleasant to live in the world, and be married to a handsome young man who would love you dearly."

"May the blessed saints refuse to listen to such abomination," cried the withered old hag, holding up her hands in horror at the supposition. "I must tell Father Juan of your expressions."

"No, pray don't," pleaded the little beauty, the tears starting to her eyes. "I should have to do penance, and I have already performed many. I did not become a nun of my own free will, and so a few of my repinings should be excused."

"Excused!" shrieked the old lady; "I shall not excuse you, but, for the good of your soul, take care to tell Father Juan of your conduct. Away with you to your chamber, and sleep without supper if you can."

The little beauty was slowly moving away to do the bidding, when I interposed.

"Pardon, senora," I said, in the worst gibberish that I could possibly assume. "Pray forgive the sister, and let her keep me company in the garden. You shall not suffer by your generosity, on the word of an English lady."

It was only by the most painful contortions that I succeeded in making myself understood, but I accompanied my words with a small gold piece which was a most powerful persuader.

"O, if the senora desires Sister Sara for a companion, I am willing, and shall readily overlook her disrespect for the holy life of a nun. You may remain, Sara, and if the English lady desires anything, you may supply her."

The antique virgin once more glanced at her gold in a sly manner, and left us alone.

"O, senora," cried the beautiful nun, her large black eyes filled with tears, "how can I thank you for the interest you have taken in me? By your influence I have escaped a severe punishment;" and with uncontrollable emotion, the little girl threw her arms around my neck and kissed me.

For a while I forgot my assumed character. That is, I think I did, for I have a very indistinct recollection of the scene, so confused was I. It seems to me that I threw my arms around the slight form of the nun, and pressed her with more than woman's strength to my heart. I have also a misty remembrance of kissing the tears from her eyes, and then kissing her lips. But the recollection of the event is dream-like and indistinct. The poor girl seemed somewhat surprised at the warmth of my affection; but on the whole, I am inclined to think that she did not dislike the treatment she received.

"There, dear, don't cry any more," I whispered. "As long as I am in the convent, I will protect you. You shall attend upon none but me, and I assure you that your duties shall be light."

"O, senora," the nun said, with a voice as sweet as a bird's, "I am but too grateful for your kindness, and shall never forget it. I hope you will remain here long, but not as a nun, for they don't treat us well. I tell you this in confidence, and I hope you won't tell old Mother Barbara, the mean thing, for if you did, she would make me eat bread and water. But I am dying to have you tell me something about the world. I can listen to you forever on that topic. We can talk all the afternoon, and if you ask Barbara, she will let me sleep in the room with you, so that we can talk all night also."

Here was a proposition from a girl not more than sixteen years of age, that was not calculated to strike a modest man in a favorable light. Poor thing! had she known that I was a wolf in lamb's clothing, she would have died before she suffered the words to pass her lips.

"Tell me," the pretty little nun continued, putting her arms around my waist, and leaning her head upon my shoulder, as confiding as though she had known me for years, " are the men as bad as Sister Barbara represents. Father Juan says they are, and that they only dream of wickedness, and when awake, are continually thinking of sin. I am sure if such is the case, I am glad I am here; but I sometimes get a glimpse of men in the street, and they look as gentle and harmless as doves. I am sure I know some sisters that look much crosser than men. Alas! I never had a chance to speak to one, excepting the priests, — and I don't like them, but you mustn't say so, — since I was seven years of age, and that is a long, long time ago."

"There are bad men in the world," I replied, "but all are not so; and I am sure that, if you mingled with the world, no one would be heartless enough to injure you. You would be loved most devotedly by some young man, who would only live for your happiness."

"O, I should like that," the little beauty cried, clapping her hands with joy at the thought. "I am sure it must be delightful to know that a brave man is thinking of one all the time; and for the matter of that, I shouldn't suppose it would do any harm if half a dozen men loved one at the same time."

Here was a confession from a child of nature that was most amusing to hear, and in spite of my attempts at gravity, I could not prevent laughing, at which the little nun pouted, and then relented, and threw her arms around my neck, and kissed me most heartily.

"Just reverse the case," I said, kissing her in return; for I thought that she would feel slighted unless I did so. "How would you like the idea of half a dozen girls loving the man whom you loved?"

"I would scratch their eyes out," was the true woman's answer; and by the sparkle of her own, I had no doubt that she spoke as she felt. A Spanish maid generally speaks as she feels, and when she loves she is not backward in manifesting it, even before the world; but she is careful to exact full obedience on the part of her lover, and if he is not faithful, her love can change to hate with most wonderful rapidity.

I thought, as I wound my arm around the little beauty's waist, that, if I had never seen Teresa, I should have felt but too happy in giving Sara my heart, and securing hers in return. But the exchange was now impossible, for Sara was bound to a convent life by vows which could not be broken except by the pope alone. I pitied the poor girl from my heart, and I would have willingly assisted her to escape; but the risk was too great, and if I even entertained the idea, I banished it from my mind.

"I hope you will stay at the convent a long, long time," Sara said, "for I have but few companions that I care to speak to, and those know nothing about the world, as you do. Most of them are old, and think only of saints and heaven, and the time when they are to leave this world for another. For the past two days a lady has been stopping here whom I really love and pity, and she has been like a true friend, but so full of her own griefs that she can't listen to mine. If I ask her if she is married, she begins to cry and call upon some one to save her. Father Juan told me to attend on her, and say that the life of a nun was the happiest in existence; but I won't say such a thing, for I don't believe it. But, if I was disposed to talk as he desires me, the lady would not listen; for she is proud and haughty, and very beautiful. I never saw any one half so handsome."

I knew that she was speaking of my wife, and only by a powerful effort could I command my agitation, and listen in silence to what was said.

"I think," Sara said, speaking very low, and very confidentially, "that there is some mystery connected with the handsome lady which Father Juan don't want the nuns to know. He left orders that only six of us should be allowed to speak to her, and that every word she said should be repeated to him on his return home. I am certain that I'm not going to play the spy for any one, and especially for a man I don't like, and who keeps me here contrary to my will."

I was about to inquire where Teresa was at the present time, but the little nun's tongue got the start of me, and I could not interrupt her.

"I suppose you wonder why I am here," Sara said. "I can tell you in a few words. It is not my choice that I took the veil, I assure you, and if my mother had not died when I was young, I don't think she would have been willing that I should have buried myself alive in this old building. I was in hopes that the earthquake, the other night, would shake it down and set us free, and I even prayed the saints to that effect; but the saints didn't pay any attention to my prayers. I suppose it is because I am not good enough, for some of the nuns say that they have only to ask the saints for a favor and it is granted. I don't believe it, though; for, if it was so, some of them would ask for more beauty than they have got — wouldn't they?"

I told her that, having no knowledge of the charms of her sister nuns, I couldn't safely answer that question. I then reminded her that she was about to tell some important facts regarding herself.

"O, yes; so I will. Well, when I was nine years of age my mother died, and I can remember of crying myself to sleep every night, when I thought that I should never ride on the Calsarda again, as I used to do when she was well. O, how I used to enjoy it! The cavaliers, on horseback, would gallop up to us, and tell me that I was handsome, and would one day break their hearts; and that used to make me laugh. I am sure that the prophecies were false, for I shall break my own heart, and never have a chance to make the men feel unhappy. I only wish I could. What sport it would be — wouldn't it?"

I shook my head, for the honor of my sex was concerned.

"Well, at any rate, I could tease them, as I sometimes tease Sister Barbara; and then she scolds me, and threatens to tell Father Juan; but she don't always. But I must inform you how I came here, or you will never know. A short time after my mother died, my father married a second wife, and she used to hate me, although for what reason I can't tell, as I always spoke pleasantly to her, and filled my hair with flowers when she was married. She was not a kind woman, by any means, and a servant told me one day, that my father married her because she was rich. If such was the case, I wish she had kept her riches and lived by herself, for I was never happy after she entered the house."

Here the young girl wiped the tears from her large black eyes, and seemed to think of her childish days with a good deal of sorrow.

"At length," Sara continued, "my new mother said that I must go to school, and I was sent to this convent to learn music, and here I have remained ever since; then all the nuns told me what a delightful and pious life they led, and how happy they were; and, like a silly girl, I believed them. I took the veil; but I cried when they cut off my hair, and I believe that I have cried every day since. I have never seen my father from the time I took the veil, or his wife, either. I think now that they should have prevented me from committing so rash an act — don't you? You are silent, my friend," the nun said, leading me from the direction of the arbor, where I so longed to go, but feared to enter. "Do you not think that I could serve the Virgin and the saints much better outside of these gloomy walls than within them?"

"It is the blessed hereafter that you are expected to look forward to, my poor child; and whether you are in a convent, or mingling with the world, your prayers should be directed to secure that happiness beyond the grave which all expect to enjoy. The world is beyond your reach. Think not of it, and you will soon get accustomed to your lot."

"But the world is not beyond my reach," the little nun said, pettishly; and then sinking her voice, she whispered, "You won't tell of me — will you?"

"The saints forbid," I answered.

"Well, sometimes I have fancied I would try and escape from the convent dressed in boy's clothes. I can look from the top of the convent and see many vessels in the bay, and I have thought if I could once get clear of the walls, that I might find refuge on board of a big ship which would take me to some country where I could earn a livelihood by teaching music. Even that would be better than staying here, and seeing none but cross faces from morning till night. O, I should so like to see foreign countries, and learn their customs! But I never shall."

The poor girl bowed her head, and once more the tears poured forth; but just at that moment we heard voices in advance of us, and saw half a dozen white-dressed females, sitting on some rough benches, at work embroidering.

The little nun's tears were dried instantly, and her look of grief was exchanged for one of composure.

"Who are they?" I asked.

"O, those are sisters Prudencia, Cartola, Clotilda, Juana, Sabina, and Dorotea. They are talking scandal, I'll warrant you. They are real ill-natured, and, I dare say, will find some fault in your dress; but you mustn't mind them — will you?"

Of course I said that I shouldn't care in the least, but I'm afraid I rather prided myself on my costume too much for that.

"Suppose that I should pretend not to speak Spanish," I remarked. "I could then learn all they said about me, and we could laugh about it some time when alone."

"O, that would be delightful!" cried the little beauty. "I should so much like to tease them, for they tell me that I'm plain, and that my form is not good, although I'm sure it is better than theirs. Just feel, and see how fat I am;" and to my surprise and nervous consternation, she placed my arm around her waist to verify her words.

We were too near the nuns to make a good inspection, and as I saw that the aged virgins were regarding me with some interest, found I had got to attend to my deportment or be exposed. I felt the warm blood rush to my cheeks, and by a careless movement dropped my veil partly, so that they could not see the whole of my face and detect its masculine outlines, if they were well posted in *man*-ology.

"What is your name?" whispered Sara, just as she was ready to introduce me.

"Guillermo," I replied, forgetting, in my confusion, that I had given my proper cognomen.

"Guillermo!" repeated the little nun in surprise; "why, that is a man's name. You must not mention the name of a man here."

"O, it's the name of my lover," I whispered, softly. "I was

thinking of him;" and while I was talking I was endeavoring to consider what woman's name would sound the best.

The six thin, bilious-looking nuns stared at me, and began to whisper to each other.

"Confound them," I thought, "they are already beginning to pick me to pieces. I know it by the snapping of their eyes."

"Your name," cried Sara, with a poke of her elbow in my ribs.

My wits had fairly deserted me, I believe, for I could think only of Teresa and Gracia. I determined to choose the name of my wife, and run the risk.

"Miss Teresa," I answered; in return for the poke that Sara gave me; and I was careful to give the English pronunciation in preference to the Spanish.

"Sisters," cried my guide, "this is Ris Teresa, who intends to beard at the convent for a few days while her lover is absent."

"Sara!" cried the eldest and most sour-looking of the nuns.

"Sara!" cried the most bilious one.

"Sara!" echoed the others, rolling up their eyes as though suddenly seized with cramp in the region of the stomach.

"Now, what have I done?" whispered the little nun, her black eyes full of fun.

"You have spoken of a lover within these sacred walls. Such a word should not be heard here, where religion reigns supreme."

"Well, I didn't know that it was wrong to speak the word. I thought it was only wicked to have a lover. But I won't mention the word again, if I can help it. At any rate, this English lady don't know what we are talking about; so we have spared her feelings."

I saw that they were agreeably surprised at the information, for it enabled them to pick me to pieces without mercy.

"I have always heard that English ladies had large feet and hands, and now I am assured of the fact," the old virgin remarked, comparing her black and bony paws with my rather small (for a man) hands.

"But her feet are larger in proportion than her hands," another said, sticking out one foot; and, by the saints, it had no stocking on, and what made the matter worse, she was not over particular how much of the accompanying portion of the leg she also exposed to view. It was lark, very dark, and didn't look remarkably clean.

"You had better not say anything about your feet," my little nun said, "for I am sure that the English lady has as good a foot as I, or you. Just see if she has not;" and down went her narrow foot close by mine for comparison.

After that demonstration the elder nuns turned on my dress, and left my bodily defects alone.

"What a frightful thing she has got on her head!" one remarked, alluding to the bonnet which I wore, and which, I have no doubt, the lady from whom it was borrowed considered the most perfect thing of its kind that ever doubled Cape Hope.

"But it's nothing compared to her dress — it is high in the neck, and looks as though intended to suffocate her. How can people be so foolish as to wear such things?"

"Perhaps, Sister Juana, she is as destitute of — "

The little nun did not have a chance to finish her remarks, for the antiquated virgins made common cause, and commenced a war upon her that threatened to last as long as the Trojan siege. They called her a fool, or very near one, an impudent little hussy, and concluded by threatening to report her to Father Juan as soon as he returned; and while the war of words was raging loudest, the sudden ringing of a bell was heard, and the nuns gathered up their work and rushed towards the building as though not a moment was to be lost. Sara and myself were left alone once more, and very thankful I was.

"There they go," cried the little nun, looking after her sisters with some contempt, "and I should not care if I never saw their faces again."

"But where have they gone?" I asked, somewhat anxious to discover what could have started them so suddenly.

"O, that bell was intended to call the old nuns to dinner. We young ones have but two meals a day — morning and night; and very hungry we get sometimes."

Once more I directed my steps towards the arbor, and had nearly reached it, when Sara suddenly stopped.

"We won't go there," she said, "for a lady is in the arbor, and she don't care about talking with any one. She is even cross to me, sometimes."

I did not heed her words, but walked on, and rather reluctantly the little nun accompanied me. We reached the door, and I saw a lady sitting with her back towards us; but she did not move until Sara ran up to her and put her arms around her neck. Then she turned her head, and to my great joy I saw that I was standing in the presence of my wife!

CHAPTER XII.

MEETING ONE'S WIFE. — A LONG CONVERSATION. — THE DISCOVERY. — PLANS FOR ESCAPE, &C., &C., &C.

TERESA merely glanced at me, and as my face was somewhat shaded by my veil, she could see nothing to startle her. In fact I thought that she appeared amazed at my intrusion, although she was very gentle with the little nun, and even returned her kiss, which I considered an aggravation. I saw that there were traces of tears in her eyes, and she looked as though she had been weeping when we entered the arbor.

"You are still pining for your liberty," Sara said, seating herself by Teresa's side, and putting an arm around her waist.

"And my husband," the wife replied, but in so low a tone that I barely heard it; and I thought that I saw the tears steal into her eyes again, although I knew that she was struggling to repress them.

"Well, don't grieve any more to-day. You will soon, perhaps, gain your liberty, and then whom shall I have for a companion? Even now your husband may be laboring for your liberation."

"Alas! I fear more for him than myself. He is a stranger in the country, rash and headstrong, and not calculated to cope with the Jesuits who surround him on every side. I know not even if he be living at this moment;" and the tears of my wife fell fast.

How I longed to comfort her! yet I did not dare to make myself known in the presence of Sara.

"But surely he can apply to the archbishop for your liberation," Sara said.

"Even that is denied him, for we were married without his consent; and besides my husband is a Protestant."

"May the saints preserve us," cried Sara, in a tone that showed how much prejudice she entertained against the creed. "Did you think of your soul when you gave yourself to a heretic?"

"No; I thought only of our happiness, and how much my husband loved me. O, if you could only see him you would not wonder at my marriage. He is so kind, and gentle, and virtuous; in fact, so different from other men, that I fear even you would love him."

"Well," replied Sara, after mature consideration, "I don't know but I might, for I feel very much like loving some one, and perhaps it would not make much difference in heaven if he was a Protestant or Catholic. But while I have been chatting with you I have forgotten my new friend, who is to board with us for a few days. Perhaps she can give you some information regarding your husband, for she is an English lady, but speaks Spanish as well as I."

Teresa looked at me eagerly, and I ventured to appoach and take a seat beside her.

"Do you know the Senor Guillermo — ?" she asked.

"I have met with him often in society lately," I replied, disguising my voice as much as possible; but in spite of my precautions I saw her face flush at the sound of it, and her eyes scrutinized my looks as though trying to trace the features of her husband.

"Is he well and happy?" she asked.

"He is well, but far from being happy," I replied. "I have heard from him the story of his wrongs, and hope that he will soon devise means to procure your escape or liberation. He has not been idle since your incarceration, and once or twice, when he thought that your place of imprisonment was discovered, has been prevented from seeing you through unforeseen events. He and his friends are working quietly, but most diligently, so that you have no cause to feel discouraged as yet."

"You may think I have not cause for grief; but if you knew to what indignities I have been subjected since the night I was abducted, how I have been entreated and threatened that unless I took the veil, and renounced my fortune to the couvent and Father Juan, you would only wonder that my reason remaiued, or that I was not dead. But I have prayed for life and sense, and the saints have granted my supplications."

I could see some of the old pride in her last words, and I longed to embrace her for her unyielding spirit in spite of priestly persecution. .

Just at that moment I heard a bell ring, and at its sound Sara started to her feet.

"My dinner is ready," she cried, "and unless I am prompt I shall find the table bare. The young sisters, when not thinking of prayers and penance, are apt to concentrate their ideas on table joys, and on such occasions strive for more than their share. You will both excuse me for a short time, for it will not take me long to eat six spoonfuls of rice and a banana."

She darted out of the door while the bell was still ringing, and we heard her footsteps as she ran over the gravelled walk towards the convent. Teresa and myself were left alone for the first time since our marriage, and yet our meeting was likely to prove somewhat embarrassing; for how to make myself known and convince her that I was her husband, taxed my ingenuity. Only for a short time did we remain silent, yet never was there a more impatient bridegroom than myself just at that moment.

"I hope that your visit to the convent is not to be of long duration," Teresa said, "and that when you leave you will manage to carry a letter to my husband. Even if I should not have the pleasure of seeing you again, I trust that you will inform him that my thoughts are his day and night, and that if we never meet again on earth, we shall in heaven, where the plots against our happiness will fail, and where we shall be united, never more to part."

"I will bear your message faithfully," I replied; "but perhaps you may soon see your husband and inform him of your sentiments without my aid. He may be nearer than you suppose."

I spoke in natural tones, and saw that she was surprised while she listened.

"Your voice is so much like the one I love that if I shut my eyes I should think he was by my side."

"Then try the experiment," I said, taking a seat close beside her.

"No, no," she replied, with a faint smile; "you are a woman, and my husband is too manly to resemble a female. The only resemblance is your voice."

"There are many deceptions in the world," I replied. "Suppose, after all, I should prove to you that I was a man."

She started and cast an apprehensive glance at me, as though she feared that she was being tricked by the priest in whose power she was.

"The conversation has become mystical," she remarked, with a haughty wave of her hand, as though she desired its discontinuance. She took up a book and opened its pages, and seemed to have forgotten my presence altogether.

I remained for a few moments undecided what to do. I feared the return of Sara, or the other nuns, every instant, and it was necessary for my plans that I should make myself known. The only thing I dreaded was woman's favorite disease, hysterics, which is sometimes assumed without the slightest cause, and once started, never knows when to stop. A sudden cry from Teresa would be apt to bring half a dozen nuns to the spot, and if they should find her in my arms and calling me endearing names, the secret would be discovered, and my death by torture most certain. While I thus sat motionless, thinking of the best plan for enlightening Teresa, she glanced from her book to my face for the purpose of seeing, I suppose, if I was offended at her words.

"Senora Teresa," I said, laying a hand upon her arm and speaking slowly and cautiously, "your friends are working hard for your liberty, and to secure it I have been sent to your assistance."

She did not believe me. I could see that she did not by the calmness of her eyes. She evidently supposed that Father Juan was endeavoring to deceive her or intrap her by some snare. For the purpose of being recognized, I found that I should have to be more explicit.

"Teresa," I whispered, "do you not know me? Do you not suspect who I am?"

I threw my veil aside, but the bonnet and its lining of roses and artificial fruits concealed too much of my features for her to recognize me. I knew that her husband's name was on her lips, but it was dismissed as an impossibility.

I untied the bonnet and threw it off, and then raised the wig which the priest was so kind as to borrow for me.

"Teresa," I said, "do you not know your husband?"

She knew me then. With a glad cry she threw her arms around my neck, and her head upon my bosom, and there she wept; but the tears now shed were those of joy.

"Be calm, darling," I whispered, "and remember that my life depends upon your discretion. If you give the least sign that shall lead the nuns to suppose I'm a man, our happiness is destroyed."

She was calm enough then, so calm that I considered I was justified in kissing her red lips a few times, just to see if they had lost any of their sweetness; and while I held her dear form in my arms, I forgot my past of misery, and only thought of present happiness. We were too excited to speak for some moments; but at length my wife removed her arms from my neck, and gazed long and anxiously at my face.

"Yes," she said at length, "you have mourned for me during my absence. I can see it in spite of your disguise. Your face is pale and thin. You have missed me — have you not?" and down upon my bosom went her head again, and more tears fell from those dear eyes, which were usually so bright and clear.

"Day and night I have sighed for you," I replied, "and not only sighed, but have worked for your deliverance. On the night that I pursued your abductors in the banco, I was almost sure I should recover you, yet came near finding a watery grave. But the saints were merciful, and spared me for this meeting."

I thought I would not speak of visiting a ship that night, and drinking half a dozen glasses of punch with old Captain Miller. Women are so confounded particular sometimes, when their affections are concerned? If I had hinted at such a thing, she would have pouted for ten minutes, just as likely as not.

"O, Guillermo," she murmured, putting up her mouth to be kissed with the innocent frankness of a child, "no sooner did I see you strike the water than I attempted to throw myself into the river, but was prevented by Father Juan and his steward. When you sank I fainted, and did not regain consciousness for a long time. When I revived I found myself in this convent, and an old nun standing over me chafing my temples. The saints forgive me, but I wished that I was dead, and beyond the reach of priests."

"But you no longer have such thoughts — you desire to live and enjoy many years of uninterrupted happiness with your husband," I whispered.

"Yes, Guillermo, without you life would indeed be a burden. But tell me, how came you here in this disguise?"

"Because I could not come in my proper character. Gentlemen are generally excluded from convents, I believe."

"But did you think of the danger?" she asked.

"Of course I did, and resolved to brave it all for the purpose of once more seeing you, and attempting to set you free."

"And can you do so?" she demanded, eagerly.

"I shall try," I replied. "But all will depend upon your calmness and obedience to my wishes."

"Am I not calm? And as for obedience, you have but to command, and love and duty alone will prompt me to obey you. As my husband, you have a right to expect it. As a wife, I shall yield it."

Bless her little heart! how I looked at her with admiration and astonishment, and wondered for a brief moment where some of her haughty spirit was concealed, with which she used to pester me during our courting days! She was a woman now — a trusting, loving woman; and I sincerely hoped she would always let me govern her as willingly as she seemed disposed to allow me while reclining in my arms at the Convent of San Sebastian. But I had my doubts, although I did not fail to reward her confession with a few tokens of affection quite common during the early stages of our courtship.

"Tell me, Guillermo," my wife said, "when shall you make the attempt for my removal from this dismal abode? If I should be compelled to remain here a month, and listen to the continued whining of the priest's creatures respecting the beauties of a nun's life, I should become insane. Do not let me remain here any longer than you can possibly help."

"The attempt, Teresa, is to be made this night; and in less than ten hours I hope to see you free. But there are difficulties in the way, and on you much will depend."

"So soon?" she cried. "O, how happy I feel at even the information! Impose the severest discipline upon me, and you shall see how readily I will bear it for your sake."

Just then I heard steps upon the walk. I hastily replaced my bonnet, and Teresa and myself took seats at some distance from each other.

"Remember, you know me only as an English lady," I whispered to my wife.

She smiled, and just at that moment Sara, the little nun, entered the arbor.

"I ate my dinner in a hurry, for I thought you would feel lonely, and want company. To be sure, there was but little to eat, for, in spite of my exertions to be first, I was last, and the first had devoured most of the rice. I do wish they would give us food in the same proportion that they give us prayers and religious exercises. We should feel more like thanking the saints for their favors."

The girl little suspected that her presence was not required just at that moment.

"I spoke to Sister Barbara," Sara continued, turning to me, "and she says that I can sleep in your room, if you are willing."

I saw a frown gather upon my wife's brow, and I feared that her jealous nature would break out; but to my intense satisfaction she remained quiet. She looked as though an explanation would be satisfactory, however, and I hastened to give one.

"When you made the proposal to occupy part of my room," I said, addressing Sara, "I did not return an answer, for fear you would take offence. A few moments since, I forgot your proposition, and agreed to room with this lady," pointing to Teresa. "If she is willing to relinquish my society for the night, I am sure I shall be happy to oblige you."

"Would you?" muttered my wife, a portion of the cloud disappearing from her brow.

"Won't you let me have her to-night? You can have her to-morrow night," Sara pleaded.

"No, indeed, I shall do no such thing; and I am astonished at your making such a request," was Teresa's decided answer.

I felt very well satisfied to have these two beautiful creatures quarrelling for the honor of my company, but I had much rather it would have been outside of the convent walls.

"It seems to me that I am crossed at every step. If I make

friends, they are taken away from me by some one who has not half as good a claim as I have. It is too bad!" and once more the tears fell from Sara's black eyes; but this time my wife hastened to console her, and after a while she succeeded; but I noticed she did not yield the contested point, or even promise that I should enjoy the little nun's company during my stay in the convent.

While the two were talking, a third bell was rung, and Sara intimated that the boarders' table was ready; and proposed to show us to it, for the sake of our society; and although my wife (who, I think, was a little jealous of the nun) protested that she knew the way, and would spare her the trouble, it made no difference; Sara would not take the hint and leave us alone for even a moment.

The table for the private boarders at the convent was somewhat better supplied than the one for the nuns, if Sara was to be believed. We found rice and curry, and chicken boiled, and then stuffed with various kinds of seasoning, among which red pepper predominated. There were two kinds of fruit also — oranges and bananas; and perhaps in honor of my arrival, Sister Barbara, who acted in the capacity of housekeeper, superior, and general scolder, placed a bottle of weak wine upon the table, which caused Sara to open her eyes to the widest extent, and declare that never in her whole experience had she seen such great liberality, and never expected to again. Poor child! she little knew what magic there was in gold outside as well as inside of a convent.

My appetite, as well as my wife's, was poor. I was too deeply impressed with the important part I had to play that night to care for food, and Teresa was too much excited at our unexpected meeting to be able to eat even an orange. I saw that our friend Sara was looking at the chicken with longing eyes, and without waiting for advice or consent from Barbara, I made her sit down and attack it. There was a disposition to scowl, but when Barbara saw that the nun was under my protection, she made no public demonstration of her rage. What was said in private I never knew.

I did manage to induce my wife to drink a glass of wine, while I helped myself to several; but its quality was so bad that I didn't blame her for not wishing for more. We three were the only persons at the table, but I saw that a door leading to the chapel was opened frequently, and several heads were thrust in for the purpose of scrutinizing us, and perhaps noticing how an English lady took her food. I sat with my bonnet on, however, so but few of them could see my face and false hair; for I feared that every moment some of the prying sisters would steal behind me, and finger my curls for the purpose of seeing if nature or art supplied them so profusely.

It was dark by the time we had finished our supper, or dinner, as they called it, and then Sister Barbara politely informed me that I could retire to my room, or hear evening vespers in the chapel. I wanted to be alone with my wife, if possible; so I declined the invitation to prayers, and Teresa did the same, much to my joy, for I feared that her coyness, which we so much admire in a bride, would impede the preparations I had to make for our escape. There were bars of iron to be sawed off and removed, and much other work that I desired to perform before the night was far advanced.

Sara looked rather dispirited when she saw that we were to leave her; but her duties required her presence in the chapel, and with a brief remark that she would room with me the next night, she left us, and Teresa and myself were soon in the apartment that was allotted us, one that overlooked the street.

We were not allowed a lamp, and perhaps it was just as well that we were not, although I am sure the blushes upon my wife's face were well worth seeing, when she found that I fastened the door to prevent interruption from the sisters; but if the reader expects that I am about to disclose a love scene, he or she is mistaken. I had too much work to perform, and there was too much at stake to allow such agreeable recreation; but I promised to make amends, if ever we escaped from the convent, and to insure that result, I commenced an inspection of the premises.

I found that there was but one window in the room, and that was guarded by four iron bars, each the size of a man's thumb. I commenced a careful examination, and found that the ends of the bars were fixed firmly in the wood-work, and held in their places by lead. The irons were too close together to admit of one's looking into the street; so I could not tell whether my friends were beneath me, or had not yet reached the rendezvous agreed upon. I looked at my watch and found that it was just nine o'clock; and they did not promise to be near me until twelve. I had three hours for using my saw or jimmy, and I did not doubt but I could make some impression by that time, if no one interrupted me.

As for Teresa, she was all excitement, and insisted upon lending me all the aid in her power; but I feared she would fatigue herself; so I desired that she should sit perfectly still, and only help me with her prayers. She obeyed me; but I could see, even in the dark, her large black eyes turned towards me, and watching every motion that I made with intense interest.

At length I found that I should have to use my saw for the purpose of removing the iron bars, for they were too firmly imbedded in the wood to be started by the jimmy; but the slight grating noise which the saw made, I feared, would alarm those in the other chambers, for the nuns had returned from the chapel, and we could hear Barbara lock them in their room, as though they were so many prisoners, and destined to escape unless extra precautions were used to prevent them. I suspended labor, and heard the usual amount of giggling, whispering, and praying, which the nuns indulged in after they were left for the night; and I could also hear my ancient friend Barbara apply her ear to the crack of my door, for the purpose of discovering if we were plotting mischief, or had gone to sleep like Christians. She seemed satisfied, after a while, that the latter supposition was correct, for she moved away, and I hoped went to bed, if ever such a faded specimen of humanity went to bed for the purpose of sleeping, of which I had grave doubts, for she seemed to me destined, like the Wandering Jew, to travel around, and never know rest or happiness.

At length all sounds, excepting the low tones of some nun who was repeating a number of prayers as a penance, ceased, and I recommenced my work; but, to my horror, found that the noise was too distinct not to attract attention, and for a few minutes I was in despair. A little cocoa-nut oil would have obviated the difficulty, and enabled the saw to run without the least jar; but unfortunately I had none with me, and lights were not allowed in the rooms.

"Why do you pause?" my wife asked, laying her hand on my shoulder, and bringing her fair face in dangerous proximity to my lips.

22

I stated my reasons, and my fears of awakening the nuns by endeavoring to cut the iron.

"Our door is not locked outside," she said, "and in the corridor is a lamp. I will dip my handkerchief in the oil, and return to you without detection."

I called her an angel, and allowed her to undertake the errand. The door was opened slowly, and by the dim light no one was seen listening or posted at the head of the stairs. She glided towards the light like a spirit of the other world, but her mission was not exactly an angelic one. She dipped one end of her handkerchief in the oil, and without the least noise or confusion, returned to me in triumph. How I praised her for her quietness!

"Now, Guillermo," she said, "while you are at work I will sing, and perhaps my voice will drown all the noise you make."

She raised her sweet voice, and sang in low, mournful tones a song that I was very fond of during our courtship.

"Nay," she cried, supending her song, "you stop to listen to me, instead of performing your task. Work now, and listen to me hereafter."

"That song carries me back to the time when our acquaintance first began. You remember that you sang it on the night of the earthquake, soon after my arrival in Manila."

"On the night you saved my life, and more than once perilled your own in the attempt. Yes, I remember, O my husband!"

She came to me and put her arm around my neck, and kissed me, and I was too happy to hold her to my heart, to think of renewing my work.

"Even then I loved you, but I knew it not," she whispered. "I longed for your society, and was always melancholy when you were from my side, but I did not know the nature of my love. Now that you are all mine, can I trust you will be always faithful to me, and never tire of your Manila wife?"

"Faithful always," I replied, fervently; and I really meant what I said. Men promise anythiug during courtship, or the first stages of the honeymoon.

"They told me cruel stories respecting your habits," my wife continued, in a dreamy sort of manner, as though we were standing in one of our parlors, and free from danger. "They said that you were unfaithful, and cared more for pleasure than for me. I did not believe them — did I?"

I told her that I rather thought she did not, to judge from appearances. I also informed her, in a calm tone, that all good men were liable to be slandered in the same way, but that I hoped my future life, if allowed to live long enough, would completely refute all the charges that were ever brought against me. At which information she seemed satisfied, and resumed her song with considerable spirit.

I worked with renewed exertions to make up for lost time, and in a few minutes had the satisfaction of severing one iron bar, and by the aid of the jimmy, bending it in such a manner that it would not interfere with our egress. One more bar was to be cut before an opening large enough to squeeze through was afforded, and I was just about to apply my saw when I heard a noise in the corridor.

"May the saints defend me!" cried my wife, flying to my side. "That is Father Juan's voice."

It was the most unwelcome announcement that could have been made, and, man as I was, I felt my heart sink with dread at the exposure which I anticipated. I put my hand in my pocket and felt for my revolver, determined to sell my life at a dear price, if the worse came to the worst.

"We are lost," my wife cried; and around my neck went her arms, as though they were anchors, and she had but to cast them loose to find harbor and shelter.

"Courage, darling," I whispered. "If the priest has returned, he may leave us unmolested until morning, and by that time we shall be in a place of safety."

I heard the shrill voice of Barbara raised, as though in angry reproach at some infringement of her rights, and then the stern tones of the priest met my ear. We listened attentively, and could distinguish every word that was spoken, for they had stopped opposite our door.

"I tell you that you are an old fool!" cried the priest, sharply.

"May the saints forgive me, but what can you expect? They wanted to sleep together, and I consented. It can do no harm that I know of, and I think you might be better employed than pulling me out of bed, at this hour of the night, for the purpose of hearing your complaints. Wait until morning, and then raise the devil if you will."

"You should have known better. But this is always the way. I can't leave the convent for twenty-four hours but something goes wrong. Just as my plans are well laid, somebody thwarts them. The convent and its inmates would go to ruin very speedily, if I was not here to look after you."

"We shall all go to the devil, at any rate, if you keep on as you have done for the past fortnight," I heard Barbara say, in a more subdued tone. "The Donna Teresa will never consent to take the veil, and all your urging is lost. Better make terms with her while you can, and let her go. A lady with her wealth must have many powerful friends, and they won't fail to make search for her."

"Let them search!" the priest cried, fiercely; "they cannot enter this convent without my consent, and I will allow my hands to wither before I yield. I have made a bold stroke for fortune, and I will succeed or fall. I hold the lady a prisoner, and as long as she is in my power I can make terms."

"May the saints protect me," murmured my wife, clinging more close to me.

"Well, let them alone for to-night, and to-morrow I will see that they are separated," Barbara said. "They are asleep now, and it will be useless to disturb them. Besides, you may alarm the English lady, and I can assure you that her friendship is worth having. She has gold in abundance, and is free with it. Let everything appear fair to her, and who knows but she can be converted to the true faith, and the convent receive a donation?"

"Poh!" interrupted the priest; "the English are pig-headed, and care nothing for our religion. I should sooner think of converting a Mohammedan than one of them. If they have gold, they give only as they take a freak. Liberal to-day, and mean to-morrow. I hate the English."

"But this lady seems different," suggested Barbara.

"Then I will see her, and judge for myself. If she is pretty, who knows but she would prefer a change of quarters for the night."

"You are an old fool!" yelled Barbara; "and if you offer to open that door, I will scratch your eyes out. Do you think that all women are bound to love your shaven head and sallow face? Go to your bed, and dream of me."

" May the saints forbid ! " the priest exclaimed, in so hearty a manner that I had no doubt of his sincerity. " Your charms are rather stale, Barbara. You are not as young as you were fifteen years ago."

" The saints be thanked, for now I am allowed some peace," was the response; and I rather think the priest was hit by that random shot, for he remained silent for a few moments, as though meditating what he should do next; and then, to my joy, I heard them moving off as though they had concluded to leave us unmolested for the night, at least.

Fearful of their returning, I resumed my work, and sawed away with patient industry, until the iron was severed and bent from its upright position. I put my head through the opening, and looked into the street. The night was too dark to discern if any one was lurking beneath the shadow of the convent wall, and I did not dare to make a signal for fear of attracting the attention of some spy, who would instantly have given the alarm to Father Juan. I looked at my watch, and by the aid of a match found that it was but eleven o'clock, while the time agreed upon for the meeting was twelve. A whole hour was to elapse before I could call myself free, and that hour, I calculated, was to be the most tedious of my stay in the convent. A dozen times in as many minutes I looked from the window, and at last, to my great delight, heard people moving on the sidewalk, and stop directly beneath me. I waited impatiently for some signal that should prove to me they were friends, and at length, to my joy, it was manifested. The tune of " Hail, Columbia," was whistled in so low a key, that even the watch dogs in the convent yard did not take the alarm, and make night hideous with their howlings. Twice that familiar tune was sounded, and then all was quiet excepting the loud calls of the soldiers on the city walls, as they announced that " all was well " as far as heard from.

In an instant I had my cord out, and a weight attached for the purpose of enabling those in the street to find it. I threw it out with nervous haste, and the next instant knew it had reached ground by an exclamation that was accompanied by an oath. The weight had struck the priest on his head, and nearly knocked him down.

"For Heaven's sake, keep quiet!" I heard Allen whisper.

"It's all very well to say keep quiet; but curse it, man, here's a half pound weight struck my head, and raised a swelling as big as my hand. If I supposed that it was done on purpose —" and Benventuro muttered something that I could not hear.

"But you know it was an accident, and that the swelling will all be erased by good wine. Here, hand me the stout cord, and stop your noise," Allen said.

The promise of the wine must have restored the priest to good humor, for he made no more remarks, and in a few moments' time I heard a whisper, —

"Pull up;" and a twitch of the cord showed me that the larger rope was fastened to my lighter one. I hauled the line in slowly, for fear the weight of the large one would break it, and after a few moments' suspense had the satisfaction of grasping the end of a piece of "ratling stuff," which was capable of sustaining two or three hundred pounds.

"Have you got it?" Allen whispered, so softly that it did not seem possible for any one to hear him excepting myself.

"I have," was the response.

"Then pull up the ladder."

I found that was no trifling feat, for the ladder was considerable heavy, and the "ratling stuff" cut my hands, unused to hard labor as they were. But by working little at a time I succeeded in getting one end to the window, and securing it firmly to the remaining iron posts.

"Are you all right?" the party below asked.

"Yes."

"Then come on without delay."

It was all very well for them to say come on, but I had a wife in the room who weighed, as near as I could guess, one hundred and thirty pounds; and it was necessary to get her to consent to attempt the novel performance of walking down that rope, when she knew three men were at the end of it, waiting for her. Women are sometimes very sensitive, and would die rather than abate one particle of their modesty.

"Come, darling," I whispered, putting my arm around her waist, and leading her to the window; "the time has now arrived for our escape. With courage and firmness we can be free in a few minutes."

"But how am I to go?" she asked. "I can't fly, and to jump would cost me my neck, which, you say, is very dear."

"Angel," I murmured, "I am glad you are so earthly that the air would refuse to sustain you, and I don't intend that your graceful neck shall be in the least damaged, if I can prevent it. The distance to the pavement is only thirty feet, and those thirty feet must be overcome by the aid of this rope-ladder, which you see is firmly secured to iron bars. A terrible rumpus the inmates of the convent will make, when they see it hanging here in the morning. A little nerve and good resolution, and you will soon be safe."

My bride put her pretty head from the window and looked down, and in the darkness she could just discern the outlines of my friends. She drew back with a shudder.

"I can't do it," she whispered.

"Why not, love?"

"Those men. My modesty — "

"Must be laid aside for once. For my sake make the attempt without a moment's delay."

"For your sake I would do many things," she answered. "But don't ask me to go down before those men."

"But I will ask them to move off a few yards, while you are descending," I said.

"And if you will request them to keep their eyes upon the sidewalk, I should feel much more comfortable," she urged.

"Angel of modesty," I replied, "your wishes shall be granted;" so I spoke to my friends, and made known her wishes, and, I may as well add, my wish also. They were kind enough to comply without stopping to argue the question; and when I had informed Teresa of the fact, a new difficulty arose. She manifested many fears of falling, and a few minutes were spent in assuring her that, if she would but grasp the rope with a firm hand, and step cautiously, she would reach the sidewalk in safety. And to insure that important fact, I tied the "ratling stuff" under her arms, so, in case she did let go with her hands, I could save her from falling by the small rope.

I don't think that crinoline was understood by the Spanish ladies in the days of which I write. In fact, as far as my observation went, the ladies were rather proud to show their well-rounded forms with as little artificial work as possible, perfectly content that old ladies should confine themselves to the "stuffing" process if desirable. Such being the case, the reader will readily understand that I had but little trouble to get my wife through the bars, and to place her hands firmly upon the ropes, while her feet also caught the ladder for a resting-place. When she was once in this position, my next trouble was to get her to move, and all of my persuasion had to be brought into use. She trembled so violently that I feared she would faint every moment; but I knew she could not fall, owing to the rope which I had tied around her waist. I expected every moment that she would utter a violent shriek, and not only alarm the inmates of the convent, but the sentinel, who was posted at the corner of the street a few blocks off.

"O, the saints protect me," she cried, "for I shall fall and be killed."

"There is not the least danger," I urged. "Step slow, and you will soon reach the sidewalk."

But like many other ladies placed in the same position, she had her private opinion on that point; and the more I coaxed, the worse she cried, and the more timid did she become. I saw that my friends were getting impatient, for there was too much at stake to waste precious moments when the field was clear; so at length I resolved to try a bold plan.

"Hark!" I said; "I think I hear Father Juan's voice in the corridor. If he discovers us we are lost."

The announcement was magical in its effect. His name was sufficient to excite terror in her mind, for her imprisonment had not been of the most agreeable description. Without uttering another word, she released her hold of the window sill, and began to descend much more rapidly than I dared to anticipate. I watched her with anxiety until I saw her reach the sidewalk, where she was received in the arms of my friends. Then her courage and strength deserted her, and she was obliged to be supported to prevent falling.

The next instant I had reached the sidewalk, and had my wife clasped in my arms.

"What a pleasant picture to contemplate!" muttered the priest. "It looks like two women embracing each other."

I had but time to shake hands with my friends, and exchange

a few words of congratulation with them, when the priest interfered.

"This is no time to talk," he said, in hoarse whisper, "for we are liable to be picked up at any moment by a guard of patrolmen. That cursed ladder would hang every member of the party higher than the gates of the castle, for it is no joke to get implicated in entering a convent, unless you go with a bottle in your hand. We must get away from this vicinity as fast as possible."

He started across the street, and we followed close at his heels. My wife had recovered sufficiently, under my treatment, to be able to walk with some slight support, such as an arm around her waist. She was so overjoyed at her escape that she hardly realized she was outside of the convent's walls, and seemed to fear that every moment some one would command her to return.

The priest, who was familiar with that section of the city, passed through an alley-way, and then crossed the main street, keeping a careful lookout for sentinels, and escaping observation as much as possible.

"Where are you leading us?" I ventured to inquire; for I saw that my wife was nearly exhausted with her trouble and fatigue, and was greatly in need of rest.

"To a place of safety," was the brief answer; and no other reply could I extort from the priest.

Suddenly Benventuro stopped in front of a small house on St. Joseph's Street, and nearly half a mile from the city gates. Before I had time to ask a question, the priest tapped lightly with his hand, and a voice from the court-yard asked, —

"Who's there?"

"Those whom the saints have befriended," was the response.

The door was instantly opened, and without a word of explanation we entered a dark court-yard. No sooner were we in the yard than the door was quickly shut and barred.

"Where is your light, Antonio?" the priest asked.

"Here, senor, under the barrel," was that worthy's answer; and lifting up a barrel that stood near the gate, a lamp was exposed which revealed the dark, melancholy face of Antonio. "The senor has escaped, I see," was the only greeting he bestowed upon me; for he appeared to take it as a matter of course that I must escape with such a splendid lot of burglar's tools in my pocket.

"Yes," I replied; "thanks to your plans and the large quantity of wine you poured down the convent steward's throat."

"Ah, senor, I left him so drunk that he could not tell a saint from a sailor, and he will have such a glorious headache for two days to come, that curses, not prayers, will escape his lips. But I pray you walk up stairs, where you will find refreshments and beds for the night."

"I supposed that we were to leave the city to-night," I said, as we followed the priest up the stairs.

"It would not have been judicious," replied Benventuro, "for the officer of the guard has a foolish habit of asking questions, which we could not have answered to his satisfaction; and as for applying for a pass for such a party as this, I did not dare to. Here we can be comfortable for the night, and in the morning go where we please. The house belongs to a friend of mine, who, with his family, is absent from the city, and has kindly placed everything at my disposal. Antonio, did you bring over the wine?"

"Yes, senor, and it is already cooling."

"And did you think to bring me my proper clothes?" I demanded, thinking more of them than the wine.

"The senor will find them in his chamber, which has been expressly prepared for himself and wife."

The rascal — I could have hugged him for his consideration. Things began to look brighter. I began to think that being married was not so very bad, after all.

The house was furnished, like the general run of Spanish gentlemen's houses, with plain but convenient furniture, and a few pictures of saints hanging on the walls. The dining-room contained a table, covered with dishes and glasses, and I was not long in detecting that the priest had made preparations for one of his pleasant suppers, as he termed them. But my appetite was poor, and my wife was too embarrassed to care to remain with my friends. She was not, however, half as anxious to get away from them as I; and while the priest was detained for a moment by Allen and Tom, who pretended that they desired his opinion on some *winish* point, my wife and myself slipped from the room, and sought the chamber that had been appropriated for our use. I had barely locked the door before the priest discovered the *ruse*, and made most pathetic appeals to induce me to return; but wine and the pleasures of the table were no temptation, when placed in contrast with the society of my bride; and when she put her arms around my neck, and whispered, "You won't go — will you?" I don't think I should have left her for a moment, if I had not dined for a week.

The night passed quietly, but almost before I could realize that it was daylight, I heard Allen pounding at the door of my room.

"It is past eight o'clock," he said, "and time for us to be moving up the river. We are awaiting your motions."

I did not keep them waiting long, for, dressing hastily in my proper habiliments, I joined my three friends in the dining-room.

"There is the devil to pay at the convent," Allen said, when I made my appearance. "Antonio has been there, and gathered the whole particulars from his friend, the steward. Father Juan is wild with rage. He has kicked Sister Barbara, and put all his nuns on bread and water, thinking they were concerned in the conspiracy. A crowd of people is around the convent, asking what has happened, and who has run off with a nun. That rope ladder first started them, as I supposed it would. It is a pity we could not have carried it away with us."

"Well, what do you propose we shall do?" I inquired.

"That is what we wanted to ask you about. Shall we remain here in concealment, as though we rather shunned investigation, or shall we start for home, and let the priest see that we are no longer fearful of his arts?"

"I will do what you think is for the best," I replied.

"Then I counsel you to start for the factory," Allen replied, "and remain with us for a few days. By that time matters can be arranged with the archbishop, and your marriage published in an official form. I will assume all the risk of an attempt to molest you at the factory. Even Father Juan would not be so imprudent."

I looked towards the priest for his opinion, but that worthy man was busy with the bones of a chicken, and could only grunt his approval or disapproval, I could not tell which. As for Tom, he was at his old tricks, trying to make the acquaintance of a pair of black eyes living in the opposite house.

"Then I had better request my wife to dress for the journey," I said,

"Certainly, and without much delay, for I should like to leave the city before there is more excitement."

I communicated the intelligence to Teresa, and in a remarkably short time for a woman, she was ready for her departure. We gave Antonio instructions to follow us at a short distance after we left the house, and to be ready to lend us all the assistance that he could command, in case we should encounter Father Juan; for I had some misgivings that we should meet that astute gentleman before we could reach a place of safety. I did not confide my suspicious to Teresa, but suffered her to suppose that all danger was passed. I could not disturb her quiet happiness, for she looked so contented while leaning on my arm, that I felt as though capable of any sacrifice on her account.

But little notice was taken of us as we walked through the streets, and it was not until we supposed all danger was passed, and in a few minutes should be beyond the city gates, that, in turning a corner, who should we run against but our worst enemy, the holy Father Juan, looking as though his blood had turned to gall, and all his better feelings had been traded away for a large stock of malice, with which he seemed pretty well loaded!

He stopped when he saw us, and his eyes lighted up with such a ferocious gleam that my wife clung to me in terror, and would have fallen, had I not supported her.

I merely bowed, and attempted to pass the priest, but he placed himself directly before me; so I could not move without stepping off the sidewalk.

"Are you aware that you are in a Catholic country, sir?" he asked.

"I am acquainted with the fact, and if I was not, I see that before me which would convince me of it," I replied.

"Speak to him kindly," whispered my wife, who trembled so violently that I feared she would faint every moment.

"And do you know the penalty of enticing from a convent those under the protection of the holy church?" the priest asked, emboldened by the shrinking timidity of my wife.

"I neither know nor care," I replied.

"And were you aware that death is the penalty for entering a convent in disguise?" was the next question; and a grin of triumph was on the man's face as he asked it.

I made no answer, but sought to pass on.

"You lo not leave me thus," he said. "You and your abettors shall now learn what it is to interfere with the affairs of the church. All of you shall go to prison, and be tried by an ecclesiastical council."

"What cursed nonsense!" muttered Benventuro. "Listen to reason for a moment — can't you?"

But Father Juan was not inclined to do any such thing. His rage was too excessive to admit of argument, and, as I expected, he speedily collected a crowd of ignorant Mestizos, who were ready to take advantage of every tumult to rob and stab if necessary.

"My children," cried the padre, "the sanctity of my convent has been violated by a cursed heretic, who, under the garb of a woman, has stolen away a daughter of the church. Death to the heretic, my children, death!"

The cry was instantly taken up by the crowd of fanatics, and they shouted, "Death to the heretic!" with much more fervor than I liked.

The rabble moved towards us in a threatening manner. I put my hand to my revolver, determined to sell my life dearly; but a word of caution from Benventuro restrained me.

"Manifest no alarm," he whispered, "and, above all things, offer no resistance at present. Crowds are fickle, and easily swayed for good or evil. I will speak to them. — My children," cried Benventuro, raising his voice, which was like the bellowing of a bull, "you all know me, and know that I am a priest."

"Yes, we know you," was the response.

"Well, I declare to you that the Padre Juan is mistaken, and that no wrong has been committed. This lady is my friend's wife, and is a Catholic as well as himself. I know it. Father Juan is mistaken."

"It is false!" roared Padre Juan. "It is only a trick to escape punishment. Death to the heretic — death!"

And a few in the crowd re-echoed the cry with startling earnestness, but a majority seemed astonished at the complicated aspect of affairs, and were mute.

"My children," cried Benventuro, "you will feel satisfied if our beloved father, the archbishop, investigates the matter?"

"Yes, yes!" yelled the crowd.

"Then let us repair to his palace, and ask his advice."

"To the archbishop, to the archbishop!" the crowd, which had now increased to some five hundred people, shouted.

"You need not think to escape by such means," Father Juan said, addressing the priest Benventuro. "Before him you dare not tell an untruth. I shall triumph, and you will be disgraced."

"We shall see," was all the remark Benventuro made.

We started for the palace, the crowd leading the way, and receiving fresh accessions to its ranks every moment. The distance was but short, so I cheered and strengthened Teresa with consoling words while we were walking, although I feared every moment that she would display her womanly feelings by fainting with terror.

While we were thus escorted through the streets, by as desperate a band of cutthroats as ever lived by robbing, I noticed that Antonio, the priest's steward, kept close by my side, and that he seemed to have some connection with many of the most ferocious-looking Mestizos that composed the rabble.

"Fear nothing, senor," he whispered to me. "I have a hundred friends in the crowd, and they will all obey me. If violence is attempted, we will let these dogs feel our knives. If the cowards dare to attack you, they shall pay dearly for it."

And I had no doubt the fellow meant what he said, for he looked as though the taste of blood would be acceptable.

In five minutes' time we were opposite the palace of the archbishop, when the crowd suddenly ceased its murmurings, and maintained an orderly deportment that was most astonishing. It showed the power of the church over the ignorant fanatics, and proved that the people could be led to good or evil, if the priests were so disposed.

The Mestizos opened to the right and left, and allowed us to pass in without a word of insult; but after we had once entered the door, they closed up all avenues of escape, and, with uncovered heads, awaited the decision of the archbishop.

"How is this to terminate?" I asked Allen, in a whisper.

He shook his head with a puzzled look.

"It's a struggle between the priests, and the smartest will win," he answered.

We were ushered into a large reception-room, and informed that his highness would see us in a few minutes; and he kept his word, for presently a stout, healthy-looking man, about fifty years of age, entered the room and took a seat that somewhat resembled a chair of state. His only attendant was a servant, dressed in linen of the whitest hue. The great man bowed gracefully to all in the room, and seemed somewhat interested in the appearance of Teresa.

"Let the lady be seated," he said, seeing from etiquette that she remained standing when it was only by an effort she was enabled to do so.

"There is a large crowd in front of the palace, and the people appear to be in an unusual state of excitement. What is the meaning of it?" demanded the bishop, after a moment's silence.

"It means, your highness," Father Juan said, every appearance of anger having vanished from his shrewd-looking face, "that the sanctity of my convent has been violated by a heretic, and that I demand the extreme punishment of law upon his head."

"If what you say is true, you shall have the justice you ask for; but we must have proof," was the bishop's reply.

"Your highness shall have proof. This young man, whom I have brought before you, has dared to enter my convent in the garb of a woman, and entice away the lady Teresa, who was under my charge. Last night they made their escape, and were leaving the city this forenoon, when I came upon them unexpectedly."

"Your charges look grave, Father Juan; but what says the young man to them?" demanded the bishop, calmly, gently agitating a fan, and regarding Teresa and myself with more attention than I thought we deserved.

"Will your highness permit me to intercede for them?" Benventuro demanded, speaking for the first time.

"If you know any extenuating circumstances, or can give me any facts regarding the matter, I should be pleased to hear them. Take care, Benventuro, that you confine yourself to what you personally knew."

"I shall do so, your highness," the priest replied; "and I feel the more confidence in this case, from the fact that I married them a month since."

A frown spread over the full face of the bishop.

"You know the penalty for marrying a Catholic heiress to a Protestant?" he demanded.

"I knew the penalty, your highness, but I also knew I should have the satisfaction of converting a Protestant to Catholicism, and placing in your highness's hand the sum of five thousand dollars for the benefit of the church; and the money would have been forthcoming long since, had not my friend, Father Juan, sought to enrich his convent by abducting the lady, and confining her, regardless of her will."

"It's false!" cried Father Juan, when he saw the frown disappear from the bishop's face. "The lady went of her free will."

"I did not," cried Teresa, starting up. "You carried me away by force."

"Father Juan," the bishop said, "it seems that your conduct has been extremely reprehensible; and I am astonished that a priest, in my jurisdiction, should have so far forgotten his duty."

"But I claim the life of the heretic for daring to enter my convent disguised as a woman. That charge he cannot refute."

"He can, and does refute it," Benventuro cried. "He hired an English lady to enter the building, and the result was the escape of his wife, who was unjustly detained there. This we can prove."

"What a splendid pleader he is!" I thought, but took good care not to say as much, for I thought it might damage my cause. I knew the bait of five thousand dollars was producing its effect, and determined to let it work.

"There must be a mistake," the archbishop said. "I don't think a man so respectable-looking would be willing to violate any law of this land. I find no reason to detain the bride or bridegroom longer, and have no doubt that, after their long separation, they would gladly be alone."

The bishop left his seat and came towards us, and shook hands with us warmly.

"You have a handsome bride," he said, "and many of our gallants will envy your good fortune. I hope you will make this country your future home. We like the Americans when they don't come as filibusters. Join the church, love your wife, and you will suffer no more persecution."

I turned to look for Father Juan, but, baffled and disappointed, he had left the room.

"The money which I intend for the church shall be placed in

your hands this week," I said to his highness, at which information he smiled, and looked far from being displeased.

We moved towards the door, and when we reached the street, the bishop raised his hands over us as though bestowing his benediction. In an instant every hat worn by those in front of the palace was removed, and then the crowd scattered to the right and left, and in five minutes not ten men could be seen.

"Victory, victory!" cried Benventuro, in triumph. "You are safe and happy."

"But you are *not* safe, damned, treacherous villain!" cried a voice; and from behind a tree started Father Juan, his eyes flashing with rage, and his thin face convulsed with the agony of defeat.

I saw a quick movement of his arm, and then my friend, Father Benventuro, fell to the pavement, the blood spurting from a terrible wound in his side.

"I'm a dead man," he gasped; "but don't let me die unavenged."

I knelt by his side and endeavored to stanch the blood which flowed so freely, but it was in vain. He never spoke again. In ten minutes he breathed his last.

"He is dead, and my secret dies with him," I heard a voice say; and on looking up I saw Antonio. "You have a clear field now," he cried. "Your friend and enemy are dead. What more could you desire?" and off he walked, and I never saw his face again in Manila. That which bound him to Benventuro I never knew.

Allen, who had started in pursuit of Father Juan, did not overtake him until the same knife that ended Benventuro's days had terminated the Jesuit's life. He cut his throat in his flight, and he cut it deeply, too. Both of the bodies were removed to the nearest convent, and were buried privately, to prevent excitement among the people.

My story is now ended; but before I close, will state that as soon as I could settle up my affairs and my wife's estate, we left the country and never returned. My wife is a treasure, and has several small ones to. her great gratification and my pride. She is as handsome as ever, and twice as quick tempered. Before we left the country I succeeded in getting Sara released from the convent, and she was married in a short time to my friend Tom. They are now residing in New York, contented with their lot. Allen was at Manila a few years ago, but I understand that he acquired a fortune, and settled in China for the purpose of establishing a house. Gracia married a Spaniard, and I gave her a thousand dollars as a nuptial present. Her father is in the chain gang, and likely to remain there for several years. The factory at Santa Mesa is still continued, and worth a visit. With these explanations I bid the reader a long farewell, for this book ends the Ocean Life Series.

www.ingramcontent.com/pod-product-compliance
Lightning Source LLC
Chambersburg PA
CBHW020241240426
43672CB00006B/599